ATHANASIUS

Athanasius was an enigmatic and fiery Egyptian bishop of the fourth-century Church. He was a principal architect of Christian doctrine and has been a controversial figure, from his own time to the present day. Much of his work focused on the question of the identity of Jesus Christ, and the nature of his relationship to God.

This book presents the fundamental elements of Athanasius's response to this question. It also provides a much-needed, up-to-date introduction to his life and work, focusing on the tumultuous doctrinal controversies in which he played a crucial part.

The majority of the book is made up of new translations of his key writings. These have been chosen with a view to presenting the rationale for Athanasius's fundamental theological positions: the divinity and humanity of Christ, human redemption, the divinity and work of the Holy Spirit, the logic of Christian worship, and the scriptural basis for the doctrinal formulations of the Council of Nicaea.

Khaled Anatolios is Associate Professor of Historical Theology at Weston Jesuit School of Theology, Cambridge, MA. He is the author of *Athanasius: The Coherence of His Thought* (Routledge, 1998).

THE EARLY CHURCH FATHERS
Edited by Carol Harrison
University of Durham

CYRIL OF JERUSALEM
Edward Yarnold, S. J.

EARLY CHRISTIAN LATIN POETS
Carolinne White

CYRIL OF ALEXANDRIA
Norman Russell

MAXIMUS THE CONFESSOR
Andrew Louth

IRENAEUS OF LYONS
Robert M. Grant

AMBROSE
Boniface Ramsey, O.P.

ORIGEN
Joseph W. Trigg

GREGORY OF NYSSA
Anthony Meredith, S.J.

JOHN CHRYSOSTOM
Wendy Mayer and Pauline Allen

JEROME
Stefan Rebenich

TERTULLIAN
Geoffrey Dunn

ATHANASIUS
Khaled Anatolios

ATHANASIUS

Khaled Anatolios

Routledge
Taylor & Francis Group

LONDON AND NEW YORK

First published 2004
by Routledge
11 New Fetter Lane, London EC4P 4EE

Simultaneously published in the USA and Canada
by Routledge
29 West 35th Street, New York, NY 10001

Routledge is an imprint of the Taylor & Francis Group

Typeset in Garamond by Taylor & Francis Books Ltd
Printed and bound in Great Britain by TJ International, Padstow,
Cornwall

British Library Cataloguing in Publication Data
A catalogue record for this book is available from the British Library

Library of Congress Cataloging in Publication Data
Anatolios, Khaled, 1962–
Athanasius / Khaled Anatolios.
p. cm. — (The early church fathers)
Includes bibliographical references and index.
1. Athanasius, Saint, Patriarch of Alexandria, d. 373. I. Title.
II. Series.
BR1720.A7 A53 2004
270.2'092—dc22   2003026829

ISBN 0–415–20202–7 (hbk)
ISBN 0–415–20203–5 (pbk)

22 439

DEDICATED TO BRIAN E. DALEY, S.J.

CONTENTS

ACKNOWLEDGMENTS

I am most grateful to Carol Harrison for her patient and gracious oversight of this project from its inception to its completion. I am also much indebted to Andrew Louth, who read the entire manuscript and made very valuable suggestions, as well as to Johan Leemans and Andrew Don, both of whom provided very helpful responses to an earlier version of Chapter 1, and to Paul Russell, who provided valuable consultation on Syriac material. Finally, I would like to express my thanks to my children, Elias and Maria, who are always unfailing in providing both inspiration and cheerful distraction.

1
INTRODUCTION

Life and times

When Athanasius became bishop of Alexandria in 328 CE, at around the age of 30, he assumed leadership of the Christian community in one of the most prominent cities of the Roman empire. With its two great harbors, the *Portus Magnus* and the *Eunostus*, Alexandria was the major gateway of trade in the Mediterranean world, linking together the Roman empire with the markets of India, China, and Arabia. It was also a great manufacturing and producing center in its own right, famous, among other things, for its shipbuilding and for the production of papyrus, the most common writing material of the ancient world. Egypt, of which Alexandria was the administrative center, was virtually the breadbasket of the empire, its grain representing a significant portion of the food supply of Rome and Constantinople. Egypt was not governed by a "proconsul," as was the case in other provinces of the empire, but by a "prefect," a viceregal governor appointed by the emperor as his direct representative. The prefect of Egypt resided in Alexandria, his authority undergirded by a military commander, or "dux." As well as being Egypt's administrative center, Alexandria was also a major center of culture for the whole Roman empire. It had been the site of the majestic "Great Library," which was reputed to have contained half a million papyrus rolls, and which was likely destroyed by a fire in the early 270s. Closely associated with the Great Library was "the Museum," a society of scholars who shared erudition and common meals, and had a "Priest of the Muses." All the major schools of philosophy were well represented there, and the city was famed for its contribution to the arts and sciences of the day. Ammianus Marcellinus, a fourth-century historian, lauds the intellectual vitality of the city, noting that "a doctor who wishes to establish his standing in the profession can

1

dispense with the need for any proof of it by saying (granted that his work itself obviously smacks of it) that he was trained at Alexandria."[1]

Sociologically, Alexandria was a melting pot of native Egyptians, Greeks, and Jews, as well as other immigrants. The combination was not always harmonious. The Alexandrian Jewish theologian Philo paints a lurid picture of a violent persecution of the Alexandrian Jews by the Greeks, during the reigns of Tiberius and Gaius,[2] and the Jews themselves were involved in a violent revolt in 115–117, which greatly reduced their presence in Egypt. Relations between the local populace and the Roman authorities were strained and sometimes bloody. In 215, the emperor Caracalla ordered a massacre of Alexandrian youth, in response to a rumor which had gained ground in the city that he was involved in plotting the murder of his brother. On the other hand, Alexandrians had a reputation for being independent and rebellious; we are told that governors entered the city in fear of its reputation.[3] Riots and urban violence were not infrequent, and were often associated not only with religious and political motives but also with the theater, chariot races, and the public spectacles, to which Alexandrians were notoriously reputed to be addicted. The struggle between Athanasius and his opponents in Egypt would sometimes manifest this streak of violence; we are told of prefects inciting violent riots against Athanasius's supporters and of the lynching of an unpopular rival bishop, George of Cappadocia, by Athanasius's supporters.

Alexandria was also the ecclesiastical center of Egypt. By Athanasius's time, it was a well-established custom, which came to be ratified by the Council of Nicaea in 325, that the Patriarch of Alexandria had direct authority over the whole Egyptian Church and was responsible for appointing bishops throughout Egypt, Libya, and the Pentapolis.[4] The bishop of Alexandria was custodian of a rich and complex tradition. Egyptian early Christianity had a strongly Jewish character, as would be expected given that Alexandria contained the largest Jewish population outside of Palestine. It was also eclectic, manifesting "gnostic" variations under the leadership of Valentinus and Basilides,[5] as well as Manichaean communities,[6] and the early importation of the writings of Irenaeus, the great antagonist of the Valentinians.[7] We also hear of a catechetical school of Alexandria which at one time was headed by the great Origen, and, in Athanasius's own time, by Didymus the Blind. Athanasius's lifetime also saw the beginning and dramatic rise of the monastic movement in Egypt, and it would be part of the achievement of his episcopate to transform this conglomeration of desert-dwellers who were suspicious of authority and its pomp into a fairly cohesive group who were intensely loyal to him and zealous for doctrinal orthodoxy.

Athanasius, the man who was destined to maintain a tumultuously intermittent reign over the Egyptian Church for almost half of the fourth century, was born ca. 295–299 CE.[8] We know very little about his early years. The Arabic *History of the Patriarchs of Alexandria*, composed by the tenth-century Egyptian bishop Severus Ibn al-Muqaffa, indicates that his parents were not Christians, describing the young Athanasius as "the son of an eminent woman who was a worshipper of idols and very rich."[9] The same text contains an account of how Athanasius as a young man was baptized along with his mother and taken under the tutelage of the bishop Alexander. It speaks of the efforts of his mother to try to procure for her son a suitable bride, which were continually rebuffed, whereupon she arranged for him to have the opportunity of being persuaded by "a wise man":

> She brought an Alexandrian who was a wise magician, from among the wise men of Saba, and she told him about how things stood with her son. He said to her, "Let me dine with him today." So she was overjoyed and prepared a great feast and the man met with her son and they ate and drank. But the next day the philosopher came to her and said, "Do not trouble yourself. You have no control over your son for he has become a Galilean and subscribes to the views of the Galileans, and he will become a great man." She said, "Who are the Galileans?" He said to her, "They are the ones who belong to the Church, who have destroyed the temples and demolished the statues. When she heard this, she said to herself, "If I distance myself from him, he will leave me and I will be left alone." So she immediately got up and took him with her and went to Alexander and related to him the situation of Athanasius her son and his whole story. Then she and her son were baptized. After some time, she died and Athanasius remained like a son with the Father Alexander, who educated him with gentleness in every art. He memorized the gospels and read the divine scriptures and when he was mature, Alexander ordained him a deacon and made him his scribe and he

3

became like an interpreter of the father and a minister of the word which he wished to speak.[10]

Leaving to one side the question of the historical veracity of all the details of this story, it is valuable nevertheless to note some of its features which bear tangible correspondence with more direct evidence. The tradition that Athanasius was of "pagan" parents might partly explain his concern with the theme of Christianity vs. "the Greeks," taken up in his first major doctrinal work, *Against the Greeks – On the Incarnation*.[11] It would also explain the indirectness of his testimony, in his *History of the Arians*, about the persecution of Maximin in 311–312.[12] The story also strikingly conveys the close relationship between Athanasius and Alexander, a relationship that by all accounts must have begun while the former was a very young man. Particularly intriguing is the designation of the young Athanasius as Alexander's "scribe," "interpreter," and "minister of the word which he wished to speak."[13] Such a characterization not only emphasizes the clear continuity in the theological perspectives of the two Patriarchs but seems to lend some credence to the theory that at least one of the important doctrinal letters of Alexander was actually written by Athanasius.[14]

That Athanasius was "educated" by Alexander at least indicates the lack of a formal course of education, which is also conceded by the panegyric of Gregory of Nazianzus.[15] This is not to say that a man of Athanasius's intelligence did not avail himself of whatever store of knowledge was readily available to him. Especially his early writing displays at least a colloquial familiarity with philosophical concepts of the various schools, in particular a Stoic cosmology which is employed to speak of the Word as the principle of harmony in the cosmos, and a Middle Platonic ontology in which God is characterized as true being, to which creaturely being is linked by participation.[16] His use of classical rhetorical techniques has also been noted.[17] The reference to Athanasius's familiarity with and study of the Scriptures represents an enduring portrait of Athanasius as a theologian steeped in the Scriptures. Gregory of Nazianzus speaks of him in a similar vein as "meditating on every book of the Old and New Testament with a depth which no one else has reached with even one of them."[18] Quite naturally, a formation under the shadow of the bishop of Alexandria would include a substantial diet of the principal texts of the Alexandrian tradition. In his later debates with the "Arians," Athanasius would refer respectfully to "the diligent Origen,"[19] and he quotes his episcopal predecessors Dionysius and Alexander, as well as Theognostus.[20] Some close textual parallels and similarity of perspective would also indicate a close familiarity with the theology of Irenaeus, whose writings, as we noted above, were readily available in Egypt soon after their composition.[21]

As evidence of his precocious abilities, we find Athanasius already a deacon and the principal secretary of Bishop Alexander at the Council of Nicaea of 325, when he was barely 30 years old, if not younger. Three years after the Council of Nicaea, on 17 April 328, Alexander died and Athanasius was elected bishop. His consecration was immediately contested. There were accusations that he was under the canonical age of 30, that he was consecrated by a group of seven bishops who withdrew from a larger synod in order to ordain Athanasius secretly, and, according to one version, that Athanasius himself lured two bishops into a church, shut the door behind him, and forced them to consecrate him as bishop. These accusations come from Athanasius's opponents, of which there was never a lack, and they were to be roundly refuted by an Egyptian synod in 338.[22] The historical context of these charges and their rebuttal partly predates Athanasius's ecclesiastical career and stems from internal conflicts within the Egyptian Church that began during the Diocletian persecution and were then complicated and intermingled with the doctrinal debates associated with the Council of Nicaea. Thus, from the moment of his consecration, the biography of Athanasius is inseparable from doctrinal and ecclesiastical issues in a way that bears out Harnack's characterization of him as "a man whose biography coincides with the history of dogma of the fourth century."[23]

The Melitian schism

The fourth-century historian Epiphanius tells us that the source of the Melitian schism was a disagreement between a newly appointed bishop, Melitius of Lycopolis, and the bishop of Alexandria, Peter, over the status of those who lapsed during the Diocletian persecution.[24] According to this account, Peter was disposed to a more lenient stance, which was rejected by the more rigorist Melitius. Melitius's ordaining of presbyters sympathetic to his views in dioceses which were not under his jurisdiction then led to his excommunication by Peter. More recently, it has been persuasively argued that the issue of the proper disposition toward the lapsed was not a central one in the Melitian schism,[25] and that Melitius was simply responding – whether out of ambition or pastoral concern – to the void created by imprisoned bishops who were unavailable to administer their own dioceses. The real issue, according to this rendering of the matter, was the challenge represented by Melitius to the traditional authority of the bishop of Alexandria, "the refusal, by a dissident bishop, of Alexandrian oversight and the monopoly exercised by the capital over the rest of the country."[26] But whatever be the original circumstances, the result was a split in the Egyptian Church that persevered after the end of the persecution in 313, and resulted in two parallel Church bodies tensely juxtaposed. In a synodal letter addressed to the Churches of Egypt, Libya, and the Pentapolis, the Council of Nicaea attempted to resolve this schism by allowing Melitian clergy to continue to serve, albeit "after being confirmed by a holier imposition of hands," but prohibited Melitius himself from administering any more ordinations, and stipulated that Melitian clergy be subject to the jurisdiction of the "catholic bishop," Alexander.[27] These terms, along with the reaffirmation of the authority of the bishop of Alexandria over Egypt, Libya, and the Penatapolis, constituted a resolution that was decidedly more favorable to Alexander than it was to the Melitians. Nevertheless, it seems that after some resistance which drew the intervention of the emperor Constantine himself, Melitius was able to persuade his supporters to accept the terms of Nicaea, and presented his clergy in person to Alexander. Shortly afterwards, however, Alexander died, and the ensuing process of choosing a successor again alienated the Melitians, who were excluded from the proceedings, perhaps after trying to consecrate one of their own number.[28] The accession of Athanasius to the episcopal throne of Alexandria thus led to a reopening of the Melitian schism, though the Melitians themselves seem to have fragmented into various factions. One of these factions, led by John Arcaph, eventually forged an alliance with the sympathizers of Arius that would lead to Athanasius's first exile.

Origins of the Nicene crisis[29]

We do not have any reliable records to indicate the precise date and exact order of the events that initiated the doctrinal debates of the fourth century.[30] We know that sometime between 318 and 320 a crisis erupted within the Egyptian Church, which quickly spread outwards and eventually enveloped the whole empire in a controversy that was arguably the most significant moment in the development of Christian doctrine. The original parties in the controversy were Arius and Alexander, the former an ascetic and charismatic priest of Alexandria, and the latter Patriarch of Alexandria. At this early stage of the controversy, Arius's position was associated with the provocative slogan "there was once when the Son was not," while Alexander strongly insisted on the doctrine of the eternal generation of the Son. The early Church historians Socrates (ca. 380–450) and Sozomen (fifth century) give somewhat divergent accounts as to the impetus of the controversy. Socrates seems to assign the initiative to Alexander, whom he describes as attempting "too ambitious a discourse" on the subject of Triune unity, to which Arius reacts out of a fear of Sabellianism, a modalist reduction of the Trinity into a singular unity.[31] Sozomen, on the other hand, characterizes Arius as "a most expert logician" who initiated investigations into hitherto unexamined questions and thus came up with a novel doctrine which "no one before him had ever suggested."[32] Of these two accounts, the more plausible is surely that of Socrates. Given that Christian piety has always centered on the worship and exaltation of the figure of Christ, it is highly unlikely that an ecclesiastical figure would simply come up with a doctrine that would seem to militate against that momentum unless it were as a reaction to a perceived exaggeration. So the more natural scenario is that Alexander delivered a sermon that put emphatic stress on the correlational unity of the Father and the Son, which Arius construed as endangering both the clear distinction between the Father and the Son as well as the monarchy of the Father. To Arius's ears, Alexander's doctrine then would have seemed to obfuscate both divine unity and trinity, collapsing the Trinity into a modalism and violating the unity by "portioning" the divine essence.

What Socrates' and Sozomen's accounts have in common, however, is a recognition that the controversy, from its opening stage, was moving into somewhat uncharted waters. Whether it was Alexander who was "too ambitious" or Arius who began to enquire into "what had not until then been examined," a clarification of the nature of the relation between the Father and the Son was rather overdue, and both Arius and Alexander pushed the question considerably further than their predecessors. The underlying ambiguity that proved to be such fertile ground for the ensuing controversy can perhaps best be illustrated by reference to another great Alexandrian theologian, Origen (ca. 185–ca. 251). On the one hand, Origen taught that the Son was eternally generated by the

Father,[33] although his doctrine in even that regard was placed in an ambivalent context, since he also asserted that creation was always coexistent with God.[34] On the other hand, Origen maintained subordinationist language in speaking of the relative status of the Father and the Son, saying, for example, that while the Son transcends creation, he is himself transcended by the Father,[35] who is "better and greater than the Word."[36] Such ambivalence could not endure for long. As the doctrine of *creatio ex nihilo* became an accepted element of Christian doctrine, it became increasingly necessary to clarify the status of the Son relative both to creation and to the Father. The process of such clarification was likely already an ongoing project in Alexandrian theology before things came to a head with the confrontation between Alexander and Arius. Later fourth-century debates between Athanasius and his opponents would advert to a tense exchange of letters in the mid-third century between Dionysius, bishop of Alexandria, and his namesake, the bishop of Rome.[37] The bishop of Alexandria is reported to have been upbraided by Dionysius of Rome for rejecting the application of the term "*homoousios*" (of one being) to the Son. In controversy with a group of Libyan Christians whom he considered to be Sabellian in their lack of differentiation between the Father and the Son, Dionysius is said to have referred to the Son as "something made (*poiēma*) which came into being (*genēton*)" and "not belonging (*idios*) by nature but alien in being (*ousia*) from the Father."[38] According to this account, Dionysius likens the relation of the Father and the Son to that between the planter of the vine and the vine, or the shipbuilder and the ship, adding that the Son "was not before he came into being."[39] Athanasius defended Dionysius by emphasizing the anti-Sabellian context in which Dionysius was expressing himself and by citing supposedly later texts in which Dionysius of Alexandria modified and defended his views to his namesake in Rome and clarified that there was never a time when God was not Father. According to Athanasius, the compromising analogies were replaced by others that sought to underline the correlational coexistence of Father and Son, such as the example of the light and its radiance.[40]

Athanasius also cites another Alexandrian contemporary of Dionysius and previous head of the catechetical school, Theognostus (d. 282). Theognostus's articulations are much more readily conformable to Athanasius's own position. The being of the Son, says Theognostus, is not "external" and not procured from non-existence but is from the Father's being. The analogies he uses include that of the sun and the ray, as well as water and vapor.[41] On the other hand, it is reported by the ninth-century Patriarch of Constantinople, Photius, that Theognostus spoke of the Son as a creature, *ktisma*.[42] But in the context of Origenian theology, which is the proper framework for understanding Theognostus, such an affirmation does not equate to derivation from nothing, but simply to the fact of derivation. The construction of a difference between "creation" and "generation" is a later development, which owes much to Athanasius himself and the problematic of the Arian controversy.

In the figure of Theognostus (as well as Dionysius, if his exchange with Dionysius of Rome is indeed authentic), we see attempts to hold in tandem both the affirmation of a correlational coexistence between Father and Son, as well as an acknowledgment of the derivative status of the Son. This tension, whose Alexandrian history is traceable, as we have seen, at least as far back as Origen, comes to somewhat of a breaking point in the original controversy between Arius and Alexander. Alexander emphasized especially Origen's doctrine of the eternal generation of the Son and of the Son's being a perfect "Image" of the Father. As the Father's perfect image, the Son is eternally present with the Father and is not derived from non-existence, and there is no "interval" between Son and Father.[43] Arius, on the other hand, radicalized a subordinationist streak that could also base itself on one tendency in Origen's theology, now viewed from the perspective of a doctrine of creation that unambiguously posited its origination from nothing. If the Son is derived from the Father, then he also comes into being from non-existence; hence the infamous slogan "there was once when the Son was not." Arius did not hesitate to draw out the implications of this statement in order to make his doctrine consistent. Thus, God is described as "supremely unique"; he was not always "Father" of the Son, but existed "before" the Son. Conversely, the Son belongs to (*idios*) the category of things which have come into being and are created, although he is of a pre-eminently higher rank than all other creatures. He comes into being, by the will of the Father, for the sake of accomplishing God's act of creating. The divine Trinity therefore is constituted of dissimilar entities (*hypostases*). Moreover, as a creature whose glory is infinitely transcended by that of the Father, the Son does not fully comprehend the Father, nor indeed his own essence. Again, as a creature, the Word is by nature changeable, though he is rendered *de facto* unchangeable by God's grace, in anticipation of his merits.[44]

By Athanasius's report, Arius popularized his theology by

casting it in poetic form and setting it to a melody, while his supporters preached it vigorously in the marketplace, accosting dock-workers and pregnant women to engage them in questions of human and divine generation. Responding to Arius's teachings, Alexander summoned a council of Egyptian bishops, which drew up a "confession of orthodoxy" to which Arius was asked to give his assent. He refused to sign and was excommunicated by Alexander. With the departure of Arius from Alexandria, the Arian controversy was exported beyond the confines of the Egyptian Church. He and his supporters traveled to other sees in search of support, and their efforts met with some success, most notably in their gaining the sympathy of Eusebius, bishop of Nicomedia, the city where the emperor lived. Eusebius was a powerful ally and could boast of connections and influence at the imperial court. He would become the emperor Constantine's primary ecclesiastical advisor and the one who administered his baptism when the emperor was on his deathbed.

The result of Arius's protestations to other bishops and his alliance with Eusebius of Nicomedia was a council held in Bithynia in 320 which validated his views as orthodox and demanded his reinstatement by Alexander, only to be rebuffed by the latter. In 324, the emperor Constantine, until then emperor of the Western part of the empire, defeated his rival in the East, Licinius, and became sole emperor. He then directly intervened in the matter, sending a blustering letter to both Alexander and Arius, urging them to stop their public quibbling over "a matter of futile irrelevance."[45] In the absence of this desired outcome, Constantine appointed the bishop of Cordoba, Hosius, to deal with the controversy. Hosius summoned a synod in Antioch, which denounced the doctrine of Arius and announced a wider council to deal with the issue. Originally to be held in Ancyra, the council was moved at the last minute to Nicaea, with the explanation that the air there was nicer, although the fact that Nicaea was closer to the emperor's residence in Nicomedia was probably not irrelevant. While by far the greater majority of participants were Easterners, the Council of Nicaea nevertheless represented the first attempt to convene a general council of the whole Church of the Roman empire. Thanks to the subsequent reception of its doctrine, this council was to become known in the Christian tradition as the first "ecumenical" council.

The Council of Nicaea

We do not have exact figures for the number of bishops attending the Council of Nicaea. By the end of the fourth century, the prestige accorded to it is indicated by the midrashic headcount of 318, the number of men led by Abraham to rescue Lot (Gen 14:14).[46] Among those in attendance was the young deacon Athanasius, acting as secretary to Bishop Alexander. The council opened in May 325 and continued its deliberations until July of that year. Among the secondary issues on the agenda, it pronounced on the date of Easter, forbade the translation of bishops from one diocese to another, and tried to address the rupture of the Egyptian Church due to the Melitian schism. But its primary concern was the controversy between Alexander and Arius. As recounted by Athanasius,[47] the main challenge for those who wanted to decisively refute Arius's doctrine was to find a way to articulate the relationship between the Son and the Father that could not be co-opted by Arius and his supporters and interpreted in a sense consonant with the belief that the Son had a beginning of his existence. Such biblical terms as "Image," for example, could be accepted by Arius's supporters, with the caveat that even human beings are God's image, despite being creatures. Eventually, it became necessary to resort to the unscriptural term "*homoousios*" (of one being), in order to rule out any suggestion of the Son's being a creature. Those who opposed Arius's doctrine prevailed, and so a creed was drawn up which included the litmus test of the "*homoousios*" formula, and anathematized anyone who would say that "there was once when [the Son] did not exist, and that he did not exist before he came into being and who allege that he came into being from nonexistence, or that he is from another subsistence (*hypostasis*) or substance (*ousia*), or is alterable or changeable."[48] Arius was exiled and Athanasius's mentor, Alexander, seemed to be vindicated.

The aftermath of Nicaea

The declaration of Nicaea, however, by no means put an end to the controversy. In many quarters, the employment of the term "*homoousios*" to describe the relation between the Father and the Son was frowned upon both because it was an unscriptural term and because it seemed vulnerable to a "Sabellian," or modalist, interpretation. Arius was recalled from exile by Constantine himself, and pressure was brought to bear on Alexander to readmit him to communion in the Egyptian Church.[49] This he steadfastly refused to do. When Alexander died

11

three years after the council, in 328, the young Athanasius became his successor, to the evident displeasure of some Melitians. In strict continuity with both the theology and ecclesiastical policy of his mentor, Athanasius also staunchly refused any compromise in the opposition to Arius and his doctrine, rejecting overtures on Arius's behalf by both the emperor Constantine and Eusebius of Nicomedia. Instead, the new bishop moved quickly to consolidate his position, traveling throughout Egypt with a large entourage and fostering his association with the growing monastic movement in the Thebaid.[50] It is perhaps to this period, in the aftermath of his controversial episcopal ordination, that we should attribute his first doctrinal treatise, *Against the Greeks – On the Incarnation* (ca. 328–335).[51] While making no mention of Arius, this work clearly defends the full divinity of the Word who became incarnate in Jesus Christ. Only one who fully shares in the reality of the Father can save us from ignorance, corruptibility, and death, which are the fruits of human sinfulness. Integral to the apologetic argument of the work is a triumphalist strain that points to the holiness and peace of the Church as concrete evidence that the crucified Christ is risen and active, and manifests through the Church a mode of activity that can only derive from genuine divinity. Such a triumphalist reading of the current state of the Church makes it implausible that Athanasius wrote this work during his first exile, as has been suggested.[52] It rather invokes the situation of a young embattled bishop who is discreetly avoiding direct mention of his opponents, but who wishes to implicitly convey the message that the judgment of Nicaea on behalf of the full divinity of the Word is part of the manifest victory of Christ through the Church. Despite the strategic adoption of such a triumphalist posture, the new bishop of Alexandria soon found himself in a precarious position, with enemies among both the Egyptian Melitians and the supporters of Arius. The ranks of the latter group now included powerful figures outside of Egypt. Eusebius of Nicomedia, who had been advocating on behalf of Arius, forged an alliance with the Egyptian Melitians, which enabled them to bring their case against Athanasius to the emperor's court. This would set off a course of events that would lead to Athanasius's first exile.

The Council of Tyre and Athanasius's first exile (335–337)

The Melitians' charges against Athanasius were serious: that he had ordered Macarius, one of his priests, to break the chalice and overturn the altar of a Melitian priest, Isychras; that he had arranged for the murder of a bishop by the name of Arsenius; and that he had facilitated his own election, below the canonical age, through bribery. Athanasius's defense, which involved an audience with the emperor and the finding of the allegedly murdered Arsenius quite alive and hiding in Tyre, persuaded Constantine to dismiss the charges brought against the Alexandrian.

Athanasius appeared before Constantine and defended himself adequately enough to have the charges against him dismissed.[53] But under the leadership of Eusebius of Nicomedia, the persistence of the protestations against Athanasius on the part of the defenders of Melitius and Arius eventually persuaded the emperor to call a council, in Tyre, to put the issue to a close. This council set up the "Mareotic" commission to go to Egypt and investigate the charges brought against Athanasius. The membership of the commission was immediately protested by the Egyptian bishops on the grounds that it was biased. Nevertheless, the composition of the commission was maintained and it proceeded to the judgment that the charge that Macarius had broken the chalice of Isychras was legitimate. The Council of Tyre thereupon affirmed Arius's views as orthodox, admitted the Melitians to communion, and deposed Athanasius, who had already fled, having become convinced that he was not getting a fair hearing. Departing from Tyre, Athanasius made his way to Constantinople to make an appeal to the emperor. According to Athanasius's telling, Constantine, initially sympathetic to his cause, became alarmed when Athanasius's opponents produced the further charge that he had threatened to withhold the exportation of grain shipments from Egypt. On this matter, which involved the vital livelihood of the empire, Constantine was less disposed to give Athanasius the benefit of the doubt.[54] Whether due to this new accusation or simply Constantine's desire to consolidate the unity of the empire by neutralizing Athanasius's dogmatic opposition to Arius, the Alexandrian bishop was exiled to Trier, in Gaul, in 335. The removal of Athanasius from his see was protested by riots in the streets of Egypt, and pleas on his behalf by the popular monk Antony.[55] But Constantine's resolve was not shaken, and Athanasius's exile persisted until the emperor's death, two years later, in 337.

Athanasius's homecoming and second exile (339–346)

Upon the death of Constantine, government of the empire was divided among his three sons, Constantinus, Constans, and

Constantius. During his exile, Athanasius had already developed a friendship with Constantinus, who was residing in Trier. Constantinus accepted Athanasius's account of the Council of Tyre as a partisan affair conducted by the Alexandrian's enemies and tried to smooth over his father's exile of Athanasius by interpreting it as an imperial intervention on behalf of the bishop's safety.[56] Following the death of Constantine, Constantinus prevailed upon his brothers to issue an imperial edict, in the name of all three emperors, stipulating that exiled bishops be allowed to return to their sees. Athanasius made his way back to Alexandria in 337, by a roundabout route, stopping to plead his cause with Constantius, the new emperor of the East.

In Alexandria, the returning bishop was met with cheering crowds, but his triumph was to be short-lived. The "Eusebians," as Athanasius styled his opponents who were headed by Eusebius of Nicomedia, were not about to dispense with their efforts to rid Egypt of him. Within the year, they convened a council which reiterated the accusations of the council of Tyre and appointed a certain Pistus as the bishop of Alexandria. Pressing their case against Athanasius to all three emperors, they brought a new accusation against him, that of personally appropriating funds that were generated by the sale of wheat and intended for the benefit of widows. Athanasius's self-defense was waged both on the domestic and international fronts. Both the Egyptian bishops and Athansius's opponents sent delegations to Pope Julius in Rome, who discountenanced the appointment of Pistus on the ground of his earlier support of Arius. Athanasius also undertook a trip to Cappadocia to defend himself personally before Constantius. Inside Egypt, Athanasius convened a council in 338, which, in a published encyclical, defended Athanasius from the charges brought against him, and rejected the appointment of a rival bishop.[57] He also persisted in his efforts to consolidate monastic support, arranging for the popular monk Antony to come to Alexandria to enlist the weight of his now prodigious esteem on the side of the Nicene cause.[58] A later account, penned by Athanasius, of this appearance by Antony hints at rival claims by Arians to enlist monastic support and manifests Athanasius's ability to condense the complex issues of Nicea to core themes that are popularly digestible.[59] Athanasius has Antony make the crucial point, which was already clearly implicit in *Against the Greeks – On the Incarnation*, that to impute anything less than the fullness of divinity to the Son is a regression to "paganism," and renders Christian devotion to Christ a form of idolatry:

> When the Arians lied, claiming that he [Antony] held the same views as they, he became indignant and astonished when he heard about it. Then, on the request of the bishops and all the brothers, he came down from the mountain to Alexandria. He publicly condemned the Arian heresy, saying that this heresy was the last and the precursor to the Anti-Christ. He taught the people that the Son of God is not a creature and did not come into being from nothing but is the eternal Word and Wisdom of the being of the Father: "So it is impious to say that 'there was when He was not'. The Word exists eternally with the Father. So do not have any thing to do with these most impious Arians. 'For light has no fellowship with darkness' (2 Cor 6:14). You are pious Christians but they, who say of the Son who is from the Father and is the Word of God that He is a creature, differ in no way from the pagans, worshipping a creature instead of God the Creator (cf. Rom 1:25). Rest assured that the whole creation itself is indignant at them, because they number among created beings the Creator and Lord of all, in whom all things came into being." So all the people rejoiced to hear so great a man anathematizing the heresy which fights against Christ.
>
> (*Life of Antony* 69–70)[60]

However, Athanasius's successes at home and in enlisting the support of Pope Julius in Rome were offset by the tide of events in the East, which was decisively moving in the direction of his opponents. Stationed in Antioch, in the course of a campaign against the Persians, the Eastern emperor Constantius was prevailed upon to be present at a synod of bishops gathered there during the winter of 338–339. This synod included the members of the investigatory commission that had previously condemned Athanasius at the Council of Tyre. The Council of Antioch of 339 reiterated the charges that had been brought against Athanasius in Tyre and they also brought against him the new charges that he was responsible for violence that had ensued in the course of his return to Egypt, and that his return to Alexandria was itself illegitimate, since the decision of Tyre was still binding and had not been overturned by another Church council. This council then set about to find a replacement for Athanasius, whose reinstatement in Alexandria they considered to be illegitimate. With Pistus discredited, they offered the Alexandrian see to a Eusebius, future bishop of Emesa, who declined it, apparently citing the attachment of the Alexandrian people to their bishop.[61] They finally settled upon a cleric from Cappadocia, by the name of Gregory. Athanasius would later press the point that if he were to be replaced, it should at least have been done by a properly constituted Egyptian synod, "and not that a person brought by the Arians from a distance, as if trafficking in the title of bishop, and with the patronage and strong arm of pagan magistrates, should assert himself over those who neither requested nor desired his presence."[62] Athanasius's remarks here are indicative of his strategy to exploit the fact that the opposition to him inside Egypt constituted a negligible minority relative to the support for him which only steadily increased throughout his episcopal career. Increasingly, Athanasius could characterize the forces arrayed against him as an external imposition on the internal affairs of the Egyptian Church.[63]

The deposition of Athanasius and his replacement by Gregory of Cappadocia was facilitated by the reappointment of the prefect Philagrius, who had assisted the investigatory commission of the Council of Tyre, but had since been replaced by another prefect, Theodorus, who was considered to be a supporter of Athanasius.[64] Philagrius took the unprecedented step of publishing an imperial edict declaring Gregory of Cappadocia to be the bishop of Alexandria. On 23 March 339, Gregory entered the city and forcibly assumed the episcopal see of Alexandria. The prefect Philagrius energetically pursued his mission of seizing churches and handing them over to Gregory. The resultant plundering apparently drew even crowds of non-Christians who participated in the mayhem. Athanasius cites a litany of outrages: a church and baptistry set on fire, virgins and monks subjected to physical abuse, and the offering of pagan sacrifices at the altar.[65] The danger to his own person was such that Athanasius was forced to go into hiding. A month later, he left Egypt and, on the invitation of Pope Julius, went to Rome. Thus began his second exile, less than two years after his return from the first. His festal letter for 339, addressed to his flock in preparation for the celebration of Easter, is revelatory both of Athanasius's sense of anxiety and of his characteristic determination to adopt a stance of indefatigable, even triumphal perseverance. Manifesting a theme that is clearly a cornerstone of both his personal spirituality and his preaching, that of the imitation of the biblical saints,[66] he exhorts his flock to persevere in confessing the unqualified divinity of the Son and to imitate the steadfastness of the "righteous and faithful servants of the Lord":

> Although they may be surrounded by external trials and tribulations, they conform themselves to the words of the apostle and "enduring in tribulations and persevering in prayers" (Rom 12:12), and in contemplation of the law, they endure everything which happen to them. They are pleasing to God and recite what is written, "Though afflictions and anguish have come upon me, your commandments are my meditations" (Ps 119:143).
>
> (*Festal Letter* XI:6)[67]

> Let us make a joyful sound, along with the saints, and let no one neglect his duty. Especially at this time, let us consider as nothing the afflictions or the tribulations which the party of Eusebius has caused us because of their jealousy. Even now they still want to harm us and to achieve our death by their accusations, because we cling to that piety whose sustenance, however, is provided by the Lord. But, as God's faithful servants, we know that he is our salvation in time of trouble – for our Lord gave us this promise when he said "Blessed are you when people insult you and persecute you and utter every kind of evil against you falsely because of me. Rejoice and be very glad, for your reward is great in heaven" (Mt 5:11–12). The Redeemer's own words are that afflictions are not for every one in this world, but only for those who have a holy fear of him – therefore, the more we are cornered in by our enemies, the more free we should be; although they abuse us, let us maintain our gatherings; and the more they try to dissuade us from piety, the more boldly we should preach it, saying: "'Although all this has come upon us, we have not forgotten you' (Ps 44:18); and we have not shared in the evil of the Arian fanatics, who say that you have your being from non-being. The Word who is eternally with the Father is also from the Father."
>
> (*Festal Letter* XI:12)[68]

In the same festal letter, the Alexandrian bishop makes it clear to his flock that the theological issues involved in the controversy with the "Arians" are not a matter of arcane speculation but have everything to do with the authentic celebration of the great feast of Christ's Resurrection, which they are about to liturgically commemorate: "They say that he is not the Creator but a creature. If he was a creature, he would have been captured by death; but if, according to the Scriptures, he was not captured by death, then he is not a creature but the Lord of the creatures and the subject of this immortal feast."[69]

While exiled in Rome, Athanasius had occasion to make the acquaintance of another staunch opponent of Arius and his supporters, Marcellus of Ancyra. Marcellus, who had been deposed by a synod at Constantinople in 336, refused all talk that seemed to ascribe to God numerical differentiation and was widely regarded among Eastern bishops as a "Sabellian," who held that "Father" and "Son" were simply identical. Marcellus had written a treatise directed against another supporter of Arius, Asterius "the Sophist." Asterius, who hailed from Cappadocia, had capitulated and offered sacrifice to pagan gods during the persecution of Diocletian. He was thus ineligible for ecclesial office but was a prolific lay theologian and exegete. Asterius had written his *Syntagmation* some time before the Council of Nicaea. In it, he followed Arius in asserting that the Son is a creature and inferior to the Father, not integral to the divine essence of "the God" (*ho theos*) but produced as an effect of the Father's will and for the sake of being a "mediator" of God's creative agency. Because the Scriptures identify Jesus Christ as the Son of God and also as the "power," "wisdom," and "Word" of God – terms that in the scriptural idiom seem integral to divinity – Asterius also adopted Arius's distinction between the innate wisdom and Word of God which is integral to the divine essence, and the created word and wisdom which is the created "Son." At the same time, Asterius decisively modified the tenor and sometimes the substance of Arius's doctrine in some important respects. No longer is there any mention of the Son's creation "from nothing," and the notion that God was not always Father is replaced with the explanation that "the God" was always Father in the sense that his generative capacity is eternal and precedes the generation of the Son.[70] Even more strikingly, Asterius speaks of the Son as "the exact image of the substance, will, glory and power of the Father,"[71] although Arius himself had struck a much different note in asserting that Father, Son, and Spirit are "wholly and infinitely unlike each other in substance and splendor."[72] In general, the strongly apophatic character of Arius's theology, which led him to state that even the Son does not know the Father or his own essence, is very much attenuated in the theology of Asterius. The latter placed greater stress on the title of "Unbegotten" as revelatory of the divine being, and on the Incarnate Son as fulfilling the mediatorial role of positively manifesting divinity to creation.[73]

The theology of Asterius, along with that of Arius, is the target of a comprehensive refutation of various strands of anti-Nicene theology that Athanasius undertook while in exile, in Rome. In the three *Orations against the Arians*,[74] Athanasius's defense of Nicene theology is for the most part confined to the scriptural domain. He largely eschews the Nicene formulation of the relation between the Father and the Son as "*homoousios*," whose lack of scriptural provenance was one of its central liabilities, and concerns himself instead with attacking the scriptural bases of anti-Nicene theology. This anti-Nicene theology found support in scriptural references that seemed to indicate that the Son's divinity was not something natural, eternal, and equal to that of the Father. Such were references to Jesus Christ as having "received" exaltation and divine prerogatives, suggesting that his divinity was attained "by grace" or divine favor, rather than "by nature." A central example was Phil 2:9, which seemed to indicate that the exaltation of Christ and his gaining of "the name that is above every name" was something that was bestowed upon him by God as a reward for his salvific labors. References to the Son's human weaknesses (his hunger, fear, lack of knowledge, etc.) were also taken as indicative of the subordinate rank of his deity. At the heart of the scriptural debate was the key text of Prov 8:22, "He created me as the beginning of his ways for his works," which was taken as referring to the originated rather than eternal being of the Word. On the other hand, the anti-Nicene positions that Athanasius is countering were challenged by such scriptural titles of the Son as "God," "Lord," "Wisdom," "Light," "Truth," and "Image," the very titles that were incorporated in the "Dedication" creed of Antioch. Athanasius's theological opponents dealt with these scriptural titles by asserting that they belonged to the Son not by nature but by participation "as a grace." In response, Athanasius constructs a Trinitarian hermeneutics which seeks to ground Nicene Trinitarian theology firmly in the narrativity and linguistic intertextuality of the scriptural witness. His three *Orations against the Arians*, which were likely penned between 339 and 343, during his exile in Rome,[75] represent the doctrinal substance of Athanasius's mature reflections "which would serve as a main literary reference during the next three decades of his long episcopate."[76]

Meanwhile, Pope Julius had been trying for some time to convene a council which would gather together Athanasius and his supporters as well as the "Eusebians," with the aim of adjudicating the charges brought against Athanasius at the Council of Tyre. After being rebuffed by the Eusebians, Julius proceeded to summon a local council in Rome, early in 341, which judged in favor of Athanasius and determined the accession of his replacement, Gregory, to be uncanonical. Marcellus produced a confession of faith which apparently couched his modalist views such that they were acceptable to the Roman synod, and he too was reinstated. This proved to be a fateful step which considerably complicated matters, for it gave the Eastern bishops some ground for asserting that the Nicene formula was at least susceptible or even hospitable to a "Sabellian" interpretation. Pope Julius's intervention, far from bringing the matter to a resolution, had the effect merely of intensifying the breach between East and West. The Eastern bishops declined his invitation to participate in a council dealing with the charges against Athanasius on the principle that Athanasius had already been condemned at the Council of Tyre, and that the judgment of one Church council cannot be re-examined by another. In an indignant and dismissive response, Julius questioned how this reasoning can be consistent with the readmission of Arians to communion and the appointment to the Alexandrian see of Pistus, whom Julius reports to have been condemned by the Council of Nicaea as a supporter of Arius. Julius asserted his firm belief in the innocence of Athanasius and, adhering to Athanasius's own reading of the situation, noted that the predominantly external pressure to dispose of Athanasius cannot be privileged over the supportive testimony of the Egyptian bishops themselves, "especially considering that you are far away while they are on the scene and they know the man and the events that took place there and write in testimony to his manner of life and clearly confirm that he has been the victim of a conspiracy all along" (*Defence against the Arians* 27).[77] At this point, the issue of the legitimacy of the intervention of the bishop of Rome in matters relating to other churches becomes intricately interwoven with that of the intervention of other bishops in the affairs of the Egyptian Church. It is to be gathered from Julius's letter that the Eastern bishops saw his intervention as meddling in manners that had been decisively settled and were not open to reexamination, while he saw himself as coming to the defense of a local church whose integrity was being violated:

> And yet after all this you fault us for departing from the canons? ... Consider, then, who it is who is acting in transgression of the canons: we, who have received this man after so many proofs [of his innocence], or those in Antioch, who from the distance of a thirty-six days' journey, named a foreigner as bishop and sent him to Alexandria with military force? ... What ecclesiastical canon or which apostolic tradition is this, that while a church was at peace and there were so many bishops in unanimity with Athanasius, the bishop of Alexandria, Gregory should be sent there, a foreigner to the city, who was neither baptized there nor known to the people, nor requested by the presbyters or the bishops or the people – someone who was appointed in Antioch but then sent to Alexandria, accompanied not by priests nor by deacons of that city nor by the bishops of Egypt but by soldiers?
>
> (*Defence against the Arians* 29–30)[78]

The estrangement between Rome and the Eastern churches was further confirmed by the Easterners' meeting separately in Antioch, later in the same year of 341. Gathered in order to dedicate the "Golden-Domed" church, built by Constantius, the Eastern bishops took the opportunity to convene a council in response to Julius's council in Rome and his trenchant missive. In addressing the doctrinal concerns underlying the conflict, this "Council of the Dedication," of which Asterius was a participant, inaugurated attempts to conjure up a doctrinal alternative to the "*homoousios*" of Nicaea with its Sabellian evocation. It produced three creeds, while a fourth was issued a few months later by yet another gathering in Antioch. Most significant of these, as indicative of a rather "mainstream" Eastern response to the Nicene Council, is the second, or "Dedication," creed, which shows unmistakable signs of the influence of Asterius. This creed tries to carve out a middle way, shunning both the "*homoousios*" and the assertion that the Son is from non-being. It simply abstracts from the problematic of making a precise distinction between the Son's ontological status and that of creation, and refers to the Son mainly by his key scriptural titles: "living Wisdom, true Light, Way, Truth, unchanging and unaltering, the exact image of the Godhead and the substance, will, power, and glory of the Father." With an anti-Sabellian, anti-Marcellan thrust, it is emphatic in its assertion that the Trinity is three in *hypostasies*, but one in "agreement" (*symphonia*).[79]

On the political front, both Pope Julius and Athanasius were pleading the latter's case to the Western emperor Constans. In sympathetic response, Constans called a council in Sardica (now Sophia, Bulgaria) in 343. This time, the Easterners sent a delegation of bishops which included five of the six members of the original Mareotic Commission that had condemned Athanasius at the Council of Tyre. On seeing that the Western contingent included Athanasius, Marcellus, and other exiled bishops, the Easterners refused to participate unless those who were the object of accusations were excluded from the proceedings. On the other hand, the Westerners insisted that since the purpose of this council was to re-examine these very accusations, the accused must be allowed to be present. In light of this stalemate, the news of Constantius's victory over the Persians provided an opportune occasion for the Eastern bishops to withdraw, explaining that they must return to congratulate the emperor on his victory. Making their way back into the Eastern part of the kingdom and the jurisdiction of Constantius, they stopped at Philoppolis, where they excommunicated Athanasius, Marcellus, and Pope Julius, as well as Hosius of Cordoba, who had convened the Antiochian council which anticipated the Council of Nicaea in denouncing Arius. They published a document, which singled out Marcellus of Ancyra for heretical views and reiterated accusations that Athanasius engaged in violent behavior both before the Council of Tyre and after his return from exile. The attempts to exonerate Athanasius from the condemnation of Tyre were interpreted as inaugurating the unacceptable precedent that Eastern bishops are to be judged by Western. On the other hand, the Western bishops gathered among themselves and reasserted their support of both Athanasius and, once again, Marcellus, and, for their part, announced the deposition of a number of Eastern bishops whom they considered to be Arian. Moreover, with an eye to the troubles of Athanasius and other deposed bishops, it was decided that bishops deposed from their sees could appeal to the see of Rome. They also published a profession of faith which took aim at what they considered to be an equivocation on the question of the unqualified divinity of the Son: "We disqualify and expel from the catholic church those who assert that Christ is indeed God, but that he is not true God, that he is Son, but not true Son; that he is begotten and at the same time has come into existence; for this is the way in which they regularly interpret 'begotten,' professing, as we have said above, that 'begotten' is 'having come into existence.'"[80]

The rupture between East and West was thus broadened, with the Western bishops tending to interpret the anti-Sabellian caution of the Eastern bishops as "Arian", while the Eastern bishops were disposed to see the strongly anti-Arian stance of the West as tending to Sabellianism.[81] This ecclesiastical divide between East and West was reflected in the opposing postures of the emperors Constantius in the East and Constans in the West. But in the aftermath of the Council of Sardica, some rapprochement between the two emperors seemed to be in the offing. The Western Constans sent a delegation to his brother in the East requesting the reinstatement of the pro-Nicene exiles. This mission seems to have softened Constantius somewhat, and he wrote a public letter forbidding the persecution of Athanasius's supporters in Alexandria.[82] The momentum toward reconciliation was further reflected in yet another council in Antioch, in 344, which attempted to arrive at a mediating position by issuing a creed (the "*Macrostich*" or "Long-lined" creed) rejecting the teaching that the Son is from "non-being," while maintaining that the Son is to be "subordinated" to the Father, as deriving from the Father "by intention and will."[83] Certainly, by the standards of Athanasius's theology, such a statement would not have passed muster. Nevertheless, a delegation was sent to Milan with this creed in order to present it to the Western bishops. The Western bishops were unwilling to consider the Eastern creed unless the Antiochian delegation passed the litmus test of condemning Arius. This the Antiochenes indignantly refused to do, and so the attempted reconciliation was aborted.

However, a reconciliation of sorts between Athanasius and the Eastern emperor Constantius was still in the making. Constantius invited Athanasius personally to plead his own cause before him and, with his replacement, Gregory of Cappadocia, now recently dead (d. 345), intimated that Athanasius would be restored to his see. After some hesitation and delay, Athanasius eventually made his way to Constantius, where he was given assurances that the emperor's disfavor of him was now to be reversed. After what seems to have been an unexpectedly cordial meeting, Athanasius was allowed to return to Alexandria, to jubilant welcome. He was able to spend the next decade in his own see, the longest period of uninterrupted residency in his 46 years as bishop.

"The Golden Decade": 346–356

The return of Athanasius to Alexandria was an event of great public celebration and personal triumph. A modern historian comments that "his triumphant progress into Alexandria resembled less the return of an exiled bishop than the *adventus* of a Roman emperor."[84] It is consistent with Athanasius's own psychological disposition, pastoral deportment, and apologetic strategy that he himself interprets his own deliverance as a triumph for the whole Egyptian Church, and he depicts this ecclesial triumph in terms of a joyful renaissance of Christian discipleship. Signaling his steadily growing engagement with the monastic movement and his consolidation of it under his own tutelage, Athanasius would later associate his triumphant re-entry upon the episcopal throne of Alexandria particularly with a renaissance of asceticism:

> I hardly need to speak of the bishops of Egypt and Libya and of the people of these lands and of Alexandria. They all assembled together and their joy was unspeakable, for not only had they received their friends back alive, which was beyond all their hope, but they were delivered from the heretics, who were like tyrants and raging dogs. Great was the delight of the people as they gathered in worship and incited each other to virtue. How many single women who were previously preparing themselves for marriage remained virgins for Christ! How many young men, witnessing the examples of others, fell in love with the monastic life! How many fathers urged their children and how many were persuaded by their children not to shirk back from the ascetic discipline in Christ! How many wives convinced their husbands and how many were persuaded by their husbands to "devote themselves to prayer," as the apostle said (1 Cor 7:5)! How many widows and orphans, who were previously hungry and unclothed, received both food and clothing through the great zeal of the people. In short, the contest for virtue was such that one would have thought every family and household to be a church, on account of the virtuous nobility of its members and their prayers offered to God. There was a deep and wonderful peace among the churches, as the bishops wrote from everywhere to Athanasius and received from him the customary letters of peace.
>
> (*History of the Arians* 25)[85]

Such an idealized picture doubtless reflects Athanasius's fond memories of the relatively peaceful times that immediately followed his return. But the first intimation that this peace was about to end came in 350, with the death of Constans, the Western emperor and supporter of Athanasius. Constans was killed by his general, Magnentius, who then took over control of the Western empire. In the East, Constantius initiated a campaign against his brother's usurper, which by 353 had succeeded to the point where Magnentius acknowledged defeat by committing suicide. As long as the outcome of the rivalry between Constantius and Magnentius was in doubt, both vied for the support of Athanasius, coveting the weight of his authority and popularity among the Egyptian people. The situation became quite different when Constantius attained sole control of the Roman empire. Not having to reckon with his brother's restraining presence, Constantius could now pursue his anti-Nicene policies with far more rigor, a state of affairs that would not bode well for Athanasius.

An ominous sign of the turning tide was a council held in Sirmium, in 351, with Constantius himself present. The resultant "First Sirmian" creed now discountenanced the Nicene doctrine of the relation between the Father and the Son as "one in essence" (*homoousios*), which it interprets as implying that the Son is an "extension" of the Father's being. In response, Athanasius's own position became even more entrenched. Up to this point, he had largely avoided the controversial term "*homoousios*," and tried to articulate the Nicene theology of the full divinity of the Son in strictly scriptural terms. Beginning with the writing of *On the Council of Nicaea* (*De Decretis*; ca. 352–353),[86] his position henceforth becomes increasingly defined by an insistence on the unimpeachable authority of the Council of Nicaea and the necessity for adhering to its definition of the relationship between the Father and the Son.

At the same time, Constantius's policy was becoming more aggressive. In 353, he summoned a council in Arles, and in 355 yet another in Milan. In these two councils, imperial pressure was brought to bear on the Western bishops to depose Athanasius and accept a doctrinal formula antithetical to Nicene doctrine.[87] Subjected to intimidation and threats, the bishops largely capitulated; the few who withstood imperial coercion were deposed from their sees and exiled. As opposition to the Nicene formulation grew under the tutelage of Constantius, he prepared to make his move directly on Athanasius. He sent his secretary, Diogenes, to seize

Athanasius by force, an attempt which proved unsuccessful in the face of public support for the bishop. Diogenes' mission, however, was merely transferred into the hands of the *dux* Syrianus, who began concentrating imperial forces from around the area into Alexandria. Alarmed, Athanasius and his supporters recalled to Syrianus the past overtures of goodwill on the part of Constantius, and were assured by Syrianus that he would not take any action until the matter was adjudicated by the emperor. But any sense of security generated by this apparent concession merely gave Syrianus the advantage of surprise. Just past midnight, on 8 February 356, Syrianus and his troops stormed the church of Theonas, where Athanasius was celebrating with his congregation. Athanasius's account of the incident, which in its substance can hardly be dismissed as fallacious given the public setting of the event, drama-tizes a classic instance of his capacity for self-possession in times of danger:

> It was now already night and some of the people were keeping vigil, in anticipation of the coming service. The general Syrianus suddenly appeared with more than five thousand soldiers bearing arms and drawn swords, bows, spears, and clubs, as I said before. He surrounded the church and stationed the soldiers nearby so that no one would be able to pass by them and leave the church. I considered it unreasonable to abandon the people in the midst of such turmoil, and not rather to endanger myself for their sakes. So I sat upon the throne and urged that first the deacon should read a psalm and the people respond, "For his mercy is forever" (Ps 136), and then everyone should leave and go away to their homes. But the general then entered by force and the soldiers surrounded the altar in order to arrest us. The clergy and the people who were there shouted and demanded that we also depart. But I refused, saying that I would not leave until each and every one of them had left. And so, getting up and exhorting everyone to prayer, I commanded that everyone else leave first, saying, "It is better for me to endanger myself than to have any of you come to harm." When most of the people had gone out and the remaining were following them, the monks who were with us and some of the clergy came up and dragged us away. And so, as truth is my witness, while some of the soldiers were standing around the altar and

others were going around the church, we passed through. Guided and protected by the Lord, we escaped their notice and went away, greatly glorifying God in that we had not abandoned the people, but had first sent them off and were then enabled to save ourselves and flee from the hands of our pursuers.

(*Defence of his Flight* 24)[88]

The third exile: 356–362

Now in hiding, Athanasius at first sought to defend himself and attempt a rapprochement with the emperor in his *Defence before Constantius*. He had originally intended to present his defense personally to the emperor in Milan, but the notion of a direct encounter with the emperor was abandoned upon his hearing of the banishment of the prominent pro-Nicene bishops Hosius of Cordoba and Pope Liberius, as well as that of a considerable number of Egyptian bishops. Constantius had also sent a letter to the Egyptian people, full of invective against Athanasius, excoriating him as "a man who had come from the lowest pits," who had won over the simple people by deceit and demagoguery, and who deserves to be killed "ten times over."[89] In the same letter, Constantius announced Athanasius's replacement, another Cappadocian named George, who was recommended by Constantius as a "learned man" but of whom Athanasius disdainfully noted that he had amassed a fortune by selling pork to the army.[90] Although the supporters of Athanasius maintained control over the churches of Alexandria for the next several months, an intensified policy of coercion eventually resulted in their being transferred over to the control of the imported George. George presided over a violent persecution of Athanasius's supporters, with the aid of the *dux* Sebastianus, a policy which would later provide motive for his own violent execution at the hands of an Egyptian mob.

During the 350s, the doctrinal controversy became considerably more complicated with the appearance of Aetius and Eunomius, who advocated the position that the Son was simply "unlike" (*anomios*) the Father. The materialization of this "Anomian" position seems to have been an attempt, from an anti-Nicene perspective, to resolve the inherent ambiguity of the "homoian" position. The latter maintained that the Son was "like" (*homoios*) the Father, but then had to differentiate itself from Nicene doctrine precisely by setting limits to this likeness, by insisting, for example, that only the Father was "unoriginated." Unlike the earlier opponents of Nicene theology, these "anomeans" were prepared to use *ousia*-language to unambiguously assert the secondary status of the Son and the tertiary status of the Spirit. The "Anomians" thus represented both a radicalization and a critique of the original position of Arius. In particular, they rejected his teaching that the Son does not know the Father and espoused the principle that names were revelatory of essences. The essence of the Father is indicated by the name of "Unoriginate/Unbegotten" (*agen(n)ētos*), and therefore is unlike the essence of the Son, which is signified by the name of "Begotten" (*gen(n)ētos*).[91] The Holy Spirit was considered to be a creature of the Son, sent by him for the work of sanctification.

Yet another manifestation of the trend away from cautious ambiguity was the Council of Sirmium of 357. This council issued a statement which came to be known pejoratively among its opponents as the "Blasphemy of Sirmium." While it eschews the original slogans of Arius, such as "there was once when the Son was not," the creed of Sirmium manifests its Arian sympathies quite clearly in its denial of Nicaea and its strong and explicit emphasis on the subordination of the Son and the unique glory of the Father. Such an extreme statement prompted a reaction in the East, which was led by Basil of Ancyra, who had succeeded the deposed Marcellus in 336, and had been a member of the Eastern delegation at the Council of Sardica in 343. In 358, a year after the Council of Sirmium, Basil assembled his own council in Ancyra. The result was a doctrinal statement (likely penned by Basil himself) which bore significant similarities to the Athanasian logic.[92] As a central point, Basil makes the argument that the relation between Father and Son must be distinguished from that between creatures and the Creator, and that the only way to safeguard that distinction is to speak of the likeness between Father and Son, as a likeness of being, or essence (*ousia*). Thus, he advocated the designation *homoiousios*, "like according to essence," as a way of asserting the essential likeness of the Father and the Son without reverting to the Nicene "*homoousios*."

Basil of Ancyra's council sent a delegation to personally deliver this doctrinal statement to the emperor Constantius. Constantius seemed to have rapidly concluded that this position could be the breakthrough in finding a consensus. He immediately championed this new position, maintaining that it had always been his own view, and sent Aetius and Eunomius into exile. He then called for an ecumenical council to rally around Basil of Ancyra's proposal.

Constantius's attitude at this point shows some signs of battle-fatigue on the ecclesiastical front, expressed in a tendency to tightly control and predetermine the outcome of such a council. It was arranged that the Western and Eastern bishops would meet separately. Moreover, even before this divided "meeting" was to occur, a document was drawn up to be presented to the respective synods. The creed that was produced announced its date as 22 May 359, and thus became known as the "Dated" creed. A small number of bishops were invited to compose this declaration, including Basil of Ancyra. The result was a compromise statement that aimed to appease both the "*homoians*" who wished to avoid language of being and the "*homoiousians*," led by Basil of Ancyra. A compromise was reached by rejecting reference to likeness of being and replacing it with the designation of "like in every way":

> The word *ousia*, because when it was naively inserted by our fathers though not familiar to the masses, it caused disturbance, and because the Scriptures do not contain it, we have decided should be removed, and that there should be absolutely no mention of *ousia* in relation to God for the future, because the Scriptures make no mention at all of the *ousia* of the Father and the Son. But we declare that the Son is like the Father in all respects, as the holy Scriptures also declare and teach.[93]

This declaration was placed before the Eastern bishops, who met in Seleucia. The *homoians* and *homoiousians* could not come to any common understanding and the Eastern contingent dismantled without any significant results. The Western contingent, meanwhile, asserted its fidelity to Nicaea and its resistance to the production of any new creed. They sent a letter to the emperor, followed by a delegation of ten from their number, beseeching him to allow them to return to their sees. The emperor declined to meet with the Western delegation and kept them waiting. With the winter approaching, the Western bishops reiterated their request to be allowed back to their sees, but to no avail. Eventually, the waiting game of the emperor proved to be efficacious and, after being removed from Ariminum to Nice, in Thrace, the Western contingent were cajoled into signing a document that was practically equivalent to the Dated creed. The significant difference was that it spoke of the likeness between Father and Son in even more diluted form, omitting the phrase "in all respects." After the

Western delegation signed this creed ("the creed of Nice"), the Eastern delegation followed suit. It was in response to this event that Jerome uttered his famous cry: *"ingemuit totus orbis, et se Arianum esse miratus est"* ("the whole world groaned and was astonished to find itself Arian").[94] In 360, the *homoian* Acacius convened another council in Constantinople, and ratified the creed of Nice, which thus became the official creed of the Church. Basil of Ancyra and most of his *homoiousian* supporters were deposed and exiled.

At this time, Athanasius was still hiding out in the desert of Egypt, sheltered by his monastic supporters. This, his third exile, was his most prolific, resulting in more than half of his extant writings. He defended his conduct and formulated his own account of the Nicene controversy in a series of treatises, including the *Defence before Constantius*, *Defence of his Flight*, and the compendious *History of the Arians*, all completed in 357, as well as *On the Councils of Ariminum and Seleucia*, written in 359. His consolidation of the monastic contingent of the Egyptian Church is evidenced by the *Life of Antony* (ca. 356), in which the great Egyptian monk is presented as a model of Athanasius's own conception of Nicene orthodoxy.[95] It is also during this period that Athanasius undertakes a defense of the divinity of the Holy Spirit, along similar lines to his efforts on behalf of the divinity of the Son. There had apparently risen up a group of Christians in Egypt who acknowledged the divinity of the Son but considered the Holy Spirit to be a creature. In response to these *Tropici* ("the Metaphoricals"), so styled because of their manner of interpreting the scriptural passages in question, Athanasius penned his *Letters to Serapion* (357–359), which notably apply the designation "*homoousios*" to the Holy Spirit.[96] On this score, Gregory of Nazianzus, who had chided his friend Basil of Caesarea for not being bold enough to do the same, lauded Athanasius as the first complete theologian of the Trinity: "He was the first and only one, or with the concurrence of but a few, to venture to confess in writing and with entire clearness and distinctness the unity of Godhead and essence of the three Persons and thus to attain in later days, under the influence of inspiration, to the same faith in regard to the Holy Spirit as had been bestowed at an earlier time on most of the Fathers in regard to the Son."[97]

In 360, Constantius died and the government of the empire passed to his cousin, Julian. Once again, the death of an emperor changed the atmosphere of Church politics. With the death of Constantius, Athanasius's prospects immediately brightened. In 361, his replacement, George, whose tenure had been steadfastly

opposed by the Egyptian people and whose authority was maintained only by the ruthless coercion of imperial forces, was brutally
attacked and killed by a vengeful Egyptian mob.[98] In 362, Julian
issued an edict allowing all bishops banished by Constantius to
return to their sees. Twelve days later, Athanasius appeared in
Alexandria, though his stay would last only eight months.

The final decade: 362–373

Anxious to consolidate the ranks of those who confessed the full
divinity of the Son, Athanasius quickly convened a council to deal
with a terminological controversy that had arisen in Antioch but
which was reflective of terminological and conceptual divergences
that were significant and pervasive. One side, of *homoiousian* ("like
in essence") sympathies, wished to speak of Father, Son, and Spirit
as three *hypostases*; the other (steadfastly pro-Nicaea) spoke of one
hypostasis. The latter group's terminology was more consistent with
the linguistic usage of Athanasius himself, as well as that of the
Council of Nicaea and its Western supporters. The former group
represented the Eastern usage and the Origenist concern to safeguard the distinct subsistences of the three in God.
Characteristically, Athanasius is less concerned with terminological
usage than he is with the substantive signification which such usage
is meant to convey. The Council of Alexandria of 362 declared that
both usages were legitimate, provided that those who spoke of three
hypostases did not thereby deny the unity of the Godhead, while
those who spoke of one *hypostasis* also acknowledged a real distinction among the three. It also anathematized those who maintained
that the Holy Spirit was a creature, and affirmed that the *Logos* did
not lack a human soul and mind.

However, Athanasius's activities in Alexandria were soon to be
once again interrupted. Emperor Julian, called by his Christian
opponents "the apostate" for having renounced Christianity, was
intent upon propagating a revival of the Greek and Roman reli-
gions. Displeased and alarmed by the towering figure that
Athanasius now assumed in Egypt, Julian issued an unlikely interpretation of his original decree, explaining that he meant only to
allow bishops back to their country of residence, rather than to the
resumption of their episcopal duties. He insisted that Athanasius in
particular ("that contemptible little fellow"),[99] who has been so
often deposed, cannot be allowed to remain in Alexandria.[100] As
Athanasius and his supporters protested, Julian became more

obdurate, now insisting that Athanasius depart not only from Alexandria but from Egypt altogether. Having re-entered Alexandria on 21 February 362, Athanasius was thus forced to make his way out again on 23 October of the same year, his fourth exile. He retired to the desert, where he was received by the monks with much fanfare. This time, his exile would last only a little over a year, whereupon the death of Julian in the course of battle with the Persians provided another respite for the Alexandrian bishop.

Upon his return, Athanasius quickly took the initiative and traveled to Edessa to present himself to the new emperor, Jovian, who was returning from Persia to Antioch.[101] Jovian proved amenable to Athanasius's cause and gave him a letter assenting to the resumption of his episcopal duties, despite the protestations of Athanasius's opponents. Responding to Jovian's request that he submit a doctrinal statement, Athanasius enjoined him simply to adhere to the creed of Nicaea, and warned against any compromise with the "*homoian*" party, stressing that the Council Fathers of Nicaea "did not merely say that the Son is like (*homoios*) the Father, so that it should be believed that he is merely like God instead of true God from true God. But they wrote '*homoousios*' which is what properly applies to a genuine and true Son, who belongs to the Father truly and by nature."[102]

Imperial support, which Athanasius had so long lacked, proved to be short-lived. Jovian died on 20 February 364, to be succeeded by Valentinian, a general. Valentinian governed the Western part of the empire, and appointed in the East his brother Valens, a sympathizer of the anti-Nicene "*homoians*." Valens set about reversing the policy of his predecessor and sent out an edict demanding that all the bishops who had been recalled to their sees by Jovian resume their exile. For a time, Athanasius demurred, his supporters contending that the edict did not apply to the complex past circumstances of their bishop.[103] But Valens persisted, and when his commander finally stormed the Church of Dionysius to arrest Athanasius, the latter had already made his getaway. He had set off for his fifth exile, which was also his shortest and last. A few months later, the tide of imperial politics turned again, this time in favor of Athanasius. The authority of Valens was challenged by a rebellion led by a relative of the deceased emperor Julian. Anxious to contain the unrest in Egypt during this time of instability, Valens reversed his position and announced that Athanasius was to be recalled to his episcopal duties in Alexandria. He was escorted back to the Church of Dionysius by the imperial *notarius*, Brasidas.[104]

Athanasius spent the remaining years of his life in relative tranquility in Alexandria. His support among the Egyptian people was now so widespread and fervent that when another anti-Nicene bishop was sent to Alexandria from Antioch, he had to be directly escorted back under imperial guard to avoid the fate that had earlier befallen George. In the last years of his life, Athanasius's doctrinal writings engage emerging Christological debates about the nature of Christ's humanity and its relation to the divinity. In response to these questions, Athanasius penned several doctrinal letters which were to carry great authority in the subsequent Christological debates of the fifth century, among which are the *Letter to Adelphius* and the *Letter to Epictetus*. The latter was considered to be one of the benchmarks of Christological orthodoxy at both the Councils of Ephesus (431) and Chalcedon (451). Referring to it, Pope Leo the Great, one of the principal figures at the Council of Chalcedon, wrote of Athanasius that "he construed the Incarnation of the Word so clearly and carefully that he defeated Nestorius and Eutyches in the persons of the heretics of his own time."[105]

Athanasius died on 2 May 373. Having attained to the epsicopal throne of Alexandria as a young man approximately 30 years old, he had spent 17 of his 46 years as a bishop in exile. With the triumph of Nicene theology at the Council of Constantinople, Athanasius would be looked upon henceforth as a standard of orthodoxy. In his funeral oration, Gregory of Nazianzus declares: "His life and conduct form the ideal of an episcopate and his teaching the law of orthodoxy."[106] Cyril, Athanasius's eventual successor to the throne of Alexandria, had an even greater regard for Athanasius's authority and based his own Christological reflections in large part along the lines of his predecessor. Traditionally considered in both the Eastern and Western Churches as a premiere authority in Christological and Trinitarian doctrine, he continues to be especially venerated by the Coptic Orthodox Church of his native Egypt.

Judgments of Athanasius's character

For the greater part of the Christian tradition, the triumph of Nicene theology has gone hand in hand with a lionization of Athanasius as the stalwart and inspired defender of the orthodox Christian faith. Athanasius's uncompromising stance toward his opponents and his indefatigable persistence were seen as illustrious reflections of his inalterable and incorruptible faith in the fullness of the Son's divinity. Into the modern era, the figure of Athanasius has been championed by such notable theologians as the English Cardinal John Henry Newman and the German Johan Möhler. In his journal entry for 14 April 1838, the great Danish philosopher Sören Kierkegaard can still reflect the traditional fascination with an Athanasius drawn in heroic proportions: "These last few days I have been reading Görres' *Athanasius* not only with my eyes but with my whole body – with a throbbing heart."[107] However, the traditionally high estimate of Athanasius's person has been increasingly brought into question since the nineteenth century. One extreme portrait presents him as a vicious tyrant, the equivalent of a modern American gangster, and a "Pharaoh" who only lusted for power and used doctrinal debates as a means to that end.[108] Given the fact that our predominant access to Athanasius's personality is that writ large over the tumultuous events of the Nicene crisis, it is hard to escape the inclination either to concur completely in Athanasius's own tendency to identify his person entirely with the Nicene cause or to dismiss such a strategy as a sham ploy for power. Clearly, Athanasius was sincerely dedicated to Nicene theology as he interpreted it and was willing to incur great personal cost as the price for upholding it. Nevertheless, this does not of itself sanction all his words and actions as if they were merely a direct extension of the presumed validity of Nicene theology, to the point where Athanasius's own personality is construed as "consubstantial" with Nicene orthodoxy. On the other hand, we also have to concede that the application of historiography to rendering moral judgments of personal character is a complex and perilous matter, especially if it ignores the historicity and variability of norms of conduct in different cultures and times. In this regard, one modern commentator wisely exhorts, "we should be very cautious in drawing large conclusions about a figure as strange to us as a fourth-century Coptic patriarch."[109] Perhaps such conclusions are after all inevitable, but then we should acknowledge the inevitability of our own prejudices in rendering such judgments. It is striking, for example, that a typical modern complaint about Athanasius lays special stress on his intransigence, his undeniable aura of being sure of himself and his position.[110] But this complaint has its own culturally bound history, having at least as much to do with the Western post-Kantian construction of a virtue of epistemological humility as it does with Athanasius himself. For his closer contemporaries, this "intransigence" was interpreted as a courageous steadfastness and an inspired perception of what was radically at stake. Moreover, his withering ridicule of opponents and sometimes bombastic rhetoric, objectionable (though far from non-existent) according to the academic standards of our day, was rather standard fare for the times. Above all, a judicious evaluation of Athanasius's character must give due weight to the undeniable fact, conceded even by the most vehement of his modern critics, that he eventually gained the overwhelming support and admiration of his own people.

It is true, nevertheless, that Athanasius was accused even during his own time of employing violent means to assert and maintain his authority. But it is very hard to evaluate these accusations objectively, especially considering that some of the most egregious of them (such as the "murder" of Arsenius) were proven, as we have seen, to be artificially contrived by his enemies. There can be no doubt, however, that outbreaks of violence occurred throughout the conflicts between Athanasius's supporters and their Melitian and anti-Nicene opponents. One testimony to this state of affairs was the finding of a papyrus, LP 1914, dating from 335 and comprising a letter sent by a Melitian, Callistus, to two Melitian priests. In this letter, Callistus complains bitterly of the sufferings of his fellow Melitians at the hands of the "adherents of Athanasius." While certain corruptions in the manuscript make the exact construal somewhat in doubt,[111] the document seems to provide clear evidence of violence perpetuated by Athanasius's supporters. For his own part, Athanasius's public pronouncements on the use of violence tend to repudiate it as a distinctly Arian mode of behavior. In recounting the imperially sponsored atrocities of his opponents, he contends:

> This is how the devil acts, since there is no truth in him. With "axe and hammer" (Ps 74:6), he breaks down the doors of those who do not receive him. But our Savior is so gentle that he teaches by saying: "If any one wishes to come after me ..." and "whoever wishes to be my disciple" (Mt 16:24). When he comes to someone, he does not force them but knocks at the door and says, "Open to me, my sister, my bride" (Song 5:2). If they open, he enters but if they delay and do not wish him to enter, he leaves them. For the truth is not proclaimed with swords or darts or soldiers; but by persuasion and advice.
>
> (*History of the Arians* 33)[112]

It is true enough that imperial forces hostile to Athanasius and his supporters were given to quashing them with a heavy hand. As one eminent historian who was no admirer of Athanasius conceded: "Even allowing for exaggerations, we must accept that Constantius's troops never had any hesitation in forcing their way into churches and suppressing popular demonstrations ruthlessly."[113] Nevertheless, it is somewhat implausible to assume that Athanasius's Egyptian supporters, who eventually constituted by far the majority of Egyptian Christians and who associated their "Arian" opponents with imperial force, persevered in an unbroken stance of non-violence. For one infamous instance, the public lynching of the unpopular George, is terrible evidence to the contrary. While there is no extant evidence of Athanasius's explicit authorization of such violence,[114] it must be conceded that the general tenor of his language was not so strictly pacific as the above quote would seem to imply. Even if he did not attempt to proclaim the truth "with swords or darts or soldiers," neither were his efforts at "persuasion and advice" free from continual recourse to verbal abuse and insult. Indeed, just as he could find scriptural warrant for shunning the use of physical violence, he was no less industrious and considerably more prolific in extricating from the Scriptures a seemingly endless supply of insults to hurl at his opponents.

To modern ears, far from the heat and tumult of the actual events, such a haranguing style can easily seem gratuitous and heavy-handed. However, from the point of view of Athanasius's own self-understanding, he is a persecuted shepherd of an embattled flock who is not only at pains to provide his people with cogent and persuasive reasons for denying "Arian" doctrine, but who is also quite desperate to coach them in the appropriate affective repugnance which they ought to feel toward such "blasphemy." We find Athanasius to be manifestly shaken by the observation that the "Arian heresy" has deceived many Christians who have either adopted it or seemingly concede that it is a permissible interpretation of the Christian faith,[115] while he is quite convinced that the denial of the full divinity of the Son simply deconstructs the whole edifice of Christian faith: "For how can he who denies the Son be truthful about the Father who is revealed by the Son? Or how can he who speaks falsely about the Son think rightly about the Spirit who is given by the Son? Who will give credence to one who speaks of the Resurrection but denies that it is the Lord who became 'first-born of the dead' (Col 1:18) for us? Or how can one who is ignorant of the genuine and true generation of the Son from the Father not be manifestly mistaken about his presence in the flesh?" (Or. Ar. 1:8).[116] Here, as in many other places, Athanasius is at pains to disqualify those who do not accept the full divinity of the Son from any claim to the name of "Christians," and he clearly considers it to be his pastoral duty to do so.

For Athanasius, this confession of the unqualified divinity of the Son was the cornerstone of genuine Christian "piety" (*eusebeia*), a term which he evokes frequently. Such a confession is also the only authentically "pious" interpretation of Scripture. His opponents, on the other hand, are not only portrayed as "inept" and "impious" interpreters of Scripture but are also assimilated to biblical personages who deny the lordship of Christ; they are like the Jews and Pontius Pilate. They are also generally assimilated to every scriptural image of villainy. Such a polemical strategy, whatever its unattractive features, must be seen in its integral context as indicative of a central feature of Athanasius's own approach to Christian piety. In his *Letter to Marcellinus*, Athanasius applies a rudimentary "form-criticism" by categorizing the psalms according to their different subject matter and type; such categorization is then employed in service of the practice of reciting the psalm that properly applies to one's current situation.[117] This practice of applying the Scriptures to the various circumstances of one's life seems to have been a mainstay of Athanasius's spirituality. Nothing is more characteristic of his approach than the tendency to render every situation and every question into scriptural categories, and to assimilate contemporary persons with scriptural personages. In this way, the struggle with his "Arian" opponents was itself subsumed into and assimilated to the scriptural language-world and thus conceived as a struggle between the supporters of the Word and the "Christ-fighters," "whose father is the devil," and whose patron is the "most impious" Constantius, "precursor to the Antichrist."

More positively, this practice of reading his situation into the scriptural world provided Athanasius with a foundational principle in his own moral code and spirituality, that of the imitation of Christ and the biblical saints.[118] When he is forced to give an explanation of his own actions, as in the *Defence of his Flight*, Athanasius's consistent standard is the biblically recounted actions of Jesus Christ and "the saints" (*hoi hagioi*), a term which in his vocabulary is generally reserved for biblical personages. It is this same principle which he employs pastorally in order to fortify his flock and which is centrally constitutive of his own celebrated resilience. By way of example, we find him reminding his flock from exile in Rome, in 341, that tribulations and afflictions are simply the allotted portion of those who seek to reverently follow the Lord. He bases this outlook on various scriptural texts and persons, from Job to Jesus himself, and he urges his flock to train themselves in perseverance by contemplating the examples of the scriptural saints who endured affliction. Inevitably, all of this is cast within a stark dichotomy between "those who revere God" and the "Christ fighters" who "deny the Lord":

> What does this mean, my beloved, but that we also should "glory in afflictions" (Rom 5:3) when enemies cause us suffering and that we should not become downcast in spirit when we are persecuted but should rather press forward toward the crown of the upward calling in Jesus Christ our Lord (Phil 3:14)? I entreat you, therefore, that when we are afflicted and injured, we should not be troubled but rather give our cheek to the one who strikes us (Mt 5:29) and stoop the shoulder (Gen 49:14, LXX). For the lovers of pleasure and strife are subjected to temptation "when they are lured and enticed by their own desires," as the blessed apostle James says (Jas 1:14). But as for us, we know that we suffer for the truth and that it is those who deny the Lord who attack and persecute us. Therefore, according to the words of James, we have hope that we shall attain to "the fullness of joy when we encounter various trials, knowing that the testing of our faith produces patience" (Jas 1:2). Let us, then, rejoice in spirit, my brothers, knowing that our salvation is being stored up for us in the midst of the time of affliction. For our Savior did not redeem us by resting but destroyed death by suffering for us. Therefore, he told us beforehand, "In the world you shall have affliction" (Jn 16:33). He did not say this to everyone but to those who serve him in constancy of faith, for he knew beforehand that those who revere God will be persecuted.
>
> *(Festal Letter* XIII:6)[119]

The above exhortation provides something of a snapshot of Athanasius's typical self-portrait and self-understanding: embattled and persecuted by those who are betrayers of Christ, struggling to be constant in defending the orthodox faith, and fortifying his flock as well as himself by attending to the imitation of Christ and the biblical saints. There has always been a competing image of Athanasius painted by his ancient opponents and modern critics: an unscrupulous, heavy-handed, tyrannical, and unbearably arrogant addict of power. What is of enduring significance for the Christian tradition, however, is not ultimately so much the personality of Athanasius – which cannot be wholly reconstructed with any objective certainty – as his central conviction that genuine Christianity stands or falls by the confession of the full divinity of the Word. It is as a theologian who gave consistent and tireless expression to this claim of faith, and not as a paragon of meekness, mildness, and *politesse* in debate (conceived according to modern standards!), that Athanasius continues to be a towering figure among the pioneering architects of the Christian tradition.

The theological vision of Athanasius

Athanasius's theological writings span a period of over four decades permeated with intense doctrinal debate. Throughout this tumultuous time, he maintains a remarkable consistency in his theological vision and even vocabulary, albeit with some notable developments and variance of emphasis. The most obvious division in Athanasius's corpus of doctrinal writings is between the early *Against the Greeks – On the Incarnation*, in which he makes no explicit mention of Arius, and the later works which are manifestly preoccupied with defending Nicene doctrine and refuting the "Arians". Compared to *Against the Greeks – On the Incarnation*, the later writings tend to be more properly *theo*-logical, concerned in a sustained and focused way with the ontological status of the relations between the Father, the Son, and the Holy Spirit. They also tend to be more closely exegetical, preoccupied with refuting anti-Nicene proof-texts and devising "right-minded" interpretations of these texts that are consistent with Nicene doctrine. But the theological-Trinitarian arguments of Athanasius, which are sometimes focused specifically on a linguistic analysis of the vocabulary which the Scriptures apply to Father, Son, and Holy Spirit, are always aligned with a particular vision of the nature and character of Christian salvation. This soteriological vision, in turn, is based on a particular conception of the relation between God and creation which is given foundational systematic expression in *Against the Greeks – On the Incarnation* and then seems to be presumed throughout Athanasius's theological career. His conception of the relation between God and creation may thus be considered as the architectonic center of Athanasius's theological vision; his account of this relation provides the overarching framework in which his various doctrines acquire their distinctive resonance. Yet it must be remembered that this central focus on the relation between God and creation is at the same time always a Christological focus. Precisely because Athanasius was deeply immersed in debate on whether the Son is a creature, the issue of the relative status of God and creation was always directly a Christological issue for him. His account of the relation between God and creation is thus ultimately a Christology conceived in the most universal terms.

God and creation: the correlation of theology and anthropology in Athanasius

In *Against the Greeks – On the Incarnation*, the relation between God and creation is conceived in terms of the interlocking of two sets of dialectics: the one, theological; the other, anthropological. In terms of the doctrine of God, Athanasius places dramatic emphasis on the simultaneous contrast and interplay between the "beyondness" of divine nature (*physis*) and God's goodness and loving-kindness (*philanthropia*):

> God, the creator of the universe and king of all, who is beyond all being (*hyperekeina pasēs ousias*) and human conception, inasmuch as he is also good and utterly noble, has made humanity in his own image through his own Word, our Savior Jesus Christ.
>
> (*Against the Greeks* 2)[120]

> God, being good and the lover of humanity, cares for the souls that he has fashioned. Since he is invisible and incomprehensible by nature and beyond all created being, the human race would have failed to achieve knowledge of him insofar as they were made from nothing while he was without origin (*agenētos*). Therefore, God arranged creation through his Word so that, although his nature is invisible, he might nevertheless become known to humanity from his works.
>
> (*Against the Greeks* 35)[121]

Thus, the dialectical simultaneity of God's beyondness and the divine love that mitigates this beyondness characterizes God's relation with created humanity from the very beginning of creation. Creation is understood as the act whereby the one who is "beyond all being" becomes the generous source of created being, and desires to grant humanity knowledge of and communion with himself.

This divine dialectic is reflected in an anthropological dialectic between human "nature" and "grace."[122] According to its nature (*physis*), humanity is incapable of knowing and relating to God. This aspect of the human being corresponds to the utter "beyondness," or transcendence, of God and the incommensurability of divine and human beings; if God's nature is that of true being, who is utterly self-sufficient and inaccessible, human nature is characterized by its origination from nothing. This *ex nihilo* is by no means merely a historical datum or a punctiliar "moment" in the story of humanity's beginning; it is an ontological determination that characterizes humanity's existence, and that of creation in general, as deriving from and thus inherently tending toward non-being: "for the nature of the things that come to be (*genēta*), inasmuch as they exist out of non-being, is unstable, weak, and mortal when considered in itself" (*Against the Greeks* 41). However, this aspect of human "nature," or *physis*, cannot, by definition, characterize the actual constitution of the human being as such. It merely refers to the radical nothingness which underlies human existence and indicates humanity's inherent lack of self-possessed being and thus its radical incapacity to preserve itself in being through its own power. For human beings to actually exist, human "nature" must be radically complemented by the dynamic of "grace", *charis*, which corresponds to the divine *philanthropia*. The aspect of "grace" in the human being is the gift that is granted to humanity of participation in God the Word, in whom all created things have their consistence. Thus, humanity is conceived simultaneously as being of a corruptible nature that tends toward nothingness, in contrast to the perfect and transcendent nature of God, and yet as possessing the grace of participating in divine life, because of the divine *philanthropia* which overcomes the natural disparity between the God who is and the creation that comes to be from nothing:

> God is good – or rather, he is the source of goodness. But the good is not begrudging of anything. Because he does not begrudge being to anything, he made all things from non-being through his own Word, our Lord Jesus Christ. Among all the things upon the earth, he was especially merciful toward the human race. Seeing that by the logic of its own origin it would not be capable of always remaining, he granted it a further gift. He did not create human

beings merely like all the irrational animals upon the earth, but made them according to his own Image, and shared with them the power of his own Word, so that having a kind of reflection of the Word and thus becoming rational, they may be enabled to remain in blessedness and live the true life of the saints in paradise.

(*On the Incarnation* 3)[123]

It is vital to distinguish this dramatically dialectical conception from later schematizations of "nature" and "grace" in the later Western tradition, where "nature" refers to the inherent structure of the human being as created by God, while "grace" is associated with the unmerited gifts which are granted by God over and above the original act of creation. For Athanasius, the aspects of "nature" and "grace" are both constitutive of the human being as created by God, "nature" referring to the whence of creation's being, which is also an intrinsic orientation to nothingness, and "grace" to the reality of its establishment in being through the Word. It might seem that Athanasius lays extreme stress on humanity's fragility, which indeed he does. But it would be a mistake to construe this as a "pessimistic" account of the human condition. Ultimately, it is a conception of the human being as an entity whose very existence is radically gifted. Precisely because its whole being is gifted, humanity has no hold on being apart from that irreducibly radical gift. The reality of its being nothing apart from the gift of participation in God is humanity's nature, or *physis*. That it does exist, and even shares in the life of God himself, is due to the grace, or *charis*, that reflects the divine philanthropy. Although all creation partakes of this dialectic of the simultaneity of intrinsic nothingness and participation in the Word, humanity's participation is unique, as the above passage asserts. Whereas all other creatures participate in the Word's power in the strictly passive mode of being "governed" by the Word, humanity's participation is in the mode of a conscious sharing in the active "rationality" of the Word; among all creatures, only humanity possesses the "greater grace" of being *logikos*. As such, humanity actively and intentionally shares in the power of the *Logos* and rejoices in this participation.

In his later writings, Athanasius does not maintain an articulation of the human being by recourse to the terminological contrast of "*physis*" and "*charis*." Nevertheless, the essential content of this framework perseveres. *On the Council of Nicaea* asserts that human beings are "incapable of existence in their own right" because of the fact of their origination from nothing, whereas the reality of their existence is grounded in the gift of their participation in the Word.[124] Athanasius's theological anthropology, as already laid out in *Against the Greeks – On the Incarnation,* also looms quite large, albeit implicitly, in his arguments for the unqualified divinity of the Son. As we have seen, the fact of being created from nothing means for Athanasius a radical ontological instability and a need for the "grace (*charis*)" of divine assistance. Against his theological opponents, Athanasius insists untiringly that the Word is the one who sustains humanity and compensates for the ontological poverty of its origination from nothing and is not himself susceptible to the radical weakness of created being. The Word is the giver and not the receiver of *charis.*

The divine dialectic between transcendence and accessibility also remains as a consistent motif in Athanasius's later writings: God is "in all things according to his own goodness and power and outside all according to his proper nature (*physis*)."[125] In these later polemical writings, Athanasius often employs the Platonic framework of "participation" (*metochē*) to articulate the simultaneity of God's transcendence and accessibility. God is altogether other than creation precisely as the one who generously grants creation a participation in the divine Word. The Word is participated and does not participate; he is "external to" creation precisely as the one in whom creation comes to be and subsists.[126] By contrast, Athanasius reports the "Arians" as maintaining that the Word is himself made divine "by participation."[127] In one significant case, Athanasius allows the conception that the Son himself participates the Father, provided that this be understood in the unique sense of a "whole participation" in which the very being of the Son is coextensive with his participation of the Father.[128] But this unique case simply underscores the contrasting fact that creation's participation in God has its point of departure in nothingness. Athanasius thus rejects the Origenian as well as "Arian" notion that the Father is in any sense "beyond" the Son, while affirming that the Son himself is both beyond creation and yet provides creation with access to God and thereby to existence itself.

Divine condescension and human ascent

In *Against the Greeks – On the Incarnation,* we find a dynamic complementarity between the movements of divine condescension and human ascent, which corresponds to the dialectic of distance and nearness between God and humanity. The ontological distance between God and humanity is overcome by God's stooping down to humanity and humanity's rising up to God. The climactic termini of the movements of both divine condescension and human ascent converge in the event of the Incarnation of the Word, whose condescension to the point of suffering death effects humanity's deification. This characterization of the central Christian mystery of the Word's Incarnation, life, and death is also read by Athanasius into the doctrine of creation. Thus, the creation of humanity is itself characterized as an act of divine condescension and mercy.[129] On the other hand, the fundamental human stance, which constitutes the very integrity of the human being, is one of conscious ascent toward God. Humanity is ordained, by the radical logic of its constitution, to rise up above itself and maintain its being by virtue of its "conversation" (*sunomilia*) with God, whence its being is derived and sustained. This framework is consistently central to Athanasius's theological vision throughout his career. It is given systematic expression in *Against the Greeks – On the Incarnation*, where Athanasius sketches a comprehensive portrait of the ascending structure of the human being according to the original creation, the inversion of this structure of ascent by humanity's descent into sin, and the salvific descent of the Word that effects humanity's renewed ascent unto deification.

The ascending structure of the human being and its inversion through sin

In *Against the Greeks*, Athanasius sketches an image of the primordial vocation of the human being to Godward contemplation which mingles Platonic and biblical vocabulary:

> He fashioned humanity to be capable of contemplating and understanding reality through its likeness to him, giving it also a knowledge and conception of its own eternity, so that as long as it retained this likeness, it might never fall away from the conception of God or forsake the fellowship of the saints. But holding on to the grace of the Giver and the power which is granted to it as its own and which is from the Father's Word, it might rejoice and converse with God (*sunomilē to theiō*), living a secure and truly blessed and immortal life. For having no impediment to its knowledge of the divine, through its purity it always contemplates

God the Word, the Image of the Father, in whose image it came into being. It is filled with great admiration when it perceives the providence exercised by him toward the universe. It is above sensible realities and all bodily images as it binds itself to the divine and intelligible realities in heaven by the power of its mind. For when the human mind is not engaged with bodily things and has no bodily desires mingled with itself from outside but is completely above that and engaged with itself, as it was created from the beginning, then it transcends what is sensible and all human things and it rises to sublime heights, and seeing the Word, it sees also in him the Father of the Word.

(*Against the Greeks* 2)[130]

Although Athanasius here sounds the characteristically Platonic note of contemplation as the forsaking of the sensible for the sake of the intelligible, his framework is not one of a dualistic opposition between the corporeal and incorporeal. Whereas the Platonic tradition tends to portray the body as representing an estrangement from the true intelligible self,[131] for Athanasius the significance of the body is precisely that it is "what is closest" to us and thus represents the danger not so much of self-estrangement as of self-indulgence. The body is meant to be the point of departure, as it were, for the ascent of self-transcendence. When it becomes instead the end-point of an orientation to self-indulgence, its proper ontological dynamism is inverted. This is one model by which Athanasius conceives of human fallenness:

But human beings, despising better things and becoming reluctant to comprehend them, pursued rather what was closer to themselves. But what was closer to them was the body and its sensations. Thus they averted their minds from intelligible realities and began to be concerned with themselves. By being concerned with themselves and seizing upon the body and other sensible realities, they became deceived about their own identity and they succumbed to their desires, preferring what is their own to the contemplation of divine things.

(*Against the Greeks* 3)[132]

Athanasius also speaks of the structure of the human being in terms of "soul" (*psyche*) and "mind" (*nous*). In distinguishing between the "soul" and "mind," he appears to presume the Platonic tripartition of the soul into appetitive, reasonable, and spirited parts.[133] Yet these are analytical categories for Plato, delineating parts of the soul, whereas for Athanasius, the distinction between "soul" and "mind" refers more to determinations of the self in its relation to God. If the body is conceived as the starting point of the Godward ascent, the "mind," or *nous*, conceived along the lines of the biblical notion of the "heart," is the locus of communion with God. The "soul," on the other hand, is an intermediate category, generally correlated by Athanasius to the body as its "pilot" or governor.[134] It governs the body precisely by orienting it toward the divine contemplation whose locus is the "mind." "Mind" therefore refers to the determination of the soul which is properly ordered toward communion with God. Thus, body, soul, and mind are hierarchically ordered within a continuum of self-transcending ascent.

Sin, however, is a movement in the "opposite direction," in which the mind orients itself toward the body; similarly, the soul, instead of piloting the body in conformity with the ascent of the mind, becomes enmeshed in the desires and fears of the body, inverting the proper teleology of the human structure and replacing it with a sheer indulgence in its own undirected and self-intoxicating movement. The result is that the body also then performs actions that are "the opposite" of its natural movements of self-transcending ascent. Athanasius depicts this derailment of the natural motion of the soul in terms that combine the traditionally Platonic image of the soul as "charioteer"[135] with biblical vocabulary. In the course of this description, Athanasius also makes explicit the positive role of the body in humanity's communion with the divine:

> The body has eyes in order to see creation and to recognize the Creator through this harmonious order, and it has hearing in order to listen to the divine sayings and the laws of God, and it has hands in order to accomplish necessary actions and in order to extend them toward God in prayer. But when the soul turned away from contemplation of the good and from movement within the good, it was henceforth deceived and moved toward the opposite. Then, having in view its own power, as we said before, and abusing it, it realized that it can also move its bodily members in the opposite direction. So instead of looking at creation, it turned its eyes toward desires, showing that it

can do that too. It thought that as long as it was in motion it would preserve its own dignity and would not be in error in actualizing its capabilities. It did not realize that it was brought into being not merely to be in motion but to move toward what it should. Therefore, the apostolic saying commands, "All things are possible but not all are expedient" (1 Cor 6:12). But human presumption, not regarding what is appropriate and fitting but only its own power, began to do the opposite. So it moved the hands toward the opposite of what they should do and people committed murder; it led the hearing into disobedience and the other members into adultery instead of lawful procreation, the tongue into blasphemy, invective, and perjury instead of fair speech, the hands, to stealing and striking fellow human beings, the sense of smell to all kinds of erotic perfumes, the feet toward the hasty shedding of blood, and the stomach to drunkenness and insatiable gluttony. All these are evils and sins of the soul. They have no other cause but the turning away from what is better.

It is like a charioteer who mounts his horse in the stadium and then pays no attention to the goal toward which he is supposed to be heading; turning away from it, he simply drives the horse whichever way he can – and his capacity corresponds to his wishes. So he would often crash into people he comes across and drive out of bounds, carried wherever the speed of the horses carries him and thinking that by racing like this he will not miss the goal, for he only looks at the track and does not see that in fact he has got away from the goal. So it is with the soul when it has turned from the path to God and moves the members of the body to what is improper, or rather is itself moved by itself along with them. Thus it sins and creates evil for itself, not seeing that it has strayed from the path and missed the goal of truth, in regard to which the blessed Paul, that Christ-bearing man, said: "I press onward toward the goal, the prize of the upward call of Jesus Christ" (Phil 3:14).

(*Against the Greeks* 4–5)[136]

The climactic stage of this inversion of the intrinsic structure of human ascent is when the soul, having departed from its proper task of assimilating the body to the divine realities which it perceives through the mind, ends by projecting onto divine realities the desires, fears, and impressions of the body.[137] That is what happens in the case of idolatry, which is employed by Athanasius as a paradigm of the inversion of the divinely ordained human ascent to God.

Thus, the alternative to the intrinsic human vocation to Godward ascent is not, for Athanasius, some neutral state of "being human" apart from God. No such possibility exists in his conception, given humanity's inherent lack of hold on being. Instead, the only alternative to the ascent toward God is a rapid descent into the nothingness which is humanity's only natural possession apart from God. What determines humanity's actual situation relative to these opposing movements – upwards, toward communion with God, or downwards, toward nothingness – is the exercise of free will. But free will is itself pre-determined in the scope of its movement by the fundamental ontological dialectic of the contrast between God and nothingness. So long as humanity chooses to exercise its free will in assenting to the Godward pull effected by the *philanthropia* of divine condescension, its participation in God is assured. However, if humanity exercises its free will by choosing to turn away from God and toward itself, it finds itself inexorably drawn toward corruption and nothingness. For Athanasius, the history of humanity since the fall of Adam is the story of an accumulating momentum of decline which was bound to lead to humanity's utter destruction. Because sin inverts the divinely ordained anthropological dialectic whereby humanity is created from nothing (*physis*) and constituted by participation in divine power (*charis*), and replaces it with the opposing momentum of humanity's decline from divine participation into the corruption of nothingness, it would not be an exaggeration to say that, within the Athanasian framework, sin is quite literally a process of "de-creation."

Against the Greeks – On the Incarnation presents the most detailed depiction by Athanasius of the ascending structure of the human being and its inversion through sin. Such detailed anthropological reflection became considerably more sparse as his theology became more explicitly polemical and preoccupied with more specifically Christological and Trinitarian concerns. Yet, his Christological and soteriological assertions about the necessity for the Son's not being a creature presume this anthropology. And when he does have occasion in his later works to return to the sort of anthropological reflections articulated in *Against the Greeks – On the Incarnation*, his perspective and vocabulary remain largely unchanged. Thus, his idealized picture of the monk Antony presents the latter as enunciating an exhortation to align the will with the ascending momentum ordained by creation and subverted by sin. As in *Against the Greeks*, Athanasius here mingles a philosophical vocabulary of contemplation with biblical language. But whereas in a Platonic or Stoic anthropology, the existence of virtue "within" the self is an indication of the natural divinity of the soul, for Athanasius it is the result of the divine creative act whose benefits we receive. Human virtue, then, is a matter of protecting and maintaining the "deposit" entrusted to us of God's creative work:

> For the Lord already told us, "The kingdom of God is within you" (Lk 17:21). Therefore, virtue requires only our willing, since it is in us and issues from us. For virtue exists when the soul maintains its intellectual aspect according to nature. It does this in accordance with nature to the extent that it remains as it was made, and it was made to be beautiful and perfectly straight. Therefore, Joshua, the son of Nun gave this exhortation to the people, saying, "Set your heart straight toward the Lord God of Israel" (Josh 24:23). And John said, "Make your paths straight" (Mt 3:3). The rectitude of the soul consists in its intellectual aspect being according to nature, as it was created. But when it strays and deviates from what is according to nature, then we speak of the vice of the soul. So it is not a difficult task. For if we remain as we were made, then we are in virtue; but if we turn our thoughts to what is worthless, then we are condemned as evil. If it was something that we had to procure from outside of us, it would be a difficult thing. But if it is within us, let us guard ourselves against contemptible thoughts. Having received the soul as a deposit, let us preserve it for the Lord so that he may recognize it as his own work, being the same as he had made it.
>
> (*Life of Antony* 20)[138]

The drama of divine descent

If, for Athanasius, human virtue consists in intentionally maintaining the gifts granted by God's creative work, God's ongoing providence and interaction with humanity also has for its goal the maintenance of the divine–human communion established in the act of creation. Like Irenaeus before him, Athanasius's theology is focused on the unity of creation and redemption. In *On the Incarnation*, Athanasius explains the necessity of beginning his discourse about the humanization of the Word by speaking of creation: "First we must speak of creation so that we may consider it fitting that its renewal was effected by the Word who created it in the beginning. For it will prove to be not the least bit contradictory if the Father worked its salvation through the same one by whom he created it."[139] Thus, before elaborating on the fittingness of the Incarnation of the Word, he deals with different theories of creation in order to make the point that a correct conception of creation will make it manifest that the Word's humanization is in keeping with the ethos of the divine work of creation. Among other false conceptions, Athanasius counters the Platonic notion of creation from pre-existent matter and the Manichaean belief that the true God is not the creator of this world. The former conception compromises divine power and makes God to be "weak" by denying that he is the source of all being; the latter offends against the divine goodness, shown forth in the liberality of bringing this world into existence. On the other hand, as we have already seen, the divine act of creation manifests both divine power and goodness. Sin, however, which we have characterized as "de-creation," renders ineffectual both God's capacity and God's desire to bring humanity into communion with himself. *On the Incarnation* does not shy away from presenting this "de-creation" effected by sin as posing a dilemma also for God the Creator. Humanity's destruction would seem to signal a defeat not only for human welfare but even for divine glory:

> What use was it then for humanity to have been created in God's image from the beginning? For either it should have been created simply as irrational or else, once it has been made rational, it should not live the life of irrational beings. Or what use was it at all for humanity to be endowed with the conception of God from the beginning? For if it is now unworthy of this endowment, it should not have been given it from the beginning. And of what benefit would this be to the God who made humanity, or what kind of glory would there be for him if the humanity which was made by him did not worship him, but thought that others had created it? It would then turn out that God had made them for others and not for himself.
>
> (*Inc.* 13)[140]

God's very glory is thus implicated in the fate of creation, especially in the fate of humanity. The divine traits manifested in the act of creation, God's strength and love, are undermined by the de-creation of sin and need to be reasserted by God himself. If sin is a de-creation by which humanity reverts toward nothingness, redemption requires a "re-creation," or a "renewal" of creation, that can be effected only by the same philanthropic creative power of the Word, a power that is not vulnerable to the inherent nothingness of all created nature. For Athanasius, it is therefore self-evident that the definitive redemption from sin can only be the work of the Creator-Word.

The Incarnation is the divine act which supremely manifests the very same attributes manifested by God in the act of creation, strength and love, and displays their overcoming of the challenge presented by human sinfulness. In *Against the Greeks – On the Incarnation*, a motif that unifies the depiction of the divine work of both creation and redemption is that of the "condescension" of the Word. As Creator, the Word "strengthened all things into existence" (*Against the Greeks* 46) and "condescends (*sunkatabainōn*) to created beings" (*Against the Greeks* 47). While human sinfulness is articulated through the terminology of fall (*peptō*) and descent (*katabaino*), the Incarnation, which culminates in Christ's salvific death, is represented as an act of powerful and loving divine solidarity with human abasement, a divine descent that accompanies, supplants, and reverses human fallenness, even while reasserting the divine glory that was manifest in the act of creation.[141]

This contrast of sinful human descent and saving divine descent is woven into the structural contrast drawn by the work between idolatry and deification. Idolatry inverts the divinely ordained ascent of humanity from nothingness to communion with God, insofar as it involves human beings in claiming for themselves a rank lower than animals and non-existents by ascribing worship to them:

When human minds strayed from God, and human thoughts and reasonings began their descent, they first ascribed the honor of divinity to the heaven and the sun, moon, and stars ... Then, descending further in their dark reasonings, they called the ether and air and the things in the air "gods". Advancing yet further in evil, they praised as gods the elements and the principles of the constitutions of bodies ... As those who have completely fallen down

crawl on the ground like snails, so also these most impious
people fell down and fell away from the contemplation of
God and came to the point of ascribing divinity even to
human beings and to the images of human beings – to
some, while they were still alive and to others, after their
deaths. Attaining to even worse things in their wills and
reasonings, they now transferred the divine and transcendent title of "God" to stone and wood and to reptiles on sea
and land, paying them every divine honor while rejecting
the true and really existing God, the Father of Christ.

(*Against the Greeks* 9)[142]

The definitive response of God to humanity's accumulating fall is
the sinless "fall" of God himself, through the Incarnation and
human death of the Word. In *Against the Greeks – On the Incarnation*,
the reversal of human fallenness by the divine fall is a theme that is
associated with that of Christ's redemption as bringing about the
restoration of humanity's knowledge of God. The conception of
humanity's relation to God in terms of knowledge (*gnosis*), albeit a
knowledge that is based on divine revelation and grounded in a life
of virtue and ecclesial participation, is a marked feature of the
Alexandrian tradition. Athanasius appropriates this tradition, but
within the terms of his own kenotic theology of divine descent. In
Against the Greeks – On the Incarnation, Athanasius speaks of four
ways in which God has made knowledge of himself accessible to
humanity: the structure of the human being itself, which is constituted by its participation in and accessibility to the Word; the order
and harmony of creation, which "cries out" that its governor and
harmonizer is the divine *Logos*; the law and prophets (the Old
Testament), which safeguard the life of participation in the Word;
and, finally, when these three ways proved insufficient to quell the
tide of human iniquity, the humanization of the Word.[143] The
Incarnation is conceived as the nadir point of divine condescension,
wherein God encounters humanity at the very place to which it had
fallen:

As a good teacher cares for his students and comes down to
the level of those who cannot take advantage of more
advanced things in order to teach them by simpler means,
so does the Word of God. As Paul says, "For since in the
wisdom of God the world did not come to know God
through wisdom, it pleased God to save those who have

faith through the foolishness of the gospel" (1 Cor 1:21).
For since human beings had turned away from the contemplation of God and become mired in the depths, with their
eyes cast down, looking for God among created things and
the realm of the senses and contriving gods for themselves
from among mortal men and demons, the Savior of all and
Word of God, who loves humanity, took to himself a body
and lived as a human being among humanity ... Since
people's reasoning had fallen to the level of sensible things,
the Word submitted himself to being revealed through a
body so that, as a human being, he might carry human
beings over to himself and direct their senses to himself,
and so that, although they saw him as a man, he might
persuade them by the works which he accomplished that he
is not only a man but God, and Word and Wisdom of the
true God. This also Paul wished to signify when he said,
"that you, being rooted and grounded in love may have
strength to comprehend with all the holy ones what is the
breadth and length and height and depth, and to know the
love of Christ that surpasses knowledge, so that you may be
filled with all the fullness of God" (Eph 3:17–19). For the
Word extended himself everywhere: above and below, in
depth and in breadth – above, in creation; below in his
humanization; in the depth of Hades; in the breadth of the
cosmos. Everything has been filled with the knowledge of
God.

(*Inc.* 15–16)[144]

While in *Against the Greeks – On the Incarnation* the characterization of Christ's salvific work as a loving "condescension" is a
structural motif that is played against that of humanity's sinful
descent into idolatry, it is used in an explicitly "anti-Arian" context
as a defining characteristic of the genuine proclamation of the
gospel, over and against the inverted proclamation of the "Arians".
In his *Orations against the Arians*, Athanasius characterizes the choice
between his theological position and that of his opponents as
reducible to that between a self-humbling God and a self-
promoting "god." As Athanasius presents it, the debate concerns
two alternative readings of salvation which respectively identify two
very different characterizations of the nature of the Son in relation
to the benefits of his work. Either the Son is by nature the true God
who humbled himself in order to bring about our exaltation, so that

his salvific work is the result of the abasement that he undertakes
for our benefit; or he was himself "promoted" to divinity as a
reward for his work in the flesh. The choice then is between the
God of loving condescension and the self-promoting, upwardly
mobile God! In one instance, this question comes up in the context
of debate over the text of Phil 2:9–10: "Therefore, God greatly
exalted him, and bestowed on him the name that is above every
name." The "Arian" interpretation, according to Athanasius's
rendering, sees this verse as indicating the "progress" of the Son and
his attainment of a privileged status and a graced divinity.
Athanasius's counter-exegesis manifests the inevitable intertwining
of Christological and Trinitarian issues involved in the Arian
controversy. He does not deny that the humanity of Christ was
promoted and exalted, but he insists that the exaltation belongs
exclusively to the humanity, whereas the humiliation pertains to the
divine Word's appropriation of the human condition. But the principal underlying question, for Athanasius, is the overall thrust of
the whole Christian *kerygma* in its characterization of Christ as God:
Is it of a God who promotes humanity by his self-humbling or of a
God who is himself promoted through his dealings with humanity?
Is it of a God who is the giver of grace and condescends for our
benefit or of a God who himself attains grace?[145] Clearly, it is the
first set of alternatives that represents the thrust of the Christian
kerygma for Athanasius. But, in that case, "He was not human, and
then became God, but he was God, and then became human, in
order to deify us" (*Or. Ar.* 1:39); for "the advance belongs to
humanity but the Son of God humbled himself so that in his
humbling we may be able to advance" (*Or. Ar.* 3:52).

A similar reasoning is used by Athanasius to argue for the Son's
divinity in the context of his discussion of the Word's role in the act
of creation. Arius and Asterius conceived the Word as a created
mediator of God's creative activity. Such a conception is unacceptable to Athanasius on at least two fundamental counts. First, the
notion that God needs any intervening mediator in order to relate
himself to creation is repugnant to him, and he expresses this
repugnance in a way that seems indebted to Irenaeus, the second-
century bishop of Lyons. In countering the "gnostic" systems in
which the creator of this world is a defective or evil being, different
from the true God, Irenaeus insisted that the true God is no other
than the Creator of this world, whose majesty is manifest in his
presence to and loving solicitude for creation.[146] Athanasius shows
clear dependence on Irenaeus when he insists that creative activity

belongs only to God and cannot be exercised by any subordinate or intermediate level of divinity. Thus, if the Word is Creator, as the Scriptures intimate and as the "Arians concur, then he must be fully God and not a creature. The divine condescension which brings creation into existence and sustains it is not exercised by a lower level of divinity but is a joint work of Father and Son, for creation "would not have withstood his nature, being that of the unmitigated splendor of the Father, if he had not condescended (*sunkatabas*) by the Father's love for humanity and supported, strengthened and carried them into being" (*Or. Ar.* 2:64). Thus, Athanasius transposes Asterius's theology of the Son as mediating the transcendence of the Father by speaking of the Son's condescension as mediating the transcendence of the *Son's own nature*, which he shares with the Father.

Secondly, according to Athanasius, the "Arian" conception of "a created Creator" again reverses the fundamental ethos of the Christian message, which is gratitude for God's gratuitous condescension. If, according to this conception, the Word himself came to be in order to facilitate our creation, then "he owes thanks to us, not we to him" (*Or. Ar.* 2:30). Again, we see that Athanasius leads the argument to the question of whether Jesus Christ embodies the gracious God, the God who is giver of grace, to whom we owe a radical debt of gratitude, or whether he represents merely the instrumental means which a transcendent God employs because creation cannot withstand immediate contact with such a God. In the first case, according to Athanasius, Jesus Christ is the natural Son of the Father who creates us out of loving condescension then redeems us to the point that we become divine by grace, sharing in the divine sonship of the Son. In the second case, however, Jesus Christ does not directly represent divine condescension and gratuity, since he himself owes his being to us – as if our existence is a sufficient end in itself, but the Son's existence is functionally oriented toward our existence (*Or. Ar.* 2:29). In his conception of the Christian accounts of creation and salvation, Athanasius thus ties the natural and ontological "belonging" of the Son to the Father to an account of the gratuitous descending love of God which is manifested in the life and death of Christ. The Son is the fully divine Creator who is other than creation, to whom creation is indebted for its being. The Son is also the fully divine Savior, as the God who humbled himself for the sake of our advancement. In Athanasius's theological vision, Trinitarian theology and a kenotic Christology are closely intertwined and mutually correlative; both are consistent with a core emphasis on the divine posture toward humanity as one of *philanthropia*, the divine love that bridges the transcendent natural inaccessibility of the divine essence.

The body and death of Christ

The centrality of the motif of divine condescension is also the appropriate context for noting Athanasius's emphasis on Christ's body and Christ's death, inasmuch as both themes indicate the extremity of the Word's descent into our condition. If, according to Athanasius, the human body is "what is closest to ourselves," the assumption of the human body by the Word indicates the point at which the Word becomes "closest" to us. Athanasius's Christology has been subjected to modern criticism particularly in reference to his typical manner of speaking of the Word and his body (or flesh), and for not figuring Christ's human soul into the equation. For this reason, he is sometimes associated with his admirer Apollinarius, who explicitly rejected the doctrine that Christ had a human soul and asserted that the *Logos* replaces the human soul in Christ and directly animates Christ's human body.[147] However, such an analytical approach to the inner constitution of Christ's person is altogether absent from Athanasius. A much more fruitful approach to his Christology is one that seeks to discern the framework and intentionality of his use of Christological terms in the context of his understanding of Christ's saving work. We have already seen him articulate the significance of Christ's body in terms of its being the locus of Christ's descent to the sensible level to which humanity had become bound. Even more primarily, the significance of Christ's body, for Athanasius, is its being the medium by which the Word encounters and triumphs over human death:

> So the Word of God himself came in order that he who is the image of the Father might be able to renew the creation of the humanity which is in the image. But this could not have been done apart from the destruction of death and corruption. Therefore, it was fitting that he took a mortal body, in order that henceforth death could be destroyed in it and humanity might be renewed in the image.
>
> (*Inc.* 13)[148]

As this passage intimates, and contrary to some misperceptions,[149] the death of Christ thus occupies a central place in Athanasius's

presentation of the rationale and salvific efficacy of the humanization of the Word. He refers to Christ's death as "the capstone of our
faith" (*Inc.* 19), and the significance which he attaches to it in large
part explains his emphasis on the bodiliness of Christ. It is the
death of Christ and its culmination in resurrection that undoes
humanity's subjection to sin and death, which are the consequences
of the transgression of Adam. This subjection is elaborated by
Athanasius both in terms of the biblically depicted divine judgment (Gen 2:16–17) and in terms of the ontological dialectic by
which humanity, once having turned away from participation in
divine life, inevitably is reduced back to its intrinsic nothingness.
But it was also fitting that the divine creative power undo the "de-
creation" of sin, consistently with God's glory as manifested in his
love for humanity. Moreover, for humanity to be truly and intrinsically free from subjection to death, the victory of sin and death
must take place from within the human being, and not simply be
ordained by God as an "external" commandment.[150] All these
conditions were met when the Word took a mortal human body and
offered it to death on behalf of all, thus repaying the debt incurred
by our transgression:

> Knowing that the corruption of humanity could not be
> undone except by the death of all, and being unable to die,
> inasmuch as he is the Word and Son of the Father, he took
> to himself a body that was capable of death so that this
> body, which participated in the Word who is above all,
> could suffice for death on behalf of all and remain incor-
> ruptible because of the Word's indwelling of it, and so that
> henceforth all corruption in humanity might be stopped by
> the grace of the resurrection.
>
> (*Inc.* 9)[151]

Associated with the centrality of Christ's death in Athanasius's
soteriology is the sacrificial terminology which he tends to use in
this context, and which gives another indication of the significance
of his emphasis on the bodiliness of Christ. Once again, Athanasius
is not concerned with the analytical question of how the human
body is animated by the *Logos*, but with the soteriological dynamics
of what the *Logos* does with the human body in order to save us.
Most primarily, for Athanasius, what the *Logos* does with his human
body for our salvation is to die on our behalf. Moreover,
Athanasius's employment of sacrificial language in this context

resonates with Eucharistic overtones.[152] While much has been made of a single instance in which Athanasius defends the plausibility of the Incarnation by alluding to the Stoic conception of the universe as "a body" animated by the *Logos*,[153] a much more typical conception is that in which Christ's body is conceived as an offering (*prosphora*) presented by the Incarnate Word to the Father. Thus, he speaks of the Word's "interceding" (*presbeuō*) for all before the Father,[154] primarily by "offering" (*prospherō*) his own body as a sacrifice (*thusia*) and ransom (*lutron*, *antipsychon*) for human sins, thus liberating humanity from its "descent" into death and reasserting the divine goodness whose efficacy was threatened by human sin:

> For the human race would have been destroyed if the Lord and Savior of all, the Son of God, had not come to bring about the end of death. Truly, this great work was particularly suited to the goodness of God. For if a king builds a house or city, which is then besieged by bandits on account of the negligence of its inhabitants, he by no means abandons it but avenges and rescues it, regarding not the negligence of the inhabitants but what is becoming for himself. By so much the more did God, the Word of the all-good Father, not neglect the human race which was made through him, when it descended into corruption. Instead, he brought to dissolution the death that had come about, by the offering (*prosphora*) of his own body; by his own teaching, he corrected their negligence; and he reformed everything that pertains to humanity by his own power.
>
> One can be assured of these things if one avails oneself of the writings of the Savior's own theologians, in which they say: "For the love of Christ impels us, once we have come to the conviction that one died for all; therefore, all have died. He indeed died for all, so that those who live might live no longer for themselves but for him who for their sake died and was raised" from the dead, our Lord Jesus Christ (2 Cor 5: 14–15). And again, "We see Jesus crowned with glory and honor because he suffered death, he who for a little while was made lower than the angels, that by the grace of God he might taste death for everyone" (Heb 2:9). And then he indicates the reason why no other than God the Word himself should have become human by saying, "For it was fitting that he, for whom and through whom all

things exist, in bringing many sons to glory, should make the leader of their salvation perfect through suffering" (Heb 2:10). In saying this, he means that it belonged to none other to bring back human beings from the corruption that had come about except the Word of God, who had also made them in the beginning. He also indicates that the Word himself took to himself a body as a sacrifice (*thusia*) on behalf of similar bodies, when he says: "Now since the children share in blood and flesh, he likewise shared in them, that through death he might destroy the one who has the power of death, that is, the devil, and free those who through fear of death had been subject to slavery all their life" (Heb 2:14–15). For by the sacrifice (*thusia*) of his own body, he put an end to the law that was against us and made a new beginning of life for us, granting us the hope of resurrection. For since it was through human beings that death had assumed power over humanity, so it was through the humanization of the Word of God that the dissolution of death and the resurrection of life came to be. And this is what that Christ-bearing man says: "Since death came through a human being, the resurrection of the dead came also through a human being; for just as in Adam all die, so too in Christ all shall be brought to life" (1 Cor 15:21–22), and so forth. For now we no longer die in condemnation but, as those who rise from the dead, we await the universal resurrection of all which God has accomplished and granted to us and which "He will reveal in his own time" (1 Tim 6:15). This then is the first reason for the humanization of the Savior.

(*Inc.* 9–10)[155]

This implicitly Eucharistic framework, evoked by the language of "offering" and "sacrifice" and much indebted to the *Letter to the Hebrews*, remains constant and becomes if anything more explicit in Athanasius's later works. In the *Orations against the Arians*, he explicates the reference to Jesus as the "apostle and high priest of our confession" (Heb 3:1) by weaving together Christ's Incarnation, death, resurrection, and atoning priesthood:

When did he become "apostle" except when he put on our flesh? And when did he become "High Priest of our confession" except when he offered himself for us and raised his

body from the dead, and now brings near and offers to the
Father those who approach him in faith, redeeming all and
making expiation to God on behalf of all? ... "In the
beginning was the Word and the Word was with God and
the Word was God" (Jn 1:1). But when the Father willed
that ransoms should be paid for all and grace given to all,
then the Word took flesh from the earth, as Aaron put on
his robe, and Mary, like untilled earth, became the mother
of his body, so that having an offering as a high priest he
may offer himself to the Father and cleanse us all from sins
in his own blood, and raise us from the dead.

(*Or. Ar.* 2:7)[156]

Athanasius's much-noted emphasis on the Incarnation should not be
seen therefore as a de-emphasis on the death and resurrection of
Christ, which are cited by Athanasius as the very purpose of the
Incarnation: "He came for this reason: that in the flesh he might
suffer and the flesh be made impassible and immortal" (*Or. Ar.*
3:58).[157]

Another possible misreading of Athanasius is to suggest that he
construes the universal efficacy of the Word's Incarnation and death
in Platonic terms – as if the Word became incarnate in the universal
"form" of humanity.[158] However, Athanasius never actually says
anything near to that effect. In fact, he tends to place considerable
stress on the similitude of Christ's body to ours; a recurrent refrain
is that his body is "like" (*homoios*) ours.[159] The salvific efficacy of
Christ's body is explained not in terms of its idiosyncratic structure,
but rather in terms of its similitude to ours and its unique relation
to the Word – its being *the Word's body*. When Athanasius tries to
explain why the offering and sanctification of the Word's body
should have a universal effect, he resorts not to a Platonic conception of Christ's body as a universal but to an evocative analogy that
is much more relational and, as it were, environmental:

When a great king has entered a large city and taken up
residence in one of the houses in it, such a city becomes
worthy of great honor and is no longer assaulted by any
enemy or bandit descending upon it, but is rather deemed
worthy of every attention because of the king residing in
one of its houses. Such is the case with the King of all. As
soon as he came to our realm and took up residence in one
body, like our own, the whole conspiracy against humanity

by its enemies has been stopped and the corruption of
death which had formerly ruled over them has been obliter-
ated.

$$(Inc. \ 9)^{160}$$

But in the last analysis, the Alexandrian's strong conception of the
applicability of Christ's salvific Incarnation to all humanity is based
on a strict adherence to scriptural assertions of the universal applicability of Christ's death, as is witnessed by his reference to such
scriptural testimony as 2 Cor 5:14, "For the love of Christ impels
us, when we consider that if one died for all, then all have died,"
and Heb 2:9, "that by the grace of God he might taste death on
behalf of all."[161] Moreover, once again we cannot ignore the
implicit Eucharistic overtones of his assertion that Christ's offering
of his own body as a sacrifice applies to us through our "kinship"
(*Or. Ar.* 1:43) with his body and our being "co-bodied" (*sussōmoi*)
with him (*Or. Ar.* 2:74).[162]

The renewal of the relation between God and creation through Christ

While Athanasius does speak of the salvation wrought by Christ as
a "renewal" of creation,[163] it is clear that this renewal does not
entail for him simply a return to the original condition of the
prelapsarian Adam. In order to characterize the new relation
between God and creation that obtains through Christ's work of
redemption, Athanasius has recourse to a series of structural motifs
that pervade his writings. Among the most important of these are:
(1) the definitive stability and security worked by Christ; (2) the
climactic "internality" of divine grace through the work of Christ;
and (3) the transformative "appropriation" of the human condition
by the divine Word.

Stability, security, and "remaining"

Athanasius had inherited from his Alexandrian predecessor Origen a
concern for the inherent instability of the human condition, and a
correlative emphasis on salvation as the attainment of stability and
immutability.[164] The provenance of this notion, however, extends
beyond Origen and has roots in both the biblical and the Greek
philosophical traditions. The Hebrew Scriptures speak of the election of Israel, its anointed king, and the just person in terms of the

promise that they "shall not be moved."[165] The Epistle to the Hebrews, hearkening back to Isa 66:22, refers to Christ's establishing an "unshakeable kingdom" which "remains" (*menei*).[166] The Platonic philosophical tradition posits a fundamental dualism between the world of becoming which is "easily movable" (*eukinētos*) and the immutable stability of the world of forms. Athanasius evokes these various resonances but integrates them into his own theological vision. In the context of creation and divine providence, he speaks of the active agency of the Word in terms of granting "protection" and "security" to an inherently unstable creation.[167] Correspondingly, one of the principal ways in which he highlights the transformed relation between God and creation through Christ is to assert that it is only through Christ's saving work that humanity attains an ultimate security, *bebaiotēs*, in its communion with God.[168]

Often, this understanding is articulated through the allied terminology of "remaining" (*menein/diamenein*). The latter is as key a structural motif in Athanasius's theology as it is for the Gospel of John, in which the "remaining" and "abiding" in Christ is a central image.[169] Athanasius's characterization of humanity's relation to God is expressed in saying that humanity cannot "remain" in existence apart from divine assistance and participation in the Word. As part of created reality, humanity is subject to the double pull by which it is intrinsically drawn to "remain" either in nothingness or in God. The economy of salvation is correspondingly characterized in terms of God's pedagogic efforts to orient humanity away from "remaining" in its own nothingness and toward "remaining" in the life of communion with him:

> He led them into his paradise, and gave them a law, so that if they guarded the grace and remained (*menoien*) good, they would possess the life in paradise that is without sorrow or pain or care, as well as the promise of incorruptible life in heaven. But if they transgressed and turned back and became evil, they would know that they would suffer in death the corruption that is according to their nature and that they would no longer live in Paradise but would henceforth die outside it and remain (*menein*) in death and corruption. The divine Scripture also foretells this, saying in the person of God: "You shall eat of every tree in Paradise. But do not eat of the tree of the knowledge of

good and evil. On the day that you eat of it, you shall die by death" (Gen 2:16–17). This "dying by death": what else could it be than not only to die but to remain (*diamenein*) in the corruption of death.

(*Inc.* 3)[170]

The finality and irreversibility of sin, as far as the powers of merely human agency are concerned, is that in depriving humanity of the "grace" (*charis*) of participation in the Word, it merely confirms the intrinsic tendency of their "nature" (*physis*) to revert to nothingness. But if the power of sin lies in its capacity to lead humanity into the condition of "remaining" in its orientation to nothingness and so exploits humanity's inherent ontological weakness, the final and definitive "remaining" in the "grace" of participation in the Word happens only through the humanization, death, and resurrection of the Word. Only the divine Word, who is not subject to the "remaining in death" that comes through sin's confirmation of humanity's inherent nothingness, can definitively liberate humanity and cause it to "remain" with God. While we find a fairly systematic presentation of this understanding already in *Against the Greeks – On the Incarnation*, the point is also made on behalf of the full divinity of the Son in Athanasius's explicitly anti-Arian polemic:

If the Son was a creature, humanity would have remained (*emenen*) none the less mortal and not united to God. It was not a creature that united creatures to God, for in that case this creature would be itself in search of one to unite it to God. Nor would a part of creation be the salvation of creation, that part itself being in need of salvation. To prevent this, God sends his own Son who becomes the Son of Man by taking created flesh, so that he may offer his own body to death on behalf of all, since all were sentenced to death but he was other than all. Henceforth, the utterance of that sentence is fulfilled, in so far as all have died through him – for "all have died" in Christ (2 Cor 5:14) – and henceforth all can be freed through him from sin and the curse that comes from it and may truly remain (*diamenosin*) forever as risen from the dead and as putting on immortality and incorruptibility.

(*Or. Ar.* 2:69)[171]

The "internality" of grace through Christ

Alongside the explication of the newness of Christ's redemption in terms of its effecting a definitive "remaining" and security for humanity, Athanasius also lays emphasis on our access to communion with God as becoming "intrinsic" to the human condition through Christ. It is typical of Athanasius to think in categories of "internality" and "externality," often making the point in his anti-Arian polemic that the world is "external" to the divine being, and that the divine Word is, by nature, "outside" creation.[172] With reference to the Incarnation, however, he is concerned to maintain that the salvation worked by Jesus Christ does not take place "outside" us or extrinsically, by divine decree, but is a transformation from "within" the human being. Linking the motif of "remaining" with that of "internality," he asserts that the reign of sin would "remain within" us unless it were superseded by the internality of the divine agency which renders sin "external" to us. This is what occurs in the Incarnation of the Word:

> Even Plato, who is so esteemed by the Greeks, says that when the one who created the world saw it in distress and in danger of lapsing into the realm of disharmony,[173] he sat at the helm of the soul and lent it his aid and corrected all its defects. So then what is so unbelievable in our saying that when humanity had gone astray, the Word sat at its helm and appeared as a human being, so that, through his guidance and goodness, he might save distressed humanity? But perhaps, being shamed into agreeing with this, they will then wish to say that when God wanted to rehabilitate and save humanity, he should not have brought his Word into contact with a body but should have done it with a mere command, just as he had done before, when he fashioned humanity from non-being. But against this objection of theirs, it would be appropriate to respond as follows: Before, when nothing existed at all, all that was required for the creation of the universe was a command and an act of will. But once humanity came into being, there was a need to cure not what did not yet exist but what had already come into being. So it was fitting and appropriate for the Healer and Savior to make himself present among those who were already in existence, in order to heal these existent beings. Therefore, he became a human being and made use of the body as a human

medium. But if it should not have happened in this way, then by what medium should the Word have appeared when he wished to do so? And from where should he have received it if not from those who already existed and needed access to his divinity through what had similitude with them? For it was not the non-existent that had need of salvation, so that a mere command would suffice, but humanity, which was already in existence and beset by corruption and ruin.

Then also, it must be understood that the corruption which had taken place was not outside the body, but attached to it. So it was necessary for life to cleave to the body in the place of corruption, so that just as death had come to be in the body, so now life would come to be in it. If death had come to be outside the body, life also would have come to be outside the body. But if death had become intertwined with the body, and in being joined with the body was in fact ruling over it, it was necessary for life to be intertwined with it, so that the body could put on life and cast off corruption. Otherwise, if the Word had come outside the body and not in it, death would still have been defeated by him – which is most natural, since death cannot overpower life – but the corruption attached to the body would nevertheless remain in the body. Therefore it was fitting that the Savior put on a body, so that the body might be permeated with life and would no longer, as mortal, remain in death, but as putting on immortality, would henceforth rise up and remain immortal. For once it had put on corruption, it would not have risen unless it had come to put on life. Moreover, death does not appear by itself but only in the body. Therefore, he put on a body, so that he might find death in the body and banish it. How indeed was the Lord manifested as Life, if not by vivifying what was mortal?

(*Inc.* 43–44)[174]

While Athanasius's doctrine of creation emphasizes that humanity's ontological vulnerability is due to its origination from nothing, his articulation of Christian salvation indicates that the definitive "remaining" in divine grace and humanity's new access to this grace "from within" constitutes nothing less than a "new origin" for humanity. Humanity's origin from nothing is now "transferred" into the humanity of the Word himself, whose sacrificial death has destroyed the intrinsic bond, confirmed by sin, between humanity and nothingness: "For by the sacrifice of his own body he both put an end to the law which lay over us, and renewed for us the origin of life by giving hope of the resurrection" (*Inc.* 10). Thus, whereas apart from the Incarnation, human existence is a movement of receptivity from nothingness to God, a movement that always threatens to relapse into nothingness, those who are united to Christ "now have the origin of their receiving in him and through him" (*Or. Ar.* 1:48). While this conception resonates strongly with Athanasius's exposition of the metaphysics of *creatio ex nihilo*, he is also able to render it according to the biblical motif of the First and Second Adam:

> When his flesh is born of Mary the Mother of God, he who provides others with their birth into being is himself said to be born so that he may transfer our origin into himself. Thus we are no longer merely earth which returns to earth (cf. Gen 3:19), but being intertwined with the Word who is from heaven, we are raised up by him into heaven. Therefore, it was not unfitting for him to transfer also the other passibilities of the body into himself, so that we may participate in eternal life, being no longer merely human but belonging to the Word. We no longer die in Adam in accordance with our first birth (cf. 1 Cor 15:22) but because our birth and all the weakness of the flesh are henceforth transferred into the Word, we are raised from the earth and loosed from the curse of sin by him who is in us and who was made a curse for our sake (cf. Gal 3:13). And rightly so! For, just as we all die in Adam, being from earth, so are we all made alive in Christ (1 Cor 15:22) when we are reborn from above by water and the Spirit (cf. Jn 3:5). Henceforth, our flesh is no longer earthly but becomes Worded[175] through the Word of God, who became flesh for our sake (cf. Jn 1:14).
>
> (*Or. Ar.* 3:33)[176]

"Appropriation"

It is likely that Athanasius's predecessor Alexander referred to the Son as *idios*, "belonging to" or "proper to" the Father. Although we have no extant records of his use of this term, Arius's explicit repudiation of it in the course of his rejection of Alexander's theology indicates its prior use by the latter.[177] Athanasius also cites Theognostus, head of the catechetical school of Alexandria in the mid-third century, who speaks of the Son as "not external" (*ouk exōthen*) to the essence of the Father.[178] The combination of the affirmation that the Son is *idios* to the being of the Father and the negation that he is "from outside" the Father's being became a cornerstone of Athanasius's own Trinitarian terminology. To say that the Son is *idios* to the Father indicated the substantial correlativity of the Father and Son; both eternally exist in relation to one another. Conversely, the irreducible contrast between the Triune God and all creation is indicated by saying that creatures are "external" to the Father's being. But Athanasius's depiction of the radical newness in the relation between God and creation that is secured by Christ's salvific work includes a reversal of this contrast. The startling *novum* of the Incarnation is that the eternal divine Word whose nature is "outside" the created order "appropriated" created human nature so that henceforth humanity was not "external" to his being but has become his very "own."

Athanasius's use of the category of "appropriation" (*idiopoieō*) issues from a soteriological focus on the ontological transformation of humanity which the Word, in unity with his human body, effects. While it is true that Athanasius does not concern himself with an analytical exposition of how the constitutive elements of Christ (i.e. human body, human soul, divinity) fit together, his language of "appropriation" does indicate a kind of unity in which a subject brings an "external" reality into his own sphere of reality, influence, and agency. In the case of the enfleshed Word, such a unity is linguistically signified by the application of human predication to the subject of the Word. But this linguistic maneuver mirrors the salvific reality that the properties of the human condition are transformed and deified when they are thus appropriated by the Word, to the point where humanity becomes "incorruptible" and "impassible." It is this appropriation by the Word that finally enables humanity to pass over from the "remaining" in the corruption of sin to the "remaining" in incorruptible communion with God:

> If the works of the Word's divinity were not accomplished through the body, humanity would not have been divinized. On the other hand, if the properties (*idia*) of the flesh were not attributed to the Word, humanity would not

have been completely freed from them. Even if they had
abated for a little while, as I said before, sin and corruption
would still remain in humanity, as is shown to be the case
with human beings before him. For there have been many
holy people who were pure of all sin. Jeremiah was sanctified from the womb (Jer 1:5) and John, while still in the
womb, leaped with joy at the voice of Mary, the Mother of
God (Lk 1:44). And yet "death reigned from Adam to
Moses, even over those who did not sin after the pattern of
Adam's transgression" (Rom 5:14). Thus did humanity
remain no less mortal and corruptible, being vulnerable to
the possibilities that pertain to its nature (*physis*). But now
that the Word has become a human being and appropriated
the properties of the flesh, these no longer harm the body,
on account of the Word who has come to be in the body.
They are rather destroyed by him, so that henceforth
human beings may no longer remain in sin and death, in
accordance with their own passibilities, but may attain to
resurrection, in accordance with the power of the Word,
remaining always immortal and incorruptible.

(*Or. Ar.* 3:33)[179]

Conceived within this transformative perspective, the relation
between the Word and his humanity constitutes a unity that is
decidedly asymmetrical. For Athanasius, as for classic Patristic
Christology in general and later Alexandrian (Cyrillian) Christology
in particular, the fact that Jesus Christ is equally human and
divine[180] does not at all imply that his humanity and divinity are in
fact equal. The inequality between the divinity and humanity of
Christ is typically emphasized by Athanasius in terms of the active
agency of the divinity in relation to the humanity. This
Christological framework is consistent with Athanasius's cosmology
in which the universe as a whole is sustained by its receptivity to
the creative and providential agency of the Word. It also evokes the
contrast in Stoic cosmology between the active (*poioun*) and passive
(*paschon*) principles by which the universe is constituted,[181] as well
as the Platonic framework of participation in which entities in the
realm of becoming are constituted by their participation in the
forms of the realm of being. In Athanasius's usage, these evocations
are used to illustrate the soteriological principle that the unity of
humanity and divinity in Christ is not a mere juxtaposition but an
active transformation of the humanity by the divinity. Thus, when

the Word becomes flesh, the divinity and lordship of the Word is not reduced but "extended,"[182] so that the sovereignty of the Word may be salvifically manifest within human flesh. Against the "Arians", Athanasius insists that the "new origin" thereby granted to humanity should not be seen as applying to the essence of the Word but to the extension of the eternal lordship of the Word into the realm of sinful flesh. The saving condescension of the Word is ultimately a glorious affirmation of his irreducible and irreducibly active sovereignty:

> It was not he who attained an origin of his being then [at the time of the Incarnation], but it was we who attained to the beginning of having him as our Lord. God, who is good and the Father of our Lord took pity on us and, wishing to be known by all, he made his own Son put on a human body and become a human being called Jesus, so that in this body he may make an offering of himself on behalf of all and liberate all from their estrangement from God and from corruption and so that he may become Lord and king of all. That he became in this way the Lord and king of all is what Peter says: "He has made him Lord" (Acts 2:36) and "he has sent Christ" (cf. Acts 3:20). This is the same as saying that the Father has made him a human being – for to be made is something that pertains to human beings. But he did not merely make him as a human being but as one who is Lord of all and who sanctifies all by his own anointing. For even if "being in the form of God, he took the form of a servant" (Phil 2:6–7), the reception of the form of a servant did not render servile the Word who is Lord by nature but rather brought liberation from the Lord for all humanity. He who is Word and Lord by nature was made a human being through the form of a servant as well as Lord of all and "Christ" – that is to say, the one who anoints all by the Spirit.
>
> (*Or. Ar.* 2:14)[183]

As can be seen from this passage, Athanasius's emphasis in the loving "descent" of the Word does not entail any speculation in the direction of a *kenoticism* of the divine essence or a passible God. While modern speculation on the notion of divine passibility frequently concerns itself with the question of what happens to the divine essence when the Word takes on human suffering,

Athanasius's much more concrete perspective is preoccupied with what happens to human suffering and corruptibility when they are assumed by the divine Word. The descent of the Word does not diminish the divine nature or amount to a reversal of divine sovereignty; rather, it is the negativities of the fallen human condition that are reversed by the Word's appropriation of them:

> For he suffered to prepare freedom from suffering for those who suffer in him. He descended so that he may raise us up. He took upon himself the ordeal of being born that we might love him who is unbegotten; He went down to corruption that corruption might put on immortality. He became weak for us that we might rise with power. He descended to death that He might grant us immortality and give life to the dead. Finally he became human that we who die as human beings might live again and that death may no longer have sovereignty over us; for the apostolic word proclaims, "Death shall not have dominion over us."
>
> (*Festal Letter* X:8)[184]

Athanasius's creative use of this model of "appropriation" allows him to handle issues of Christological predication with a sophistication that is precocious, given its pre-Chalcedonian setting. Such sophistication can be easily missed if one focuses one-sidedly on his denial of the predication of human attributes to the Word – in saying, for example, that it was not the Word who suffered. Or else, his paradoxically simultaneous affirmations and negations of such attributes (that Christ "suffered and did not suffer"[185] or was "weak himself though not himself weak"[186]) may easily appear to be nonsensical. However, within the framework supplied by his model of "appropriation," we can discern in Athanasius a double concern to distinguish the reality of the Word *qua* Word from the reality of the human condition which he appropriates, while simultaneously affirming the fact that the human condition has in fact been appropriated by the Word to the extent that it has become "his" reality. Typically, Athanasius is concretely concerned with the intelligibility of biblical language which refers human predications to the subject of the Word:

> Therefore, when the scriptural authors[187] who speak of him say that he ate and drank and was born, you should understand that it was the body, as body, which was born and fed

70

with appropriate nourishment. But God the Word, who was united to the body while ordering all things, made it known through the works which he accomplished in the body that he was not a human being, but God the Word. Yet these things were said of him because indeed the body which ate and was born and suffered was not another's but the Lord's.

(*Inc.* 18)[188]

The *Orations against the Arians* provide a wider context for interpreting Athanasius's meaning when he uses such paradoxical language. There, Athanasius is dealing with the "Arian" interpretation of Prov 8:22, wherein Wisdom (*Sophia*) declares: "He created me as the beginning of his ways for his works." The interpretation against which he is contending is that the figure of Wisdom in this passage, understood by both sides to be the pre-existent Christ, is "created" and therefore not co-eternal with the Father. One of the ways in which Athanasius deals with this text is to make the linguistic-logical point that predications of creatureliness do not necessarily apply to the very essence of the subject of whom these predications are made. Characteristically, he makes the point by scriptural examples:[189] "A clean heart create in me, O God" (Ps 51:12) is not a petition to have one heart replaced by another one that is different in its very essence. Rather, it is an appeal to have one's heart undergo a change and conversion. Similarly, according to Athanasius's interpretation, when Wisdom says, "He created me," the predication of creatureliness does not define the subject of Wisdom but speaks of an event which is nevertheless truly predicated of that subject: "The phrase, 'He created,' does not of itself simply signify the being or the generation, but can indicate that something else comes to be in reference to the one of whom it speaks" (*Or. Ar.* 2:45).[190] It is in the context of arguing this very point that Athanasius presents one of his articulations of the theme of the paradoxical applicability and non-applicability of human attributions to the Word: "By receiving our weaknesses, he himself is said to be weak – though not weak in himself, for he is the power of God. And he became sin for us and a curse, though not having sinned himself, but because he himself bore our sins and our curse" (*ibid.*). The logic propounded here is that the predication refers to an "event" that is correctly attributed to the subject and thus belongs (*idios*) to the subject, but that such predications do not define the subject as such, independently of that event. Thus, all creaturely predications properly belong to the subject of the Word, through the Incarnation, but do not essentially define the Word as subject, independently of the Incarnation: "Let it be known that while the Word himself is impassible in his nature, these things are said of him because of the flesh that he put on, since they belong to the flesh and the body itself belongs to the Savior" (*Or. Ar.* 3:34).[191] While Athanasius is clearly concerned to guard the divine impassibility of the Word, he also stresses that what is specifically unique and salvific about the Incarnation is precisely that these human attributes are predicated of the Word himself:

> In earlier times, the Word came to each of the saints and sanctified those who received him rightly. But neither when they were born was it said that he had become a human being, nor when they suffered was it said that he himself had suffered. But once he came from Mary to dwell among us, at the end of the ages for the remission of sins (for so it was pleasing to the Father to send his own Son, born from woman, born under the law) (Gal 4:4), then it was that it was said of him that he had taken flesh and become a human being and that in this flesh he suffered for us, as Peter says: "Christ suffered for us in the flesh" (1 Pet 4:1).
>
> These things are said so that it might be shown and so that we all might believe that, being always God and sanctifying those to whom he came while also ordering all things according to the Father's will, he later became a human being for our sakes and divinity dwelt bodily in the flesh, as the apostle says (cf. Col 2:9). This is as much as to say: Being God, he took possession of a body as his own and employed it as a means by which he became a human being for our sakes. Therefore, since he was in the flesh, the properties of the flesh are attributed to him – such as hunger, thirst, suffering, fatigue, and so on – to which the flesh is susceptible. But through his own body he also accomplished the characteristic works of the Word himself, such as raising the dead, making the blind to see again, and healing the hemorrhaging woman. While the Word bore the weaknesses of the flesh as his own – for the flesh was his own – the flesh itself rendered service to the activities of the divinity – for the divinity was in the flesh and the body belonged to God. Thus, the prophet spoke well when he

said, "He bore [our weaknesses]" (Isa 53:4); he did not say, "He healed our weaknesses," as if he merely healed the body, as he had always done, while being outside it, thus leaving humanity still subject to death. But he bears our weaknesses and sins, so that it may be manifest that he has become a human being and that the body which bears these in him, is his own. He himself was not harmed by "bearing our sins in his body upon the tree," as Peter says (1 Pet 2:24), but we human beings were redeemed from our own passibilities and filled with the righteousness of the Word.

(*Or. Ar.* 3:31)[192]

Athanasius's handling of issues of Christological predication was highly influential on his episcopal successor, Cyril of Alexandria, whose own work was so foundational for the Christological Councils of Ephesus (431) and Chalcedon (451). In the Christological controversies that erupted between Cyril and his Antiochian opponent Nestorius, Cyril argued on behalf of the application of human attributes to the Word by recourse to much of Athanasius's logic and to the language of "appropriation" and internality.[193] He insisted that it is legitimate and necessary to say that Mary was the "Mother of God" (*Theotokos*), and that the eternal Word was born, suffered, and died. While the human attributes are not directly applicable to the Word's nature, they are nevertheless appropriately predicated of the Word himself, insofar as the Word has made the humanity "his" and inasmuch as this humanity is not "external" to the Word:

> This is how we speak of him as suffering and rising again; not as if the Word of God suffered blows or nail-piercings or any of the other injuries in his own (*idian*) nature (for divinity is impassible because it is incorporeal). But since the body that had become his own (*idion*) suffered these things, he himself is said to have suffered for our sake. For the Impassible was within the passible body.[194]

The essential core of Cyril's Christology, and indeed of Chalcedonian Christology, is that there are two distinct sets of predications that are applicable to the single subject of the Word. That is the linguistic and scriptural model that underlies the philosophical vocabulary of two natures and one person. It is a model which is already given fairly mature expression by Athanasius:

For while he is Word of God, so afterwards "the Word became flesh" (Jn 1:14); and though "in the beginning was the Word" (Jn 1:1), in the fullness of time the virgin came to be with child (Isa 7:14, Mt 1:23) and the Lord became a human being. It is one who is thus doubly signified, for "the Word became flesh" (Jn 1:14). But what is said concerning the divinity is distinct from what is said concerning the humanity; each of the sayings has its appropriate interpretation. The one who writes[195] concerning the human attributes of the Word knows also of those that pertain to his divinity and the one who explicates what pertains to the divinity is not ignorant of the characteristics of his advent in the flesh; like an expert and reputable auditor he distinguishes each from the other and so walks in the way of piety. So, in speaking of the Lord's weeping, he knows that, since the Lord has become human, he manifests his humanity by weeping, although he raises Lazarus, as God. He knows also that while he hungered and thirsted in the body, he divinely fed five thousand with five loaves of bread and that while it was a human body that lay in the tomb, it was raised as God's body by the Word himself.

(*On the Thought of Dionysius* 9)[196]

Trinitarian doctrine

The range and development of Athanasius's Trinitarian theology can be gleaned by a brief overview of his thought in three important works: *Against the Greeks – On the Incarnation* (328–333), *Orations against the Arians* (339–341), and *Letters to Serapion*. In his early work *Against the Greeks – On the Incarnation*, Athanasius places primary stress on the economic activity of the Father and the Son and largely abstracts from mention of the Holy Spirit. Insofar as the work is constructed as an *apologia crucis* which seeks to fortify the claim that the same one who died on the cross is God, it identifies God the Creator and Savior in terms of the mutual relation between the divine Word who became incarnate and the Father. As Creator, "the true and real God" is "the Father of Christ,"[197] and our approach to God is an access to the Father through his Word, in whom the Father is seen, known, and worshipped. The first part of the treatise presents God the Creator in terms of this correlation between Father and Son, though the underlying logic of this position requires the further argument of the second part of the treatise, *On the Incarnation*. *On the Incarnation* tries to show that the fruits of Christ's life, death, and resurrection, as manifest in the life of the Christian community, demonstrate the truth of Christ's genuine divinity. If that is so, then the true God and Creator is none other than the "Father of Christ," to whom we only have access through his Son and Word.

The economic co-activity of Father and Son is equally evident in Athanasius's presentation of Christ's work of redemption. While we have already noted some of the terms in which Athanasius explicates the contents of Christian salvation (e.g. "appropriation," "internality," "remaining" in grace), all of these can be subsumed within the central conception that Christ "brought all humanity to himself and through him to the Father" (*Inc.* 37). *On the Incarnation* presents two ways in which Christ saved humanity: his sacrificial death, and his showing forth the knowledge of God in the material human realm. Both of these are explicated dialogically in terms of the relation between Father and Son: Christ's sacrificial death is a priestly offering to the Father,[198] and his pedagogic condescension to the realm of the material shows forth in sensible terms the knowledge of the Father.[199]

While focusing primarily on the common activity of Father and Son in the realms of creation and salvation, Athanasius's early double treatise also makes some ventures toward an articulation of the ontological status of the relation between Father and Son. At one point, Athanasius has recourse to a "psychological analogy" to depict the correlativity of Father and Son, though he bases this analogy on a perception of God's providential power in the universe:

> Just as when one looks up to heaven and see its order and the light of the stars, one becomes aware of the Word who brings these into order, so when we contemplate the Word of God, we must think of God his Father, from whom he proceeds and who is thus fittingly called the Father's interpreter and messenger. We can see this by reference to ourselves. For when a word is uttered by human beings, we understand that its source is the mind and, by attending to the word, we attain by thought to the perception of the mind that is thereby expressed. All the more, by a greater imagination and an incomparable preeminence, when we

see the power of the Word, we attain to the apprehension of
the good Father, as the Savior himself says: "The one who
has seen me has seen the Father."

(*Against the Greeks* 45)[200]

There is also the attempt, in *Against the Greeks – On the Incarnation*,
to express the correlativity of Father and Son by drawing together
the different scriptural titles (such as Word, Wisdom, Power,
Image) by which Christ is identified in his relation to the Father, a
strategy that will become much more prominent in his later explicitly anti-Arian polemic:

> Being with him as Wisdom and beholding the Father, as
> Word he created and formed and ordered the universe. And
> being the power of the Father, he endowed all things with
> the strength to exist. As the Savior says, "Everything which
> I see the Father doing, I also do likewise" (Jn 5:19). And
> his holy disciples teach that everything was created
> through him and for him (cf. Col 1:16) and that he is the
> good offspring of the good Father and true Son and power
> of the Father and his Wisdom and Word. He is these
> things not by participation, nor as if they were added to
> him from outside of himself, as is the case with those who
> participate in him and are made wise through him and are
> empowered and made rational in him. But he is Wisdom
> itself, Word itself, the very Power which is the Father's
> own, Light itself, Truth itself, Righteousness itself, Virtue
> itself, and indeed the imprint and radiance (cf. Heb 1:3 –
> character, *apaugasma*) and Image of the Father. To sum up,
> he is the perfect offshoot of the Father; He alone is Son, the
> precise Image of the Father (cf. 2 Cor 4:4, Col 1:15).

(*Against the Greeks* 46)[201]

Finally, the ontological mutuality of the Son and the Father is
expressed by saying that the Son is "proper to" or intrinsically
belongs to (*idios*) the Father.[202] The natural and ontological
"belonging" of the Son to the Father is thus distinguished from the
Son's making humanity "his own" through the Incarnation.

Perhaps the starkest development in Athanasius's thought from
the time of the writing of *Against the Greeks – On the Incarnation* to
Orations against the Arians is in his presentation of the role of the
Holy Spirit. We have already noted that *Against the Greeks – On the*

Incarnation shows a rather surprising neglect of the work of the Spirit in Christian salvation. Like the early apologists, this work identifies the Spirit as the inspirer of the Scriptures but abstracts from the role of the Spirit in the divine work of redemption. In contrast, the *Orations against the Arians* indicate an implicit acknowledgment of the full divinity of the Spirit and manifest a much more integrated conception of the Spirit's role in redemption. As to the first point, Athanasius argues that the Son is equal to the Spirit in order to demonstrate that the Son is equal to the Father, thus clearly implying the premise that the Spirit himself is equal to the Father.[203] With regard to the Spirit's role in redemption, he now aligns Christ's divinity with the role of giving the Spirit, and Christ's humanity with the role of receiving the Spirit on our behalf.[204] By receiving the Spirit derivatively from Christ's human reception of it, we thus become conformed to his divinity. The Spirit is here conceived primarily as the Spirit of adoption, the one "in whom" we participate the Son, and thus become divinized.

As in *Against the Greeks – On the Incarnation*, Athanasius depicts the divinity of the Son dialogically, in terms of his relation to the Father. He also retains and intensifies usage of the terminology whereby the Son is described as "proper to" or "belonging to" (*idios*) the Father's being. There are two important developments in his argumentation, however. First is the recourse to the argument from Christian worship, specifically the rite of baptism, and, secondly, we find a much more focused linguistic analysis of the specific titles by which the Scriptures characterize Christ.[205] With regard to the first point, Athanasius argues that the characterization of the Son as a creature means that our initiation into divine life in baptism is actually into a hybrid mixture of Creator and creature.[206] This is an important line of argument whose implicit logic of the necessary correlation of worship and faith will find mature and explicit expression in St. Basil's *On the Holy Spirit*.[207] As to his linguistic analysis of scripture, Athanasius follows a line of development that hearkens back to his predecessor Origen's Christology of scriptural titles (*epinoiai*).[208] Like Origen, Athanasius identifies a set of titles (Word, Wisdom, Power, Image, etc.) which scripturally converge around the figure of Jesus Christ, and which are thus used by him as providing an integral and mutually related "lexical field" for the identification of Christ. Typically, Athanasius justifies the individual constituents of these clusters by citing New Testament texts which apply these titles to Christ. From there, he is concerned to show that the scriptural titles applied to Christ are linguistically correlative to the scriptural designations of divinity. This linguistic correlativity of scriptural titles is then taken to be an authoritative disclosure of the ontological correlativity of Father and Son. For example, the Scriptures speak of God as the "fountain of life" (Ps 36:10), but Jesus in the gospel identifies himself as "the life"; thus Jesus is the life that issues from the fountain of life. Without this life issuing from the fountain, the fountain itself is barren, "destitute of life and wisdom" (*Or. Ar.* 1:19). Similarly, the same psalm says, "In your light we shall see light" (Ps 36:10), while Christ is also called the light and "the radiance of [God's] glory" (Heb 1:3). Christ, the Word, is therefore the radiance that issues from the Light.

In his anti-Arian polemic, Athanasius exploits the scriptural overlapping of predications applied to God and to Christ by pressing "Arian" propositions about the Son to yield discomfiting conclusions about the Father. Thus, if the Son is scripturally identified as "Truth," then the proposition that the Son "once was not" must be reinserted into the scriptural language-world, yielding the conclusion that Truth was not always in God (*Or. Ar.* 1:21). Athanasius employed this strategy most forcefully with reference to the scriptural titles of Christ as Word and Wisdom. Contending against the slogan of Arius that "there was once when the Son was not," Athanasius repeatedly accuses the "Arians" of "robbing God of his Word" and of asserting that God was once without Wisdom and Reason (*Logos*). On the face of it, these charges seem to be a willful distortion of his opponents' doctrine and an example of faulty rhetoric.[209] For they certainly would not agree that God was once without Wisdom; rather, they distinguished the Wisdom which was an essential attribute of the singular divine essence from the "Wisdom" who is the distinct *hypostasis* of the Son and who came into existence and is called "Wisdom" by virtue of his participation in God's essential Wisdom. However, it is essential to note that Athanasius is here not simply making an abstract theological argument on some neutral ground – as if he were saying that a God who does not eternally beget an Image as his Wisdom cannot be eternally wise. To interpret Athanasius's argument in its proper context, one must keep in mind the scriptural background that was determinative for him, and to which his opponents also claimed recourse. Within the context of the linguistic field of the Scriptures, Athanasius's deeper point is that there exists a correlation *in the Scriptures* between God and his Wisdom, wherein Christ is also identified as Wisdom. The force of Athanasius's point lies in his protestation that the "Arians" are tearing asunder that scriptural correlation. To say that "there was once when the Son was not" is to abstract from this scriptural correlation where the Son is aligned with Wisdom, and thus correlated to God. Therefore, when Athanasius asks, "when was God without his Wisdom?," the context in which he says this indicates that his question is primarily anchored in the scriptural language-world, and bears direct reference to that world. This, of course, is not to say that he considered this biblical language-world in postmodern fashion, as being merely the play of signifiers without an external ontological reference. The Scriptures efficaciously mediate the truth of God and creation, but precisely for this reason, the mediation of the Scriptures cannot be bypassed, and so the way things are described, related, and distinguished in scriptural language is truly revelatory of the way these things are. For this reason, scriptural language and scriptural imagery are taken very seriously by Athanasius. He considers the images afforded by Scripture to represent paradigmatic illustrations or symbols (*paradeigmata*) of divine truths that are not directly accessible to human comprehension.[210] Therefore, one has to be extremely attentive to the "exact" patterns of these images in order to glean the divine mysteries that underlie them.[211] Thus, the scriptural dynamics of intertextuality by which there exists a series of linguistic correlations between the designations of the person of Christ and the characterizations of God are taken to be representative of the Trinitarian mystery of the ontological correlativity of the Father and the Son. Athanasius's consistent strategy is to press the scriptural linguistic correlation into an ontological correlation, and then to rhetorically represent the "Arian" position as a deconstruction of this ontological correlation.

On the other hand, Athanasius makes positive use of the sets of linguistic correlations that he draws up, not only to affirm the ontological correlation of the Father and the Son, but also to acknowledge the mutual distinction within that correlation. The "exactness (*akribeia*) of scriptural language" indicates a certain order within the correlation. Reason (*logos*), for example, is always *from* and proper to the being of the one whose reason it is; if the Father is the fountain of living water (Jer 2:13) and the "fountain of wisdom" (Bar 3:12), then the Son is the life (Jn 14:6) and the wisdom (1 Cor 1:24) that pours out from the fountain; if the Father is light (1 Jn 1:5), the Son is the "radiance" and "expression" of that light (Heb 1:3). All these relations are non-reversible, even while they designate equality. Thus, for Athanasius, these images indicate intrinsic correlationality as well as distinction: the outpouring is not the same as the fountain ("for what coexists does not coexist with itself but with another" (*Or. Ar.* 2:38)), but the fountain is not a fountain apart from the outpouring. Father and Son are irreducibly and eternally distinct, and while the Son is the exact image of the Father, he is, in a sense, a reverse image of the Father; he remains inalterably like the Father by remaining inalterably Son.[212]

Conversely, Athanasius searches the Scriptures to make the point that the linguistic field by which both the Old and the New Testaments identify Christ not only correlates and distinguishes Christ and the Father, but also distinguishes the Son from the realm of creation. To make this point, Athanasius considers not only the attributions applied directly to the person of Jesus Christ, but those associated with "Word," "Wisdom," and divine "Power," insofar as all these are themselves scripturally integrated into the identification of Jesus Christ. He contends, citing various examples, that the "Arian" vocabulary which applies to the Son language of temporal specificity, such as "when" and "before," are applied by the Scriptures to creatures (*Or. Ar.* 1:13). On the other hand, affirmations of the divine attribute of eternity are applied generally to God, but also to Christ: "who is and who was and who is to come" (Rev 1:4); "who exists before the ages ... by whom [God] made the ages" (Heb 1:2); "Christ who is over all, God blessed for ever" (Rom 9:5). Similarly, as against the doctrine that the Son, as creature, has a will that is changeable by nature, Athanasius marshals texts that contrast the impermanence of creation with the inalterability of God: "You, O Lord, established the earth and the heavens ... they will perish but you remain" (Ps 102:26); "I do not alter" (Deut 32:39). Once again, Christ is shown to be scripturally associated with the latter kind of predication: "Jesus Christ is the same yesterday, today, and forever" (Heb 13:8).

Of course, Athanasius has to admit that not all predications referred to Jesus Christ can be assimilated directly to the scriptural patterns of identifying divinity. Some clearly belong to the realm of creaturely and human existence. But in this context, Athanasius's Trinitarian hermeneutics, which aims to probe the correlativity of the identifications of God (the Father) and Jesus Christ (as Word, Wisdom, Radiance, Image of the Father), becomes integrated with a Christological hermeneutics, which interprets the sayings about Christ-Word-Wisdom-Radiance-Image in light of the overarching plot (*skopos*) of the Word's becoming flesh.[213] In this context, Athanasius lays down the main principles for executing a correct exegesis: one must be aware of the time, the person, and the occasion to which the text refers.[214] The crucial distinction in scriptural "times" for Athanasius is before and after the enfleshment of the Word, a point he makes by inner-scriptural references, for example to the opening of the letter to the Hebrews: "In past times, God spoke in partial and various ways to our ancestors through the prophets. But in these last days, he has spoken to us through his Son, whom he made heir of all things and through whom he created the universe" (Heb 1:1–2). Thus, the overall "scope" or main story-line of Scripture, for Athanasius, is "a twofold proclamation of the Savior":

> Therefore the scope and characteristic feature of the holy
> Scripture, as we have often said, is its twofold proclamation
> of the Savior: that he was always God and Son, as being the
> Father's Word, Radiance, and Wisdom, and that afterwards
> he took flesh from Mary, the Virgin Mother of God, for our
> sake, and became a human being. One can find this indi-
> cated throughout the entire divinely inspired Scripture, as
> the Lord himself has said: "Search the Scriptures, for it is
> they which testify to me" (Jn 5:39). But so that I may not
> extend my writing excessively by collecting everything said
> on this point, it will suffice to recall the following repre-
> sentative passages. For John says, "In the beginning was the
> Word and the Word was with God and the Word was God.
> Everything was made through him and without him
> nothing was made" (Jn 1:13). Then: "And the Word
> became flesh and dwelt among us and we have seen his
> glory, the glory of the Father's only-begotten Son" (Jn
> 1:14). And Paul writes: "Who, being in the form of God,
> did not regard equality with God as something to be
> grasped but emptied himself, taking the form of a servant,
> and coming in the likeness of human beings, he was found
> human in appearance. He humbled himself, becoming
> obedient to death, even death on a cross" (Phil 2:6–8).
> Therefore, if one goes through the whole Scriptures on the
> basis of these passages and the sense indicated therein, one
> will see how in the beginning the Father said to him, "Let
> there be light" (Gen 1:3) and "Let there be a firmament"
> (Gen 1:6) and "Let us make human beings" (Gen 1:26).
> But at the consummation of the ages, he sent him into the
> world, not in order to judge the world but so that the

world might be saved through him (cf. Jn 3:17). And so it is written: "Behold, the Virgin shall be with child and bear a son and they will call his name 'Emmanuel', which means 'God with us'" (Isa 7:14, Mt 1:23)

(*Against the Arians* 3:29)[215]

A proper reading of Scriptures, therefore, is one that discerns the overall scope of Scripture in terms of the central storyline of the Incarnation of the Word, which, as we have seen, represents for Athanasius the supreme and exhaustive expression of God's loving condescension. Read in this way, the Scriptures identify Jesus Christ as both fully God, existing in mutual correlation to the Father, and yet made a creature for the sake of human salvation.

Athanasius becomes the first person to write a treatise on the Holy Spirit in his *Letters to Serapion*, which are indicative of his mature Trinitarian theology. This writing is occasioned by the controversy with the Tropici, an Egyptian group who acknowledged the full divinity of the Son but denied that of the Spirit. At this stage, Athanasius presses his arguments on behalf of the divinity of the Son in the service of the Holy Spirit. The creative and sanctifying work of the Spirit, which extends to the point of effecting our deification, indicates that he can be nothing less than God. As in the *Orations against the Arians*, Athanasius here also makes use of the argument from worship and baptism to characterize as "idolatry" a worship that mixes together Creator and creature. Moreover, the arguments based on scriptural linguistic correlation are now also applied to the Spirit. The images or paradigmatic illustrations (*paradigmata*) by which the Scriptures identify the Spirit align the Spirit with the Father and the Son. For instance, the Son is the outpouring from the fountain, while we drink of the Spirit; or the Son is the radiance streaming from the light, while we are enlightened by the Spirit.[216] As in certain conceptions in contemporary theology, these scripturally derived characterizations of the Spirit identify the Spirit with the actualization or application to humanity of the work of the Son: the Spirit is the "vital activity and gift whereby [the Son] sanctifies and enlightens";[217] "all creation partakes of the Word in the Spirit."[218] For Athanasius, these scriptural correlations indicate that the Spirit is integral to the organic unity of divine agency, while the inseparability of the activity of Son and Spirit indicates that the Spirit has the same ontological unity with the Son as the Son has with the Father.[219] On the basis of this scriptural witness, Athanasius extends his own ontological vocabulary which he had used to indicate the natural unity between the Father and the Son to the Spirit. The Spirit also is "proper to" and "belongs to" (*idios*) the Father and Son, by nature. At the same time, and contrary to some misinterpretations, Athanasius insists that Father, Son, and Holy Spirit are truly distinct subsistents.[220] Only the Father is the source; the Son and Spirit are distinguished from one another according to the biblical pattern of imagery, in which the Spirit seems to be the one in whom the work of the Son is actualized in humanity. In keeping with the apophatic tenor of the Greek Fathers, Athanasius is reluctant to go any further than strictly scriptural warrant in characterizing the distinction between the three. What the Scriptures indicate is that Father, Son, and Spirit all share in the divine work of creation and deifying salvation; their relations are indicated by the patterns of scriptural language; they are thus equally constituents of the divine realm and not creatures: "This much suffices for the faithful and this is the extent to which human knowledge attains, at which point the cherubim make a covering with their wings (cf. Isa 6:2) ... For the things that are handed down by faith should be understood not by human wisdom (cf. 1 Cor 2:13) but by the hearing of faith (cf. Gal 3:2)" (*Letters to Serapion* 1:17).

Eusebeia: *theology and holiness*

Athanasius occupies a central place in Christian tradition primarily because of his teachings on doctrinal matters. But for the Alexandrian himself, the true perception of the contents of Christian faith is inseparable from a life lived in intimate communion with God and modeled after the examples of the scriptural saints:

> The investigation and true knowledge of the Scriptures requires a good life and pure soul and the virtue that is consonant with Christ, so that the mind, in following this path, may be enabled to reach and comprehend what it desires, as far as it is accessible to human nature to learn about the Word of God. For without a pure mind and the imitation of the life of the saints, one cannot comprehend the words of the saints. If someone wishes to see the light of the sun, he would certainly clean out and brighten his eye and purify it until it approaches a likeness of what he desires to see; when the eye becomes light in this way, it

may see the light of the sun. Or, when someone wishes to
see a city or country, he certainly goes to that place in order
to see it. Likewise, the one who wishes to comprehend the
mind of those who speak of God needs to begin by living
the kind of life that washes and cleanses the soul and then
go to the saints themselves, approaching them by imitation
of their deeds, so that becoming aligned with them
through a common way of life, he may come to understand
the things that have been revealed to them by God.
Henceforth, as being in a close bond with them, he may
escape the peril of sinners and their fire at the day of judgment, and may receive what has been stored up for the
saints in the Kingdom of Heaven, "which eye has not seen,
nor ear heard, nor has entered into human hearts" (1 Cor
2:9), whatsoever has been prepared for those who live virtu-
ously and love the God and Father, in Jesus Christ our
Lord, through whom and with whom to the Father himself
with the Son and the Holy Spirit be honor and power and
glory for ever and ever. Amen.

(*Inc.* 57)[221]

The disposition described in this passage, which Athanasius elsewhere
frequently calls "piety" (*eusebeia*), is thus considered by him to be
constitutive of theological reasoning.[222] Conversely, Athanasius never
tired of accusing his theological opponents of "impiety," of saying
things that are unworthy of God and discordant with devotion to
Christ. In this way, it is quite true, as some modern critics have
pointed out, that Athanasius often begs the question in his debates
with the "Arians". It might seem maddeningly disingenuous and
circular for Athanasius to demand rhetorically of his opponents,
"Which of the two theologies manifest our Lord Jesus Christ as God
and Son of God?" (*Or. Ar.* 1:10). Yet, Athanasius's deeper point is
that begging the question of the absolute lordship of Christ is a
methodological *a priori* of Christian reflection. It is first of all the
pattern of Christian life, with its unqualified dedication to the
virtue "according to Christ," which pre-empts any questioning of
the absolute lordship, and hence authentic and absolute divinity, of
Christ. The absolute lordship of Christ is thus simultaneously an
implicit epistemological principle for Athanasius's theology and a
foundational rule for Christian living, the two aspects mutually
reinforcing one another. As a pastor, Athanasius exhorted his flock
to organize their perception of time in accordance with the celebra-

tion of the Paschal mystery of Christ;[223] he lauded the practice of pilgrimage to places sanctified by the Lord's presence and evocative of the "Father's house" which is beyond this earthly realm;[224] and he insisted that both marriage and virginity are paths to genuine communion with God in Christ,[225] although the path of virginity has special pre-eminence as an undivided offering to the divine Bridegroom.[226] In general, Christians are always ordained to make their bodies and minds hospitable to the lordship of Christ. While it may be said that those who did not accept Nicene doctrine also followed these practices and aspirations, Athanasius's fundamental argument implied that there was a radical inconsistency to such a stance. If Christ is not truly God, the Christian's submission to the sovereignty and adoration of Christ would be mere idolatry, and humanity would still be alienated from God. In the end, Athanasius was quite incapable of entertaining with sobriety any doctrine that attenuated the Son's divinity, as if this was simply one plausible interpretation of Christian faith among others. Any such doctrine, whatever its qualifications and accoutrements, was reducible for him to an "Arian" betrayal of the cornerstone of Christian faith. While the modern reader may well cringe at his constant hammering away at the "senselessness" of the "Arians", it is important to see at least that a Christian denial of the full divinity of Christ really did not make any sense at all for Athanasius himself.

Indeed, insofar as Athanasius was given to a global characterization of the Christian dispensation as one of divine condescension to which the appropriate human response is gratitude, he ultimately traces the anti-Nicene denial of the full divinity of the Son to the spiritual vice of ingratitude. In his estimation, such ingratitude is due to an incapacity to discern the true mystery of divine condescension, which leads these "Arians" to "look down upon" the Savior for the lowliness that he took upon himself out of love for humanity:

> The Arian fanatics, being opponents of Christ and heretics, did not think upon these things and so they lash the one who brought them aid with their tongues and blaspheme the one who brought them freedom and entertain all kinds of strange notions about the Savior. They deny his substantial Godhead because he came down on behalf of humanity. They doubt that he is truly the Son of God because he came forth from the Virgin. They deny his eternity because they are aware that he has become incarnate in time. They do not

confess him as the incorruptible Son of the incorruptible
Father because they see that he has suffered for us. Finally,
they reject the eternity of his substance because of what he
endured for our sakes. In all this, they avail themselves of
ingratitude, despising the Savior and insulting him instead
of acknowledging his grace. Justly may we speak to them
in these words: O ungrateful opponent of Christ ... if you
had understood the Scriptures and listened to the saints,
who said, "May your face shine upon us and we will be
saved" (Ps 43:3), or again, "Send out your light and your
truth" (Ps 80:7), you would have known that the Lord did
not come down for his own sake but for ours and so you
would have admired his love for humanity all the more ...
If you had understood his love for us, you would not have
estranged the Son from the Father and you would not have
made him who reconciled us to his Father a foreigner [to
the divine essence].

(*Festal Letter* X:9)[227]

To put the matter more positively, the emphasis on gratitude as
central to Christian "piety" may be taken as the subjective correlative to Athanasius's fundamental characterization of the objective
contents of Christian faith. We have noted the centrality for
Athanasius of the characterization of the God revealed in Jesus
Christ as a gracious "lover of humanity" whose merciful condescension overcomes the difference between his own transcendent nature
and the inherent weakness of human nature which is exacerbated by
sin. *Eusebeia* is a grateful acknowledgment of the descending love of
the transcendent God, climactically manifest in the condescension
of the Incarnate Word who "presents us to the Father" in the Spirit.
For Athanasius, the foundation of such piety is the confession of the
absolute and unqualified divinity of the Word who became flesh
and died so that humanity may be rescued from death and deified.

2

SELECTIONS FROM
ORATIONS AGAINST
THE ARIANS

Introduction

The first two of the *Orations against the Arians* were written in
Rome, ca. 339–340, during Athanasius's second exile. Pope
Julius, who was extending hospitality to Athanasius at the time,
was endeavoring to arrange for a council to deal anew with the
charges brought against Athanasius at the Council of Tyre of 335.
It is quite possible that Athanasius anticipated that such a council
(which did not in fact occur) would include a showdown between
pro-Nicene and anti-Nicene forces, and the *Orations* could have
been composed in preparation for such an impending battle. It is
also clear from the contents of this polemical treatise that
Athanasius is anxious to thwart a growing acceptance of
"Arianism," or at least a lessening of the opposition to it. Such a
development was perhaps associated with the adjustment and
selective attenuation of some of Arius's doctrines by his supporter
Asterius. In Rome, Athanasius had ready access to Asterius's writings through his companion in exile, Marcellus of Ancyra, who
had recently composed a refutation of Asterius. While the figure
of Eusebius of Nicomedia occasionally makes an appearance,[1] the
Orations show Athanasius in direct debate principally with
Asterius and Arius, selectively exploiting both the similarities and
the differences between the two in order to defend the Nicene
doctrine of the full divinity of the Word as the only cogent and
authentic version of Christianity. Athanasius veers eclectically
from one "Arian" theology to the other, the various strands of his
attack finding their center in the denunciation of the doctrine that
the Son is not eternal and integral to the divine essence. Thus, he
will mock Arius's teaching that the Son is "foreign" to or "other"
than the divine essence, and then argue that the Son can only be
"like" the Father as his "image" (as Asterius taught) only if he is

actually divine by nature. He will ridicule Arius's assertion that God was not always Father, but then exploit Asterius's teaching that God is always generative by insisting that the generated "Son" of the Father must be identified with the eternal Word and Wisdom of God. By creating an amalgam of "Arian" doctrine, he is able to exploit one anti-Nicene teaching to counteract another as well as to create the impression, which he often explicitly states, that such anti-Nicene teaching is self-contradictory and willfully shifty. At the same time, Athanasius is occupied throughout these *Orations* with defending Nicene doctrine against the exegetical attacks of its opponents. His overarching goal is to show that the Scriptures, when properly read according to their "ecclesiastical sense," reveal Christ to be nothing less than the eternal Word who is fully divine by nature, whose fullness of divinity is the ultimate "security" for human redemption and deification.

A critical edition of the text can be found in *AW* I/I.

Selection 1: Arianism must be distinguished from authentic Christianity (*Or. Ar.* 1:1)

The first selection offered here in translation, from the first book of the *Orations*, reveals Athanasius's perturbance at the fact that "Arianism" is making inroads in the Church. It is also indicative of the various layers of Athanasius's polemic. He is not simply engaged in a theological battle between what he considers to be the true faith in Christ's divinity and the "heresy of the Arians," but addresses himself pointedly to the "simple" who are in danger of being deceived by the "Arians" and "the foolish" who do not see Arian doctrine as a threat.[2] Consequently, Athanasius constructs his pastoral role in the composition of these *Orations* to be not merely that of a calm and rationally convincing debater but, perhaps even more, that of a shocked devotee of Christ who seeks to communicate his shock and dismay to his companions in "true piety." The constant haranguing of the "Ariomaniacs" is deliberately part of this strategy to induce an esthetic disgust for anti-Nicene doctrine, a disgust at the disfiguring of the proper glory of Christ which Athanasius is all too ready to model for his supporters. The double effort to argue for the theological inadequacy of "Arian" doctrine and to induce an affective disgust at its "impiety" is summed up in Athanasius's stated goal in the treatment of anti-Nicene theology in these *Orations*: "to reveal the stink of its foolishness."

Text

1:1. It has become evident that all the heresies which have turned aside from the truth were manufacturing madness, and their impiety (*asebeia*) has become manifest to all long ago. For the fact that the inventors of these heresies have "gone out from among us" (1 Jn 2:19) makes clear, as the blessed John has written, that their minds neither were nor are now with us. Therefore, as the Savior has said, "they do not gather with us but scatter" with the devil (Lk 11:23), and they are on the lookout for those who are sleeping so that, by sowing their own poison of destruction, they may have companions to die with them. But this one heresy, called the Arian, which is the last and which has now emerged as forerunner of the Antichrist, being deceitful and cunning and seeing that the other heresies which are its elder siblings have been openly denounced, hypocritically shrouds itself in the language of the Scriptures, as did its father the devil (cf. Mt 4:1ff.), and forces itself again into the paradise of the Church, so that, by pretending to be Christian, it may deceive some to turn their minds against Christ by the persuasiveness of its false reasonings – for it lacks any good sense. And it has already deceived some of the foolish, so that they are not only corrupted by hearing, but they take and eat like Eve (Gen 3:6), and finally, in their ignorance, they come to consider the bitter as sweet (Isa 5:20) and they say of this disgusting heresy that it is good. Therefore, urged by you, I have considered it necessary to pierce through the "folds of the breastplate" (Job 41:5) of this loathsome heresy, and to reveal the stink of its foolishness, so that those who are far from it may continue to flee it, while those who have been deceived by it may repent and, opening the eyes of their hearts (Eph 1:18), may understand that just as light is not darkness, nor falsehood truth, so neither is the Arian heresy good. Indeed, those who call these people "Christians" are greatly and seriously deceived, as not having studied the Scriptures and not knowing at all what is Christianity and the Christian faith.

Selection 2: Against the doctrine that the word is changeable by nature (*Or. Ar.* 1:35–51)

The second selection (*Oration against the Arians* I:35–51) is concerned with the various scriptural texts that "Arian" theologians have used to argue the view that the Son is by nature changeable (*treptos*) and alterable (Phil 2:9–10 and Ps 45:7–8). This appears to be among the original teachings of Arius. The *Encyclical Letter of*

Alexander of Alexandria reports Arius as asserting that the Son "is changeable and alterable in his being like all rational beings,"[3] while Arius's own *Thalia* clarifies that while the Son is "changeable by nature," he freely chooses to be good and it was in anticipation of this consistent choice that God proleptically bestowed glory upon the Son.[4] Alexander himself responded with an emphatic assertion that the Son is "unchangeable and inalterable like the Father,"[5] an affirmation echoed by the Synod of Antioch of 325, while the Council of Nicaea anathematized those who held that the Son is "a creature or alterable or changeable" (*ktistos ē treptos ē alloiōtos*).[6]

It has been argued that this emphasis on the changeability of the Son is part of a soteriological focus on the Son as an exemplary model for human salvation.[7] While such a soteriological application might indeed have been derived from this teaching,[8] it does not seem likely that a soteriological motive simply generated such a teaching. Its provenance, however, becomes intelligible once it is placed in the framework of Origen's theological system.[9] Origen maintained that the Son/Word/Wisdom of God is "unalterable and unchangeable," since "every nature which is alterable and changeable ... cannot be said to possess a glory that is sincere and bright, by reason of the fact that its righteousness and wisdom are accidents, and whatever is accidental may also be separated and lost."[10] When he turns to the treatment of rational beings, however, Origen is strenuously concerned to maintain that the status and condition of each is not dictated by God's arbitrary will but is providentially arranged by God in accordance with the merits of each. In short, for Origen, "there is none among rational creatures who is not capable of both good and evil except the nature of God" (ibid, I, 8, 3). Moreover, Origen's Christology places considerable emphasis on Christ's human soul, which is conceived as one of the souls of the intelligible realm which surpassed all others in clinging to the Word with unbroken ardor. This soul was assumed by the Word in preparation for the Incarnation. Maintaining his stress on the correspondence between divine gift and human merit, Origen insists that "the taking up of his soul was not accidental or due to personal preference, but ... a privilege conferred upon it as a reward for its virtues" (ibid, II, 6, 4). He gives scriptural proof for the rightness of his view by citing Ps 45:7: "You have loved righteousness and hated iniquity; therefore God has anointed you with the oil of gladness above your fellows."[11] Origen is careful, however, not baldly to characterize the soul of Christ as changeable. Although indeed changeable by nature, it consistently chose the good, and thus "what formerly depended upon the will was by the influence of long custom changed into nature" (ibid, II, 6, 4).

Once these fundamental elements of Origen's system are seen in the background, the doctrine of the changeable nature of the Son becomes readily comprehensible. If the Son is created, his nature must be alterable, as is the case with all rational beings. The unparalleled prerogatives of the Son are therefore the proleptically bestowed reward for his merits. The phrases used by Origen to indicate the correspondence between the free acts of rational beings and divine providential design (i.e. "prize of virtue," "reward for progress") recur in the language reported by Athanasius to have been used by Arius and his supporters in reference to Christ. Yet Athanasius, for his part, also could draw on the Origenian legacy inasmuch as Origen clearly attributed immutability to the Word and the Spirit.[12] Furthermore, Athanasius could draw on Origen's association of creaturely mutability with instability and insecurity to underline his own soteriological teaching that our salvation is definitively secured only if it is ultimately anchored in the immutability of the fully divine Word. But since the main terrain of battle are the Scriptures themselves, Athanasius's predominant mode of offensive is to reinsert "Arian" doctrinal statements into the language of Scripture: i.e. how can the changeable Son be completely in the unchangeable Father (cf. Jn 14:10)? Conversely, he labors to interpret the various scriptural texts in light of the overall Christological plot and goal (*skopos*) of Scripture, which is characterized by the divine condescension of the Word effecting human exaltation and not, as he construes the Arian version, by the promotion of the Word himself through humanity.

Text

1:35. As to their discussion about whether the Word is changeable (*treptos*), that is something which hardly requires investigation. It suffices for me merely to write down what they say in order to show the boldness of their impiety (*asebeia*). They vent their nonsense by asking these questions: "Does he have free will or not? Is he good by choosing to be good through his free will and so is able to change, if he wills it, as one who is changeable by nature? Or is he like a rock or a piece of wood, not having a choice that is free to be moved and to incline toward this or that?"[13] Indeed, it is not inconsistent with their heresy to say and think these things. For once they have fashioned for themselves a god out of nothing and a created Son, it follows that they would compile for themselves these little phrases that are suitable for a creature. But since they fight against those who belong to the Church and even when they hear from them about the one true Word of the Father still dare to say these things about him, who can find anything more disgusting than their doctrine? Who would not be greatly disturbed merely to hear these things, even if one were unable to reply to them?[14] Who would not shut his ears in astonishment at the vain things which they say, the very mention of which is blasphemy?

For if the Word is changeable and alterable (*treptos kai alloioumenos*)[15] where will he end up and what kind of end will there be to his progress?[16] Or how can the changeable be like (*homoios*) the unchangeable?[17] And how can the one who has seen the changeable be considered to have seen the Unchangeable (cf. Jn 14:9)?[18] Or what level should he come to in order that one can see the Father in him? Clearly, one will not always see the Father in him, since the Son is always changing, and is changeable by nature. For the Father is unchangeable and inalterable, and is forever identical and the same. Whereas, if the Son is changeable, according to them, and is not always the same but rather is always alterable by nature, how can such a one be the "Image" of the Father, if he lacks the likeness of the Father's unchangeability?[19] Or how can he be wholly "in the Father" (Jn 14:10) if he has a faculty of choice that is ambivalent in its inclination? Perhaps, since he is alterable and advances every day, he is not yet perfect! But let such madness of the Arians be banished; let the truth shine out and show that they are senseless. For how can what is not perfect be "equal to God" (Phil 2:6; cf. Jn 5:18)? Or how can he not be unchangeable who is "one with the Father" (Jn 10:30) and who is the Father's Son and belongs (*idios*)[20] to his essence? For, since the Father's essence is unchangeable, the proper (*idion*) offspring from that essence would also be unchangeable. But if they falsely ascribe change to the truly existent Word and Reason (*Logos*), let them know that their own reason is in danger![21] For "the tree is recognized by its fruit" (Mt 12:33),[22] and so the one who "has seen the Son has seen the Father" (Jn 14:9) and the knowledge of the Son is knowledge of the Father.

36. Therefore, the Image of the unchangeable God has to be unchangeable, "for Jesus Christ is the same yesterday, today, and forever" (Heb 13:8). David sings of him, saying "You, Lord, in the beginning established the earth and the heavens are the works of your hands. They will perish but you remain. They will all grow old like a cloth; and like a garment you will fold them up and they

will be changed. But you are the same and your years will not fade" (Ps 102:26–28, Heb 1:10–12). The Lord himself says of himself through the prophet: "Behold me; Behold that I am" (Deut 32:39), and "I do not change" (Mal 3:6). Even if it can be said that this passage signifies the Father, it still befits the Son to say these words, especially because when he became human, he showed his unvarying identity and his unchangeableness to those who consid-ered him to have changed on account of his flesh, and to have become something else.[23] So the saints,[24] or rather the Lord, are more reliable than the perversity of the impious. For Scripture, according to what is said in the psalm above, declares all things that come to be and all of creation (for this is what is signified by "heaven and earth") as having a nature that is changeable and alter-able. But it excludes the Son from these and shows that he is not at all one of those that come to be (*genēton*), teaching rather that it is he who changes all things and is not himself changed, saying, "But You are the same and your years will not fade" (Ps 102:28, Heb 1:12). And this is aptly said; for things which are originated (*genēta*) and which are from non-being and do not exist at all before they come to be have a nature that is alterable – since they are not, then come to be. But the Son, being from the Father and belonging (*idios*) to his essence, is inalterable and unchangeable as the Father himself. For it is improper to say that from the essence of the Unchangeable there comes to be a changeable Word and an alterable Wisdom.

For how is he still the Word if he is changeable? Or how is that which is alterable still Wisdom? Unless, as they like to construe it, it is perhaps like an accident in a substance,[25] as if it were a certain grace or habit of virtue which is accidental to a particular substance and which in this way is called word and son and wisdom, as if it could be subtracted and added. They conceive such things and have said them often! But this is not the faith of Christians. Nor does this conception proclaim him as the one who is truly Word and Son of the Father, nor the Wisdom which is true Wisdom. For how can that be true which changes and alters and does not stand in one and the same state? But the Lord says, "I am the Truth" (Jn 14:6). If then the Lord himself says this about himself and shows his inalter-ability, while the saints have learned it also and give witness to it – indeed, even our conceptions of God provide us with the knowledge that this is the pious course – from where did these impious people conceive such inventions? They have vomited them out of their hearts, as if from corruption itself (cf. 2 Pet 2:12).

37. But since they make a pretext out of the divine sayings and violently distort them to accommodate their own minds, it has become necessary to respond to them to the extent of vindicating the sayings of Scripture and showing that these have a right sense, while it is they who understand them badly. They say that it is written by the apostle, "Therefore God has highly exalted him, and has given him a name above every name, so that in the name of Jesus every knee should bend, of things in heaven, on earth, and under the earth" (Phil 2:9,10). And it is written by David, "Therefore God, your God, has anointed[26] you with the oil of gladness above your partners" (Ps 45:8, Heb 1:9). Then they press their point, as if they were saying something clever: "If he was 'therefore' exalted and received grace and he was 'therefore' anointed, then he received a reward as a consequence of his deliberate choice. Thus, having acted through deliberate choice, his nature is altogether changeable."[27] Eusbeius[28] and Arius have not only dared to say these things but also to write them, and their followers have not drawn back from saying them in the middle of the marketplace, oblivious of the insanity of what they are saying. For if he received what he had as a reward for his deliberate choice, and did not have possession of it except by showing forth the work of the one who gave to him, and thus came into the possession of it through virtue and advancement, then it follows that he is called Son and God on account of these things which he received, and is not true Son. For a true offspring is from another according to nature, as Isaac was in relation to Abraham, and Joseph to Jacob, and as the radiance is to the sun. But those who attain to that status through virtue and grace are only called so; instead of nature, they have the grace of receiving and they are other than what is given to them. Such is the case with those who receive the Spirit by participation, of whom it is said, "I have begotten sons and exalted them but they have rebelled against me" (Isa 1:2). Of course, since these were not sons according to nature, when they changed, the Spirit was withdrawn from them and they were disowned. On the other hand, when they repent, God, who at the beginning had given them grace, will receive them again and grant them light and call them sons.

38. If, however, they speak in this way about the Savior also, it will turn out that he is not true God nor true Son, nor is he like the Father, nor does he have God in any way as the Father of his being, according to essence, but only by a grace given to him and thus, as far as essence, he would have God as the Creator of his being, as do all other things. If so, it will be apparent furthermore that he did

not possess the name of "Son" from the beginning – if indeed he came into possession of that name as a reward for the works that he accomplished and as a consequence of that advance which he gained only when he became a human being and "took the form of a servant" (Phil 2:7).[29] For it was when he "became obedient unto death" (Phil 2:8), that it says he was "highly exalted" (Phil 2:9) and received as a grace that name, "so that in the name of Jesus every knee may bend" (Phil 2:10). What then was he before this, if he was only exalted and began to be worshipped and to be called "Son" when he became a human being? It would seem that rather than having advanced the flesh, it was he himself who was advanced through the flesh, if indeed, according to their malicious thinking, it was only when he became human that he was exalted and called "Son." But then what was he before this? It is necessary to address the question to them yet again, so that the final consequence of their impiety may be made evident. For if the Lord is God, Son, and Word – and yet he is none of these things prior to his becoming human – then either he was something else other than these things and later acquired participation in them on account of his virtue, as we have said, or else (may this fall back upon their own heads!) they must say that he did not exist before becoming human, but is simply human by nature and nothing more. But this is not the mind of the Church, but of the Samosatene[30] and of the present-day Jews.[31]

If they hold to these views, why do they not become circumcised like the Jews? Why do they make a pretense of Christianity, while in fact they are hostile to it? For if he did not exist prior to becoming human – or even if he did exist but was promoted later – how is it that "all things were made through Him," and "in him" (cf. Col 1:16, Jn 1:3)? Or how is it that the Father delighted in him (cf. Prov 8:30), if he was not perfect? And if he has only been promoted now [that he has become human], how is it that before then he "rejoiced in the presence" of the Father (*ibid.*)? If he received worship only after death, how is it that Abraham appears worshipping him in the tent (Gen 18:2) and Moses in the bush (Ex 3:6)? Indeed, as Daniel saw, "myriads of myriads and thousands of thousands were ministering to him" (Dan 7:10). If, according to them, he only now attained advancement, how is it that he makes mention of his own glory that was before the world and transcends the world? For the Son himself said, "Glorify me, Father, with the glory which I had with you before the world was" (Jn 17:5). If, according to them, he is only now exalted, how is it that, before [his becoming human], he "bowed the heavens and descended" (Ps 18:10) and, again, "The Most High bestowed his voice" (Ps 18:14)? Therefore, if even before the world came to be, the Son possessed glory, and was both "Lord of Glory" (1 Cor 2:8) and "Most High," and descended from heaven, and is always to be worshipped, then he was not promoted on account of having descended but rather he himself promoted those things which were in need of advancement. And if he descended to accomplish the grace of their advancement, then he did not come to be called "Son" and "God" as a reward, but rather he himself made us sons for the Father and divinized human beings when he himself became a human being.

39. So he was not a human being and later became God. But, being God, he later became a human being in order that we may be divinized. For if he was called Son and God when he became a human being, and yet before he became human God called the ancient people "sons" and Moses referred to the Pharaoh as "God" (Ex 7:1) and Scripture says of many, "God is in the assembly of the gods" (Ps 82:1), then it is clear that he was called "Son" and "God" after all these. But how then were "all things through him" (Jn 1:3, Col 1:16) and "he was before all things" (Col 1:17)? Or how is he "the firstborn of all creation" (Col 1:15) when there were others before him who were called "sons" and "gods"? And how is it that those who were first in their participation in divinity did not have participation in the Word?[32] Such a supposition is not true; it is a false invention of these present-day Judaizers. For in that case, how could anyone at all have come to know God as Father, since there is no adoption[33] apart from the true Son, who says himself, "No one knows the Father except the Son and the one to whom the Son reveals him" (Mt 11:27).

How then can there be deification without the Word and before him, when he himself says to their brothers, the Jews: "If he calls these gods, to whom comes the Word of God ..." (Jn 10:35). But if all who are called sons and gods, whether on earth or in the heavens, are adopted and deified through the Word, while the Son himself is the Word, then it is clear that all is through him, and he himself is before all. Or rather, he alone is the true Son and he alone is "true God from true God," not by receiving these titles as a reward for virtue nor as being himself other than them, but as being these things by nature and essence. For he is the offspring of the Father's essence. Therefore, no one should doubt that, in accordance with his likeness to the unchangeable Father, the Word also is unchangeable.

40. Up to this point, we have countered their irrational fabrications by providing correct conceptions about the Son, as the Lord himself has granted us. But, for the remaining, it would be good to set before us the divine sayings, in order to demonstrate even more conclusively the unchangeableness of the Son and his inalterable nature, which is that of the Father – and, by contrast, their perversity.

The Apostle, writing to the Philippians, says, "Have this attitude among yourselves, which is in Christ Jesus, who being in the form of God, did not consider equality with God as something to be grasped. Rather, he emptied himself and took the form of a servant and came in the likeness of human beings. And being found in human form, he humbled himself, becoming obedient to death, even the death of the cross. Therefore, God also highly exalted him and granted him a name which is above every name, so that in the name of Jesus every knee should bend, of those who are in heaven and on the earth and under the earth and every tongue confess that Jesus Christ is Lord to the glory of God the Father" (Phil 2:5–11). What can be clearer and more evident than this? He did not become greater, as one who was lesser; but, rather, being God, "he took the form of a servant" and in the taking of it, he was not advanced but rather humbled himself. So where then is their "reward of virtue," or what kind of promotion and advance is there in humiliation? For if he is God, and became human, and, having descended from the heights, is said to be exalted, to where is he exalted, since he is God? For it is clear that if God is Most High, necessarily so is his Word the Most High. So where can he be exalted higher – he who is in the Father (Jn 10:38) and "like the Father in all things (*homoios kata panta*)"?[34] Therefore he has no need for any gain and is not as the Arians presume him to be. For even if the Word descended in order to be exalted – and these things are written in the Scriptures – how was he in any need at all of humbling in order to seek to receive what he already had? Or, what kind of grace did he receive, who is the giver of grace? Or how did he, who is forever to be worshipped in his own name, receive the name to which worship is due? Indeed, before he became human, the holy ones called upon him, saying, "O God, in your name, save me" (Ps 54:3). And again, "Some exult in chariots and some in horses, but we in the name of the Lord our God" (Ps 20:8). And he was worshipped by the Patriarchs, while it is written of the angels, "Let all the angels of God worship Him" (Heb 1:6).

41. And if, as David sings in the seventy-first psalm, "His name endures, before the sun and before the moon, from generation to generation" (Ps 72:17), how did he receive what he forever had, even before his receiving it now? Or, how is he exalted, being the Most High before he was exalted? Or how did he receive the prerogative of being worshipped? For before having received it now, he was forever worshipped. This is not a riddle but a divine mystery! "In the beginning was the Word and the Word was with God and the Word was God" (Jn 1:1); but, later, for our sakes, "the Word became flesh" (Jn 1:14). And to refer to him now as "highly exalted" is not to signify that the essence (*ousia*) of the Word is exalted. For he always was and is "equal to God" (Phil 2:6; cf. Jn 5:18); but the exaltation pertains to the humanity. These things were not said of him before but only when the Word became flesh, so that it may be evident that "humbled" (Phil 2:8) and "exalted" (Phil 2:9) are spoken of the humanity. For it is the one of humble status who may undergo an exaltation. And if "humbled" is written of him on account of his taking flesh, it is clear also that "highly exalted" is on the same account. For humanity was in need of this exaltation because of the lowliness of the flesh and because of death. Therefore, since he is the Image of the Father and Immortal Word, "He took the form of a servant" (Phil 2:7) and, for our sakes, as a human being, he suffered death in his own flesh, so that through death, he may thus offer himself for our sakes to the Father. Therefore, as a human being, he is said to be "highly exalted" because of us and for our sakes, so that, as in his death "we all have died" in Christ (2 Cor 5:14), so also in this same Christ we again may be "highly exalted" and, being raised from the dead, we may ascend into heaven, "where Jesus has entered as a forerunner, for our sakes" (Heb 6:20), not "into the figures of true realities but into heaven itself, now to appear in the presence of God, for our sakes" (Heb 9:24). But if now Jesus has entered into heaven itself for our sakes, even though, before this occurred, he is forever Lord and Creator of the heavens, then the "being exalted" is here written for our sakes. And, as he himself sanctifies all things and yet says to the Father that he sanctifies himself for our sake (Jn 17:19) – not in order that the Word may become holy but in order that he may make us all holy in himself – thus also it is now said that "[God] highly exalted him," not so that he himself may be exalted, for he is Most High, but in order that he may "become righteousness" for us (cf. 1 Cor 1:30), and so that we may be exalted in him and enter through the gates of the heavens, which he himself has reopened for

us, as the forerunners have said, "Lift up your gates, O rulers, and be lifted up, O everlasting gates, and the King of glory shall enter" (Ps 24:7). For in this case also, these gates were not shut on him who is the Lord and Maker of all things, but this too is written for our sakes, against whom the door of Paradise was closed shut. Therefore, it is with respect to the humanity, because of the flesh that he carried, that it is said of him, "Lift up [the gates]"; and it is said, "He shall enter," referring to his entrance as a human being. On the other hand, with respect to the divinity, since "the Word is God" (Jn 1:1), it is said of him that he is the Lord and "King of glory" (Ps 24:7). In the eighty-eighth psalm, the Spirit proclaimed beforehand this same exaltation which has transpired for us, saying: "And in your righteousness they shall be exalted, for you are the boast of their strength" (Ps 89:17). But if the Son is righteousness, then it is not he himself who is exalted as being in need of exaltation, but it is we who are exalted in the righteousness which he is (cf. 1 Cor 1:30).

42. And also, "He gave to him" (Phil 2:9) is not written in reference to the Word himself. For, as we have said, even before he became human he was worshipped by the angels (cf. Heb 1:6) and by all creation, inasmuch as he belonged to the Father.[35] But, again, this is written about him because of us and for our sakes. For just as Christ died and was exalted as a human being, so it is as a human being that he is said to "receive" what he possessed forever as God, in order that the giving of such grace may reach us. For the Word was not lessened by his taking a body, so that he would seek to receive grace, but rather he divinized what he put on, and, what's more, he gave this to the human race. For as he is worshipped forever, being Word and "in the form of God" (Phil 2:6), so also, being what he is, while becoming a human being and being called "Jesus," he nevertheless has the whole creation "under his feet" (cf. 1 Cor 15:27), bending the knees to him in this name (cf. Phil 2:10) and "confessing" (Phil 2:11) that the Word has become flesh (Jn 1:14) and has undergone death in the flesh, not to the detriment of the glory of his divinity, but "to the glory of God the Father" (Phil 2:11). For it is the Father's glory that humanity,[36] made and then lost, should be found again, and having died, should be made to live again and to become "the temple of God" (1 Cor 3:16).[37] And this is the grace and the exaltation that has come to us: that even the angels and archangels who forever worship the Word, and who worship him now "in the name of Jesus" the Lord, continue to worship the Son of God who has become human, and the heavenly

powers are not astonished to see all of us, who are joined to his body,[38] enter into their realms. And this indeed could not have happened unless the one who was "in the form of God had taken the form of a servant and humbled himself to the point of death" (Phil 2:6–8) by yielding up his body to death.

43. See then that what people consider to be the "foolishness of God" (1 Cor 1:25), through the cross has become more honorable than all things, for our resurrection is "stored up" (Col 1:5) in the cross. Henceforth, as the prophet had spoken beforehand, not only Israel but all the nations have abandoned their idols (cf. Tob 14:6), and acknowledge the true God, the Father of Christ, while the illusion of demons is dissipated and only the real God is worshipped in the name of our Lord Jesus Christ.[39] Moreover, even when the Lord came to be in the body and was called Jesus, he was still worshipped and believed in as the Son of God, through whom the Father was known.[40] This makes it clear, as has been said, that it is not the Word, as Word, who received the grace of exaltation, but us. For we have become "the temple of God" (1 Cor 3:16) through kinship with his body[41] and henceforth have been made into "sons of God" (Gal 3:26), so that already the Lord is worshipped even in us, and those who see us "proclaim," as the apostle said, "that truly God is in their midst" (1 Cor 14:25). As John also says in the Gospel, "To as many as received him, he gave power to become children of God" (Jn 1:12). And in the epistle, he writes, "By this we know that he remains in us, through his Spirit which he gave us" (1 Jn 3:24). It is a manifestation of the goodness that has come to us from him, that we ourselves are exalted on high through the Most High Lord being in us, and grace is given through us because the Lord who is the giver of grace has become a human being for our sakes. But, as for the Savior, he "humbled himself" (Phil 2:8) by taking "our lowly body" (Phil 3:21) and received "the form of a servant" (Phil 2:7), putting on the flesh that had become enslaved by sin (cf. Rom 8:3). It was not he who attained an advancement from us, for the Word of God is full and without need. Rather, it is we who were promoted through him. For he is "the light which enlightens every person who comes into the world" (Jn 1:9).

So it is useless for the Arians to lean upon that conjunction, "therefore," just because Paul said, "Therefore God highly exalted Him" (Phil 2:9). When Paul said this, he was not alluding to any prize for virtue, nor to an advancement of progress, but he was signifying the cause of the exaltation that has come to us. And what is this cause, except that he who is "in the form of God" (Phil 2:6)

and is the Son of the noble Father "humbled himself" (Phil 2:8) and
became a servant on our behalf and for our sakes? For if the Lord
had not become a human being, we would not have risen from the
dead by being loosed from our sins but would have remained dead
beneath the ground. We would not have been exalted to the
heavens, but would be lying prostrate in Hades. So it is because of
us and for our sakes that it is said, "He was highly exalted," and
"He was given ..." (Phil 2:9).

44. This, therefore, is what I consider to be the meaning of the
passage and it is a very ecclesiastical meaning.[42] Nevertheless, there
is also a second way in which one may render the sense of this
passage, saying the same thing in a parallel way. This is to say that
it indicates not that the Word, as Word, is exalted – for, as has just
been said above, he, like the Father (*homoios tō patri*), is Most High –
but refers rather to his resurrection from the dead, on account of his
becoming human. Thus, upon saying, "He humbled himself unto
death" (Phil 2:8), there immediately follows, "Therefore, he highly
exalted him" (Phil 2:9), with the intention of showing that while he
is said to have died as a human being, nevertheless, being Life, he
was exalted in the resurrection. "For he who has descended is the
same as he who has ascended" (Eph 4:10). For he descended bodily;
but he ascended because he was God himself in the body. And it is
again for this reason that he added the conjunction "therefore," in
keeping with the same sense, not to indicate a "reward for virtue"
nor a progress, but to demonstrate the cause why the resurrection
took place, and on account of which all other people from Adam
until now have died and remained dead (cf. 1 Cor 15:22), while he
alone rose as whole from the dead. And this cause, as he previously
said, is that, being God, he became human. For all other people
who are merely from Adam have died and have had "death ruling"
over them (Rom 5:14). But he is the "second human being from
heaven" (1 Cor 15:47), for the "Word became flesh" (Jn 1:14). Such
a one is said to be "a human being from heaven" (1 Cor 15:47) and
"heavenly" (1 Cor 15:48) because the Word "descended from
heaven" (Jn 6:38), and so he was not "subject to the power of death"
(Acts 2:24). And although he "humbled himself" (Phil 2:8) by
giving up his own (*idion*) body to death, since it was susceptible to
death, nevertheless he was "highly exalted" (Phil 2:9) and raised up
from the earth, since he was the Son of God in the body.

So what is said here, "Therefore God has highly exalted him," is
equivalent to what is said in the *Acts* by Peter, "He whom God
raised, having loosed him from the pangs of death, because it was

not possible for him to be held by its power" (Acts 2:24). As it is written by Paul, "Since, being in the form of God, he became human and humbled himself to death, therefore God has highly exalted him" (Phil 2:6,8,9), so it is said by Peter, "Since, being God, he became human, and signs and wonders proved him to eyewitnesses to be God, therefore 'it was not possible for him to be held by the power of death'" (cf. Acts 2:22–24). But this achievement is not possible for a human being, for death is proper to human beings. Because of this, the Word, being God, became flesh, so that "having been put to death in the flesh" (1 Pet 3:18), he might "enliven all" (1 Cor 15:22) by his own power.

45. But, since it is said that he was "exalted" (cf. Phil 2:9, Jn 3:14), and that God "gave" to him (Phil 2:9), and so the heretics consider this to indicate a deficiency or passibility of the essence of the Word, it is necessary to say in what sense these things are spoken. He is said to be highly exalted "from the lower regions of the earth" (Eph 4:9) because the death is said to be his. Both events are spoken of as his, since the body that was highly exalted and raised up from among the dead and also taken up into heaven, was his and not another's. Since the body was his, and was not external to the Word, it is fitting that when the body was highly exalted, he himself, as a human being, is said to be highly exalted on account of the body. If he had not become human, these things would not have been said of him. But if "the Word became flesh" (Jn 1:14), it is necessary that both the exaltation and the resurrection are referred to him, as a human being, so that the death which is said to be his may be a ransom for the sins of human beings and an abolishment of death, and so that the resurrection and exaltation may be rendered secure[43] for us through him. He has said both these things of him, "God highly exalted Him," and "God gave to him," in order to show that it is not the Father who has become flesh, but it is his Word who has become a human being, "receiving" humanly from the Father, and "highly exalted" by him, as has been said. But it is clear, and no one would doubt it, that what the Father gives, he gives through the Son.[44] And what is wonderful and truly astounding is that the Son himself is said to have received the grace which he gives from the Father, and to be himself "highly exalted" by the same exaltation which he effects and grants from the Father. For he who is the Son of God became himself the Son of Man. As Word, he gives from the Father, for all that the Father makes and gives he makes and grants through the Son. But, as Son of Man, he is said to receive humanly what is from himself, on account of the

body being not another's but his own, and having the nature which receives grace, as has been said. For he received the humanity in such a way as to grant it exaltation and this exaltation was its deification. But the Word himself was forever in possession of this, according to his own divinity and perfection, which are of the Father.[45]

46. This is the meaning of what is written by the apostle and it serves to refute the impious. On the other hand, what the psalmist says also has the same right meaning, which they distort, but which the psalmist shows to be pious (*eusebē*). For he says, "Your throne, O God, is for ages of ages. The scepter of your kingdom is a scepter of rectitude. You have loved righteousness and hated unrighteousness. Therefore God, your God, has anointed you with the oil of gladness above your partners" (Ps 45:7–8).[46] Look, you Arians, and acknowledge the truth that is found here. The psalmist says that we are all partners and partakers of the Lord.[47] But if he were "from nonbeing" and was one of those who come into being, he himself would have been one of those who participate. But since the psalmist hymned him as Eternal God, saying, "Your throne, O Lord, is unto the age of ages," whereas he has made it clear that all other things participate in him, what should one possibly think but that he is other than things that come to be, and is rather the One True Word, Radiance, and Wisdom of the Father, of which all things that come to be participate and are sanctified, in the Spirit? Therefore, he is here "anointed" not so as to become God, for he was God before this; nor in order to become king, for, as the verse shows, he was reigning forever, being the "Image" of God (2 Cor 4:4, Col 1:15). But again, this is written for our sakes. For, in the case of the Israelite kings, they became kings when they were anointed, as happened to David and Hezekiah and the others, and they were not kings before then. The Savior, on the contrary, being God, and forever ruling the kingdom of the Father, and being himself the supplier of the Spirit, is nevertheless now said to be anointed by the Spirit, so that, being said to be anointed as a human being by the Spirit, he may provide us human beings with the indwelling and intimacy of the Holy Spirit, just as he provides us with exaltation and resurrection.[48]

The Lord himself provides this meaning when he says, in his own person, in the gospel according to John: "I have sent these into the world, and I sanctify myself for their sakes, that they may be sanctified by the truth" (Jn 17:18–19). By saying this he showed that he was not the one who is sanctified but the one who sanctifies. For he is not sanctified by another, but he sanctifies himself, in order that we may be sanctified in the truth. But the one who sanctifies himself is the Lord of sanctification. How does this happen? How does he speak the way he does, except as if to say, "I, being the Word of the Father, give the Spirit to myself, having become a human being. And, in the Spirit, I sanctify myself, having become human, so that henceforth all may be sanctified in me by the truth, 'For your word is truth' (Jn 17:17)."

47. But if it is for our sakes that he sanctifies himself, which he did when he became a human being, then it is quite clear that the descent of the Spirit upon him in the Jordan was a descent upon us, because of our body which he carried. This did not take place for the advancement of the Word but for our sanctification, so that we may share in his anointing and so that it may be said of us, "Do you not know that you are the temple of God, and the Spirit of God dwells in you?" (1 Cor 3:16). For when the Lord was washed in the Jordan, it was we who were washed in him and by him. And when he received the Spirit, it was we who were made recipients of the Spirit by him. For this reason, he was not merely anointed with oil like Aaron and David and all the others. But altogether differently from "all his partners," he was anointed with "the oil of gladness" (Ps 45:8, Heb 1:9), which he himself interprets to be the Holy Spirit, when he says, through the prophet: "The Spirit of the Lord is upon me, because he has anointed me" (Isa 61:1, Lk 4:18). Likewise, the apostle said, "As God anointed him with the Holy Spirit" (Acts 10:38). But when were these things said of him, except when he came in the flesh and was baptized in the Jordan and "the Spirit descended upon him" (Mt 3:17)? In fact, the Lord himself says to his disciples, "the Spirit will take from what is mine" (Jn 16:14), and "I will send him to you" (Jn 16:7) and "Receive the Holy Spirit" (Jn 20:22). And he who provides for others as Word and Radiance of the Father is nevertheless now said to be "sanctified" (Jn 17:19), because he has become human and the sanctified body is his own. Therefore we also have begun to receive from him the anointing and the seal, as John says: "You have an anointing from the Holy One" (1 Jn 2:20); and the apostle says, "You were sealed by the Holy Spirit of the promise" (Eph 1:13). Therefore it is because of us and for our sakes that the Scriptures speak in this way.

So what kind of progress of advancement or "reward for virtue" or for any kind of conduct is indicated of the Lord here? For if he was not God and then came to be God; or if he was not king and was promoted to kingship, your talk would contain some semblance of persuasion. But if he is God, and "the throne of his kingdom is eternal" (Ps 45:7, Heb 1:9), then how can God have advancement? What was lacking to the one who was sitting on the Father's throne? But if, as the Lord himself has said, the Spirit is his and takes from him (Jn 16:14) and it is he who sends it (Jn 16:7), then it is not the Word, as Word and Wisdom, who is anointed by the Spirit which is given by him.[49] But it is the flesh assumed by him that is anointed in him and by him, in order that the sanctification which came to be in the Lord as a human being may come to be in all human beings from him. For he says, "The Spirit does not speak on his own" (Jn 16:13); but it is the Word who gives the Spirit to those who are worthy. For this is like the passage mentioned above, in which the apostle has written: "Who being in the form of God, did not consider being equal to God something to grasp at, but emptied himself, taking the form of a servant" (Phil 2:6–7). Likewise, David hymns the Lord as the Eternal God and King who was sent to us and assumed our mortal body. He signifies this when he sings in the psalm: "Myrrh and aloes and cassia from your garments" (Ps 45:9); and this is indicated also by Nicodemus and the companions of Mary, when the one came carrying "a mixture of myrrh and aloes, weighing about a hundred pounds" (Jn 19:39), and the others brought the spices which they had prepared for the burial of the Lord's body (Lk 24:1).

48. What kind of progress, then, is it for the Immortal to assume the mortal? Or what kind of advancement is it for the Eternal to put on the temporal? What kind of reward could be greater than being the Eternal God and King, who is in the bosom of the Father (Jn 1:18)? Do you not see that this also took place and is written because of us and for our sakes, so that the Lord, having become human, may grant immortality to us who are mortal and temporal and lead us into the everlasting kingdom of heaven? Do you not blush to lie and falsify the divine sayings? For when the Lord Jesus Christ came to dwell among us, it was we who were promoted, having been freed from sin (Rom 6:18). But he is the same and, to repeat again what I already said, he did not change because he became human. As it is written, "The Word of God remains forever" (Isa 40:8, 1 Pet 1:25). To be sure, just as before his becoming human, he was the Word who granted to the saints the Spirit as his own (*idion*), so also, upon his becoming human, he sanctifies all by the Spirit, and says to the disciples: "Receive the Holy Spirit" (Jn 20:22). And he gave it also to Moses

105

and to the seventy (Num 11:16). Through him, David also prayed to the Father, saying, "Do not take away your Holy Spirit from me" (Ps 51:13). And having become human, he said, "I will send you the Paraclete, the Spirit of truth" (Jn 15:26). And he did send it, for he is without falsehood, being the Word of God.

Therefore, "Jesus Christ is the same yesterday and today and forever" (Heb 13:8), remaining and not changing. And he is the same, both giving and receiving, giving as the Word of God, receiving as a human being. So it is not the Word, as Word, who is advanced. For he had all things and has all things forever. But it is human beings who now have the principle and origin of their receiving in him and through him. For now that he is said to be humanly anointed, it is we who are anointed in him. And because he is baptized, it is we who are baptized in him. The Savior makes clear all these things when he says to the Father: "And the glory which you have given to me, I have given to them, so that they may be one, as we are one" (Jn 17:22). So it is because of us that he is glorified (Jn 17:5) and because of us that it is said that "He took" (Phil 2:7) and "was anointed" (Ps 45:8) and "highly exalted" (Phil 2:9). It was so that we may receive, that we may be anointed, that we may be highly exalted in him, just as he sanctifies himself for our sakes, so that we may be sanctified in him (Jn 17:19).

49: But if, in order to suit their own wishes, they make a pretext for themselves because of the word "therefore," when the psalm says, "Therefore God, your God, has anointed you" (Ps 45:8, Heb 1:9), let these amateurs in Scripture and experts in impiety understand that there also the word "therefore" does not signify any reward for the virtue or conduct of the Word. Rather, it again refers to the reason for his descent to us, and for the anointing of the Spirit which took place in him for our sakes. For he does not say, "Therefore he has anointed you *to become* God or King or Son or Word"; for he was this before then and is so forever, as has been shown. But rather, "Since you are God and King, 'therefore' you were anointed – since there was no other to join humanity to the Holy Spirit except you who are the Image of the Father, and according to whose image we were made in the beginning;[50] for the Spirit also is yours." The nature of things that come to be is not trustworthy for this task, for angels have transgressed, and human beings disobeyed. "Therefore" God was needed (and "the Word is God" (Jn 1:1)), so that he himself may free those who had come under the curse. If "he was from non-being," he would not have been the Anointed "Christ" but would have been himself one

among all the rest and himself "a partner" – one who participates.[51]
But since he is God, being the Son of God and Eternal King, and
Radiance and Expression of the Father (Heb 1:3), "therefore" it is
fitting that he is the awaited Christ whom the Father announces to
humanity and reveals to the holy prophets, so that as we have come
to be through him, so also there may come to be in him a redemption for all from sins, and so that all may be ruled by him. And this
is the reason for the anointing which took place in him and for the
incarnate presence of the Word, which the psalmist contemplates
when he sings, on the one hand, of his divinity and paternal
kingdom[52] – crying out, "Your throne, O God, is unto the ages of
ages. A scepter of rectitude is the scepter of your kingdom" (Ps
45:7, Heb 1:8) – and, on the other hand, he proclaims his descent
to us when he says, "Therefore God, your God, has anointed you
with the oil of gladness above your partners" (Ps 45:8, Heb 1:9).

50. But what is so bewildering or unbelievable, if the Lord who
gives the Spirit is now said himself to be anointed with the Spirit
when, due to the pressing need, he did not shrink from speaking of
himself as less than the Spirit, on account of his humanity? For
when the Jews said, "He casts out demons by Beelzebub" (Lk 8:15,
Mt 12:24), he answered and said to them, in order to confute their
blasphemy: "But if I cast out demons in the Spirit of God ..." (Mt
12:28). Look, then, the Giver of the Spirit now says of himself that
he casts out demons in the Spirit. But this was not said except on
account of the flesh. Since the nature of human beings is not sufficient to cast out demons on its own but only by the power of the
Spirit, therefore as a human being he said, "But if I cast out demons
in the Spirit" (Lk 4:14, Mt 12:28). To be sure, he also signified that
blasphemy directed at the Holy Spirit is worse than that directed
against his humanity, saying, "Whoever speaks a word against the
Son of Man shall have pardon" (Mt 12:32) – like those who said, "Is
he not the son of the carpenter?" (Mt 13:55). But those who blaspheme against the Holy Spirit and ascribe the works of the Word to
the devil shall meet with inescapable retribution.

The Lord said such things to the Jews, as a human being. But to
the disciples he showed his divinity and greatness; and no longer
manifesting himself as less than the Spirit, he indicated rather that
he was equal to the Spirit when he gave them the Spirit and said, "I
will send him" (Jn 16:7) and "he will glorify me" (Jn 16:14) and
"whatever he hears he will say" (Jn 16:13). As in that case, the Lord
who is Giver of the Spirit did not shrink from saying, as a human
being, that he "casts out demons in the Spirit" (Mt 12:28), so also

in the same way, he who is the same Giver of the Spirit did not shrink from saying, "The Spirit of the Lord is upon me because He has anointed me" (Lk 4:18, Isa 61:1). He said this because of his having become flesh, as John says (Jn 1:14). In both cases, these things are said so that it may be shown that it is we who are both in need of the grace of the Spirit for sanctification, and who are power-less to cast out demons apart from the Spirit's power. But through whom and from whom should the Spirit have been given, if not through the Son whose Spirit it is? And, then again, when were we empowered to receive, if not when the Word became a human being? Just as the apostle's words indicate that we would not have been freed and "highly exalted" if it were not that "he who is in the form of God took the form of a servant" (Phil 2:6,7), so also David shows that in no other way would we have partaken of the Spirit and been sanctified if it were not that the Giver of the Spirit, the Word himself, spoke of himself as anointed by the Spirit for our sakes. Therefore we have received securely (*bebaiōs*)[53] in that he is said to be anointed in the flesh. The flesh was first sanctified in him and he is spoken of as having received through it, as a human being, and so we have the Spirit's grace that follows from his reception, receiving from his fullness (Jn 1:16).

51. As for the verse in the psalm that runs, "He has loved righ-teousness and hated injustice" (Ps 45:8), this does not show that the nature of the Word is changeable, as you think,[54] but rather provides a direct indication of his unchangeableness. For the nature of things that come to be is changeable, and some have transgressed while others have disobeyed, as has been said, and their conduct is not stable (*bebaia*), but it is often possible that one who is now good changes later and becomes other than he was, so that one who was righteous up to now is found to be unrighteous a little later.[55] Therefore there was a need for someone who was unchangeable, so that human beings might have that immutability as an image and archetype of virtue. This reasoning makes good sense for those who think rightly. For since Adam, "the first human being" (1 Cor 15:45) changed, and "through sin death entered into the world" (Rom 5:12), it was fitting that "the second" Adam (1 Cor 15:47) be unchangeable, so that even if the serpent were to attack again, it would be "the serpent's deceit" (cf. 2 Cor 11:3) itself which would be rendered ineffective. Since the Lord is unchangeable and unalter-able, the serpent would become enfeebled in his attacks against all. For as when Adam transgressed, the deceit passed over "to all people" (Rom 5:12), so when the Lord overpowered the serpent,

such great power henceforth passed over to us to the point where each one of us can say, "We are not ignorant of his designs" (2 Cor 2:11). Therefore it is fitting that the Lord who is unchangeable forever and by nature, "loving righteousness and hating injustice" (Ps. 45:8), should be anointed and himself sent, so that, being and remaining the same while taking changeable flesh, "he may condemn sin in it" (Rom 8:3) and make it free henceforth to be able "to fulfill the righteousness of the law" in itself (Rom 8:4), so that we could say: "We are not in the flesh but in the Spirit if the Spirit of God dwells in us" (Rom 8:9).

52. So in this case also, it is in vain, you Arians, that you conceive such a supposition and it is in vain that you use the words of the Scriptures as your pretext. For the Word of God is unchangeable and is forever the same; and not merely the same, but the same as the Father is. For otherwise how is he "like the Father"? Or how is it that all which belongs to the Father belongs to the Son (Jn 16:15, 17:10) if he does not have the Father's unchangeability and inalterability? But, in fact, he does not love one thing and hate the other by inclination to one side and as one who is subject to laws, as if he shuns the one out of fear of falling and so chooses the other, for in that case changeability would again be introduced. Rather, as God and Word of the Father, he is a just judge and lover of virtue; or rather, the giver of virtue. Therefore it is as being just and holy by nature that he is said to "love righteousness and hate injustice" (Ps 45:8), which is to say that he loves and chooses the virtuous, but hates and turns away the unjust. The divine Scriptures also say the same thing with regard to the Father: "The Lord is righteous and he has loved righteousness" (Ps 11:7) and "You have hated all those who work iniquity" (5:6) and "He loves the gates of Sion more than the dwellings of Jacob" (Ps 87:2) and "I have loved Jacob and hated Esau" (Mal 1:3), while in Isaiah the voice of the Lord again says, "I am the Lord who loves righteousness and hates the robbery of injustice" (Isa 61:8). Therefore, let them take the former words in the same sense as these latter, for the former also were written about the Image of God; or else, misunderstanding these latter words as well as those former, they will contrive the notion that the Father too is changeable. But if even to hear others say this is perilous, we think well if we understand that to speak of God as "loving righteousness and hating the robbery of injustice" is not to indicate that he inclines to the one side while being capable of the opposite, as if opting for the one and not choosing the other, for this is characteristic of things that come to be. Rather, it is as Judge that he loves

and accepts the righteous and distances himself from the bad. Accordingly, we should think the same about the Image of God, that he loves and hates in this manner. For the nature of the image must be such as its Father, even if the blind Arians do not see this, nor anything else that is in the divine words. For when they are deprived of the conceptions, or rather misconceptions, of their hearts, they take refuge again in the words of the divine Scriptures, whose meaning they generally do not grasp in their insensibility. Rather, they place their own impiety (*asebeia*) as a kind of canon, according to which they subvert all the divine sayings. Upon the mere utterance of these things, they deserve to hear nothing but, "You are mistaken, knowing neither the Scriptures nor the power of God" (Mk 12:24, Mt 22:29). And if they still persist, they should be shamed by hearing, "Render to human beings the things that are human and to God the things that are God's" (Lk 20:25, Mt 22:21).

Selection 3: Exegesis of Prov 8:22
(*Or. Ar.* 2:2, 2:3, 2:18–82)

The third selection from the *Orations* which is translated below provides Athanasius's treatment of the most controverted text of the Nicene controversy, Prov 8:22, where Wisdom says, "The Lord created (*ektize*) me as a beginning of his ways for his works." The text had become a cornerstone of anti-Nicene theology and any defense of the doctrine of Nicaea had to contend with this biblical pronouncement that Wisdom was "created." As one modern commentator puts it, "this text in Proverbs ... was in the fourth century fought over by the theologians as in the *Iliad* the Greeks and Trojans fight over the body of Patroclus."[56] The same commentator goes on to point out that by the standards of contemporary biblical criticism, Athanasius would have been able "to dismiss the whole debate as a storm in a teacup because the text does not refer to Christ."[57] Of course, this option was not available to Athanasius or any of his contemporaries, who located the meaning of the text not so much in the conscious intention of the human author but in the objective reference to divine realities and to the economy of divine revelation that was placed in the biblical text by the Spirit. From the latter perspective, it was crucial for the early Christian understanding of the person of Christ to attend to the biblical identification of Jesus as divine Word, Wisdom, Power, etc. Indeed, for Athanasius's Alexandrian predecessor Origen, "Wisdom" was the most primary biblical designation for Christ.[58] Once this identification was accepted, it was to be applied consistently. So, if Wisdom says that she was "created," this had to be somehow understood in reference to the (pre-existent) person of Christ.[59] Athanasius's explication of this text again involves him in the work of attempting to show that the overall patterns of scriptural language identify the Word as God and not as a creature, and that the governing "plot" of Scripture involves "a double account of the Savior," referring alternately to his divinity and humanity.[60] Thus, he interprets Prov 8:22 in reference to the economy of the Incarnation, rather than to the divinity of the Word.

Text

2:2. If he is not Son, let him be called a work (*poiēma*). And let everything that is designated of works be applied also to him. And let it not be said of him alone that he is Son and Word and Wisdom. And let it not be said of God himself that he is Father, but merely maker and creator of the things which he brings into being.[61] And let the creature be Image and Expression of his creative will. In accord with them, let not God be of a generative nature, so that there may be no Word nor Wisdom nor any Image at all of his own essence. For if he is not Son, then neither is he Image. But if there is no Son, how then do you say that God is Creator, if indeed it is through the Word and in Wisdom that everything that is made comes to be and without which nothing comes to be, and yet, according to you, God does not possess that in which and through which he makes all things (cf. Wis 9:2, Jn 1:3, Ps 104:20,24)?[62] But if, according to them, the divine essence itself is not fruitful but barren, like a light that does not shine and a fountain that is dry, how are they not ashamed to say that God has creative energy? Denying what is by nature, how can they not blush to wish to give precedence to what is by will? If God creates things that are external [to the divine essence] and at first were not, by willing them to be, and thus becomes their Maker, how much more is he first of all Father of an offspring from his own proper (*idias*) essence? For if they grant to God the willing of what is not, why do they not acknowledge of God what supersedes the willing? But what supersedes the willing is his bringing-forth and his being Father, by nature, of his own (*idiou*) Word. Therefore, if that which is first, which is according to nature, does not exist, according to their mindlessness, how can that which is second, which is according to will, come to be? But what is first is the Word, and the creation is second. Indeed the Word exists, whatever these impious ones dare to presume; for the creation "has come to be through him" (Jn 1:3).

It should be clear then that God, being Maker, has his creative Word not from outside but as proper (*idion*) to him – this must be repeated yet again. If, on the one hand, the willing belongs to him, and his will is productive and sufficient for constituting the things which come to be, and, on the other hand, his Word is producer and creator, then it is beyond doubt that this Word is the living will of the Father,[63] and Essential Energy, and True Word, in whom also he constitutes and governs all things excellently. Indeed, no one should doubt at all that the One who arranges is prior to the arrangement and to the things that are arranged. So, as I have said, God's creating is second to his begetting. For the Son is proper to (*idion*) and truly from that blessed and everlastingly existent essence, whereas those things that are from the will have come to be constituted from outside [the divine essence], and are made through his proper (*idion*) offspring, who is from [the essence].

3. Now that our discourse has demonstrated the great absurdity of those who say that the Lord is not Son of God but a work, it is imperative that we should accordingly confess him to be Son. But if indeed he is Son, which he is, and it is acknowledged that a son is not from outside but from the one who begets him, let them not impose distinctions on the terms, as I have said before, even if the holy writers refer to the Word himself by saying "to the one who made him" (Heb 3:2),[64] instead of "to the one who begot him." The term is indifferent, in these cases, as long as the nature is confessed. For terms do not take anything away from the nature. Rather, the nature assimilates the terms to itself and transforms them. For terms do not precede essences, but the essences are first and terms are second to them. Therefore, when the essence is a work or a creature, then the words "he made" and "he became" and "he created" are spoken of it in a strict sense (*kyriōs*) and signify a work. But when the essence is an offspring and son, then the words "he made" and "he became" and "he created" are no longer applied to it in a strict sense and do not signify a work; in that case, the words "he made" are used indifferently from "he begot."[65] Thus, fathers often call the sons born of them "servants," without thereby denying that they are their legitimate sons by nature. Often, too, they lovingly call their own servants "children," without forgetting their original acquisition of them. In the first instance, they speak upon their authority as fathers; in the second, they lovingly name them so.

Thus, Sarah calls Abraham "Lord" (1 Pet 3:6), although she is not a servant but a spouse. And the apostle adjoins Onesimus the servant to Philemon the Master as "brother" (Philem 16), while Bathsheeba, even though she is a mother, calls her son "servant," saying to his father, "your servant Solomon" (1 Kings 1:19), after which Nathan the prophet entered and said the same thing to David: "Solomon, your servant" (1 Kings 1:26). But it was not an issue of any concern for them to speak of the son as a servant, for when David heard, he recognized the nature, just as those who were speaking were not ignorant of the legitimate sonship. Thus, they expected him whom they called "servant" to become his father's heir; for he was David's son by nature.

18. Let us come next to an examination of the saying in the Proverbs, "The Lord created me as the beginning of his ways for his works" (Prov 8:22), even though once it has been shown that the Word is not made (*poiēma*), it is also shown that he is not a creature. For to say "made" and "creature" is the same thing; therefore, the proof of his not being made is the same as that regarding his not being a creature. So one may well be amazed at these people who invent pretexts for themselves, for the sake of impiety, and are not put to shame by the refutations marshaled against them on every side. First they contrived to trick those who are simple and guile-less,[66] enquiring of them: "Did the one-who-is make from non-being what existed or what did not exist?"[67] and "Did you have a son before you begot him?" When that was shown to be fallacious, they invented this: "Is the Unbegotten one or two?" Then, being refuted in this also, they immediately concocted another: "Does he have free will[68] and a changeable nature?" But being overcome on this score also, they again contrived to go around saying, "being made so much better than the angels" (Heb 1:4). Now that this also has been refuted by the truth, they have proceeded to gather all these things together, thinking to promote their heresy by "made" and "creature." Yet they again mean all the other things that they said before and have not withdrawn from their perversities. They vary and alter the same things many times over so that if possible they can deceive some by this variety. Therefore, although what has been said before has amply demonstrated the foolishness of this invention of theirs, nevertheless, since they have created such a din everywhere with this saying from the Proverbs, and appear to be actually saying something to many who are ignorant of the Christian faith, it is necessary to examine the words, "being faithful to the one who made him" (Heb 3:2), as well as "he

113

created" (Prov 8:22), in order to show that in this case, as in every-thing, they are in possession of nothing more than fantasy.

19. First, then, let us look at the responses they made to the blessed Alexander when they were devising their heresy in the beginning. They said in writing: "He is a creature, but not as one of the creatures. He is made, but as one of the things that are made. He is an offspring (*gennēma*) but not as one of the offsprings."[69] Let everyone see the villainy and deceit of this heresy! For, knowing the bitterness of its own malicious thinking, it strives to embellish itself with persuasive words. So, while it does in fact speak its mind in saying that he is a "creature," it thinks that it can hide itself by saying, "but not as one of the creatures." Nevertheless, in writing this, they have convicted themselves of their own impiety all the more. For if, according to you, he is altogether a creature like us, why do you say hypocritically, "but not as one of the creatures"? And if he is simply made, how is it that he is "not as one of the things that are made"?

In these phrases, one can see the poison of their heresy. For, in saying "offspring but not as one of the offsprings," they conjure up many sons, and they assert that one of these is the Lord. So, according to them, he is no longer the only-begotten (*monogenē*) (cf. Jn 3:16, 1 Jn 4:9), but they call him "offspring" and "son" as one out of many brothers. What is the use of this pretense, then, of saying that he is a creature yet not a creature? Although you say, "not as one of the creatures," this sophistry of yours will be shown to be without any sense. For you still say that he is one of the crea-tures and, as people who are truly "foolish and blind" (Mt 23:17), you attribute to the Son the things that one would say about the other creatures. For what kind of creature is there which is just what another is, that you can say this of the Son as if it made him exceptional? The whole visible creation came to be in six days: in the first, there was light, which he called day; in the second, the firmament; in the third, he gathered together the waters and displayed the dry land and brought out the various fruits in it; in the fourth, he made the sun and the moon and all the chorus of stars; in the fifth, he created the species of living things in the sea and of the birds in the air; in the sixth, he made the four-footed creatures which are upon the earth and finally, the human being (cf. Gen 1). "His invisible things are perceived through the creation of the world and understood by the things that are made" (Rom 1:20). Yet the light is not as the night, nor is the sun as the moon is, nor are irrational things as the rational human being. Neither are the angels as the thrones, nor are the thrones as the powers. Nevertheless all are creatures, though each of the things that have come to be exists and remains as it was made, "according to its kind" (Gen 1:11) and its proper being.

20. The Word, therefore, should be set apart from the things that are made. As creator, he should be restored to the Father and confessed to be Son by nature. Otherwise, if he is simply a creature, let it be confessed that he has the same rank which the other creatures share among themselves. Let it be said of each of these creatures also: "a creature but not as one of the creatures; an offspring or made but not as one of the offsprings and things that are made." For you have said that an offspring and an object that is made (*poiēma*) are the same thing, writing, "begotten or made."[70] But even if the Son has a relative precedence over the others, he would still be none the less a creature, just as they are. For even among those who are creatures by nature, there is to be found those who have precedence over others; thus, "star differs from star in glory" (1 Cor 15:41) and everything else differs from the others when one makes comparisons. But that does not mean that some are lords and others do service to those who are superior;[71] nor that some are efficient causes and others come to be through their agency. Rather, all have a nature which comes to be and is created, and they acknowledge, of themselves, their own creator.[72] Thus David sings, "The heavens declare the glory of God, the firmament proclaims the work of his hands" (Ps 19:2). Likewise, Zorababel the wise man says, "All the earth calls on the truth, and the heaven blesses the truth, and all the works shake and tremble" (1 Esd 4:36). But if all the earth hymns and blesses and shakes before the Maker and the Truth, whereas its Maker is the Word, who says himself, "I am the Truth" (Jn 14:6), then the Word is not a creature, but he alone belongs (*idios*) to the Father. In him all things are arranged in harmony, and it is he whose praises are sung by all things, as the Maker. As he himself says, "For I was arranging beside Him" (Prov 8:30); and "My father works until now and I work" (Jn 5:17). So the "until now" shows his eternal existence in the Father, as Word. For it belongs to the Word to work the works of the Father, and not to be external to him.

21. But if what the Father works, the Son also works, and what the Son creates is the creation of the Father, then if also the Son himself is a work and creature of the Father, it turns out that he makes himself and thus will be creator of himself (since the Father's works are also works of the Son), which is senseless and impossible.

Otherwise, he is not a work nor a creature, being the Fashioner and
Creator of the Father's creation. Or else, as an efficient cause [who is
made], he will cause it to come about that other things that are
made are also [makers] like himself. But what is more to the point
is that, in such a case, he would be incapable of causing anything.
For if, according to you, "he has come to be from non-being," how
is he able to fashion into being what is not? But if, being a creature,
he also fashions a creature, then the same conception will apply to
every creature, that they are likewise able to create. If that is how
you want it, what need is there for the Word, if inferior things come
to be through the superior? Or else, each of the things which had
come to be at the beginning would have been able to hear from
God, "Become," and "Be made," and would be made in that way![73]
But this is not what is written; neither was this possible. None of
the things that have come to be is an efficient cause: "for all things
have come to be through the Word" (Jn 1:3). The Word would not
be maker of all things if he himself was one of the things created.
For neither are angels able to create, being themselves creatures
(even if Valentinus and Marcion and Basilides think such things and
you have come to imitate them);[74] nor will the sun, being a creature, ever make what is not into being; nor does a human being
make a human being; nor does a stone conceive a stone; nor does a
tree cause a tree to grow. But it is God who fashions the human
being in the womb (Isa 44:24, Jer 1:5) and fixes the mountain in
place and gives growth to the tree (cf. 1 Cor 3:7). The human
being, insofar as he is capable of knowledge, combines and remodels
this material, according to his learning, and so makes things that
already have being and is pleased to accomplish even that much.
Recognizing his own nature, he knows how to ask God if he is in
need of anything.

22. But if God is also considered to work and compose out of
matter, that would be a Greek conception and in that case God
would be called a craftsman and not a maker.[75] But let us even
suppose that the Word works upon matter, as one who is appointed
to be at the service of God.[76] It still remains the case that if God
calls into existence what is not through his proper Word, then the
Word is not one of the things that did not exist and were called.
Otherwise, we would have to search for another Word, through
whom this Word was called, for that which did not exist has come
to be through the Word (cf. Jn 1:1). And if it is through the Word
that God creates and makes, then the Word himself is not among
the things that are created and made. Rather, he is the Word of the

Creator God; and from the works of the Father, which the Word himself works, one recognizes that he is in the Father and the Father is in him (Jn 14:10–11) and that the one who has seen him has seen the Father (Jn 14:9) because of the identity of essence and the complete likeness of the Son to the Father.[77] How, then, does the Father create through him if he were not his Word and Wisdom? And how can he be Word and Wisdom if he is not the proper offspring (*idion gennēma*) of the Father's essence but himself has come from non-being?

Indeed, since all things are created from nothing and, according to them, the Son is one of the created things that once were not, how is it that he alone reveals the Father and he alone and no one else knows the Father (Jn 6:46, 10:15)? If it is possible that he is made and yet knows the Father, then all things would know the Father, each according to their own measure; for all things are made, just as [you say that] he is. But if it is impossible for things that have come to be either to see or know the Father, since both his countenance and the knowledge concerning him transcend all things and God himself says, "No one will see my face and live" (Ex 33:20), whereas the Son has said, "No one knows the Father except the Son" (Mt 11:27), then the Word is other than those things which have come to be. He alone knows the Father and he alone sees the Father, as he has said, "No one has seen the Father except the one who is from the Father" (Jn 6:46), and "No one knows the Father except the Son" (Mt 11:27), though Arius does not think so.[78] So then how did he alone know the Father unless he alone properly belonged (*idios*) to the Father? And how did he belong to the Father as his very own if he was a creature and not true Son from the Father?

For the sake of piety, we cannot hesitate to say these things and to say them often. It is indeed impious to think that the Son is one among all. It is blasphemous and senseless to say, "a creature but not as one of the creatures; made but not as one of the things made; an offspring, but not as one of the offsprings." How is he not one of them if, according to them, "he was not before he was generated"? For it is proper to things created and made not to be before they come to be and to come into subsistence from non-being, regardless of whether they surpass others in glory. For such distinctions will be found among all other creatures with respect to each other, as even visible things show.

23. However, if, according to the heretics, he was a creature or a work but "not as one of the creatures" because of his being distinguished from them in glory,[79] then the Scriptures ought to have

depicted and described him by favorable comparison to other works. They should have spoken of him, for example, as greater than the archangels and more honorable than the thrones and more radiant than the sun and moon, and greater than the heavens. Now, in fact, they do not depict him in this manner. Rather, the Father describes him as his own (*idion*) and only Son, saying: "You are my son" (Ps 2:7, Acts 13:33, Heb 1:5, 5:5) and "This is my beloved son in whom I am well pleased" (Mt 3:17). Therefore the angels served him as one who is other than them.[80] He is worshipped by them not as one who is greater in glory but as being other than them and other than all creatures and as the only one who is the Father's own (*idios*) Son by essence. If he was worshipped because he excelled in glory, then each of those who are inferior should worship the one who excels it. But it is not so. A creature does not worship a creature, but the servant worships the Master and the creature worships God. So Peter the apostle restrained Cornelius, who wished to worship him, saying "And I also am a man" (Acts 10:26). And, in the *Apocalypse*, the angel restrained John when he wished to worship him, saying "Do not! I am a fellow servant of yours and of your brothers the prophets, and of those who keep the words of this book. Worship God" (Rev 22:9). Therefore, only God is to be worshipped.

The angels themselves know this; they know that, even if they excel others in their glory, they are nevertheless all creatures and not to be worshipped but are among those who worship the Master. Thus the angel prevented Manoah, the father of Samson, when he wished to offer sacrifice to it, saying, "Do not make your offering to me but to God" (cf. Judg 13:16). But the Lord is worshipped even by the angels; for it is written: "And let all the angels of God worship Him" (Heb 1:6). And he is worshipped by all the nations, as Isaiah says: "The toil of Egypt, the gain of Ethiopia, and the Sabeans, majestic men, will come over to you and will be your servants" (Isa 45:14), and then, "and they will bow down before you and say in prayer that God is in your midst and there is no other God" (*ibid.*). And he receives the disciples who worship him and assures them of who he is, saying, "Do you not call me 'Lord and Teacher'? You speak well; for so I am" (Jn 13:13). And when Thomas calls him "my Lord and my God" (Jn 20:28), he lets him say it; instead of preventing him, he approves of him. For, as the other prophets say and as David sings, he is the "Lord of Hosts" (Ps 24:10) and "Lord of Sabaoth" (Isa 6:3), which means "Lord of the armies," and "True God and Ruler of all" (3 Macc 6:18), even if this makes the Arians explode.

24. He would not be worshipped nor would these things be said of him if he were simply one of the creatures. But since in fact he is not a creature, but the proper (*idion*) offspring of the essence of the God who is worshipped and his Son by nature, he also, like the Father, is worshipped and believed in as God and is "Lord of the armies" and has authority and is ruler of all. For he has said: "All things that the Father has are mine" (Jn 16:15). Indeed, it is proper to the Son to have whatever belongs to the Father and to be such that the Father is seen in him (cf. Jn 12:45), and all things are made through him (cf. Jn 1:3) and in him the salvation of all things has both its genesis and content.

Moreover, in order that the refutation of their heresy may become still more apparent, it is good to ask them this also: If all things are creatures and all things have their subsistence from non-being, and the Son also, according to you, is a creature and a work and one of those that once were not, how is it that God has made all things through him alone and "without him not one thing came to be" (Jn 1:3)? Or why is it the case that when reference is made to "all things," no one understands the Son as signified among the "all" but one restricts the reference to the things that have come into being? And why is it that when the Scriptures speak of the Word, they also do not conceive him as among the "all" but align him with the Father, as the one in whom the Father works the providence and salvation of all things? Yet surely all things were capable of coming into being through the same command by which he came into being "by God alone"! After all, God does not get tired when he commands nor is he weak in the face of the task of making all things, so that he "alone" would create the Son "alone" as if he is in need of the Son as an assistant and help in the making of others.[81] Nor is there any delay when he wishes for something to come into being. He merely willed and all things existed and "no one has resisted his will" (Rom 9:19). So why is it that all things did not come into being by "God alone" through the command by which the Son came into being? Let them also say why it is that all things came to be through him, if he himself had an origin to his being. This is all just nonsense on their part.

Moreover, they say this about him: that God, wishing to create the nature of all the things that were to come into being, and seeing that such a nature would not be capable of withstanding his immediate hand and creative activity, first creates by himself only one, whom he calls "Son" and "Word," so that the latter being thus a mediator, all things could finally be enabled to come into being through him. Eusebius and Arius and Asterius, the one who sacrificed, have not only said these things but have dared to write them.[82]

25. When it comes to such conclusions, how could any of them fail to condemn the outcome of the impiety which they have concocted for themselves by mixing in a lot of nonsense and which they have now imbibed to the point where they do not blush to rail drunkenly against the truth? If it is because of the toil involved for God in the making of the other things that they say that he made only the Son, the whole creation will raise a protest against them for saying things that are unworthy of God, including Isaiah, who has written: "The Eternal God, who has fashioned the ends of the earth, does not faint or grow weary and his understanding is beyond scrutiny" (Isa 40:28). But if it is because of disdaining to make the others that God made only the Son, and handed over the [task of making the] others to the Son as to an assistant, then this also is unworthy of God; for there is no pride in God.[83] The Lord shames them when he says: "Are not two sparrows sold for a small coin? And yet not one of them falls to the ground without your Father who is in heaven?" (Mt 10:29). And again: "Do not worry about your life, what you will eat; nor about your body, what you will wear. Is not life more than food, and the body more than clothing? Look at the birds of the sky; they neither sow nor reap nor gather into barns. Yet your heavenly Father feeds them. Are you not better than they? Who among you by worrying can add to his life a single moment? And why do you worry about clothing? Learn from the lilies of the field, how they grow. They do not toil or spin. But I say to you that not even Solomon in all his glory dressed as one of those. But if God so clothes the grass of the field, which is here today and tomorrow is thrown into the fire, will he not do much more for you, you of little faith?" (Mt 6:25–30). So if it is not unworthy of God to be provident even toward things so minor as the hair of the head and the sparrow and the grass of the field, neither is it unworthy of him to also make these things. Through his proper Word, he is the maker of those very things over which he exercises providence.

Moreover, an even greater absurdity presents itself to those who say these things. For they distinguish the things that are created from the creative activity and say that the creative activity is the work of the Father, while the creatures are the work of the Son.[84] But either all things must be brought into being by the Father with the Son; or, if all the things that come into being come to be through the Son, then it must not be said of him also that he is one of the things that come into being.

26. Furthermore, one may refute their nonsense in this way: If the Word also is of an originated nature, and such a nature is incapable of withstanding the direct activity of God, how is it that the Word alone among all things was enabled to come into being by the uncreated and unmitigated essence of God, as you say? For it must be the case either that all were capable of this as he was capable of it; or all are incapable and so neither is the Word capable, since, according to you, he also is one of those whose being is originated. Yet again, if the nature of originated beings needs a mediator because it is not capable of partaking in the direct activity of God, then it is altogether necessary that the Word, as a creature whose being is also originated, also needs a mediator for his creation, for he too is one of those whose nature is originated and cannot partake of God's activity but has need of a mediator. And if a mediator is found for him, then there will again be need for another mediator. Thus one will extend and pursue the argument until one ends up with a great crowd of mediators pouring in from all sides. In this way the creation will be forever unable to exist because it needs a mediator and that mediator cannot come into being apart from another mediator, for all would be of that originated nature which, according to you, is incapable of partaking of the activity of God alone.[85] How full of nonsense are these notions, through which they must arrive at the conclusion that the things which in fact did already come into being were incapable of coming into being![86] Or perhaps they imagine that these things have still not come into being because they are still seeking a mediator. According to their impious and foolish madness, the things which have come into being would not exist, since a mediator would always be lacking.

27. But they offer this pretense: "He led the people out of Egypt through Moses also and he gave the law through him, even though he was a human being. So then it is possible for things to come into being through what is like them."[87] It would have been proper for them to cover themselves when they say these things, so as not to bring upon themselves so much shame. Moses was not sent to create nor to call into being what was not and to fashion human beings like himself, but only to serve by speaking to the people and to Pharaoh. This is a very different matter. To serve is for those who have come into being; they are servants. But to make and create is for God alone and his own Word and Wisdom. Therefore, none other can be found for the work of creating than the Word of God

alone, "for all things have come to be in wisdom" (Ps 104:24) and "apart from the Word not one thing came into being" (Jn 1:3). But for the work of service, there is not only one but many who are sent from among all and the Lord sends all those whom he wishes to send. So there are many archangels and many "thrones and powers and dominions" (Col 1:16), "thousands of thousands and myriads of myriads who stand and serve" (Dan 7:10), ready to be sent. There are also many prophets and twelve apostles and Paul. Even Moses himself was not alone but Aaron also was with him and with them the seventy others who were filled with the Holy Spirit (Num 11:25). And Moses was succeeded by Joshua the son of Nun; and Joshua was succeeded by the Judges; and they were succeeded by not one but many kings. Therefore, if the Son was a creature and among those who have come into being, then there should have been many such sons, so that God may have many such servants, just as there are many of those other servants. However, if this is not the case, but rather the creatures are many while the Word is one, who would not gather from this that the Son is set apart from all things and has no equality with creatures, but rather possesses identity (*idiotēta*) with the Father? Thus, there are not many words but only one Word of the one Father and one Image of the one God.[88]

But "Look!" they say, "there is only one sun and one earth."[89] Senseless people! Let them say also that water is also one and fire is also one, and the response they will hear is that each of the things that come into being is one with respect to its own essence but none is of itself adequate and sufficient for the service and ministry entrusted to it:[90] "For God said: Let there be lights in the firmament of the heaven to illuminate the earth, and to separate the day from the night and let them be for signs and seasons and days and years" (Gen 1:14). Then it says: "And God made two great lights, the greater light to govern the day and the lesser light to govern the night. And he made the stars and placed them in the firmament of the heaven, that they may shed light upon the earth and govern the day and the night" (Gen 1:16–18).

28. So, you see, there are many lights and not the sun alone nor the moon alone. But while each is one insofar as each essence is one, they are all involved in a single and common service (*leitourgia*). The deficiency of one is fulfilled by the other, and the task of casting light is fulfilled by all. Thus the sun possesses the power of casting light only during the interval of the day, while the moon has such power during the night. Along with these the stars bring to completion the seasons and years, and each is "for a sign" (Gen

1:14) according to the requisite need. Thus also the earth is not for all things but only for plants and so as to be a ground for those who live upon it. And the firmament is for the division between water and water (Gen 1:7) and for the placing of stars therein. So also fire and water and all the other [elements] are for the constitution of bodies. In general, no one thing is simply alone; but all the things that have come to be are as "members of one another, so as to be one body" (cf. Rom 12:4–5), completing the universe. Therefore, if that is how they understand the Son to be, let them be smitten by all, since they consider the Word to be a part of "all things," and thus a part that is not adequate to the service entrusted to it, apart from the others. But if this is obviously impious, let them recognize that the Word is not of those that come into being, but the only proper (*idios*) Word of the Father and maker of the things that come into being.

But they say: "Although he is a creature and of those that come into being, he has learned to create from the Master and Maker and thus has come to serve the God who taught him."[91] Asterius the Sophist, having himself learned to deny the Lord,[92] has dared to write these things, incognizant of their absurdity. For if creating is something that is taught, let them watch out that they don't end up saying that God himself is Creator not by nature but by knowledge, so as to be capable of losing that knowledge. Then again, if the Wisdom of God has acquired the creative agency through teaching, how can it still be Wisdom if it is in need of learning? And what was it before this learning? For it was not Wisdom if it needed to be taught; it must have been something empty and void and not wisdom in its very essence. But then it would have acquired the name of Wisdom through progress and will be wisdom just to the extent that it retains what it has learned. For what does not pertain to one by nature but is added by learning is capable of being unlearned at some point.[93] But to say such things about the Word of God is not for Christians but for Greeks.

29. Furthermore, if creating is something that is acquired through teaching, then these senseless people are attributing jealousy and weakness to God – jealousy, because he did not teach many others to be creators so that there may be many creators around him, just as there are many angels and archangels; and weakness, because he was not able to create on his own and needed a co-worker or assistant. However, it has been shown that the nature of things that come into being is in fact capable of being brought into being by God alone, since, by their own account, the Son also

came into being and yet was able to be brought into being by God alone. God has no need of anyone; never! He himself said, "I am full" (Isa 1:11).[94] The Word did not become creator through teaching, but being the image and wisdom of the Father, he does the works of the Father. Nor did the Father make the Son for the sake of making the things that come into being. Just look! After all, the Father is seen to be still working even while the Son exists, as the Lord himself says: "My Father is working until now and I also am working" (Jn 5:17). But if, according to you, the Son came into being for the sake of making the things that came into being after him, and yet it is shown that the Father is also working after the Son came into being, then the making of such a Son is superfluous according to you and your argument. Moreover, why is it that he seeks a mediator at all when he wishes to create us, as if his will is not sufficient to constitute whatever is pleasing to him? And yet the Scriptures say: "Whatever he wills is done" (Ps 115:3) and "Who has resisted His will?" (Rom 9:19). But if his will alone is sufficient for the creating of all things, then the need for a mediator is again superfluous, according to your own terms; and your examples about Moses and about the sun and moon have been shown to be unsound. Moreover, this also will put you to shame: If, when he wishes to create the nature of originated things, God conceives and creates the Son for our sake in order to create us through him, see how great an impiety you have dared to utter.

30. In the first place, it appears that the Son has come into being for our sake, and not we for his, since we were not created on his account but he has been made for us. In that case, it is he who owes us gratitude, and not we him, just as in the case of the woman and the man: "The man was not created for the woman," Scripture says, "but the woman for the man" (1 Cor 11:9). Therefore, as "the man is the image and glory of God, while the woman is the glory of the man" (1 Cor 11:7), so likewise it turns out that it is we who are the image of God and for his glory, while the Son is our image and for our glory.[95] Moreover, we have come into being for the sake of our own existence, while the Word of God, according to you, has been made not for the sake of his own existence but in order to be an instrument for our need. But then it is not we who are "from him" but he who is constituted for the sake of our need.

Do not those who merely conceive such thoughts exceed all insanity? If the Word came to be on our account, then he is not prior to us in his relation to God. In that case, it is not that God, having the Word in himself, wills us; but it is as if, having us in himself, God wills his own Word. But if this is so, perhaps the Father did not even will the Son at all. For it seems that he did not willingly create him but rather fashioned him for our sake, in the course of willing us. In that case, he conceived him after conceiving us and, according to these impious people, this "Son" who has come into being as an instrument is now superfluous, insofar as those for the sake of which he was created have now come to be. But if the Son had the capacity to come to be by God alone while we, lacking that capacity, came to be by the Word, why does God not first will the one who has this capacity instead of us who do not? Or why does he not give priority to the one who is thus capable rather than to those who are weak? And why does he make him first and yet not will him first? Or why is it that he wills us first and yet does not make us first if indeed his will is sufficient for the constitution of all things? Why, instead, does he create him first and yet will us first, so that he wills us prior to the Mediator? Yet we, whom he wills and intends to create, he calls "creatures"; while the one whom he creates on our account he calls "Son" and "proper" (*idion*) to him and "heir." But it should have been we who should be called "sons," since he was made for our sake! Or, clearly, since he is the Son, it is he who is first intended and willed, and it is on his account that he makes us all.[96] But this is simply the vomit and sickness of the heretics.

31. Yet the understanding of truth must not be silenced but given large voice to proclaim especially this point: The Word of God did not come to be on our account but rather it is we who have come into being for his sake and "in him all things were created" (Col 1:16). Nor was it because of our weakness that he was brought into being as one capable of direct creation by the Father alone, just so that the Father may create us by him as by an instrument. Never! This is not true! Even if it was the Father's conception not to make things that come into being, the Word would none the less still be "with God" (Jn 1:1) and the Father "in him" (Jn 10:38, 14:10). But the things that come into being are incapable of becoming apart from the Word. They came to be through him and this makes sense because the Word is the Son of God who belongs (*idios*) to the essence of God by nature and is from him and "in him" (Jn 10:38), as he himself said, and so created things cannot come to be except through him.

Just as the light enlightens all things by its radiance, and apart from the radiance nothing would be enlightened, so also the Father worked all things in the Word, as by a hand,[97] and does nothing without him. So, as Moses tells us, "God said, 'Let there be light'" (Gen 1:3) and "Let the waters be gathered together" (Gen 1:9) and "Let the earth bring forth" (Gen 1:24) and "Let us make man" (Gen 1:26). Likewise, the blessed David also sings in the psalm: "He spoke and they came to be; he commanded and they were created" (Ps 33:9). But "he spoke" not as in the case of human beings, when an assistant hears and learns the wish of the one speaking and goes out and does the work. This is what is proper for created things but to think or speak this about the Word is unsuitable, for the Word of God is Creator and Maker and is himself the Will of the Father.[98] Therefore, Sacred Scripture does not say that the hearer heard and answered, enquiring how and in what manner the speaker wishes those things to come into being, but only that "God said, Let there be" (Gen 1:6) and then it adds, "and so it came to be" (*ibid.*). For that which was conceived and willed immediately came to be and was consummated by the Word. But when God commands angels or others, or converses with Moses, or announces to Abraham, the hearer answers back. One says, "How shall I know?" (Gen 15:8) and the other, "Choose another" (Ex 4:13) and again, "If they ask me what is his name, what shall I say to them?" (Ex 3:13); and the angel said to Zechariah, "thus speaks the Lord" (Zech 1:17), and he also enquired of the Lord, "Lord of hosts, for how long will you be without mercy for Jerusalem?" (Zech 1:12) and he waits to hear "good and comforting words" (Zech 1:13). Each of these receives the Mediator Word and the Wisdom of God which makes known the Father's will. But when the Word himself works and creates, then there is no question and answer, for the Father is in him and the Word is in the Father (cf. Jn 10:38). The willing suffices and the work comes to be; for "he said" is an indication of the willing that is for our sake; whereas "it came to be so" signifies the work which is through the Word and Wisdom, in whom is the will of the Father. And the phrase, "God said," itself implies "in the Word"; for it says, "He made all things in Wisdom" (Ps 104:24), and "by the Word of the Lord the heavens were established" (Ps 33:6) and "one Lord Jesus Christ, through whom all things are and through whom we exist" (1 Cor 8:6).

32. From all this one may conclude that the heretics are not waging the battle concerning this heresy against us; they pretend that we are their target but in fact they are waging war on the divinity itself. If it was our voice that uttered, "This is my son" (Mt 3:17), our censure of them would be a small matter. But if it is the Father's voice which the disciples heard, and the Son himself says

about himself, "Before all the hills he begets me" (Prov 8:25), are they not now waging war against God like the giants of myth, wielding their tongues like sharp swords, as the psalmist said (Ps 57:5), for the sake of impiety? They were not afraid of the Father's voice, nor did they have reverence for the Savior's words, nor are they persuaded by the saints,[99] among whom one writes: "He is the radiance of his glory and the expression of his subsistence (*hypostaseōs*)" (Heb 1:3) and "Christ the power of God and wisdom of God" (1 Cor 1:24) and the psalmist says, "for with you is the fountain of life and in your light we shall see light" (Ps 36:10) and "You made all things in wisdom" (Ps 104:24), and the prophets say, "the Word of the Lord came to me" (e.g. Jer 1:11), while John says, "In the beginning was the Word" (Jn 1:1), and Luke, "Just as those who were eyewitnesses from the beginning and ministers of the Word have handed down to us" (Lk 1:2), and again David says, "He sent his Word and healed them" (Ps 107:20). All these completely banish the Arian heresy, indicating the eternity of the Word and signifying that he is not foreign but proper (*idios*) to the essence of the Father. For when does anyone see light without radiance? Or who dares to say that the expression is alien to the subsistence? Is it not utter madness for someone to even think of God as ever without reason (*alogos*) or without wisdom?[100]

Since human nature is not capable of the comprehension of God, Scripture has placed before us such symbols (*paradeigmata*) and such images (*eikonas*), so that we may understand from them, however slightly and obscurely, as much as is accessible to us. Indeed, the creation is sufficient for the knowledge of God's existence and providence, for "from the greatness and beauty" of the created world "its author, by analogy, is seen" (Wis 13:5). Moreover, we do not learn from creatures by demanding utterances but, upon hearing the Scriptures, we believe, and seeing the very order and harmony of everything, we acknowledge that there is a God and Master and Maker of all these and we apprehend his wonderful providence and governance of all. In the same way the words that have been recited above are sufficient concerning the divinity of the Son. It is superfluous – or rather, utter madness – to doubt and enquire heretically: "How can the Son be eternal?" or "How can he be from the being of the Father and not be a part of him, since what is said to be 'from someone' is a part of him, but what is partitioned is no longer whole?"[101]

33. These are the malicious sophistries of the heterodox. Although we have already refuted the senselessness of their views in

what has been said above, the exactness (*akribeia*) of these scriptural phrases and the meaning indicated by the scriptural symbols (*paradeigmaton*) further refute the ramblings of their defiled doctrine.[102] For we see that reason (*logos*) is always from and belonging to (*idion*) the being of the one whose reason it is, without a "before" or "after." We see also that the radiance is from the sun and belongs to it, while the being of the sun is not thereby divided or lessened, but while the sun's essence is whole, the radiance also is complete and whole and does not lessen the essence of the light but accompanies it as a true offspring from it. So we also see that the Son is not from outside but begotten from his Father; and while the Father remains whole, the expression of his subsistence (cf. Heb 1:3) always endures and preserves an unvarying likeness and image to the Father, so that one who sees him sees in him also the subsistence of which he is the expression. And so from the activity of the expression we perceive the true divinity of the subsistence. The Savior himself also teaches us this, saying: "The Father who abides in me is doing the works which I do" (Jn 14:10; cf. Jn 10:25), and "I and the Father are one" (Jn 10:30), and "I am in the Father and the Father in me" (Jn 14:10).

So let this Christ-fighters heresy first try to insinuate divisions into the examples that refer to created things and let it say: "there was once when the sun was without its radiance," or "the radiance does not belong to the being of the light" or "it belongs to it but is a part of it by division." Or, again, let it divide reason from mind and say that reason is alien to mind or that "it once was not" or that it does not belong to the being of mind or that it is a divisible part of mind. Let it thus make divisions concerning also the expression and the light and the power as it does concerning reason and radiance; and then let it fantasize about whatever it wishes. But if they cannot dare to say such things, are they not really crazy to extend their foolishness to what transcends the things that come into being and even their own nature, and to delve into the impossible?

34. Even with regard to the things that come into being and are corporeal, one finds offspring that are not parts of the essences from which they are and are not passible and do not lessen the beings of their progenitors. If this is so, are they not once again crazed to conjecture and enquire about parts and passibilities in reference to the incorporeal and true God and to ascribe divisions to the impassible and unalterable God – all in order to confound the ears of simpler folk and to turn them away from the truth?[103] For who, upon hearing "Son," does not infer that which belongs (*idios*) to the

being of the Father? Who is there who has heard in his first cate-chism that God has a Son and has made all things by his proper Word and has not received this according to the sense by which we are now conceiving it? When the defilement of the Arian heresy occurred, who did not hear the things they say and immediately banish them as alien and as a sowing that overlies the word sown from the beginning? For it is sown in each soul from the beginning that God has a Son – the Word, Wisdom, and Power – who is his Image and Radiance. From these utterances flow directly the attri-butions of "always" and "from the Father" and "like" and "eternal offspring of the essence." But there is no conception of "creature" or "work" involved in these utterances. It was when the people were sleeping and "the enemy" (Mt 13:25) went over the original sowing and sowed the seeds of "creature" and "there was once when he was not" and "how then can it be?" that the malicious heresy of the Christfighters, like a weed, finally came to be. Immediately there-after, they invade like robbers destitute of all righteous and correct judgment and dare to say: "How can it be that the Son coexists eter-nally with the Father? It takes time for men to beget sons. The father may be thirty years old and then the son is begotten and at that time has a beginning. As a matter of fact, every son of man was not before he was begotten."[104] And they go on whispering: "How can the Son be Word or how can the Word be Image of God? For the word of human beings is composed of syllables and only signi-fies the will of the speaker and then straightaway it is finished and disappears."

35. So they again castigate themselves (cf. 1 Tim 6:10) with chains of impiety and keep arguing, as if having forgotten the refutations with which they were rebuffed before. But the word of truth refutes them thus: If they were arguing about a man, then let them conceive of his word and his son in a human way. But if the argument is about God, the creator of humanity, then let them conceive of him not in a human way but otherwise, as being beyond the nature of human beings. For as is the begetter, then necessarily such is the offspring; and as is the father of the word, such will be his word. So the man who was begotten in time also begets a child in time. And it is because he has come to be from non-being that his word finishes and does not remain. But "God is not as human beings" (Jdt 8:16); this is what Scripture says. Since "he is the existent one" (Ex 3:14) and exists forever, his Word also is existent and is forever with the Father, as the radi-ance of light (Wis 7:26).

Moreover, the word of human beings is composed of syllables and neither lives nor activates anything but only signifies the mind of the speaker. It merely comes and goes and then disappears, since it did not exist at all before it was uttered. So the word of human beings does not live or act, nor is it itself a human being at all. And it undergoes this [extinction], as I said before, because the human being also who begets it has a nature that is from non-being. But the Word of God is not, as it were, a mere enunciation[105] nor is it a sound of utterances nor is the Son God's command. As the radiance of the light, he is the perfect offspring of one who is perfect; therefore he is God and Image of God. For "the Word," it says, "was God" (Jn 1:1). And the words of human beings do not act. Therefore it is not by words but by hands that a human being works, for human hands have subsistence while words do not. But the Word of God, as the apostle said, "is living and active, sharper than any two-edged sword, piercing even between soul and spirit, joints and marrows, and discerns the thoughts and conceptions of the heart. There is no creature that is not manifest before it; all are naked and exposed to the eyes of the one to whom we render account" (Heb 4:12–13). Therefore, he is Creator and "without him nothing came into being" (Jn 1:3), nor can anything come into being without him.

36. But one must not ask: "Why is God's Word not like ours?" For God is not like us, as has been said before. Nor is it appropriate to ask: "How is the Word from God?" and "How is it the radiance of God?" or "How does God beget and what is the manner of his begetting?" One would be crazed to presume to ask such questions and to demand that something ineffable and proper (*idion*) to the nature of God, which is known only to God and to the Son, be explained to him in words. One might as well ask: "Where is God and how does God exist and what sort of existence does the Father have?" Just as to ask such questions is impious and shows ignorance of God, so neither is it legitimate to presume to pose such questions with regard to the generation of the Son of God nor to measure God and his Wisdom by one's own nature and weakness.[106] But neither should one depart from the truth because of this nor should one lose faith in what is written if one is at a loss in enquiring about these matters. It is better to be silent and believe when one is perplexed than to lose faith because of perplexity. The one who is puzzled can be pardoned insofar as he has been silent even while enquiring; but the one who invents what is unsuitable because of his perplexity and so utters things

that are unworthy of God attains a most severe judgment for his presumption. For one can attain some consolation in the face of these perplexities from the divine Scriptures, so as to suitably receive what is written and to contemplate, by way of analogy (*en paradeigmati*),[107] our own word. Just as our word belongs to us and is not a work that is effected from outside of us, so also the Word of God belongs to (*idios*) God, and is from him and not a work; yet it is not like the word of human beings, or else we would have to think that God is human. We see that the words of human beings are many and diverse and are produced every day because the ones before them do not remain but disappear. This happens because their "fathers" are human beings whose seasons pass away and whose thoughts succeed one another. So they speak what they have considered and reconsidered and many words come about and yet afterwards none of them is left; when the speaker stops, his word is immediately extinguished. But the Word of God is one and the same, as it is written, "the Word of God abides forever" (Ps 119:89) and does not alter (cf. Mal 3:6); nor is it antecedent or posterior to any other but exists forever the same. For it was fitting that, since God is one, his Image also is one and his Word is one and his Wisdom is one.

37. So I am amazed that, while God is one, these people introduce, according to their own conceptions, many Images and Wisdoms and Words and say that the proper and natural Word of the Father is something other than the Son. They say that in this Word God made even the Son, while the one who is truly Son is only called Word by way of the conceptions which are associated with him (*kat' epinoian*), as he is called "vine" (Jn 15:1) and "way" (Jn 14:6) and "door" (Jn 10:7) and "tree of life" (Rev 22:14).[108] They say that he is nominally called Wisdom, while there is another Wisdom which is truly so and proper to the Father and which coexists unbegottenly with the Father, in whom also he made the Son and called him Wisdom on account of his participation in that Wisdom.[109] These things have been uttered by them not only in speech but Arius inserted them into the composition of his *Thalia*[110] and Asterius the Sophist wrote these very things which we have reported above, thus:

> The blessed Paul did not say that he preaches *the* Power of God or *the* Wisdom of God (1 Cor 1:24), but omitted the adjoining article [saying], "Power of God and Wisdom of God." Thus he preaches that the proper Power of God,

which is innate and natural to him and coexists unbegottenly with him, is other than Christ, and is of course
generative of Christ and creates the whole world,
concerning whom Paul speaks when he teaches in the
epistle to the Romans: "His invisible things, his eternal
power and divinity, are perceived from the creation of the
world, being understood through the things that are made"
(Rom 1:20). Just as no one would say that the "divinity"
indicated here is Christ – it is the Father himself – so I
think that "his eternal power and divinity" also is not the
only-begotten Son but the Father who begot him. Thus he
teaches that there is another power and wisdom of God
which is manifested through Christ.[111]

And a little later, the same Asterius says:

> Although "his eternal power and wisdom," which the logic
> of truth manifests as without beginning and unbegotten, is
> indeed one and the same, yet many are those which are
> individually created by it, of which Christ is firstborn and
> only-begotten. Yet all are equally dependent on the one
> who procures them. And all are justly called "powers" of
> the one who creates and makes use of them. Thus the
> prophet says that the locust, which comes to be as a
> divinely sent judgment for the sins of human beings, is
> called by God not only "power" but also "great power" (cf.
> Joel 2:25). Moreover, the blessed David, in most of the
> psalms, exhorts not only the angels but also the "powers" to
> praise God (cf. Ps 148:2).[112]

38. Do they not deserve to be completely hated for merely saying
this? For if, as they suppose, he is Son not because of generation
from the Father and as proper (*idion*)[113] to his being, but is called
Word and Reason (*Logos*) because of his relation to rational beings;
and Wisdom because of the things that are made to be wise; and
Power, because of the things that are empowered,[114] then surely he
is called Son because of his relation to those who are made sons!
And perhaps he even has his being merely by way of our conception
of him, on account of his relation to the things that exist.

So then what finally *is* he? For he would not *be* any of these
things if they were nothing but names. In that case, his possession
of being is only phantasmal, since he is endowed with these names

because of us. But this is just diabolical dementia or even worse, since they wish for themselves to truly exist but they consider the Word of God to exist only in name. Is it not quite beyond the pale to say that Wisdom coexists with the Father but to deny that this Wisdom is Christ, and to assert that there are many created powers and wisdoms and that one of these is the Lord, who is compared by them to a caterpillar and a locust? Is it not criminal that when they hear from us that the Word coexists with the Father they immediately complain and allege, "So you say there are two Unbegottens," and yet when they say, "his unbegotten Wisdom," they do not see that they have thus pre-empted us in becoming the object of the accusation that they foolishly alleged against us? And is it not utterly foolish for them to think that the Wisdom which coexists eternally with God is simply God himself? For what coexists does not coexist with itself but with another, as the evangelists say of the Lord that he "was with" (cf. Lk 9:18) the disciples – so he was not with himself but with the disciples.[115] But perhaps they will say that God is composite and has Wisdom as something attached to and intertwined with his own essence, and that this Wisdom is also unbegotten, which they would substitute as creator of the world so as to deprive the Son of creating. For they will exert themselves to say whatever it takes to avoid thinking rightly about the Lord.

39. For where did they ever find it said by the holy Scripture or from whom have they heard that there is another word and another wisdom than this Son, so as to invent such things for themselves? It is indeed written: "Are not my words like fire?" (Jer 23:29). And in the proverbs: "I will teach you my words" (Prov 1:23). But these are ordinances and commands, of which the psalmist says, "I kept my steps from every evil path, that I may guard your words" (Ps 119:101), and which God has spoken to the saints through his proper and only true Word. The Savior indicates that such words are other than himself when he says in his own person: "the words, which I have spoken to you" (Jn 6:63). Such words are not offsprings nor are they sons nor are there many creator-words nor images of the one God nor did those many words become human for our sake. Nor was it one of these many words which, according to John, "became flesh" (Jn 1:14), but it is as the only Word of God that he is preached by John: "The Word became flesh" (Jn 1:14), and "everything came to be through Him" (Jn 1:3). Therefore it is about him alone, our only Lord Jesus Christ, and about his unity with the Father that the testimonies are written and that is what they make manifest – the testimonies of the Father which indicate

that the Son is one, and those of the sacred [writers] who learned this and who say that the Word is one and that he is only-begotten. The works that are accomplished through him are also declared, for "all things visible and invisible" (Col 1:16) "came to be through him and apart from him not one thing came into being" (Jn 1:3). But the sacred writers do not indicate by name or deed any other Word or Wisdom, nor do they conjure up any such thing as that which is identified only by these people. Such an invention and conjecture, which is hostile to Christ, is simply their own. They abuse the name of Word and Wisdom and invent for themselves other words and wisdoms, thus denying the true Word of God and the only existent Wisdom of the Father.

These wretched people end up rivaling the Manichees. For, although they see the works of God, the Manichees deny the only existent and true God and invent another for themselves, of whom they can show neither any deed nor any witness from the sacred writings.[116]

40. Therefore, since there is no other Wisdom to be found in the divine words than this Son, nor have we heard of any such thing from the fathers, while it is acknowledged and written by them that Wisdom's coexistence with the Father is without origin (*agenetos*) and that Wisdom is proper to the Father and is maker of the world, then it must be the Son himself who, even on their own terms, coexists eternally with the Father. For it is he who is Creator, as it is written: "He has made all things in Wisdom" (Ps 104:24). Even Asterius himself seems to have forgotten what he previously wrote when he comes to argue against the Greeks. Acting inadvertently, like Caiaphas (Jn 11:51), he refrains at this point from speaking of many wisdoms or the caterpillar, but ends up confessing only one. Thus he writes, "God the Word is one but rational beings are many; And the being and nature of Wisdom is one but the things that are wise and good are many."[117] A little later, he says again, "Who would those be whom they honor by naming 'children of God'? For they will not say that these also are words nor that there are many wisdoms. For since the Word is one and Wisdom is manifested as one, it is not possible for the being of the Word to be distributed and for the title of Wisdom to be granted to many children."[118]

So it is not at all amazing that the Arians battle against the truth, since they even collide against their own tenets and stumblingly contradict each other, now saying that there are many wisdoms and now affirming only one. At one time, they compare Wisdom to a caterpillar while, at another time, they say that it coexists with the Father and is proper (*idian*) to him.[119] On the one hand, they say that the Father alone is without origin; on the other hand, that his Wisdom and Power are also without origin. They wage battle against us for saying that the Word of God is eternal but then they forget their own words and say that Wisdom coexists with God without origin. So they end up in a complete fuddle about everything and deny the true Wisdom while they invent one that does not exist, just like the Manichees who deny the true God and make for themselves another one.

41. But let the Manichees and the other heresies hear that the Father of Christ is one, who, through his own Word, is also Lord of creation and its Maker. For their part, let the Arian fanatics also hear that there is one Word of God, who is the only proper and genuine Son from the Father's being and who possesses an indivisible unity with his Father, as we have said many times, having learned this from the Savior himself. Indeed if this were not the case, why does the Father create "through him" (Col 1:16) and why is he revealed in him to those whom he wills (Mt 11:27) and whom he enlightens? Why also is the Son named together with the Father in the performance of baptism? It would be impious to say that it is because the Father is not self-sufficient. But if he is self-sufficient (and that is what one should say), why is there any need for the Son, either for the sake of creating or for the holy washing? What partnership is there between the Creator and the creature? Or why is what is made counted together with the Maker in the act whereby we are all perfected (cf. Mt 28:19)?[120] Or why is the faith handed down to us a faith in one Creator and one creature, as you would have it? If it is for the sake of joining us to divinity, what need is there for a creature? But if it is in order to unite us to the Son, while the Son is a creature, then the naming of the Son in baptism is superfluous, according to your account; for the God who made him a son is sufficient likewise to make us sons. Moreover, if the Son is a creature, and the nature of rational creatures is one, then there will be no help to creatures from a creature, since all are in need of grace from God.

We have previously spoken a little on how consistent it is that "all things came to be through him" (Jn 1:3). But since the flow of the argument has moved us to mention holy baptism, it is necessary for me to say what I understand and believe – namely, that the Son is named along with the Father not as if the Father were insufficient, nor as if haphazardly or by chance, but because he is the Word of God and his proper Wisdom and Radiance, who is always with the Father. Therefore it is not possible for the Father to bestow grace except in the Son. For the Son is in the Father as the radiance in the light; not as if God were inadequate, but as Father he "has established the earth in his own Wisdom" (Prov 3:19) and "has made all things by the Word" (Wis 9:1) which is from him, and has established the holy bath securely in the Son. Where the Father is, there is the Son; just as where the light is, there is the radiance. Just as the things that the Father does, he does through the Son and the Lord himself says, "the things that I see my Father doing, these things I also do" (Jn 5:19), so also when baptism is given, the one whom the Father baptizes the Son also baptizes, and the one whom the Son baptizes is perfected in the Holy Spirit. Again, just as when the sun shines one would say also that the radiance sheds light, for the light is one and cannot be broken or separated, so also where the Father is or is named, there also and absolutely is the Son. So it is because the Father is named in baptism that the Son must also be named along with him.

42. Thus, when he bestowed his promise to the saints, he said: "My Father and I will come and make our dwelling with him" (Jn 14:23), and again, "that they may be one in us, as You and I are one" (Jn 17:21, 10:30). The grace that is given is one, which is given from the Father in the Son, as Paul writes in all his epistles, "Grace to you and peace from God our Father and the Lord Jesus Christ" (e.g. Rom 1:7). For the light must be with the ray and the radiance must be seen with its own light. Thus also the Jews, who, like them, "deny the Son do not have the Father either" (1 Jn 2:23). Having "forsaken the fountain of wisdom" (Bar 3:12), as Baruch chastised them, they said "We have no king but Caesar" (Jn 19:15) and thus they removed from their midst the wisdom which is from the fountain, our Lord Jesus Christ, for Christ, says the apostle, is "the power of God and the wisdom of God" (1 Cor 1:24). The Jews have received the penalty for their denial; their reasoning was annulled along with their city.[121] But these ones also end up endangering the very fullness of the mystery; I am speaking now of baptism. If the initiation is given into the name of the Father and the Son, and yet they are not speaking of a true Father since they deny what is from him and like his being and they deny also the true Son and invent for themselves another who is created from non-being, how is the baptism which they administer not completely empty and useless, a mere pretense which in fact is of no aid to piety? For the Arians do not give it "into the Father and the Son" (Mt 28:19) but into Creator and creature and into Maker and

136

made. As a creature is other than the Son, so also what they purport to give is other than the truth, even if they make a pretense of naming the name of the Father and the Son, because this is what is written in the Scripture. But the one who gives the baptism is not simply the one who says, "Lord" (Mt 7:21), but the one who joins calling on the name to holding the right faith. For this reason, therefore, the Lord did not merely command to baptize, but first he says to "teach" and then to "baptize into the name of the Father and the Son and the Holy Spirit" (Mt 28:19), so that right faith may come about through teaching, and the initiation of baptism may be accompanied by faith.[122]

43. There are also many other heresies which merely say the names, as I have said, but not in accordance with right understanding and sound faith. The water given by them is of no benefit and lacks piety, so that the one who is sprinkled by them is rather defiled by impiety than redeemed. Such is the case with the Greeks, who speak of God with their lips, but nevertheless warrant the accusation of godlessness because they do not acknowledge the really existent and true God, the Father of our Lord Jesus Christ. Thus the Manichees and the Phrygians and the disciples of the Samosatene speak the names but are none the less heretics.[123] Thus, afterwards, come finally those who think the way of Arius, who although they read what is written and say the names, merely play games with those who receive baptism from them, and are even more impious than the other heresies and "in a short time, outdid them" (Ezek 16:47) and made them seem righteous in comparison with their own outbursts. For the other heresies falsified some element of the truth, either falling into error regarding the body of the Lord, saying that the Lord did not have flesh from Mary, or that he did not die at all or did not actually become human but that his appearance was not true and that he seemed to have a body but did not and seemed to appear as a human being but it was an illusion, as in a dream. But these ones openly cast their impiety on the Father himself. Having heard from the Scriptures that his divinity is manifested in the Son, as in an image, they yet blaspheme and say that this image is a creature and, like a currency of mud in their wallets, they carry around everywhere their little coined phrase of "was not" and spew it out like snakes spit out their poison. Then, since their doctrine nauseates everyone, they quickly support it with human patronage, like a prop against its downfall, so that those who are more simple may see it or even become frightened by it and ignore the harm caused by their evil thinking.[124]

Are not those who are deceived by them worthy of pity? Is it not proper to weep over those, who through regard for the present, because of concern for pleasures, give up what is beneficial to themselves and fall away from the hope of what is to come? For by intending to receive baptism into what is not, they have received nothing at all; and being aligned with a creature they will have no help from the creation.[125] And believing in what is unlike (*anomoion*) and other than the Father in being, they will not be conjoined with the Father, not having his proper Son who is from him by nature, who "is in the Father, and in whom the Father is" (Jn 14:10), as he himself said. But being deceived by them, they remain destitute and end up being stripped of divinity, the wretched ones. The apparitions that belong to this earth will not follow them when they die, nor will they be able to call to their aid any of those who now deceive them when they see the Lord whom they denied sitting upon the throne of his Father and judging the living and the dead. Indeed, they will see their deceivers also being judged and repenting for their unrighteousness and impiety.

44. We have taken up these points at such length and have countered the irrational fabrications which they have devised in their hearts before dealing with the passage of the Proverbs, so that they may recognize that it is not fitting to call the Son of God a creature and may thus learn to read correctly the passage in the Proverbs, according to its right sense.[126] It is written: "The Lord created me as a beginning of His ways, for his works" (Prov 8:22). But since these are proverbs, and are spoken proverbially and by way of parable,[127] one must not take the passage in question simply at face value but rather enquire as to the person (*prosopon*) and thus piously accommodate the sense to the person. For what is spoken in the Proverbs is not spoken plainly but proclaimed in a hidden manner, as the Lord himself taught in the Gospel according to John, saying: "I have spoken to you these things in parables (*en paroimiais*). The hour is coming when I will no longer speak to you in parables but plainly" (Jn 16:25). Therefore we must uncover the sense of the passage and enquire into it as something hidden and not simply take it as spoken plainly, lest we misinterpret it and be led astray from the truth. If what is written were in reference to an angel or to any other of the things that come into being or to one of us, who are made, then let it simply be said: "He created." But if it is the Wisdom of God, in whom all the things that come into being are fashioned, who speaks about herself, how must this be understood except that in saying "he created" she is saying nothing contrary to

"he begot"?[128] It is not as if she is forgetting that she is Creator and Fashioner or as if she were ignorant of the difference between Creator and creatures that she counts herself among creatures, but she is signifying a certain hidden sense, not plainly, but as in a parable. She declares this sense in prophecy through the biblical saints, but a little later she also indicates the meaning of "He created" in a parallel way, using other words, when she says, "Wisdom has built herself a house" (Prov 9:1). Clearly, the house of Wisdom is our body, in the taking of which Wisdom became human.[129] So it is fittingly said by John: "The Word became flesh" (Jn 1:14), and through Solomon, Wisdom speaks about herself with precision inasmuch as she does not say, "I *am* a creature," but only that "the Lord created me as a beginning of his ways, for his works" (Prov 8:22); not "He created me into being," nor "I have the beginning and generation of a creature."

45. In this passage, the Word spoke thus through Solomon not as signifying the essence of his divinity nor his eternal and genuine generation from the Father, but rather his humanity and accommodation (*economia*) for our sake. Therefore, as I mentioned, he did not say "I am a creature" or "I came into being as a creature" but only "He created." For creatures come into being and have a created essence and are said to be created; and of course, a creature is simply created as such. But the phrase, "He created," does not of itself simply signify the being or the generation, but can indicate that something else comes to be in reference to the one who is spoken of as "created" and not simply that such a one *is* a creature by nature and being.[130]

The divine Scripture is aware of this difference, speaking of creatures thus: "The earth is filled with your creation" (Ps 104:24); and "creation laments together and is in travail" (Rom 8:22); while in the Apocalypse, it says: "A third of the creatures living in the sea died" (Rev 8:9). Likewise, Paul also says, "Every creature of God is good, and nothing is to be rejected which is received with thanksgiving" (1 Tim 4:4). And it is written, in Wisdom: "And in your Wisdom you fashioned humanity to rule over the creatures which you made" (Wis 9:2). Since these are creatures, they are said to be created; thus we hear the Lord saying, "From the beginning the Creator made them male and female" (Mt 19:4, Gen 1:27, 5:2). And Moses writes in the song: "Ask of the days that have gone before you, since the day in which God created humanity upon the earth; ask from one end of the sky to the other" (Deut 4:32). And Paul says in the epistle to the Colossians: "He is the Image of the invisible God, the firstborn of all creation. For in him all things were created both in heaven and on earth, the visible and the invisible, whether thrones or dominions or principalities or powers. All things were created through him and for him, and he is before all" (Col 1:15–17).

46. These examples suffice as a reminder of what is pervasive throughout the Scriptures, namely, that those who have a created essence by nature are called creatures and are said to be created. However, that the phrase, "He created," does not of itself at all signify the essence and the generation, we have the example of David in the psalm: "Let this be written for another generation and the created people will praise the Lord" (Ps 102:19). And again: "A pure heart create in me, O God" (Ps 51:12). And Paul says in his epistle to the Ephesians: "Having abolished the law of commandments contained in decrees, so that he may create of the two one new human being in himself" (Eph 2:15).[131] And again: "Put on the new human being, created in God's pattern, in holiness and in the righteousness of truth" (Eph 4:24). Now, David was not speaking of a people who are created, so far as their very being and essence are concerned, nor was he praying to receive another heart than the one he had, but he was indicating rather a godly renewal and renovation. Paul also was not indicating that the two are created [into one] in the Lord, as far as their being is concerned, nor was he counseling us to put on some other humanity. But in speaking of the human being who is "[created] in God's pattern" he was speaking of the virtuous life, and in speaking of those who are created in Christ, he meant the two peoples who are renewed in him.[132] The same goes for the saying of Jeremiah: "The Lord created a new salvation for planting, in which humanity will walk" (Jer 38:22, LXX). In saying this, he is not referring to the very essence of a creature but is prophesying about the renewal of salvation among humanity that has come to be for us in Christ.

Such is the difference between the creatures and the mere saying of "He created"! So, if you do find anywhere in the divine Scripture that the Lord is called a creature, show it and fight on. But if it is not written anywhere that he *is* a creature, though he says about himself in the Proverbs, "He created me," then let the distinction that has been indicated and the fact that the words were spoken proverbially both stand to your shame. In short, you are not to take the phrase, "He created," as if it were equivalent to "creature" but as referring to his becoming human, for being created properly pertains to this humanity. Indeed, is it not unjust that when you hear "He created" from David and Paul you do not understand it to refer to being and generation but to renewal, yet when you hear it from the Lord you count his essence among the creatures? Again, when you hear, "Wisdom built herself a house and set up seven pillars" (Prov 9:1), you allegorize the "house" but you take "He created" as it is and change it into "creature." The fact that he is the Creator does not shame you, nor does his being the only proper offspring of the Father intimidate you. But it is as if you are just set on enlisting in the ranks against him and you keep fighting on and thinking less of him than of human beings.

47. Even the passage itself shows that to say that the Lord is a creature is merely an invention of yours. For the Lord, knowing his own being as the only begotten Wisdom and offspring of the Father who is other than the things that come to be and other than those who are creatures by nature, here says in his love for humanity, "The Lord created me as a beginning of his ways." This is the same as saying, "The Father 'has prepared a body for me' (Heb 10:5) and has created me for the sake of human beings and for their salvation." Likewise, when we hear John saying, "the Word became flesh" (Jn 1:14), we do not understand that the Word himself is wholly flesh but that he has put on flesh and become human; and when we hear that "Christ became a curse for us" (Gal 3:13), and that "He made the one who did not know sin to be sin for us" (2 Cor 5:21), we do not understand that he himself has entirely come into being as a curse and sin but that he took upon himself the curse which was against us, as the apostle says, "having redeemed us from the curse" (Gal 3:13), and "carried" our sins, as Isaiah said (Isa 53:4) and as Peter wrote, "He bore them in his body on the wood" (1 Pet 2:24). So also when we hear in the Proverbs, "He created," we must not understand that the Word is wholly creature by nature, but that he put on the created body and that God created him for our sake, "having prepared" a created body for him, as it is written (Heb 10:5), so that we may be enabled to be renewed and deified in him.

What then has deceived you, you mindless people, to say that the Creator is a creature? Or from where did you procure for yourselves this cheap way of thinking that you put on parade? For the Proverbs do indeed say, "He created"; yet they do not say that the Son is a creature, but an offspring. And according to the aforementioned distinction, drawn from the Scriptures – I mean between "He created" and "creature" – the Scriptures acknowledge, on the one hand, what is proper to the Son by nature, that he is the only-begotten Wisdom and fashioner of creatures; and, on the other hand, they say "He created" not with reference to his being, but as signifying his becoming a beginning of many ways, so that "He created" (Prov 8:22) is contrasted with "offspring" (cf. Prov 8:25), and his being said to be "a beginning of ways" (Prov 8:22) is in contrast to his being the only-begotten Word (cf. Jn 1:1).

48. For if he is an offspring, how can you say that he is a creature? No one who creates something says that he begets it (cf. Prov 8:25), nor does anyone call his own offspring creatures. Yet again, if he is only-begotten, how does he come to be "beginning of the ways"? If he was created as the first of all things, then it necessarily follows that he is no longer unique since there are others created after him. So even though Reuben came to be the "first of the children" (Gen 49:3), he was not only-begotten. He was first with respect to time, but in nature and kinship he was simply one among those who came after him. Therefore, if the Word also is the "beginning of the ways," then he must be just as the "ways" are and the "ways" must be the same as he is, even if he is created as the first of them with respect to time. For the origin and foundation of a city is like the other parts of a city which, in turn, are conjoined with the foundation to form one single whole city, as "one body of many members" (Rom 12:4). It is not that one part of the city is a maker, while another part comes to be and is subject to it, but the whole city is equally constituted by its maker and is equally the object of its maker's attention. Therefore, if it is in this way that the Lord is created as a beginning of all, then he, together with all the rest, form a single creation and he does not differ from the others, even if he is the beginning of all, nor is he their Lord, even if he is older in time. Along with all, he also would have one Lord and Word, who brings about his creation.

So if he is a creature, as you say, how is it at all possible for him to be created as unique and first, so as to be the beginning of all, since it is clear from what has been said that no one among the creatures is first and of itself unique, but everything has the same origination as all the rest, even if one "differs in glory" (cf. 1 Cor 15:41) from the others? For among the stars and great lights, one did not appear first and another second, but all were called into being in the same day and by the same command. The same goes for the origination of beasts and birds and fish and cattle and plants, and the race of human beings which is in God's image. For even if Adam was alone formed from the earth, nevertheless the seeds (*logoi*) of the whole succession of the race were contained in him.

49. "From the visible creation of the world, we perceive the invisible things that are understood by means of the things that are made" (Rom 1:20), and we perceive that among these invisible things also, none is altogether unique nor is one first and another second, but they were all constituted at once, each according to their kind.[133] For the apostle did not count each individually, so as to say, "whether angel or throne or dominion or authority," but all together, according to rank: "whether angels or archangels or principalities" (Col 1:16); for such is the origination of creatures. But, as I said, if the Word was a creature, then he must have come into being not first, but together with the other powers, even if he far exceeds the others in glory. Thus also among the other creatures one finds that while they have come to be at once and there is no first or second, they yet differ from each other in glory (cf. 1 Cor 15:41); some are on the right, some on the left, others all around, and all stand and chant together, ministering to the Lord. Therefore, if the Word is a creature, he would not be first, nor the beginning of the others. But if he is "before all things" (Col 1:17), which indeed he is, and is alone first and Son, then he is not, in his being, the "beginning of all things." For the beginning of all things is counted together with all things. But if he is not a beginning nor a creature, then clearly, as far as his being and nature, he stands apart from creatures and is other than they are, being the likeness (*homoiosis*) and image of the only true God, and is himself unique and one.

For this reason, therefore, the Scriptures do not count him together with the creatures. Rather, David chastises those who would dare to even think such a thing, saying: "Who is like you among the gods, O Lord?" (Ps 89:9) and "who will be likened to the Lord among the sons of God?" (Ps 89:7). And Baruch: "This is our God; none other is to be counted with him" (Bar 3:36). For he creates, but they are created; he is proper Word and Wisdom of the Father's being, but the things that have come to be did not exist before they were made through this Word.

50. So your notorious statement that the Son is a creature is not true but only a fantasy of yours and Solomon denounces you for having falsified him so often. For he did not call the Son a creature but God's offspring and wisdom, saying, "God established the earth by wisdom" (Prov 3:19), and "Wisdom built herself a house" (Prov 9:1). Moreover, the passage in question itself refutes your impiety. It is written: "The Lord created me as a beginning of his ways for His works" (Prov 8:22). Therefore, if he is "before all things" (Col 1:17) and yet he says, "He created me" – not "in order that I may make

the works" but "for the works" – then either the event signified in "he created" is posterior to him, or it will turn out that he is posterior to the works.[134] According to the latter case, it is as if when he is created he finds these works already constituted before him, for the sake of which he then comes to be. But if the latter is the case, how is he still "before all things" (Col 1:17)? And how did all things come to be through him (Jn 1:3) and have their consistence in him (Col 1:17)? According to you, the works would have had their consistence before him and he is created and sent for their sake.

But it is not so; never! The thinking of the heretics is false. The Word of God is not a creature but Creator. It is when he puts on the created flesh that he says, in the manner of a proverb, "He created me." Moreover, there is something else that can be understood from this very passage: Being Son, and having God as his Father – for he is his proper offspring – he nevertheless now calls the Father "Lord," not because he was a servant but because he "took the form of a servant" (Phil 2:7). For it was fitting that just as in being the Word from the Father he calls God "Father" – for this is proper to a son in relation to a father – so in coming to "complete the work" (Jn 4:34) and taking the form of a servant he calls the Father "Lord." He taught this difference himself in the gospels and made an apposite distinction when he said first: "I thank you, Father," and then, "Lord of heaven and earth" (Mt 11:25, Lk 10:21). Thus he says that God is his Father but also calls him Lord of the creatures, in order to show clearly that it is when he puts on what is created that he calls the Father "Lord."[135] The Holy Spirit indicates the same distinction in the prayer of David when it says in the psalm: "Give your strength to your child and save the son of your handmaid" (Ps 86:16). For the one who is true child of God by nature is other than the children of the handmaid, which is the nature of the things that come into being. Therefore, as Son, he has the strength of the Father, whereas they are in need of salvation.

51. But if it is because he was called a child that they blabber so, let them know that Isaac too was called the child of Abraham (Gen 21:7) and the son of the Shunamite woman was called a little child (2 Kings 4:18). Since we are servants, it was fitting that when he became as we are, he also calls the Father "Lord," just as we do. He did this out of his love for humanity, so that we who are servants by nature may receive the Spirit of the Son and so have the courage to call "Father" by grace the one who is our Lord by nature (cf. Gal 4:6). Just as when we call the Lord "Father," we do not deny our

servanthood according to nature – for we are his work and "he made us and not we ourselves" (Ps 100:3) – so also, when the Son takes the form of a servant (Phil 2:7) and says "the Lord created me," let them not deny the eternity of his divinity and that "in the beginning was the Word" (Jn 1:1) and "all things came to be through him" (Jn 1:3) and "in him all things were created" (Col 1:16).

So the passage in the Proverbs, as I said before, does not signify the essence but the humanity of the Word. In saying that he was created "for the works," he clearly wishes to signify not his own essence but the economy that came to be for the sake of the works and which is secondary to being. For the things that come to be and are created are made primarily for the sake of being and existence, and only secondarily for doing, according to what the Word commands them. We see this with all things. Adam was created not in order to work but first of all in order that he may be a human being; after that he received the command to work. Noah was created not for the sake of the ark, but first of all in order that he may exist and be a human being; after that he received the command to build the ark. Anyone who looks into the matter will find that it is the same with all people. Even the great Moses first became a human being and then was entrusted with the government of the people. Therefore here too the same must be understood. You can see that the Word did not come into being by being created but "in the beginning was the Word" (Jn 1:1) and after this he was sent "for the works" and the economy pertaining to them. Before the works came to be, the Son forever was and there was no need yet of his being created. But when the works were created and when the need arose afterwards for the economy of their restoration, then it was that the Word gave himself to condescension (*eis to sunkatabēnai*) and to becoming like (*homoiōthēnai*) the works. This is what he indicates to us by the phrase, "He created." Wishing to signify the same through the prophet Isaiah, he again says: "And now thus says the Lord, who formed me as his servant from the womb, to gather together to him Jacob and Israel. I will be gathered together and I will be glorified before the Lord" (Isa 49:5).

52. With reference to this last passage also, it is not that he enters into being by being "formed" but he comes to be formed for the sake of gathering together the tribes that were already in existence before he was formed. "He created" in that passage is like "He formed" in this one; "for the works" there is like "to gather together" here, so that on all accounts it is manifest that "He

created" and "He formed" are spoken of him with reference to what is posterior to the Word's existence. Just as the tribes for the sake of which he was formed already existed before he was formed, so also the works for which he was created are shown to have been already in existence. When "in the beginning was the Word" (Jn 1:1), there was not yet any works, as I said before; but when the works came to be and the need demanded it, then it is said, "He created." It is like a son who is sent by his father to retrieve and gather together some slaves who are being destroyed by enemies through their own carelessness, in a situation in which the need is pressing. He goes out, wearing the same clothes as the slaves and taking on the same appearance so that their captives may not recognize him as the master and then flee and prevent his descending to the servants whom they have hidden under the earth. Then if somebody were to enquire of him why he did this, he would say: "My father has formed me and prepared me in this way for his works." In saying this, he is not signifying that he himself is a servant nor that he is one of the works nor is he speaking of the beginning of his coming to be, but of the task that was later given to him for the sake of the works. Likewise, when the Lord put on our flesh and "was found in human appearance" (Phil 2:7), if he were asked by those who saw him thus and became amazed, he would say: "The Lord created me as the beginning of his ways for his works" (Prov 8:22), and "He formed me to gather together Israel" (Isa 49:5).

The Spirit also declared this beforehand in the psalms when it said, "You have appointed him over the works of your hands" (Ps 8:7). And the Lord himself indicates the same about himself when he says, "I have been appointed king by him over Zion, his holy mountain" (Ps 2:6). He did not have a beginning of his being nor a beginning of his kingdom when he shone bodily in Zion. But being the Word of God and eternal King, he resolved that his kingdom should shine in Zion in a human way, so that he may redeem them and us from "the reign of sin in them" (cf. Rom 5:21) and bring us under his Father's kingdom. Likewise, when he was appointed "for the works," it was not for the sake of what did not yet exist but for what already existed and was in need of restoration.

53. Thus, his being "created," "formed," and "appointed" all have the same meaning. They indicate not the beginning of his being, nor that his essence is created, but the renewal that came to be for our sake through his bounty. Therefore, while he says those things, he nevertheless also taught that he existed before all that when he said: "Before Abraham came to be, I am" (Jn 8:58) and

"When he prepared the heavens, I was with him" (Prov 8:27) and "I was arranging with him" (Prov 8:30). So he existed before Abraham came to be while Israel came to be after Abraham. It is clear then that he pre-existed and was later "formed," so that his being formed does not signify the beginning of his being but his becoming human, in which he gathered together the tribes of Israel. Likewise, he is always with the Father as the fashioner of creation and it is clear that the works of creation are posterior to him, and "created" indicates not the beginning of his being but the economy which came about for the sake of the works and which he actualized in the flesh. For it was fitting that he who is other than the works of creation and rather their fashioner should take up their renewal in himself so that, in his being created for us, he may recreate all things in himself.[136] So when he says "created," he immediately adds the reason, which he says is "the works," in order to clarify that his being created for the works is his becoming human for their renewal.

This then is the manner of Divine Scripture: When it refers to the origination of the Word according to the flesh, it points out also the reason why he became human. But when he speaks about his divinity and when his servants proclaim this divinity, then everything is said in simple terms and in an unqualified sense and without any reason added.[137] For he is the radiance of the Father. Just as the Father does not exist for a certain reason, so also one must not seek a reason for his radiance. "In the beginning was the Word and the Word was with God, and the Word was God" (Jn 1:1); so it is written and no "why" is given. But when "the Word became flesh" (Jn 1:14), then the reason is given why he came, saying, "and he dwelt among us." Again, when the apostle says, "who is in the form of God" (Phil 2:6) he does not give a reason; but when "he took the form of a servant" (Phil 2:7), then he provides a reason, saying, "He emptied himself unto death, even death on a cross" (Phil 2:8). It was for this reason that he both became flesh and took the form of a servant.

54. The Lord himself has said many things in proverbs, but in referring to himself, he spoke without qualification: "I am in the Father and the Father in me" (Jn 14:10) and "I and the Father are one" (Jn 10:30) and "The one who sees me has seen the Father" (Jn 14:9) and "I am the light of the world" (Jn 8:12) and "I am the truth" (Jn 14:6). He does not append to each of these sayings the reason and the "what for," lest it may seem that he is secondary to those for whose sake he came into being. Such a reason would then

necessarily take precedence over him, and apart from this reason he would not even have come to be. Thus Paul, who "was set apart as an apostle for the sake of the gospel, which the Lord promised beforehand through the prophets" (Rom 1:1), was secondary to the gospel, of which he "became a minister" (Eph 3:7). And John, who was chosen to prepare the way of the Lord, was secondary to the Lord. But the Lord did not have any antecedent reason for his being Word, except only that he is the Father's offspring and only-begotten Wisdom. However, when he becomes a human being, then he offers the reason for which he intends to put on flesh. For what preceded his becoming human was humanity's need, apart from which he would not have put on flesh. What this need was, for the sake of which he became human, the Lord himself indicates, saying: "I have come down from heaven, not in order to do my will but the will of the one who sent me. And this is the will of the one who sent me, that I may not lose anything of what he has given me, but may raise it up on the last day. For this is the will of my Father, that everyone who sees the Son and believes in him should have eternal life and I will raise him up on the last day" (Jn 6:38–40). And again, "I have come as light into the world, so that everyone who believes in me may not remain in darkness" (Jn 12:46). Yet again he says: "For this I have been born and for this I have come into the world, to witness to the truth" (Jn 18:37). And John has written: "The Son of God was manifested in order that he may destroy the works of the devil" (1 Jn 3:8).

55. The Savior came in order to give witness and submit to death for our sake and raise up humanity and "destroy the works of the devil" (1 Jn 3:8).[138] This is the reason for his incarnate presence. There would have been no resurrection if there was no death. But how could the death have taken place if he did not have a mortal body? Having learned this from him, Paul said: "Since the children have shared in flesh and blood, he also equally shared in them, so that by death he might abolish the one who had the power of death, that is, the devil, and deliver those who through fear of death were subject to slavery all their life" (Heb 2:14–15). And "since death came through a human being, the resurrection also came through a human being" (1 Cor 15:21), and again, "For what was impossible for the law, in that it had been weakened through the flesh, God has done; by sending his own Son in the likeness of sinful flesh and for the sake of sin, he condemned sin in the flesh that the decree of the Law might be fulfilled in us who walk not according to the flesh but according to the Spirit" (Rom 8:3–4). And John says, "God did

not send his Son into the world in order to condemn the world but so that the world may be saved through him" (Jn 3:17). Again, the Savior says himself: "I have come into the world for judgment, so that those who do not see may see and those who see may become blind" (Jn 9:39). So he did not come for his own sake but for our salvation and for the banishment of death and the condemnation of sin and for the renewal of sight to the blind and the raising of all from the dead. But if he came not for his own sake but for ours, then neither was he created for his own sake but for ours. And if he was not created for his own sake but for ours, then he is not a creature but says these things in reference to his putting on our flesh.

That this is the sense of the Scriptures one can learn from the apostle, who says in the epistle to the Ephesians: "Having broken down the dividing wall of enmity in his flesh, abolishing the law of commands set down in decrees, in order to create in himself the two into one new human being" (Eph 2:14–15). But if the two are created in him and in his body, then it follows that he himself is created insofar as he bears these two in himself. He united those who were created in him and he was in them and they in him. Because the two were thus created in him, it is appropriate that he says, "the Lord created me." In the same way, when he takes upon himself our weakness he is said to be weak himself, although he is not himself weak, for he is "the power of God" (1 Cor 1:24). And he became sin for us and a curse, although he himself did not sin, because he bore our sins and our curse (cf. 2 Cor 5:21, Gal 3:13). So also when he creates us in himself, let him say, "He created me for the works," although he is not himself a creature.

56. According to them, it is because the being of the Word is created that he, as a creature, says, "the Lord created me." But in that case, he was not created for us and if he was not created for us, then we were not created in him. And if we were not created in him, then we do not have him in ourselves, but extrinsically (*eksōthen*), as having received instruction from him as from a teacher. But if that is the case with us, then the reign of sin in the flesh would remain internal to us and would not be expelled from the flesh (cf. Rom 5:21).[139] However, the apostle opposes such thoughts shortly before when he asserts: "For we are his work, created in Christ Jesus" (Eph 2:10). If we were created in Christ, then it is not he who is created, but we who are created in him. Therefore, the term "created" is on our account for it is because of our need that the Word, although he is Creator, submitted to the term which designates the creatures and which is not proper to him, insofar as

he is Word, but is proper to us who are created in him. The Father is everlasting, and his Word is also everlasting and, being everlasting, he says: "I was his delight every day, rejoicing before him" (Prov 8:30) and "I am in the Father and the Father is in me" (Jn 14:10). But when he became human because of our need, he, like we, fittingly says of himself what applies to us – "the Lord created me" – so that by his indwelling of the flesh, sin would be perfectly extricated from the flesh and we would have a free mind.

What, indeed, should he have said when he became human: "In the beginning I was human"? That would not be fitting for him nor would it be true. Just as it was not appropriate for him to say this, so it was fitting and proper to say of his humanity that it was "created," and "He made him." That is why the cause of his being "created" is added, which is the need of "the works." When the cause is added, surely this addition itself provides a good explication of the text. So while in reference to "created," he indicates the cause, which is "the works," he signifies the generation from the Father without qualification, adding immediately: "Before all the hills, He begets me" (Prov 8:25). He does not add the reason why – as in regard to "created," he said, "for the works" – but he says without qualification, "He begets me," just as it says without qualification, "In the beginning was the Word" (Jn 1:1). For even if the works had not been created, the Word of God still was and the "Word was God" (Jn 1:1) but his becoming human would not have taken place if the need of humanity had not become a cause. So the Son is not a creature. If he were a creature, he would not have said, "He begets me" (Prov 8:25), for creatures are works of the maker and external to their maker, but the offspring is not from outside, like a work, but is from the Father and proper to his essence. Therefore, they are creatures but he is the Word of God, the only-begotten Son.

57. Moses certainly did not say about the creation that "in the beginning he begot" it nor that "in the beginning, it was," but "in the beginning God *made* heaven and earth" (Gen 1:1). Nor did David say in the psalm, "Your hands begot me," but he says "made me" (Ps 119:73) and he always says "made" when speaking of creatures. But in reference to the Son, it is the reverse. He did not say "I made" but "I begot" and "He begets me" (cf. Ps 2:7, 110:3, Prov 8:25) and "my heart has poured forth a good word" (Ps 45:2). In reference to creation, "in the beginning he made" (Gen 1:1), but in reference to the Son, "in the beginning was the Word" (Jn 1:1).

This is the difference: the creatures are made at the beginning and have a beginning to their being that is constituted by an interval,[140] and so it is said of them, "in the beginning he made [them]." That is the same as saying that "he made [them] from the beginning," just as the Lord taught when he shamed the Pharisees, saying, "From the beginning the one who created them made them male and female" (Mt 19:4), and the Lord knows what he made. For it is from a certain beginning of non-being that the things that come to be were then brought into being and created. The Holy Spirit indicated this in the psalms, when it said: "Lord, you established the earth at the beginning" (Ps 102:26). And again: "Remember your flock, which you have acquired from the beginning" (Ps 74:2). It is clear that what came to be "at the beginning" has the beginning of being created, and that God acquired the flock at a certain beginning. Moses himself makes it clear that when he says "he made in the beginning" (Gen 1:1), the word "made" means "began to make." He says that after the completion of all things "God blessed the seventh day and sanctified it, because in it he rested from all his works, which God began to make" (Gen 2:3). As far as creatures are concerned, therefore, they "began" to be brought into being. But the Word of God, not having a beginning of being, accordingly did not begin to be and did not begin to come into being, but always was. The works of creation have a beginning in their being made and this beginning leads them forth in their coming into being. But the Word is not among those that come into being but rather becomes himself the fashioner of the things which have a beginning. Moreover, the being of things that come into being is measured out in becoming;[141] and at a certain beginning God began to make them through the Word, so that it may be known that these things were not before their becoming. But the Word does not have his being in any other beginning but in the Father who, according to them also, is without beginning. Therefore, he also, as offspring of the Father, is in the Father, without beginning (*anarchos*), and is not the Father's creature.[142]

58. That is how Holy Scripture conceives the difference between the offspring and the things that are made. It shows that the offspring is the Son, who did not begin at a certain beginning but is eternal. On the other hand, it indicates that what is made is a work which is extrinsic to its maker and has a beginning of its coming into being. Thus also John, theologizing about the Son and knowing the difference between the terms, did not say, "In the beginning he became" or "was made" but "In the beginning was the

Word" (Jn 1:1), so that everyone may conceive the offspring in association with this term "was," and no one may conceive of him in association with an interval, but rather believe that the Son exists forever and eternally.

In light of this evidence, how is it, you Arians, that you do not understand the words of Deuteronomy and here also you dare to be impious toward the Lord and to say that he is still a work or a creature even if he is an offspring? You allege that "offspring" and "work" signify the same thing. But in this also you will be shown to be no less ignorant than impious. The first passage is this: "Is he not your father who acquired you and made you and created you?" (Deut 32:6). And a little later in the same song, it says: "You abandoned the God who begot you and you forgot the God who fed you" (Deut 32:18).[143] But in fact there is a very wonderful meaning contained here. For "begot" does not come first, as if it was undifferentiated from "made." Had it been so, they would have had an excuse to say: "Though Moses tells us that God said at the beginning, 'Let us make humanity' (Gn 1:26), he also later says, 'You abandoned the one who begot you' (Deut 32:18). So the terms 'make' and 'begot' are not distinct, and an offspring is just the same as a work." The actual passage, however, manifests its true meaning in the fact that it is only after "he acquired" and "he made" that Moses finally adds, "he begot." By "made" he does in fact signify what pertains to the nature of human beings, namely that they are works and made. But by "begot" he indicates God's love for humanity that came to human beings *after* he created them. Because they became ungrateful for this, Moses rebukes them, at first saying, "Do you thus repay the Lord?" (Deut 32:6). Then, he adds: "Is he not your Father who acquired you and made you and created you?" (*ibid.*). Following this, he says: "They sacrificed to demons and not to God, to gods they did not know. New gods, newcomers, rose up, whom their fathers did not know. You abandoned the God who begot you" (Deut 32:17–18).

59. For God did not only create them as human beings but he also begot them and called them "sons." Here also, "begot" signifies "son," as he says through the prophet, "I begot sons and exalted them" (Isa 1:2). In general, when Scripture wishes to signify "son," it does so not by the word "created" but, of course, by the word "begot." This is also apparent when John says: "He granted them authority to *become* children of God, begotten not from blood nor from the will of the flesh nor from the will of man, but from God" (Jn 1:12–13). There is great precision here also; he says "become"

because they are called sons not by nature but by dispensation and he says "begotten" because they have also nevertheless received the name of "son," even though, as the prophet says, the people "despised" their benefactor (Isa 1:2). Yet the love of God for humanity is such that by grace he becomes Father of those in relation to whom he had previously only been Maker. He becomes their Father when created human beings receive "into their hearts the Spirit of the Son, crying out, 'Abba, Father'" (Gal 4:6), as the apostle says. These are the ones who, by receiving the Word, receive authority from him "to become children of God" (Jn 1:12). Being creatures by nature, they would not become "sons" except by receiving the Spirit of the natural and true Son. So it was in order to bring this about and to make humanity receptive of divinity that "the Word became flesh" (Jn 1:14).

One can learn the same meaning from the prophet Malachai when he says, "Has not one God created us? Is there not one Father of us all?" (Mal 2:10). Here again, he puts "created" first and then "Father," in order that he also may show that whereas from the beginning we were creatures by nature and God is our Creator through the Word, later we were made sons and from then on the Creator God becomes also our Father. Therefore the Father properly belongs to (*idion*) the Son and it is not the creature but the Son who properly belongs (*idion*) to the Father. So it is demonstrated here also that we are not sons by nature but the Son who is in us is. Likewise, God is not by nature our Father but Father of the Word who is in us, in whom and through whom we cry, "Abba, Father" (Rom 8:15). Accordingly, the Father calls "sons" those in whom he sees his own Son and he says "I begot" since "begetting" signifies "son," while "making" is indicative of the works. Therefore, we are not begotten first but made, for it is written, "Let us *make* humanity" (Gen 1:26). But when we later receive the grace of the Spirit, we are henceforth said to be also begotten. Therefore, the great Moses certainly speaks with aptness in his song when he first says "acquired" and then "begot" so that those who hear "begot" may not forget their original nature but may recognize that while they are creatures from the beginning, they are said to be begotten as sons by grace, even though human beings are still none the less made, as far as their nature is concerned.

60. In fact, in the Proverbs themselves the Lord himself shows that creature and offspring are not the same but differ from each other both in nature and in the signification of the terms. After he said "the Lord created me as a beginning of his ways" (Prov 8:22),

he went on to add "But before all the hills, he begets me" (Prov 8:25). But if the Word was a creature by nature and being, and there was no difference[144] between creature and offspring, he would not have added "He begets me." The fact that he had said "created" would have been already sufficient if the meaning of that word was simply equivalent to "begot." As it is, having said "He created me as the beginning of his ways for his works" (Prov 8:22), he did not merely add, "He begets me" (Prov 8:25), but also the adjoining conjunction "but," as if thereby safeguarding the distinction of the term "created." So he says, "But before all the hills He begets me." The phrase "begets me," closely following upon "created," makes the meaning coherent and shows that, while "created" is said with a view to a cause, "begets me" precedes "created." If conversely he had said first "the Lord begets me," and then added "but before all things he created me," then surely "created" would precede "begot." So, having first said "created" and then added "before all the hills he begets me," he indubitably shows that "begot" precedes "created."

Moreover, in saying "Before all things be begets me," he signifies that he is other than all things, since we have previously demonstrated[145] the truth that among creatures none preceded another but all the things that come to be subsisted at once and all together by one and the same command. For this reason the words that come after "created" are not the same as those after "begets me." After "created" comes "as a beginning of the ways," but after "He begets me," he does not say "He begets me as a way" but "before all things he begets me." However, what is before all things is not the beginning of all things but other than all things. But if he is other than all things, and the beginning of all things is contained within the category of "all things," then obviously he is other than creatures. It becomes quite clear therefore that the Word, being other than all things and before all things, is later created "a beginning of the ways for the works" through his humanization, so that, as the apostle says, "He is the beginning, the firstborn from the dead, so that in all things he might be pre-eminent" (Col 1:18).

61. This then is the difference between "He created" and "He begets me" and between "the beginning of the ways" and "before all things." Therefore, God, who is the Creator of human beings, as has been said, later becomes their Father because of his Word dwelling in them. But with the Word, it is the reverse. God, being his Father by nature, afterwards becomes his Creator and Maker when the Word puts on the flesh that is created and made and becomes a human being. Just as when human beings receive "the Spirit of the

Son" (Gal 4:6) they "become children of God"[146] (Jn 1:12) through him, so also the Word of God, when he puts on the flesh of human beings, is then said to be both created and made. So if we are sons by nature, then he is made and a creature by nature. But if we become sons by dispensation and grace, then clearly the Word said, "the Lord created me," because of the bestowal of his grace to us in his becoming human. Moreover, since when he put on what is created he became like (*homoios*) us in a bodily way, he is fittingly called both our brother and "firstborn" (Rom 8:29, Heb 2:11).[147] For, although it was after us (cf. Jn 1:15) that he became for us a human being and became our brother through the likeness of the body, nevertheless, even in that regard, he is still said to be and is the "first" (Jn 1:15). For, while all humanity was perishing because of the transgression of Adam, his flesh was the first to be saved and freed, as being the body of the Word himself. From then on, we are "incorporated" (*sussōmoi*; cf. Eph 3:6) with his body and saved through our accord with it. In this body the Lord becomes our guide into the kingdom of heaven and to his own Father, saying "I am the way" (Jn 14:6) and "the door" and all must "enter through me" (Jn 10:9). Therefore, he is also said to be "firstborn from the dead" (Col 1:18), not because he died before us – for it is we who died first – but because when he took upon himself death on our behalf, he "abolished" it (2 Tim 1:10) and was the first to rise as a human being, raising his own body for our sake. He has risen and henceforth we too, after him and from him and through him, are also raised from the dead.

62. Now, if he is also said to be "firstborn of creation" (Col 1:15), it is not as being equal to creatures and as the firstborn among them in regard to time (for how can this be, since he is "*only*-begotten"?) but it is because of the condescension (*tēn sunkatabasin*) of the Word toward creatures, through which he became the "brother of many" (Rom 8:29). For, of course, the one who is only-begotten is only-begotten because there are no other brothers; but the firstborn is so called because of other brothers. For this reason, then, it is nowhere said in the Scriptures that he is "the firstborn *of God*" or "creature *of God*." Conversely, "only-begotten" and "Son" and "Word" and "Wisdom" are terms that refer back to the Father and indicate the fact that the Son belongs to the Father. So, "we have seen his glory, glory as of the only-begotten from the Father" (Jn 1:14) and "God sent His only-begotten Son" (1 Jn 4:9) and "O Lord, your Word remains forever" (Ps 119:89), and "the Word was with God" (Jn 1:1) and "Christ the Power of God and Wisdom of God" (1 Cor

1:24) and "This is my beloved Son" (Mt 3:17) and "You are the Christ, the Son of the living God" (Mt 16:16). But "firstborn" connotes the condescension toward creation, for it is of creation that he is said to be the firstborn. And "created" (Prov 8:22) connotes the grace toward the works of creation; since he is created for the works (cf. Prov 8:22). So if he is only-begotten, which indeed he is, then his being "firstborn" needs to be interpreted accordingly. But if he is in fact "firstborn," he cannot be only-begotten. For the same one cannot be both only-begotten and firstborn, unless it is in different respects, so that "only-begotten" is in reference to the generation from the Father, as has been said, while "firstborn" is in reference to the condescension (*ten sunkatabasin*) toward creation and taking many others to be his brothers. Indeed, since these two terms are antithetical with respect to each other, one may justly say that it is the attribute of being only-begotten which has the pre-eminence in reference to the Word since there is no other Word, nor any other Wisdom, but he alone is the true Son of the Father.[148] For, again, as has been said above, it is without any adjoining explanation of cause and without qualification that he is said to be "the only-begotten Son who is in the bosom of the Father" (Jn 1:18). But to "firstborn" is adjoined the cause, which is creation, and this is added by Paul when he says, "for in him all things were created" (Col 1:16). But if all creatures were created in him, then he is other than creatures and is not a creature, being rather the Creator of all.

63. So he was not called "firstborn" because of his being from the Father, but because creation came to be in him. Just as before creation he was the Son, through whom creation came to be, so also before he was called "firstborn of all creation" (Col 1:15) he himself was none the less "the Word with God, and the Word was God" (Jn 1:1). But these impious ones, who do not understand this either, go around saying, "If he is firstborn of all creation, then clearly he is himself also one of the creation."[149] Thoughtless people! If he is absolutely the "firstborn of *all* creation," then he is other than all creation! For he did not say, "firstborn of the *other* creatures," lest he may be considered to be one of the creatures but "firstborn of *all* creation," so that he may be shown to be other than creation. Thus, Reuben is not said to be the "firstborn" of *all* the children of Jacob, but of Jacob himself and of his brothers, so that he may not be thought to be other than the children of Jacob (Gen 46:8ff.). Even in referring to the Lord himself, the apostle did not say, "so that he may become the first born of all" (Rom 8:29), lest he may be thought to have put on a body other than ours, but "*among* many brothers" (*ibid.*),

because of the likeness (*homiotēta*) of the flesh.[150] Therefore, if the Word also was one of the creatures, Scripture would have said of him too that he is "firstborn of the *other* creatures." But since what the sacred writers actually do say is that he is the "firstborn of *all* creation," it is clearly shown that the Son of God is other than all creation and not a creature. For if he is a creature, then he would be his own firstborn. How, you Arians, can he be both prior to and after himself? Then again, if he is a creature and all creation "came to be through him" (Jn 1:3) and "had its consistence in him" (Col 1:17), how can he both create the creation and be one of things which have their consistence in him? Such a conception of theirs is manifestly absurd. The truth that refutes them is that he is called "firstborn among many brothers" (Rom 8:29) because of the kinship of the flesh, and "firstborn from the dead" (Col 1:18) because the resurrection of the dead comes from him and after him, and "first-born of all creation" (Col 1:15) because of the Father's love for humanity, on account of which he not only gave consistence to all things in his own Word but brought it about that the creation itself, of which the apostle says that it "awaits the revelation of the children of God," will at a certain point be delivered "from the bondage of corruption into the glorious freedom of the children of God" (Rom 8:19,21). The Lord will be the firstborn of this creation which is delivered and of all those who are made children, so that by his being called "first," that which is after him may abide, united to the Word as to a foundational origin and beginning.

64. But I think that these impious people themselves will be brought to shame by their own interpretation. For if it is not as we have said and they rather would have him be "firstborn of all creation" (Col 1:15) as being himself, by essence, a creature among creatures, then let them take note that in this way they consider him to be like things that are irrational and lifeless and their brother in being. For these also are parts of "all creation"; and the firstborn must be first only in point of time, but is the same as all the rest as far as kinship and likeness (*homoiotēti*). Do they not then surpass all impiety when they say this? Who will stand them when they say these things? Who would not hate their merely conceiving such thoughts? For it is clear to all that he was called the "first-born" of creation not as being of himself a creature nor because of any kinship of essence with all creation, but because the Word condescended (*sunkatabebēke*) to the things coming into being when he was creating them at the beginning so that they may be enabled to come into being. For they would not have withstood his nature,

being that of the unmitigated splendor of the Father, if he had not condescended (*sunkatabas*) by the Father's love for humanity and supported, strengthened, and carried them into being.[151] Then, secondly, he was called "firstborn" because, by the Word's condescending (*sunkatabantos*), creation itself was made to be a "son" through him, so that he may become, as has been said, the firstborn of creation in every respect, both in creating it and in his being brought into this world itself for the sake of all. So it is written: "When he leads the firstborn into the world, he says: 'Let all the angels of God worship him'" (Heb 1:6).

Let the enemies of Christ then hear this and tear themselves to pieces: It is his coming into the world that made him to be called the firstborn of all. The Son is "the only-begotten" from the Father because he alone is from the Father, but he is "the firstborn of creation" because of the adoption of all as sons. Just as he also rose "from the dead as the first fruits of those who have fallen asleep" (1 Cor 15:20), so he "was created a beginning of the ways" (cf. Prov 8:22), because it was fitting that "he may be pre-eminent in all things" (Col 1:18). He "was created a beginning of the ways" so that we may walk on that way and enter through the one who says "I am the way" (Jn 14:6) and "the gate" (Jn 10:9), and so that we may share in the knowledge of the Father and hear it said of us, "Blessed are those who are blameless in the way" (Ps 119:1), and "Blessed are the pure in heart, for they shall see God" (Mt 5:8).

65. Since truth thus reveals that the Word is not a creature according to nature, it remains to say how he is said to be "beginning of the ways." The first way, which was through Adam, was destroyed, and instead of remaining in paradise we turned away into death and we heard it said to us, "You are earth, and to earth you will return" (Gen 3:19). Therefore the Word of God, who loves humanity, puts on the created flesh by the counsel of the Father, so that he himself may enliven and renew in the blood of his own body that which the first human had put to death through the transgression. In doing so, he forges "a new and living way for us," as the apostle said, "through the veil which is his flesh" (Heb 10:20) and in another place the apostle articulates the same meaning, saying: "Therefore, if anyone is in Christ, he is a new creation. The old things have passed away; behold, new things have come" (2 Cor 5:17).

But if a new creation has come, there needed to be someone to be the first of this creation. It could not have been a mere human being, merely earthly, such as we had become after the transgression.[152] For human beings had become unfaithful in the first creation, and through them, the first creation was destroyed. There was need for another to renew the first creation and maintain the new one. Therefore, in his love for humanity, none other than the Lord is created "a way," as the beginning of the new creation. He fittingly says, "The Lord created me as the beginning of His way for His works" (Prov 8:22), so that humanity may no longer live according to the old creation. But since there is now the beginning of a new creation and we have Christ as the beginning of its ways, we may henceforth follow the one who says, "I am the way" (Jn 14:6). The blessed apostle teaches this in his epistle to the Colossians, saying: "He is the head of the body, the Church; He is the beginning, the firstborn from the dead, so that he himself may be pre-eminent in all things" (Col 1:18).

66. For if, as has been said, he is called "first-fruits" because of the resurrection from the dead, and he is also "the beginning" because of it, and yet the resurrection came about when he carried our flesh and gave himself to death for our sake, then clearly his saying, "He created me as the beginning of the ways" does not signify his essence but his embodied presence. Death is proper (*idios*) to the body; and just as death is proper to the body, so also the saying, "He created me as the beginning of his ways," is proper to the bodily presence. Because the Savior is created in the flesh and becomes a beginning of those who are recreated and because "the first-fruits" – which is to say, the human body that he put on – belongs to him, it is fitting that there be a people which is created after him. So David says: "Let this be written for another generation, and the people to be created will praise the Lord" (Ps 102:19). And, again, in the twenty-first psalm, "The generation to come will declare to the Lord and proclaim his righteousness to the people that shall be born, whom the Lord has made" (Ps 22:32). Accordingly we shall no longer hear it said to us, "In the day that you eat of it, you will surely die" (Gen 2:17), but rather, "where I am, there you shall be also" (Jn 14:3), so that we may say, "We are his works created" by him "for good works" (Eph 2:10).

Yet again, since the work of God, which is the human being who was created perfect, became deficient through the transgression and dead through sin and it would have been unfitting for the work of God to remain imperfect[153] (and thus all the saints beseeched God, saying in the hundred-and-thirty-seventh psalm, "The Lord will answer me. Lord, do not despise the works of your hands" (Ps 138:8)), the perfect Word of God put on the imperfect body and is said to be "created for the works." He did this so that he may repay the debt on our behalf and perfect through himself what was lacking to humanity, and what was lacking was immortality and the way to paradise.[154] This is exactly what the Savior says, "I glorified you upon the earth. I perfected the work that you have given me to do" (Jn 17:4), and again, "The works which the Father has given me to perfect, these works which I do, bear witness to me" (Jn 5:36). The works which he here says that the Father has given him to perfect are those for which he is created, saying in the Proverbs, "the Lord created me as the beginning of his ways for his works" (Prov 8:22). For it is the same thing to say, "The Father has given me the works" (cf. Jn 5:36), and "He created me for the works" (Prov 8:22).

67. So when was it that he received the works in order to perfect them, you enemies of God? The answer to that question will also reveal the sense in which he is "created." If you say that he received the works at the beginning, when he made them from non-being into being, that would be false. For they had not yet come into being, while he seems to speak as if receiving what is already existing. Nor is it blameless to say that it was before the time of the Word's becoming flesh, for in that case his coming will turn out to be superfluous since this coming was for the sake of these works. So it remains finally to say that it is when he became a human being that he received the works, for it was then that he perfected them by healing our wounds and granting to all the resurrection from the dead.

But if it is when the Word became flesh that the works were given to him, then clearly it is when he became human that he was created "for the works." Therefore, "created" does not signify his essence, as has been said many times, but his bodily generation. It was then that, because of the works having become imperfect and deficient as a result of the transgression, it is said of him, with reference to the body, that he is created, so that, by perfecting the works and making them whole, he may "present" the Church to the Father, as the apostle says, "without spot or wrinkle or any such thing, that she may be holy and without blemish" (Eph 5:27). Thus, the human race is perfected and restored in him, as it had been in the beginning, or rather, by an even greater grace. For, rising from the dead, we no longer fear death but will reign in Christ forever in heaven. This came about because the Word of God himself, who is proper to (*idios*) and from the Father, put on the flesh and became human. If he who became human was originally a creature himself, humanity would remain none the less as it was, not conjoined to God. For how can something that is made be united to the Creator by another thing that is made? Or what kind of help can come from like to like, since those that would help are themselves in need of help? And how, if the Word is a creature, was he able to absolve the sentence of God and forgive sin, since it is written in the prophets that this capacity belongs to God: "Who is like you, O God, removing sin and overlooking iniquity?" (Mic 7:18). For it was God who said, "You are earth and to earth you shall return" (Gen 3:19), and so human beings became mortal. So then how can sin be absolved by those who had an origin to their being? But it was the Lord himself who absolved it, as he himself said: "... unless the Son will set you free" (cf. Jn 8:36). So the Son who has set us free has truly shown that he is neither a creature nor among those that came into being, but is the proper (*idios*) Word and Image of the Father's being. It was he who declared the sentence at the beginning and who "alone forgives sins" (Lk 5:21). Since it was in the Word that it was said, "You are earth and to earth you shall return" (Gen 3:19), it follows consistently that it was through the Word himself and in him that there came about freedom and the removal of condemnation.

68. "But," they say, "even if the Savior were a creature, God was able to merely speak and undo the curse."[155] They may also hear from another what amounts to the same thing: "God was able, without even his coming, to merely speak and undo the curse."[156] But it is necessary to look into what is advantageous for humanity, rather than merely considering what is possible for God. In the time of Noah's ark, it was possible for God to destroy the transgressors before the ark but he did it after the ark. He also could have merely spoken and led the people out of Egypt without Moses, but it was expedient that this be done through Moses. God also could have saved the people without the judges, but it was advantageous to the people that he temporarily raise up judges for them. The Savior also was able to make his visitation at the beginning, or having come, not to be given over to Pilate, and yet he came "at the end of the ages" (Heb 9:26) and when sought after, he said, "I am he" (Jn 18:5). Whatever he does is advantageous to humanity and it was not fitting for it to have been otherwise and he makes provisions for exactly what is fitting and expedient. Therefore he did come, "not to be served but to serve" (Mt 20:28) and to work our salvation. He was certainly capable of speaking the law from heaven, but he knew that it was advantageous to

humanity that he speak from Sinai. He did this so that Moses may be able to go up the mountain and the people may thus be further enabled to believe by hearing the word from nearby.

Moreover, one may see the fitting rationale of what happened in this: If he had spoken and undone the curse, merely in accordance with his capacity to do so, the power of he who thus issued the command would have been displayed but humanity would nevertheless have remained as Adam was before the transgression, receiving grace externally and not having it mingled with the body. For such was Adam when he was placed in paradise. In fact, perhaps humanity would have become worse because it had by now learned to transgress. So, this being the situation with humanity, if it were again deceived by the serpent, there would be again a need for God to command and undo the curse. The need would then become limitless, and humanity would remain none the less in slavery and liability to sin. Forever sinning, it would be forever in need of pardon and it would be never freed. Being, on its own, mere flesh, it would be forever defeated by the law through the weakness of the flesh.

69. Yet again, if the Son was a creature, humanity would have remained none the less mortal and not united to God. It was not a creature that united creatures to God, for in that case this creature would be itself in search of one to unite it to God. Nor would a part of creation be the salvation of creation, that part itself being in need of salvation. To prevent this, God sends his own Son who becomes the Son of Man by taking created flesh, so that he may offer his own body to death on behalf of all, since all were sentenced to death but he was other than all. Henceforth, the utterance of that sentence is fulfilled, insofar as all have died through him – for "all have died" in Christ (2 Cor 5:14) – and henceforth all can be freed through him from sin and the curse that comes from it and may truly remain forever as risen from the dead and as putting on immortality and incorruptibility. For, as has been often demonstrated, when the Word put on the flesh, he brought about the complete eradication from the flesh of every bite of the serpent and the repulsion of any evil that had sprung up from the movements of the flesh and the annihilation of the death which follows upon sin. So the Lord himself says: "The prince of this world is coming and he finds nothing in me" (Jn 14:30), and "He has been manifested for this reason," as John writes, "so that he may destroy the works of the devil" (1 Jn 3:8).

Therefore, since these works of the devil have been destroyed from the flesh, we have all been freed through the kinship (*sungeneian*) between his flesh and ours and we ourselves are henceforth united to the Word. As being united to God, we no longer remain upon the earth, but as he himself said, where he is, we will be also (Jn 14:3). Henceforth we shall no longer fear the serpent, for he has been nullified. He has been hunted down by the Savior from within the flesh, and has heard the words, "Depart from me, Satan" (Mk 8:33 and par.) and has been cast out of paradise into the everlasting fire. Nor shall we be on guard against the beguilement of woman, for "in the resurrection they neither marry nor are given in marriage but are like the angels" (Mt 22:30), and there will be "in Christ Jesus a new creation" (2 Cor 5:17) and "neither male nor female" (Gal 3:28) but "Christ is all and in all" (Col 3:11). But where there is Christ, what kind of fear or what kind of danger can there still be?

70.[157] But all this would not have happened if the Word was a creature. The devil, who is himself a creature, would persist in battle forever if he was contending against a creature. Humanity, stuck in the middle of this battle, would be always intimidated by death, not having one through whom and in whom it can be joined to God so that it may become entirely free from fear. Truth shows, therefore, that the Word is not one of the things that come to be, but rather their creator. He took to himself the body that was human and had a beginning so that he who is its creator may renew it and thus divinize it in himself and lead all of us into the kingdom of heaven, in accordance with his own likeness.

But humanity would not have been deified if joined to a creature, or unless the Son was true God. And humanity would not have come into the presence of the Father unless the one who put on the body was his true Word by nature. Just as we would not have been freed from sin and the curse unless the flesh which the Word put on was human by nature – for there would be no communion for us with what is other than human – so also humanity would not have been deified unless the Word who became flesh was by nature from the Father and true and proper (*idios*) to him. Therefore the conjoining that came about was such as to join what is human by nature to what is of the nature of divinity, so that humanity's salvation and deification might be secured.[158] So let those who deny that the Son is from the Father by nature and proper (*idion*) to his being deny also that he took true human flesh from the Ever-virgin Mary. For there would no longer be any benefit to us human beings if the

163

Word was not the true Son of God by nature or if the flesh that he put on was not true and genuine. But he did take true flesh, even if the Valentinians go crazy; and the Word was true God by nature, even if the Arians go mad. In this flesh there has come about the beginning of our new creation because he has been created as a human being for our sake and has renewed the way for us, as has been said.

71. Therefore, the Word is not a creature or a work. For "creature" and "made" and "work" are the same. If he was a creature and something made, then he would also be a work. That is why he did not say: "He created me as a work," nor "He made me along with the works," so that he may not be thought to be a creature by nature and being. Nor did he say, "He created me to make works," so that he may also not be considered to have come into being as an instrument for our sake, in keeping with the perversity of the impious.[159] Nor did he proclaim that "He created me before the works," lest he inculcate the notion that just as he is offspring before all things, so he is also created before all things, thereby making "offspring" and "created" to be equivalent. Rather, with a careful exactitude,[160] he said "for (*eis*)[161] the works," which is the same as saying, "The Father has made me into (*eis*) flesh, in order to become a human being." He said this to show that he is not a work but an offspring. For just as the one who comes into (*eis*) a house is not part of the house but is other than it, so also the one who is created for (*eis*) the works must be of another nature than the works.

But if, according to you Arians, the Word of God is a work, in what hand and wisdom did he himself come to be? For all the works that came into being came to be by the hand and wisdom of God, as God Himself says: "My hand has made all these" (Isa 66:2, Acts 7:50) and David sings, "You have established the earth in the beginning, Lord; and the heavens are the works of your hands" (Ps 102:26, Heb 1:10), and again in the one-hundred-and-forty-second psalm, "I remembered the days of old, I pondered on all your works, meditating on the works of your hands" (Ps 143:5). Therefore, if the things that were made were worked by the hand of God, while it is written that "all things came to be through the Word, and without him not one thing came to be" (Jn 1:3), and again, "one Lord Jesus Christ, through whom are all things" (1 Cor 8:6), and "all things had their consistence in him" (Col 1:17), then clearly the Son must not be a work but is himself the hand and wisdom of God.[162] Knowing this, those who became martyrs in Babylon – Ananias, Azarias, and Mishael – refute the impiety of the Arians when they

164

say, "Bless the Lord, all the works of the Lord" (Dan 3:57). They counted the things in heaven and on the earth and the whole creation as works, but they did not name the Son so.[163] They did not say, "Bless, O Word, and sing praise, O Wisdom," because they wanted to show that while all other things praise and are works, the Word is not a work and not one of those who praise but is himself praised and worshipped and confessed as God, along with the Father, and is the Father's Word and Wisdom, but Creator of the works. Making an apt distinction, the Spirit has said this also in the psalms, "the word of the Lord is true and all his works are trustworthy" (Ps 33:4), while in another place it says, "How manifold are your works, O Lord; In Wisdom, you have made all things" (Ps 104:24).

72. If the Word was a work, then surely he himself would have come to be, and Scripture would not have distinguished him from the works, nor would it have named them "works" while proclaiming him to be the Word and proper (*idian*) Wisdom of God. But in fact Scripture does distinguish him from the works and shows that Wisdom is not a work but fashioner of the works. Paul also employs the same distinction when he writes to the Hebrews: "For the Word of God is living and effective and sharper than any two-edged sword, penetrating even to the division of soul and spirit, joints and marrow, discerner of the thoughts of the heart. There is no creature that is hidden from him, but all things are naked and exposed to the eyes of the one to whom we must render account" (Heb 4:12–13). Look how he calls the things that come into being, "creature," but he recognizes that the Son is "Word of God," as being other than the creatures. Also, when he says, "all things are naked and exposed to the eyes of the one to whom we must render account," he again signifies that he is other than all things. Therefore, he is the one who judges, but among the things that come into being, each is obligated to give account to him.

Likewise, the whole creation's groaning with us to be freed from the slavery of corruption (cf. Rom 8:22) shows that the Son is other than creatures. For if he was a creature, he himself, along with all, would be one of those who groan and are in need of the one who grants sonship and freedom. But if "all creation groans" for freedom from "the slavery of corruption," while the Son is not among those who groan and are in need of freedom but is himself the one who grants sonship and freedom to all (as he said to the Hebrews then: "The slave does not remain in the house forever, but the Son remains forever. Therefore if the Son sets you free, you shall be free indeed" (Jn 8:35–36)) then it is clearer than light that the Word of God is not a creature but the true and genuine Son of the Father by nature.

Thus, regarding "the Lord created me as the beginning of the ways" (Prov 8:22), it seems to me that these words, even if they are meager, are sufficient to provide a basis for those who are more eloquent to prepare further refutation of the Arian heresy.

But since the heretics have also read the next verse in a bad sense, and think that because it is written, "He established me before the ages" (Prov 8:23), these words are spoken of the divinity of the Word and not of his incarnate presence, it is necessary to analyze this verse also, in order to show their error.

73. It is written, "God established the earth in Wisdom" (Prov 3:19). So if the earth is established through Wisdom, how can the one who establishes be the one who is established? But this also is said by way of a parable and a proverb. We must enquire into its meaning and then we will understand that while the Father fashions and establishes the earth by wisdom in order to make it abide and be steadfast, Wisdom itself is established for us in order to become a beginning and foundation of our renewal and our new creation. Therefore, here also he did not say, "Before all the ages, he made me son, or word," as if he had a beginning of his being made. So the first thing is to enquire and search the Scriptures about whether in fact he is "Son."[164] This was what Peter said when the apostles were questioned and he replied: "You are the Christ, the Son of the living God" (Mt 16:16). This was also among the first questions of the father of the Arian heresy, "If you are the Son of God ..." (Mt 4:6). For he knew that this was the truth and the chief point of our faith and that, if he was the Son himself, the diabolical tyranny would come to its end, but if he was a creature, he would be one of those who derive from the same Adam who was deceived by him and there would be no reason to worry. Because of this also, the Jews of that time were angered because the Lord called himself the Son of God and "called God his own Father" (Jn 5:18). If he had said that he was one of the creatures or "I am made," they would not have been astonished to hear this nor would they have called such words blasphemy, since they knew that even angels had visited their fathers. But since he called himself "Son," they knew that this indicated not a creature but divinity and the Father's nature.

74. So the Arians should have really spent more effort on this point, if only in imitation of their father the devil. If indeed it had said, "He has established me as a foundation to be Word or Son,"

then let them think the way they do. But if he did not say that, let them not dream up for themselves what is not real. For he did not say, "Before the ages, he has established me as a foundation, to be Word or Son," but simply, "he has established me as a foundation" (Prov 8:23), in order to show, as I have said, that he speaks this not with a view to himself but proverbially, with a view to those who are built up on him. Knowing this, the apostle too writes: "No one can lay another foundation than that which already exists, which is Jesus Christ. But each must take care how he builds upon it" (1 Cor 3:11,10). But the foundation must be the same as what is built upon it, so that they may be "fitted together" (Eph 2:20). Therefore, being Word, there is nothing which can be "fitted together" to him and is like him, insofar as he is Word. For he is only-begotten. But when he became human, then there were those who were like him, the likeness of whose flesh he put on. Thus he "was established as a foundation" according to his humanity, so that we also may be enabled to be built up as "precious stones" (1 Cor 3:12), and to become "the temple of the Holy Spirit, who dwells in us" (1 Cor 3:16). Just as he is the foundation and we are stones built up upon him, so is he also the "vine," while we are united to him as "branches" (Jn 15:5), not according to the essence of divinity (for that is impossible) but, once again, according to the humanity. For the branches must be like the vine, and we also are like him, according to the flesh.

Furthermore, since the heretics understand these matters according to human conceptions, it is fitting to refute them through their own reasonings, by using human illustrations. Thus, he did not say "He has *made* me as a foundation," lest they may find in this a shameless pretext for impiety, so as to say that he is something made, something which has a beginning of its very coming to be. Rather, he says "He has established me as a foundation." But a foundation is established on account of the stones that are to be set upon it. It does not simply come into being as a foundation, but only becomes a foundation when a stone is transported from the mountain and is placed into the depths of the earth. As long as it is simply a stone in the mountain, it is in no way a foundation. When, however, the need arises and it is transported and cast into the depths of the earth, then at last it would say (if stones could speak): "Now he has established me as a foundation, he who transported me here from the mountain." Therefore also the Lord did not have a beginning of his existence when he was established as a foundation (for he was Word before this). But when he put on our body, which

167

he excavated and took from Mary, then it was that he said, "He has established me as a foundation," which is the same as saying: "I am the Word whom he has covered with an earthly body." Thus he was established as a foundation for us by receiving what is ours so that we, fitted together into one body with him (*sussōmoi*) and bound together in him through the likeness of the flesh and thus attaining to "the perfect man" (Eph 4:13), may remain immortal and incorruptible.

75. But let no one be troubled when it says, "before the ages" and "before the earth was made" and "before the mountains were set in place" (Prov 8:23–25). These words in fact agree well with "He has established me as a foundation" and "He created [me]," for once again, this touches upon the economy according to the flesh. For while the grace of the Savior towards us has appeared now (cf. Titus 2:11), as the apostle said, and it came to pass when he journeyed among us, yet it was prepared beforehand even before we came into being, or rather, even before the foundation of the world. And how good and wonderful was the reason for this! For it was not fitting for God to determine his will for us later on, as if he were ignorant of what would happen to us. So when the God of the universe created us through his own Word, he knew what would happen to us better than we; he knew beforehand that while we were made to be good we would later transgress the commandment and be thrown out of paradise for our disobedience. Being himself good and the lover of humanity,[165] he prepared beforehand the economy of our salvation in his own Word, through whom he also created us, so that despite our falling through being deceived by the serpent, we would not remain (*mē apomeinōmen*) utterly dead. Rather, having recourse to the redemption and salvation prepared beforehand for us in the Word, we would rise again and remain (*diamenōmen*) immortal when he would be "created as the beginning of the ways" (Prov 8:22) for our sake, and so "the firstborn of creation" (Col 1:15) would become "the firstborn among brothers" (Rom 8:29) and himself rise as the "first-fruits of the dead" (cf. 1 Cor 15:20).[166]

This is what the blessed apostle Paul teaches in his writing. He provides an interpretation of the words of the Proverbs, "before the ages" (Prov 8:23) and "before the earth was made" (Prov 8:24), when he says to Timothy: "Share in the burden of the gospel through the power of God, who has saved us and called us with a holy calling, not on account of our own works but according to his own design and grace, which he has given to us in Christ Jesus before the ages, but is now made manifest through the appearance of our Savior Jesus Christ, who has destroyed death and brought life to light" (2 Tim 1:8–10). And to the Ephesians, he says: "Blessed be the God and Father of our Lord Jesus Christ, who has blessed us in Christ Jesus with every spiritual blessing in the heavens, as he chose us in him before the foundation of the world to be holy and blameless before him. In love he predestined us for adoption to himself through Jesus Christ" (Eph 1:3–5).

76. So then how did he choose us before we existed, if not, as the apostle himself said, we were prefigured "in him" (Eph 1:11)? How indeed did he "predestine us for adoption" (Eph 1:5) before humanity was even created, if not that the Son himself was "established as a foundation" (Prov 8:23) before the world, having taken upon himself the dispensation (*oikonomian*) for our sake? Or how is it that, as the apostle adds, "we were predestined for an inheritance" (Eph 1:11), if not that the Lord himself was "established as a foundation" (Prov 8:23) before the world, insofar as it was his purpose, for our sake, to take upon himself, through the flesh, the whole inheritance of judgment against us and thus henceforth to adopt us in himself? Or how did we receive grace before times and ages, when we who were created in time had not yet come into being, unless that antecedent grace was stored up for us in Christ? For in the judgment, when each will receive "according to his action" (Mt 16:27), he says, "Come, blessed of my father. Inherit the kingdom that was prepared for you from the foundation of the world" (Mt 25:34). So how or in whom was it prepared before we came to be, if not in the Lord who was established as a foundation for this before the world was, so that we may be built up on him as "precious stones" (1 Cor 3:12) and may receive life and grace from him? As I have said before and as would seem fitting to one who thinks piously, this took place so that we may be capable of eternal life, rising from a short death. As human beings who are from earth, we would not have been capable of this had not the hope of life and salvation been prepared for us, in Christ, before the world was. Therefore it was fitting that the Word came into our flesh and "was created as a beginning of the ways for his works" (Prov 8:22) and thus was "established as a foundation," insofar as the will of the Father resided in him, as has been said, "before the world was and before the earth was made and before the mountains were set in place, and before the springs of water gushed forth" (cf. Prov 8:23–25). This took place so that even if the earth and the mountains and the forms of visible things will "pass away" (1 Cor 7:31) in the consummation of the present age (Mt 13:40), and we also

like them will "grow old" (Ps 102:27), yet we will still be enabled to have life even after all this and to attain to the life and spiritual blessing that were prepared for us and for the sake of our election before all these things in the Word himself. Thus we will be enabled to have a life that is not merely transitory, and to live after all these things in Christ, since before all these things our life was established and prepared in Christ.

77. For it would not have been at all fitting for our life to be established in any other foundation except in the Lord, so that insofar as this life is in the one who existed before the world and before the ages and through whom the world came to be (Heb 1:2), we also may be enabled to inherit eternal life. "God is good" (cf. Mk 10:17), and being good, he has eternally willed this, knowing that our weak nature was in need of his help and salvation.[167] Just as a wise builder who sets out to build a house and at the same time makes plans for rebuilding it in case it is destroyed prepares a plan for its rebuilding and gives that to the builder – so that the plan for its rebuilding exists before the house itself – so in the same manner our salvific renewal was established in Christ before we existed, in order that we may be enabled to be created anew in him. The will and design for this was prepared before the world existed, though the act itself was accomplished only when the need arose and the Savior came.[168] And when he receives us into eternal life in heaven, the Lord himself will stand for us in place of the world and everything else.

This is enough then for demonstrating that the Word of God is not a creature and that the passage does have a correct sense. Since a close examination of that passage yields an altogether proper sense, it is appropriate for us to state what this is so that these mindless ones may perhaps be brought to shame by our many words. But it is necessary here to recall what was previously said; for what we are about to say refers to the same proverb and the same Wisdom. The Word did not say of himself that he was a creature by nature, but was speaking in proverbs when he said, "the Lord created me" (Prov 8:22). It is clear that this signifies a meaning that is not overt but hidden, which we can find if we "lift the veil" of the parable. For who, upon hearing Creator-Wisdom say, "the Lord created me for the sake of his works" (Prov 8:22), would not immediately investigate the meaning and consider how it can be that the Creator is created?[169] Who, when he hears the only-begotten Son of God saying that he was created as "a beginning of the ways" (Prov 8:22) would not enquire into the meaning and wonder how the only-begotten Son could become a beginning for many others? This indeed is an enigma. But it says, "The intelligent will understand a parable and a dark saying, the words of the wise and their riddles" (Prov 1:5–6).

78. Therefore, the only-begotten and true Wisdom of God is the creator and maker of all things. For it says: "In wisdom you have made all things" and "the earth is filled with your creation" (Ps 104:24). But in order that creatures may not only be but also thrive in well-being, it pleased God to have his own Wisdom condescend to creatures. Therefore, he placed in each and every creature and in the totality of creation a certain imprint (*typon*) and reflection of the Image of Wisdom, so that the things that come into being may prove to be works that are wise and worthy of God. Just as our word is an image of the Word who is the Son of God, so the wisdom that comes into being within us is an image of his Wisdom, in which we attain to knowledge and understanding. Thus, we become recipients of the Creator-Wisdom, and through her we are able to know her Father. For he says, "the one who has the Son also has the Father" (1 Jn 2:23) and "the one who receives me receives the one who sent me" (Mt 10:40). Since this imprint of Wisdom is created in us and in all created works, it is fitting that when the true Creator-Wisdom receives her own imprint into herself, she says: "the Lord created me for his works."[170] That which the wisdom within us says about herself, the Lord himself speaks as pertaining to him.

Since he is Creator, he is not created; but on account of his image that is in created works, he speaks of what pertains to them as applying to himself. Just as the Lord himself, on account of his imprint being in us, said, "the one who receives you receives me" (Mt 10:40), so he also says of himself, "the Lord created me as the beginning of his ways for his works" (Prov 8:22). He says this on account of the fact that his image and imprint (*typos*) is created in the works, although he himself is not one of the things that are created. Thus did the imprint of Wisdom come to be in created things, so that the world, as I have said, may come to know its Creator and Word, and through him, the Father. This is what Paul said, "For what can be known about God is evident to them, because God made it evident to them. Ever since the creation of the world, his invisible attributes have been able to be understood and perceived in what he has made" (Rom 1:19–20). Therefore, the Word is not a creature by essence, but the saying in the Proverbs refers to that within us which is called wisdom.

79. But if they do not believe what we are saying, let them say themselves whether there is any wisdom in creatures or not. If there is not, what about the apostle's censure, when he says, "since in the wisdom of God, the world did not come to know God through wisdom" (1 Cor 1:21). And if there is no such wisdom, how is it that we find in Scripture "many wise men" (Wis 6:24); and "the wise man is cautious and shuns evil" (Prov 14:16); and "a house is built by wisdom" (Prov 24:3). Moreover, Ecclesiastes says, "The wisdom of a man illumines his face" (Eccl 8:1), and he admonishes those who are too precipitate, saying, "Do not ask: Why were the former days better than these? For it is not in wisdom that you ask about this" (Eccl 7:10).

But if wisdom does exist [in the world] – as indeed Sirach says, "He has poured her forth upon all his works, upon all flesh according to his bounty, and he has lavished her upon those who love him" (Sir 1:8) – and yet such an outpouring does not indicate the being of Wisdom herself and of the only-begotten but of her extrapolated image in the world, why is it incredible if, as we have said, the true and Creator Wisdom herself, whose imprint (*typos*) is the wisdom and knowledge poured out into the world, should say about herself, "the Lord created me for his works" (Prov 8:22)? For the wisdom which is in the world does not create but is created in the works, and it is through this wisdom that "the heavens declare the glory of God, and the stars proclaim the work of his hands" (Ps 19:2). If they bear this wisdom within themselves, human beings will also recognize the true Wisdom of God and will know that they are really made in God's image. It is just as in the case of a king's son, whose father wishes to build a city, and who inscribes his own name on each of the works within the city so that these works may be secured and preserved on account of the appearance of his name on each of them and so that the inhabitants of the city may be enabled by the inscription of the name to remember both him and his father. If, upon completion, someone were to ask him about how the city was made, he would say: "It was made securely, for by the will of my father, I was represented in each of the works, for the inscription of my name was created within the works." In saying this, he would not be indicating that what is created is his own being, but rather his imprint (*typos*), which is represented by the name. In the same way as the example above, the true Wisdom responds to those who marvel at the wisdom in creatures by saying, "'The Lord created me for the works.' For my imprint (*typos*) is in them and thus have I condescended in the act of creating."

80. So there is no reason to become bewildered if the Son speaks of his imprint in us as something that is his own, just as (for we do not hesitate to repeat ourselves) when Saul was persecuting the Church in which was his image and imprint (*typos*), he spoke as if he himself were being persecuted: "Saul, why do you persecute me?" (Acts 9:4). Therefore, as has been said, just as no one would think it strange if the imprint of Wisdom which is in the works should say, "He created me for his works" (Prov 8:22), so if the true Creator-Wisdom of God and his only-begotten Word ascribes to himself what belongs to his image and thus says "He created me for his works," let no one bypass the wisdom that is created in the world and in the works and consider that the "created" is said of the very essence of Wisdom, lest such a person "mix wine with water" (Isa 1:22) and distort the truth.

For while Wisdom herself is Creator and Maker, her imprint is created in the works and is [made] according to the image of the Image.[172] She says "beginning of the ways," because such wisdom becomes a beginning and, as it were, a paradigm of the knowledge of God. When one embarks upon this primary path and guards it by the fear of God – as Solomon says, "The beginning of wisdom is the fear of God" (Prov 1:7) – and then ascends by intelligence and understanding and perceives in creation the Creator Wisdom, he will perceive in her also her Father, as the Lord himself has said, "The one who has seen me has seen the Father" (Jn 14:9) and John writes, "The one who confesses the Son also has the Father" (1 Jn 2:23). She says, "before the world he has established me as a foundation" (Prov 8:23), because it is in the imprint of Wisdom that the works find stability and always remain. Moreover, in order that no one, upon hearing these things said of the wisdom created in the works, may conclude that the true Wisdom and Son of God is by nature created, she necessarily adds, "before the mountain" and "before the earth" and "before the waters" and "before the hills he begot me" (Prov 8:24,25). By saying, in effect, "before all creation" – for she clearly encompasses all creation in these things – she shows that she is not created along with the works, as far as essence. For if she is created "for the works" and yet exists before the works, it is clear that she exists before being "created." Therefore Wisdom is not a creature by nature and being, but as he himself added, is an offspring (cf. Prov 8:25). As to the difference and variance in nature between a creature and an offspring, that has been shown in the preceding.

81. Now, since she goes on to say, "When he fashioned the heavens, I was there with him" (Prov 8:27), we must understand

that she is saying that the Father did not fashion the heavens or "the clouds above" (Prov 8:28) except through her. For it is beyond doubt that all things were created in Wisdom, and apart from her not one thing was made (cf Jn 1:3). But this is what she is saying: "Everything came to be in me and through me. But there was need for wisdom to be created in the works. I was in the Father according to being, but as a condescension (*tē sunkatabasei*) toward created beings, I concocted an imprint derived from myself for the sake of the works, so that the whole universe would be as one body, not discordant but in harmony with itself."[173] Therefore, all those who contemplate creatures with a right reason, according to this wisdom that is granted to them, would be enabled to say: "By your command all things stands firm" (Ps 119:91). But all those who neglect this wisdom will hear it said of them: "While claiming to be wise, they have become fools" (Rom 1:22). For "what can be known about God has been manifest to them, because God has manifested it to them. Ever since the creation of the world, his invisible attributes of eternal power and divinity have been able to be understood and perceived through the creation of the world. So they have no excuse, for although they knew God, they did not glorify him as God" (Rom 1:19–21), but "have worshipped creatures instead of the creator of all things who is blessed forever, Amen" (Rom 1:25). And they will be ashamed when they hear: "Since the world did not know God through wisdom" (according to the manner that has just been described), "it pleased God to save those who believe through the foolishness of the proclamation" (1 Cor 1:21). For God willed to make himself known no longer as in previous times through the image and shadow of wisdom, which is in creatures, but has made the true Wisdom herself take flesh and become a mortal human being and endure the death of the cross, so that henceforth all those who put their faith in him may be saved. But it is the same Wisdom of God, who previously manifested herself, and her Father through herself, by means of her image in creatures – and thus is said to be "created" – but which later on, being Word, became flesh (Jn 1:14) as John said, and after "destroying death" (2 Tim 1:10) and saving our race, both revealed himself and through himself his Father, saying, "Grant that they may know you the true God and Jesus Christ whom you have sent" (Jn 17:3).[174]

82. Therefore all the earth is filled with his knowledge. For one is the knowledge of the Father, through the Son, and of the Son, from the Father,[175] and the Father rejoices in the Son and in this

same joy, the Son delights in the Father, saying, "I was beside him, his delight. Day by day, I rejoiced in his presence" (Prov 8:30). These words again show that the Son is not other (*mē allotrion*), but belongs (*idion*) to the being of the Father. So, then, it is not for our sake that he came into being, as the impious say, nor is he in any way "from nothing." Nor did God acquire for himself a cause for rejoicing from outside of himself. Rather, these words refer to what is his own and of his likeness (*homoiou*).

When was it then that the Father did not rejoice? But if he has always rejoiced, then there was always the one in whom he rejoiced. In whom, then, does the Father rejoice (cf. Prov 8:30), except by seeing himself in his own image (*eikoni*), which is his Word? Even though, as it is written in these same Proverbs, he also "delighted in the sons of people, having consummated the world" (Prov 8:31), yet this also has the same meaning. For he did not delight in this way by acquiring delight as an addition to himself, but it was upon seeing the works that were made according to his own image, so that the basis of this delight also is God's own Image. And how does the Son too rejoice, except by seeing himself in the Father? For to say this is the same as to say: "The one who has seen me has seen the Father" (Jn 14:9), and "I am in the Father and the Father is in me" (Jn 14:10).

So now your boasting has been shown to be completely vacuous, you enemies of Christ, and your parading around and babbling everywhere about "He created me as the beginning of his ways" (Prov 8:22) is foolish. You distort the sense of the passage and proclaim your own ideas rather than the meaning of Solomon. But now your interpretation has been shown to be mere fantasy. For the passage in Proverbs and all that has been said about it make it evident that the Son is not a creature by nature and being (*tē physei kai tē ousia*), but the Father's own (*idion*) offspring who is true Wisdom and Word, "through whom everything came into being, and without him nothing came to be" (Jn 1:3).

3

ON THE COUNCIL OF
NICAEA (DE DECRETIS)

Introduction

Athanasius's treatise in defense of the Council of Nicaea was written
sometime in the 350s. A seeming reference to impending violence
against Athanasius and his supporters ("in a little while, they will
turn to outrage and after that they will threaten the cohort and the
captain" (cf. Jn 18:12)) has led some scholars to place it ca. 351,
when the anti-Nicene emperor Constantius was redirecting his
attention to Church affairs after having been preoccupied with the
Persian threat and an insurrection by the general Magnentius.[1]
Conversely, it has been argued that it is a mere rhetorical trope to
depict "the heretics" as threatening violence and that the overall
preoccupation of the treatise, which is to defend the use of *ousia*-
language, is intelligible only in light of the explicit rejection of
ousia-language in the so-called "Second Formula of the Synod of
Sirmium" in 357. Thus, the treatise would have been composed ca.
357–359.[2] While it is not possible to adjudicate the question with
absolute certainty, the earlier dating seems more plausible.
Certainly, the dissatisfaction with Nicene *ousia*-language did not
erupt *ex nihilo* at the sparsely attended Synod of Sirmium in 357,
though that event undoubtedly represented a climactic crystalliza-
tion of a growing momentum.[3] Indeed, as Athanasius himself goes
on to show, it was only with reluctance that the Nicene fathers
themselves adopted such terminology. On the other hand, while the
violence of the "Arians" is a consistent trope in Athanasius's
polemic, there is a marked difference in tone between his allegation
here of impending violence and his reporting of the misdeeds of his
opponents once he is again sent away into exile in the winter of
356.[4]

The occasion of the letter is a dispute between some Nicene
sympathizers and "Eusebians," in which the latter had criticized

Nicaea's use of unscriptural terms in designating the relation of the Son to the Father as "from the essence" and "*homoousios.*"

Characteristically, Athanasius quickly turns the tables, pointing out that it is the Arians who need to be on the defensive when it comes to the discussion of "such a great and ecumenical council" (4) at which they were condemned. Once again, his strategy of conflating all anti-Nicene factions as "Arians" gives him an opportunity to accuse his opponents of inconsistency. Eusebius of Caesarea, one of those who had sympathized with Arius's anti-Nicene views, had nevertheless subscribed to the Nicene formula. Why were these present "Arians" then turning away from the doctrines of "those who formerly taught them" (4)? Athanasius distinguishes between "those Arians" of Nicaea and "these" contemporary Arians only to underscore the assertion that, despite all variation and inconsistency, they are both the same in ultimately asserting that "the Son is not true God" (6). Having located this question as the fixed and inescapable center of the theological debate, he engages his opponents by querying their interpretation of the uniqueness of the Son. Asterius figures prominently as the source of various construals of the precedence of the Son that do not amount to a sharing in the divine nature. Athanasius counters each of these interpretations in turn (6–10) before turning to a defense of Nicene doctrine. In contrast to the varying and self-contradictory positions of the anti-Nicene factions, Athanasius presents the Council of Nicaea as one that upholds the consistent teaching of both Scripture and tradition. Because the being of the uncreated God cannot be inferred from created realities, human beings must rely on scriptural symbols (*paradeigmata*) for indications of the relation of the Son to the Father (12). The interplay of these symbols indicates that the Son is not a creature and that his being is correlative to the Father's being (12–17). It was this scriptural truth that the Nicene Council wished to teach and safeguard and it was only the obstinacy and deceitfulness of the "Arians" that forced the Nicene fathers to use non-scriptural words in order to maintain the meaning of Scripture (18–23). The *ousia*-language of Nicaea, therefore, must be understood in light of its scriptural provenance and, apophatically, in keeping with the immaterial and transcendent reality to which it signifies (24). Athanasius then attempts to trace a trajectory of tradition that includes Theognostus, Dionysius of Alexandria, and his Roman namesake, as well as Origen, in support of Nicene teaching (25–27). He concludes that it is the anti-Nicene designation of God as "unoriginated" (*agenetos*) that is unscriptural, both according to its letter and its sense (28–31). Whereas the designation of God as "unoriginated" merely contrasts the uncreated God with creatures, the title of "*homoousios*" is ultimately a way of signifying that the relation of Father and Son is enfolded within the divine being, while humanity is then enfolded within that relation through the Incarnation of the Word and the Spirit's abiding in humanity (31).

The text translated here is that of the critical edition of *AW* II/I.

Text

1. You have done well in making known to me the discussion which you had with the supporters of Arius, in which were involved some of the party of Eusebius and many of the brothers who adhere to the teachings of the Church.[5] I applauded your Christ-loving vigilance, which excellently refuted the impiety of the heresy. On the other hand, I was astounded at their shamelessness, in that, despite the fact that the Arian arguments have been shown to be corrupt and futile, and even after they have been condemned by all and convicted of every perversity, they still complain like the Jews, saying: "Why did those gathered at Nicaea put forth these unscriptural terms: 'from the essence' (*ek tēs ousias*) and '*homoousios*'?" But you, as a learned and articulate man, convicted them of talking nonsense, despite their pretences. Nevertheless, in the invention of these pretences of theirs, they are not acting inconsistently with their own evil minds. For they are as variable and unstable in their minds as chameleons in their colors; when exposed, they blush; when questioned, they are at a loss; but finally, putting aside all shame, they set about devising their pretexts. And if someone confronts them about these things, they exert themselves to invent things that have no standing in reality, and as the Scriptures say, they "plot about vain things" (Ps 2:1), only to remain in their impiety.

Such efforts on their part are nothing but an obvious indication of their irrationality, which, as I have said before, is an imitation of Jewish malice.[6] For the latter also, when convicted by the truth, and unable to face it, devised pretexts, saying: "What sign do you do, that we may see and believe in you? What work do you perform?" (Jn 6:30), when in fact there were so many signs that even they said, "What should we do? For this man works many signs?" (Jn 11:47). Indeed, the dead were raised, the lame walked, the blind regained their sight, lepers were cleansed, water became wine, and five thousand were filled from five loaves of bread.[7] Everyone marveled and worshipped the Lord, confessing that the prophecies were fulfilled in him, and that he was God, the Son of God. Only the Pharisees, despite the appearance of signs that shone brighter than the sun, still grumbled in their ignorance, saying: "Why do you, a human being, make yourself to be God?" (Jn 10:33). They were senseless and truly blind in their understanding. What they should have said, on the contrary, is: "Why did you, being God, become a human being?" For his works showed that he is God, so that they might worship the goodness of the Father, and marvel at his dispensation (*economian*) for our sake. But they did not say this, nor did they wish to see what was happening. Or, rather, they did see (for one could not help but see these things). But then they merely changed course and began to grumble again: "Why do you heal the paralytic on the Sabbath, and on the Sabbath make the one who was blind from birth to see again?" (cf. Jn 5:16, 9:1ff.). This, again, was a pretence and mere grumbling. For the Lord was healing every infirmity and disease on the other days also, but they murmured in their usual manner, preferring to have the suspicion of ungodliness imputed to them, by calling him Beelzebub (cf. Mk 3:22), rather than to recant their own wickedness. Despite the Savior manifesting his own divinity many times in many ways and preaching the Father to all, they, like those who kick against the goad, contradicted him with silly talk, only so that they may find a pretext to separate themselves from the truth, as the divine proverb says.[8]

2. Therefore, as the Jews who at that time did such wicked things and denied the Lord were fittingly dispossessed of the laws and of the promise made to their fathers, so the Arians who are now Judaizing seem to me to be in the same position as that of Caiaphas and the Pharisees of that time. Seeing that their heresy is bereft of good sense, they invent pretexts: "Why is this written and not that?" But do not be amazed if they now contrive such machinations, for in a little while, they will turn to outrage and after that they will threaten the cohort and the captain (cf. Jn 18:12); their evil thinking seems to be sustained by such things.[9] Having denied the Word and Reason of God, it is only fitting that they are utterly bereft of reason, and being cognizant of this, I would not have ventured answers to their questions.[10] But, since you, in your benevolence, have asked to know what transpired at the synod, I have not delayed, but rather immediately set forth what went on then, showing briefly the extent to which the Arian heresy is bereft of a pious disposition and how they merely invent pretexts.

See for yourself, beloved, if it is not so. If they are confident about the evil things that they invented when the devil planted this perversity within them (Mt 13:25), let them defend themselves against the accusations brought against them when they were proved to be heretics, and only then should they question, if they can, the things that were defined in opposition to them. For no one who is convicted of murder or adultery has an opportunity after the trial to censure the judge's pronouncement and ask him why he spoke in this way and not that. Indeed, to do so would not result in the acquittal of the one who is judged, but rather would aggravate the charge brought against him, on account of his rashness and presumption. Therefore, let them prove that their way of thinking is pious. For they were denounced and convicted, and had no complaints until then, and it is just that those who are under accusation should not venture beyond defending themselves. Or, if their conscience is besmirched and they see themselves to be impious, let them not censure what they do not understand, lest they bring upon themselves both the charge of impiety and the reproof of ignorance. Rather, let them enquire into the matter as those who love to learn, so that, coming to know things which they had not known previously, they may cleanse their impious ears with the stream of truth and the doctrines of piety.

3. This is what happened at the Council of Nicaea to the party of Eusebius: While the impious ones were eager for quarrel and attempted to fight against God, saying things that were most impious, the bishops assembled there (of whom there were three hundred, more or less) gently and kindly asked them to provide an explanation and show what pious foundations there are for the things they said. But no sooner did they begin speaking than they were condemned and began to fight among themselves. With the realization that their heresy was quite untenable, they fell dumb and remained so, and thus confessed through silence the shame which befell their vacuous opinions. Then the bishops, having annulled the phrases invented by them, put forth against them the sound and ecclesiastical faith, and when all subscribed to it, the party of Eusebius also subscribed to it in those same words which they now censure. I speak of "from the essence" (*ek tēs ousias*) and "one in essence" (*homoousios*) and that the Son of God is not a creature nor work nor one of the things that come to be, but that the Word is offspring from the essence of the Father (*gennēma tēs ousias tou patros*).

And the strange thing is that Eusebius, from Caesarea of Palestine, having subscribed afterwards to what he had denied the day before, wrote to his own church, saying that this is the faith of the Church and the tradition of the fathers.[11] Thus he showed clearly to all that they had previously been mistaken and were foolishly contending against the truth. Although he was embarrassed at the time to use these terms and wanted to excuse himself to his church, nevertheless, since he did not deny in his letter the "one in essence" and the "from the essence," he clearly intends to imply them. Thus he involved himself in a conundrum. For, by way of defending himself, he proceeded to denounce the Arians for having written that the Son was not before his coming to be and thus denying him existence before the coming in the flesh.[12] Acacius also knows this, even if he is now behaving hypocritically and denying the truth because he is afraid of the present circumstances.[13] Therefore, I have appended Eusebius's letter at the end, so that you may know the presumption shown against their own teachers by the enemies of Christ, and especially Acacius.

4. Are they not acting wrongfully merely by wishing to contradict such a great and ecumenical synod? Are they not transgressing in presumptuously setting themselves against the definitions that were well crafted against the Arian heresy, and that were witnessed to even by those who formerly had taught them impiety?[14] Even if those who belong to the party of Eusebius did change after they had subscribed to these definitions, and like dogs turned back to their own vomit of impiety (2 Pet 2:22), are not these present dissenters even more worthy of contempt in that they sacrifice the freedom of their own souls and want to adopt as their leaders in heresy those who are, as James said, "duplicitous people, unstable in all their ways" (Jas 1:8), not having one mind but turning now this way and now that, now speaking in approval but soon after censuring what they have said, then again approving what they have just censured? But, as the *Shepherd* has said, this is the offspring of the devil, and the mark of peddlers of cheap wares, rather than teachers.[15] For true teaching is what the fathers have handed down, and truly, this is the mark of teachers: to confess the same things among each other and not to disagree among themselves or with their own fathers. Those who are not so disposed are not to be called true teachers but knaves. Thus, the Greeks, who do not confess the same things but disagree among themselves, do not have the true teaching. But the saints, who are truly heralds of the truth, agree with each other and do not differ among themselves.[16] Even though they existed at different times, they all traveled along the same path, being prophets of the one God, and preaching harmoniously the same Word.

5. Thus Abraham had adhered to what Moses taught. And what Abraham adhered to was acknowledged also by Noah and Enoch, who distinguished the clean from the unclean and became well-pleasing to God. Abel also gave witness in the same way, having knowledge of the things which he had learned from Adam, who was himself taught by the Lord who said, when he came at the consummation of the ages for the banishment of sin, "I do not give to you a new commandment, but an old commandment which you have heard from the beginning" (cf. 1 Jn 2:7). Therefore also Paul, the blessed apostle who learned from the Lord, in setting forth matters that pertain to the Church did not wish deacons, much less bishops, to be double minded (1 Tim 3:8). In chastising the Galatians, he made an absolute declaration, saying: "If anyone preaches to you a gospel other than what you have received, let him be anathema, as I have said before and say again. But even if we or an angel from heaven should preach to you a gospel other than what you have received, let him be anathema" (Gal 1:8–9).

Therefore, since the apostle has spoken thus, let them either anathematize the party of Eusebius who have changed and now say things that are different from those to which they have subscribed; or, if they acknowledge that they had subscribed well, let them not complain against so great a council. But if they do neither one nor the other, then clearly they also are carried about by every wind and wave (cf. Eph 4:14), and dragged around by the minds of others, not their own. In that case, neither are they now trustworthy in their allegations. But let them then stop casting blame on what they don't understand. Or else, not knowing how to discriminate, they will simply "call evil good and good evil, and consider the bitter to be sweet, and the sweet bitter" (Isa 5:20).[17] In fact, they wish to grant authority to what has been judged to be bad and rejected, while they violently slander what was well defined. There should have been no need for us still to defend these things that were defined nor to make a response to their foolish pretexts, nor for them to be still eager for quarrel. But they should rather adhere to what was subscribed to by the leaders of their heresy, seeing that, whereas the later reversal of the party of Eusebius was suspicious and malevolent, the fact that they had subscribed after being able to give at least a brief defense of themselves is proof that the Arian heresy is truly impious. For they would not have subscribed earlier, unless they had condemned the heresy; and they would not have condemned it if not for their being ashamed and confounded on all sides. Thus their reversal is evidence of their querulous eagerness for impiety. Therefore these also, as I have said, should be silent.[18] But since they are impelled toward what is shameful and perhaps consider that they are better able than the others to maintain their grip on this diabolical impiety and even though I have already responded with a thorough refutation against them in the first letter that I wrote to you,[19] nevertheless let us now put them to the test as we then did those others, examining each of their statements. For it will be shown no less now as then that their heresy is unwholesome and demonic.

6. They speak, in fact, in just the same way that those others used to think and dared to speak: "Not always Father, not always Son. The Son was not before his generation but he also came to be from non-being. Therefore God has not always been Father of the Son. But when the Son came to be and was created, then it was that God was called his Father. For the Word is a creature and a work and foreign and unlike (*anomios*) in essence to the Father. Neither is the Son by nature the true Word of the Father nor his unique and true Wisdom, but he is a creature and one of the things made, and is called Word and Wisdom only improperly, for just like all things, he also came to be by the Word which is in God. Therefore, the Son is not true God."[20]

I wish to ask them first of all, in order that they may at least be able to understand the things that they are saying: What is a son and what does this name signify? For the divine Scriptures signify to us a double sense pertaining to that name. One is that of which Moses speaks in the law: "If you attend to the voice of the Lord your God, to guard all his commandments, all that I have commanded to you today, to do what is good and pleasing before the Lord your God, then you are sons of the Lord our God" (Deut 13:19, 14:1). Likewise, John says in the gospel: "To as many as receive him, he gives power to become sons of God" (Jn 1:12). The other sense is that according to which Isaac is the son of Abraham, and Jacob the son of Isaac, and the patriarchs the sons of Jacob. So according to which of these senses do they consider the Son of God to be, when they go about mythologizing in this way about him? Indeed, I know well that they will proceed into the same impiety together with those who belong to Eusebius.

For if it is according to the first sense, in which those gain the grace of the name through the improvement of their conduct and thus receive power to become sons of God (for this is what the others have said),[21] then it would appear that he does not differ from us at all; and neither would he be only-begotten, since he also would have come into possession of the name of Son by virtue. For even if, as they say, it was foreknown that he would become such, and thus received at once with his coming into being the name and the grace of the name, he would still in no way differ from those who receive the name consequent to their actions, insofar as he also is confessed to be son in that way. For Adam also received grace at once with his coming into being and he was placed in paradise. Yet he was in no way different from Enoch who was transported there some time after his birth, after pleasing God. Nor did he differ from the apostle who also, consequent to his actions, was taken up into paradise (cf. 2 Cor 12:4), nor from the thief who, through his confession, received the promise that he would immediately be in paradise (cf. Lk 23:43).

7. But when they are pressured on these points, perhaps they will respond in the same way that has often brought shame upon them: "In this way we consider the Son to have precedence over the others and he is said to be only-begotten for this reason: that he alone came to be by God alone, whereas all the others were created by God through the Son."[22] Now who suggested to you this foolish new idea that prompts you to say that "the Father alone by himself crafted the Son alone, but all the others came to be through the Son, as through a subsidiary assistant"?[23] If it is because of the labor involved that God was adequate to the task of crafting only the Son but not the others, it is indeed impious to say such things, especially for those who have heard Isaiah say: "The eternal God, the God who fashioned the ends of the earth, does not hunger nor grow weary, and his understanding is beyond scrutiny" (Isa 40:28). Rather, he is the one who gives strength to the hungry and, through his own Word, grants rest to those who toil. But if he disdained to craft by himself those who would be after the Son, as something beneath him, this also is an impious proposition. For there is no arrogance in God, who comes down into Egypt with Jacob; and corrects Abimelech for Abraham's sake, because of Sarah (cf. Gen 20); who speaks face to face with the man Moses (Ex 33:11); who comes down to Mount Sinai (cf. Ex 19:18); and wages war for the people against Amalech, by a secret grace (cf. Ex. 17).

What you say is false. "For he made us and not we ourselves" (Ps 100:3). He is the one who, through his own Word, has made all things, both the small and the great, and there can be no division among creation, such that we can say that this belongs to the Father and that belongs to the Son, but creation is of the one God, who uses his own Word as a hand and works all things in him.[24] God himself showed this when he said, "My hand has made all things" (Isa 66:2); and Paul learned it and taught it: "One God, from whom are all things, and one Lord Jesus Christ through whom are all things" (1 Cor 8:6). Therefore it is he who now and always speaks to the sun and it rises, but when he commands the clouds it rains upon a portion of the earth and the earth dries up where it does not rain. He orders the earth to give forth its fruits, and he forms Jeremiah in the womb (cf. Jer 1:5). But if he does these things now, then there is no doubt that in the beginning he did not disdain to make all things through the Word. For these things are simply parts of the whole.

8. But if it is because the rest of the creatures were not able to withstand the working of the Unoriginate's immediate hand, and it is only the Son who came to be by God alone whereas the others came to be through the Son, as through an assistant and helper[25] – for Asterius the Sacrificer[26] has written this and Arius transcribed it and gave it to his own and henceforth these deranged people use this phrase like a broken reed without knowing that it is rotten to the core – if, indeed, things that come to be are incapable of enduring the hand of God, and yet by your own account the Son is one of those things that have come to be, how is it that he himself was enabled to come to be by God alone?[27] Moreover, if things that come to be need a mediator in order that they may come into being, and yet, according to you, the Son also has come to be, then there needs to have been a mediator before him, in order for him to be created. Yet again, since that mediator would itself be a creature, it follows that it would have needed yet another mediator for its own constitution. And if you conceive of another mediator, you would have to preconceive yet another mediator for it, until you fall into infinity. So there would always be need of a mediator and creation would not be able to be constituted, since, as you say, none of what comes to be is able to withstand the immediate hand of the Unoriginate.

But if you perceive the absurdity of this and then try to say that although the Son was a creature he was made capable of coming into being through the Unoriginate, then it necessarily follows that all the other things that have come into being were also capable of being made[28] by the Unoriginate himself. For, according to you, he is a creature just like all those others are. And thus, according to your impious and foolish conception, the coming into being of the Word would be ultimately pointless since God is adequate for making all things by himself, while things that come to be are capable of enduring the immediate hand of God.[29]

Since this is such mindless madness, let us see if indeed this piece of sophistical speaking by these impious ones is not manifestly more irrational than all their others. Adam alone came to be by God alone, through the Word. Yet, for all that, no one would say that Adam has any precedence over all other people or that he was different from those after him, even if he alone was made and fashioned by God alone while all of us came to be from Adam and were constituted through the succession of the species. This makes no difference, so long as he was fashioned from the earth, and at first did not exist but later came to be.

9. But even if one grants to the first-made (*Protoplastos*) a precedence because of his being found worthy of the hand of God, such a precedence would be referred to him in respect of honor not of nature. For he came to be from the earth, just like all the rest; and the same hand that fashioned Adam then now and always fashions also those after him and constitutes them in existence. As I said before, God himself said the same thing to Jeremiah: "Before I fashioned you in the womb, I knew you" (Jer 1:5); and of everything he says, "My hand has made all these things" (Isa 66:2). And again, through Isaiah, he says, "Thus says the Lord your Redeemer, who fashioned you in the womb. I am the Lord who commands all things, who alone stretched out the heaven and spread out the earth" (Isa 44:24). David, knowing this, sang in the psalm: "Your hands made me and fashioned me" (Ps 119:73). And the one who says in Isaiah, "Thus says the Lord who has fashioned me in the womb a servant to him" (Isa 49:5), means the same thing. Therefore he does not differ from us at all, according to nature, even if he precedes us in time, since we are all constituted and created by the same hand. So if it is in this way that you conceive of the Son of God, O Arians – that he subsists and comes to be in this way – he would not differ at all with respect to nature from the others, according to you, insofar as he also was not and came to be, and the grace of the name was co-created for him because of his virtue. For, according to what you say, he also is one of those of whom the Spirit says in the psalms, "He spoke and they came to be. He commanded and they were created" (Ps 33:9). But then, through whom did God command, in order for him to be created? For there must be a Word, by whom God commands and in whom the works are created. But you have no one to present in that role, apart from the Word which you deny, unless you again invent some other notion.

"Oh, yes," they will say, "we have found another." Once I heard the followers of Eusebius saying this: "We hold that it is for this reason that the Son of God has precedence over the others and is said to be only-begotten, in that he alone participates the Father, whereas all the others participate the Son."[30] Thus have they labored in transforming and altering their words like colors. All the same, they will be exposed to be like those who are bound to the earth (cf. Jn 3:31) and devoid of reason, wallowing in the mud of their own ideas (cf. 2 Pet 2:22).

10. He is the Son of God. Now, if we were called "sons of the Son," then their fabrication would be plausible. But if we also are called sons of God, of whom he too is Son, then clearly we too participate the Father who says, "sons I have begotten and exalted" (Isa 1:2). For if we did not participate him, he would not have said, "I have begotten" (*ibid.*). But if it is he himself who begot us, then no other but he is our Father. And, yet again, it makes no difference if the Son possesses something more and has come into being first, while we have come into being later and are lesser, so long as we all participate and are called sons of the same Father. For "greater" and "lesser" do not indicate different natures but are referred to each one depending on the practice of virtue.[31] So one is placed over ten cities and another over five (cf. Lk 19:17,19) and some are seated "on twelve thrones judging the twelve tribes of Israel" (Mt 19:28); while others hear, "Come, blessed of my Father" (Mt 25:34), and "Well done, good and faithful servants" (Mt 25:23).

But since they think in this way, it is consistent for them to fantasize that God is not always father of such a son, and that such a son does not always exist himself, but came into being as a creature from non-being, and did not exist before he was begotten. But such a one is other than the true Son of God. But since their perseverance in saying such things incurs defilement – it is in fact the attitude of the Sadduccees and the Samasotene[32] – it only remains to say that the Son of God is son in the other sense, in which Isaac is the son of Abraham. It is natural knowledge, after all, that a son is one who is begotten from someone by nature and not acquired from outside the nature, and such is the signification of the name of "son."

"Well, then, is the generation of the Son one of human passibility?"[33] (For, like their predecessors, they also will likewise wish to ignorantly contradict.) In no way! For God is not like a human being, nor are human beings like God. Human beings are created from matter and this passable essence, while God is immaterial and incorporeal. If indeed the same language is sometimes applied to both God and human beings in the divine Scriptures, nevertheless those who are perspicacious will be attentive in their reading, as

Paul has counseled (1 Tim 4:13), and thus distinguish and discern what is written according to the nature of each of the things signified.[34] In this way, they will not confuse the sense by understanding the things of God humanly or by considering human things as referring to God. That would be to mix wine with water (cf. Isa 1:22) and to throw alien fire on the altar along with the divine fire (cf. Lev 10:1).

11. Indeed God creates and yet it is said of human beings also that they create. And whereas God is being, human beings are also said to be, having received being from God. Is it the case, therefore, that God creates as do human beings? Or that God's being is like that of humans? Never! We receive the terms referring to God in one way, and we conceive of those that refer to human beings in another. For God creates, without need of anything, by calling into being what is not (cf. Rom 4:17) while humans first pray and then fashion the subsisting matter, receiving the knowledge of making from the God who has created all things through his own (*idios*) Word. Moreover, humans, who are of themselves incapable of being, exist in place and are encompassed and sustained in the Word of God, while God is self-existent, containing all things and being contained by none, and is in all things according to his own goodness and power, but outside all things according to his own nature.[35] Just as the mode by which human beings create is not that by which God creates, neither do human beings exist as God exists. Therefore, the generation of human beings is other than that of the Son from the Father. For the offspring of human beings are in a way parts of those who generate them, since the nature of their bodies is not simple but composed of parts and variable. Moreover, human beings exhaust themselves in the act of generating and are replenished again by ingesting food and so men become fathers of many children over time. But God, being without parts, is Father of the Son without partition or passibility, for neither outflow nor influx pertain to the Incorporeal as they do to human beings.[36] Since his nature is simple, he is Father of the one and only Son.

Because of this, he is only-begotten and is alone in the bosom of the Father (cf. Jn 1:18), and the Father shows that he alone is from himself, saying: "This is my beloved Son, in whom I am pleased" (Mt 3:17). He is Word of the Father, in whom the impassibility and indivisibility of the Father can be contemplated. Indeed, not even the word of human beings is begotten by passibility and partition, much less that of God. Therefore he is seated at the right hand of the Father as Word, for where the Father is, there also is his Word.

But we stand in order to be judged by him, as beings that are made. And, while he is worshipped on account of his being Son of the Father who is worshipped, we worship and confess him to be Lord and God, since we are creatures and other than he is.

12. Considering all these things, let the one who wishes among them look further into the matter and let there be someone to shame them by asking if it is fitting to say of the one who is from God, as his own (*idion*) offspring, that he is from nothing. Or, once the matter has been so much as merely considered, is there any sense (*logon*) at all in the notion that what is from God has been added to him, so that one would dare to say that the Son is not always? For on this point, once again, the generation of the Son exceeds and transcends human conceptions. We become fathers of our own children in time because we ourselves later come into being after formerly not being, but God, who exists forever, is forever Father of the Son.

We infer knowledge regarding the origination of particular things by reference to similar things. But since "no one knows the Son except the Father, and no one knows the Father except the Son, and the one to whom the Son reveals Him" (Mt 11:27), the sacred writers to whom the Son was revealed have given to us a certain image (*eikona*) derived from visible things, saying, "who is the radiance of his glory and the expression of his being" (Heb 1:3), and again, "for with you is the fountain of life and in your light we shall see light" (Ps 35:10). And when the Word rebukes Israel, he says, "You have abandoned the fountain of Wisdom" (Bar 3:12). This is the fountain which says, "You have abandoned me, the fountain of living water" (Jer 2:13). And while the symbol (*paradeigma*) bears only a slight and very dim resemblance compared to what we yearn for, it is possible nevertheless to conceive from it something greater than human nature and to refrain from considering the generation of the Son to be equal to our own.[37] For who can even conceive that there was once no radiance of light, so as to dare to say that the Son is not always, or that the Son was not before he was begotten? Or who can unloose the radiance from the sun or conceive the fountain as once bereft of life, so as to insanely say of the one who says "I am the life" (Jn 14:6) that "the Son is from non-being," or to say of the one who says, "the one who has seen me has seen the Father" (Jn 14:9), that he is alien to the Father's essence? The sacred writers have given such symbols (*paradeigmata*) because they want us to form our understanding in accordance with them. So it is absurd and very impious that, while Scripture has these images (*eikonas*), we should conceive of the Lord by other ones that are neither in Scripture nor have any pious rationale.

13. Therefore, let them say where they learned these things or from whom was it handed down to them so that they should begin to conceive such things about the Savior. They will say, "We have read in the Proverbs: 'The Lord has created me as a beginning of his ways, for his works' (Prov 8:22)."[38] The followers of Eusebius also used to insist on saying this, while you have written to me showing that these ones also, although they have been overcome and refuted by many demonstrations, have gone about all the same throwing this phrase around every which way, saying that the Son is one of the creatures and counting him among the things which have come to be. But it seems to me that they have failed to properly understand this passage too. For it has a pious and very correct sense, which if they had known, they would not have blasphemed the Lord of glory (cf. 1 Cor 2:8).

Let them compare their statements above with this passage and they will see that there is a great difference between them. Who is there of right mind who will not see at once that the things which are created and made are external to the Maker, whereas our discourse has shown already that the Son exists not externally but from the Father who begets him? For it is the case with a human being also, that he creates a house but begets a son, and there is no one who would turn this around and say that the house and the ship are begotten by the one who makes them, while the son is made and created by him, nor that the house is an image of its creator while the son is unlike his begetter. Rather, one will agree that the son is image (*eikona*) of the Father, while the house is a work of art, unless one is sick in mind and has come to the point of losing one's senses. Certainly the divine Scriptures know better than anyone the nature of each thing. Regarding creatures, Scripture says, through Moses: "In the beginning God made heaven and earth" (Gen 1:1). But, regarding the Son, it shows no other but the Father himself saying, "From the womb before the morning star, I have begotten you" (Ps 109:3). And again: "You are my son, Today I have begotten you" (Ps 2:7). The Lord himself says about himself in the Proverbs: "Before all hills he begets me" (Prov 8:25). Regarding things which have come to be and were created, John says, "All things came to be through him" (Jn 1:3). But when he preaches about the Lord, he says: "The only-begotten Son, who is in the bosom of the Father, he has made him known" (Jn 1:18). Therefore: if Son, then not a creature; if a creature, then not Son. For great is the difference between these. The same one cannot be both creature and Son, as if his being can be considered to be both from God and from outside (*exōthen*) God.

14. "So is this passage simply pointless?" This is what they keep buzzing all around us, like a swarm of mosquitoes. Not at all; it is not pointless but is rather quite to the point. He is indeed said to be created also, but that is when he became a human being; for this is what properly belongs to (*idion*) being human. Such a meaning will be found to be well laid out in the sayings of the Scriptures by one who undertakes the reading of them not as if it were some subsidiary matter, but rather searches out the time and the persons and the purpose of what is written, and on this basis judges and contemplates what is read.[39] He will thus discover and come to knowledge of the time of this text: that, forever being Lord, he later, at the completion of the ages, became human; and, being Son of God, he became also the son of Man.[40] Such a reader will also perceive the purpose: that, wishing to nullify our death, he took to himself a body from the Virgin Mary so that, having offered this as a sacrifice (*thusian*) for all to the Father, "he might set free us all who, through fear of death, had been subject to slavery our whole life long" (Heb 2:15). As to the person (*prosōpon*), it is that of the Savior: but it is said when he takes a body and then says, "The Lord created me as a beginning of his ways for his works" (Prov 8:22). For just as it well befits the Son of God to be eternal and to be in the bosom of the Father, so also, upon becoming human, it is fitting for him to say, "The Lord created me." Then it was that this was said of him.

He also hungered and was thirsty, and enquired where Lazarus was laid, and suffered and rose. And just as when we hear that he is Lord and God and true light, we perceive him as being from the Father, so it is right that when we hear "created" and "servant" and "suffered" not to refer these to the divinity, for they are out of place there, but rather to measure these statements in reference to the flesh which he bore for us. For these things properly belong (*idia*) to the flesh and the flesh is not another's but is the Word's.[41] If someone wishes to learn the benefit that results from this, he will discover that also: "For the Word became flesh" (Jn 1:14) in order that he may offer it for the sake of all and so that we, receiving from his Spirit, may be enabled to be divinized. In no other way would we attain to this, if it were not that he himself put on our created body. For thus have we begun to be called "people of God" and people who are in Christ. But just as when we receive the Spirit we do not destroy our proper being (*idian ousian*), so also, when the Lord becomes a human being for our sakes and puts on a body, he is none the less God. He was not lessened by the covering of the body, but rather divinized it and made it immortal.[42]

15. These things then are sufficient for uncovering the malignity of the Arian heresy. As the Lord has granted it, out of their own words they have been routed and refuted as impious. But let us now advance and demand of them some answers. Now that they have been defeated on their own terms, it is time for them to be questioned on ours. Perhaps in this way they will even become embarrassed and recognize to what point they have fallen, these foul-minded people. We have learned from the Holy Scriptures that the Son of God, as we have said, is the Word itself and Wisdom of the Father. For the apostle says: "Christ the power of God and wisdom of God" (1 Cor 1:24). And John, having said, "And the Word became flesh," immediately adds, "and we have seen his glory, glory as of the only-begotten from the Father, full of grace and truth" (Jn 1:14). Since the Word is only-begotten Son, it is in this Word and in Wisdom that heaven and earth and all that is in them have come to be. And that the source and fountain of this wisdom is God, we have learned from Baruch, where Israel is reprimanded that it has "forsaken the fountain of Wisdom" (Bar 3:12). So if they deny the Scriptures, then they are immediately estranged from the name of Christians and they would be appropriately called atheists and the worst enemies of Christ. For they have brought these names upon themselves. But if they agree with us that the sayings of the Scriptures are divinely inspired, let them dare to openly say what they secretly think, that once God was word-less and wisdom-less, and let them madly say: "There was once when he was not," and "Before he was generated, Christ was not."[43] Let them also declare again that the fountain has not generated wisdom from itself but has acquired it from outside, so that they may dare to say, "From non-being there came to be the Son." It seems that this is no longer a fountain, but some kind of pond which receives water from outside and is gratuitously furnished with the name of fountain.

16. I believe that no one with even a little sense would doubt that this is replete with impiety. But since they keep babbling inarticulately, saying, "Word and Wisdom are only names of the Son," it is necessary to enquire of them as follows: If these are only names of the Son, then he is other than them. But, on the one hand, if he is greater than the names, it is not legitimate for what is greater to be

signified by what is lesser.[44] On the other hand, if he is lesser than
the names, then certainly there is a cause for his acquiring the
better name and this is again to impute progress to him, which is
no less of an impiety than the previous ones. To call the one who is
in the Father, and in whom the Father is (Jn 10:38, 14:10,11), who
said: "I and the Father are one" (Jn 10:30), whom "whoever has
seen has seen the Father" (Jn 14:9), as if he is improved by something external (exōthen) surpasses all madness

But once they are driven back and constrained by great diffi-
culties, like the party of Eusebius, they at last resort to this,
which Arius mythologizes in his songs and in the *Thalia* of his,
raising a new objection: "God speaks many words. Which of
these do we call Son and only-begotten Word of the Father?"[45]
You senseless ones who are anything but Christians! First of all,
to say such things about God is not far from taking God for a
human being who thus speaks and turns aside from his first
words to his second, as if the one Word of God is not sufficient to
accomplish all the work of creation and providence, by the will of
the Father. That God would speak many words would indicate
the weakness of all of them, each one in need of the help of
another. But that God should have one Word, which indeed is
the truth, manifests the power of God and the perfection of the
Word that is from him, as well as the pious understanding of
those whose thinking accords with this truth.[46]

17. If only they were willing to confess the truth, even on the
basis of what they themselves say! For once they concede that God
brings forth words, they clearly acknowledge that he is Father.
Having acknowledged this, let them observe that by not willing to
grant that there is one Word of God, they end up imagining him
to be the Father of many! And not willing to deny that there is in
fact a Word of God, they yet do not acknowledge that this Word is
the Son of God. But this is ignorance of the truth and inexperience
of the divine Scriptures. For if God is Father of a word at all, how
is it that the one who is begotten is not the Son? Moreover, who
then would be the Son of God if not his Word? For there are not
many words, so that each would be deficient, but the Word is one,
so that he alone is perfect; and since God is one, one also must be
his image (eikona), which is the Son. And the Son of God, as one
can learn from the divine oracles themselves, is himself the Word
of God and the Wisdom and the Image and the Hand and the
Power. For the offspring of God is one, and these names are indications of his generation from the Father.

So if you speak of the Son, you indicate what is from the Father by nature. And if you ponder the Word, you think upon the one who is from the Father and inseparable from him. And when you speak of Wisdom, you think just as much of the one who is not from outside (*exōthen*) but from him and in him. If you name the Power and the Hand, you speak again of what is proper (*idion*) to the essence (*ousia*). And if you speak of the Image, you signify the Son, for what would be like God except the Offspring which is from him? Certainly, the things that came to be through the Word have been established in Wisdom. And the things that have been established in Wisdom have been made in the Hand and have come to be through the Son.

We have the assurance of these things not from outside but from the Scriptures. God himself speaks through the prophet Isaiah, saying, "My hand established the earth and my right hand has made firm the heavens" (Isa 48:13). And again: "I will cover you in the shadow of my hand, in which I have made the heaven to stand and established the earth" (Isa 51:16). David, upon learning this and knowing that the hand is the same as Wisdom, sings, "You have made all things in wisdom. The earth is filled with your creation" (Ps 104:24). Likewise, Solomon also, receiving the teaching from God, says: "God established the earth in Wisdom" (Prov 3:19). And John, knowing that the Word is the Hand and the Wisdom, preached: "In the beginning was the Word and the Word was with God, and the Word was God. This was in the beginning with God. All things came to be through Him, and apart from Him nothing came to be" (Jn 1:1–3). The apostle, seeing that the Son is the Hand and the Wisdom and the Word, says: "In times past, God spoke in partial and diverse ways to our ancestors through the prophets; in these last days, he has spoken to us in the Son, whom he has appointed heir of all things, through whom also he made the ages" (Heb 1:1–2). And again, "One Lord Jesus Christ, through whom are all things and we through him" (1 Cor 8:6). Yet again, knowing that the Image of the Father is the Word and the Son and the Wisdom, he says in the letter to the Colossians, "Giving thanks to the God and Father who has made us worthy to share the inheritance of the saints in light, who delivered us from the power of darkness and transported us into the kingdom of his beloved Son, in whom we have redemption, the forgiveness of sins. He is the image of the invisible God, firstborn of all creation, so that all things were created in him, both those in the heavens and upon the earth, things visible and invisible, whether thrones or dominations or principalities or powers. All things were created through him and for him and he is before all things, and all things hold together in him" (Col 1:12–17). As all things were created through the Word, who is the Image, they are thus created in the Image. Therefore, the one who contemplates the Lord in this way will not fall upon "the rock of stumbling" (Rom 9:32), but rather will come to the brightness in the light of truth. For this is truly the outlook of piety, even if these lovers of strife burst asunder, who neither have reverence for God nor shame at being refuted by proofs.

18. At that time,[47] the party of Eusebius was thoroughly interrogated. When they ended up bringing condemnation upon themselves, as I said before, they subscribed and then fell silent and gave up. But since these ones go about swaggering with impieties and confused about the truth, busying themselves with nothing other than abusing the council, let them tell us from what sort of scriptures they have been taught or by which of the saints have they heard the sayings which they have gathered up for themselves: "from non-being" and "he was not before he was generated" and "there was once when he was not," and "changeable" and "beginning to be" and "by will," in all of which they mythologize, making child's play at the expense of the Lord.[48] For the blessed Paul in his epistle to the Hebrews says, "We understand by faith that the ages were established by the word of God, what is visible having come to be from what is invisible" (Heb 11:3). But the Word has nothing in common with the ages, for he exists before the ages, through whom also the ages have come to be. And it is written in the *Shepherd* [49] (since they use it as a pretext even though it is not from the canon): "Believe first of all, that God is one, who has created all things and ordered and made all things from non-being into being." But, once again, this is not at all about the Son. Rather, it is speaking about all the things which have come to be through him, he being other than these. One cannot count together the maker with the things which come to be by him, unless one is crazed enough to say that the architect is the same as the buildings which are made by him.

So why then do they bring forward unscriptural phrases for the sake of impiety, and yet accuse those who use unscriptural phrases piously? For impiety is in every way to be shunned, even if someone tries to cloak it in many words and persuasive sophistries. But piety is sanctioned by all, even if someone uses unusual words, providing only that the one speaking has a pious conception and wishes to signify reverently, through these words, what he has conceived.

Now it has already been shown by our discourse that the aforementioned sayings of the enemies of Christ were mere piddling words which, then as now, are full of all impiety. But if someone enquires accurately into the things written and defined by the council, he will find that it completely embraces the sense of the truth, especially if one were to enquire with a love of learning and hear the fitting reason for the use of these words. And it is this:

19. The council wished to banish the impious phrases of the Arians and to inscribe the words confessed by the Scriptures: that the Son is not from non-being but from God; that he is Word and Wisdom, neither creature nor something made, but from the Father as his own (*idion*) offspring. But the party of Eusebius, compelled by their longstanding perversity, wished the designation of his being "from God" to be taken as something in common with us and the Word of God to be no different from us in this respect, as it is written: "one God from whom are all things" (1 Cor 8:6) and "the old things have passed away; behold all that is new has come to be; and all this is from God" (2 Cor 5:17,18). So the fathers of the council, seeing their deceit and the machinations of their impiety, finally found it necessary to proclaim the "from God" more clearly and to write "the Son is from the essence of the Father" (*ek tēs ousias tou theou*), so that "from God" may not be considered to be the same and equal in the case of the Son as it is with things that have come to be; but that it may be confessed that while all others are creatures, the Word is uniquely from the Father. For even if all things are said to be from God, this is altogether otherwise than how the Son is. In the case of created things, they are said to be from God in that they do not exist randomly and unaccountably; neither do they attain their origination by chance, as those who speak of an origination that comes about from the intertwining of atoms and of like parts; nor, as certain heretics say, is there another creator, nor, as again others say, do all things have their subsistence through some angels.[50] Rather, all things are said to be from God because the existent God, by himself and through the Word, brought all things that formerly did not exist into being. But the Word is said to be and is alone from the Father because he is not a creature; and the Son's being "from the essence of the Father" is indicative of this sense, which does not pertain to anything that has come into being.[51]

Certainly, Paul does say that all things are from God, but he immediately adds: "and one Lord Jesus Christ, from whom are all things" (1 Cor 8:6), in order to show to all, that the Son is other than all things which have come into being from God. For the things which have come into being from God have come to be through the Son. Paul said this because it is by God that creation comes to be, not because all things are from the Father in just the same way that the Son is. Neither are all things as the Son, nor is the Word one of "all things," for he is Lord and Fashioner of all things. That is why the holy council proclaimed in a clearer way that he is "from the essence of the Father," in order to proclaim the confession that the Word is other than the nature of things which have come to be and is alone truly from God, and in order to leave no more pretext for the deceit of the impious. This then is the reason for their having written "from the essence."

20. Yet again, when the bishops said that it is necessary to proclaim the Word as true power and image of the Father and unchangeably like the Father in all things (*homoion te kai aparallakton auton kata panta tō patri*) and inalterable and that he is always and inseparably in the Father – for never was he not, but rather, the Word is always with the Father, as the radiance and the light – the party of Eusebius persevered, though because of their shame at the refutations leveled against them, they did not dare to contradict. Instead, they were caught winking their eyes and murmuring among themselves that "like" (*homoion*) and "always" and the name of "Power" and "in him" are also common to us and the Son, so that it would not hurt them to agree with us. As to "like," because it is written of us also, "the human being is the image and glory of God" (1 Cor 11:7); as to "always," because it is written, "we who live are always ..." (2 Cor 4:11);[52] "in him," because "in him we live and move and have our being" (Acts 17:28); "inalterable," because it is written, "Nothing will separate us from the love of Christ" (Rom 8:39); as to "Power," because the caterpillar and the locust are called "power" and "great power" (cf. Joel 2:25) whereas it is often written in reference to the people, as "all the power of God came out from the land of Egypt" (Ex 12:41); and there are other heavenly powers, for it says, "the Lord of powers is with us; our stronghold is the God of Jacob" (Ps 46:8).[53]

Asterius, who is called "the sophist," has written these things, having learned from them and, along with him, Arius also, as has been said. But the bishops, perceiving their hypocrisy here also and seeing that, according to what is written, "deceit is in the hearts of the impious who plot evil" (Prov 12:20), found it necessary again to gather together the sense of the Scriptures and to speak more clearly the things which they said before, and to write, "the Son is one in essence (*homoousion*) with the Father," in order to signify that the Son is not only like, but from the Father as the same in likeness (*tauton tē homoiōsei*), and in order to show that the likeness and inalterability of the Son is other than the imitative likeness that is ascribed to us and which we attain through virtue by keeping the commandments. For it is possible for bodies which are like each other to become in some way separated and distant from one another, which happens with the sons of human beings in relation to their begetters, as it is written concerning Adam and Seth, who was begotten of Adam and who was like him "according to his kind" (Gen 5:3). But since the generation of the Son from the Father is other than that which pertains to the nature of human beings and he is not only like (*homoios*) but also inseparable from the essence (*ousia*) of the Father and he and the Father are one, as he himself said (Jn 10:30), and the Word is always in the Father and the Father in the Word (cf. Jn 10:38) – as is the radiance in relation to the light (for this is what the phrase means) – the council, understanding all this, aptly wrote "one in essence" (*homoousion*). They did this in order to overturn the perversity of the hypocrites and to show that the Word is other than the things which come to be. For immediately after writing it, they added: "But those who say that the Son of God is from non-being or is a creature or changeable or made or from another essence (*ousia*), these the holy and catholic Church anathematizes."[54] In saying this, they made it manifestly clear that "from the essence" and "of one essence" are abrogations of the trite slogans of the impious: such as that he is a "creature" and "made" and something which has come into being (*genēton*) and changeable and that he was not before he was generated. The one who thinks such things is contradicting the council. But the one who does not think along with Arius necessarily holds and takes to mind the teachings of the council and views them appropriately, as indicating a relation like that of the radiance to the light, and in this way attains to an image of the truth.

21. Therefore, if these ones also adopt the pretext that the words of the council are alien, let them attend to the sense in which the synod wrote them and let them anathematize what the council has anathematized. Then, if they can, let them complain about the words. But I know well enough that if they were to adhere to the sense of the council, they would accept completely the words that express that sense. But if they wish to censure the sense, it should be clear to all that there is no point for them to be talking about the council's words, and that they are only inventing for themselves a basis for impiety and that is the motivation for their own words.

But if they keep murmuring that it is because the words of the council are not scriptural, then let them be cast out on those very grounds, as people who speak vacuously and whose mind is unsound. Let them accuse themselves on this very score, for it was they who first provided the cause for this when they began to fight God using unscriptural terms.[55] Nevertheless, let it be known to anyone who wishes to learn, that even if the words are not as such in the Scriptures, yet, as has been said before, they contain the sense (*dianoian*) of the Scriptures and they express this sense and communicate it to those who have ears that are whole and hearken unto piety.

This is what you should take into consideration and these ignorant ones should pay heed to it: It has been shown in the preceding and it is to be believed as true, that the Word is from the Father and is alone proper (*idion*) to him and his offspring by nature. Or else, from where or from which other should one conceive the Son to be, who is Wisdom and Word, in whom all things came to be, except from God himself? But we have also learned this from the Scriptures, where the Father says through David: "My heart has poured out a good word" (Ps 44:2),[56] and "From the womb before the morning star I have begotten you" (Ps 110:3), while the Son manifests himself to the Jews by saying, "If God were your father, you would have loved me. For I have come from the Father" (Jn 8:42), and again, "Not that anyone has seen the Father, except the one who is from God; He has seen the Father" (Jn 6:46). Certainly, to say "I and the Father are one" (Jn 10:30) and "I am in the Father and the Father is in me" (Jn 14:10) is the same as saying, "I am from the Father and inseparable from him." Having learned these things from the Father, John spoke, saying, "the only begotten Son, who is in the bosom of the Father, has revealed him" (Jn 1:18). But what else does "in the bosom" signify but the authentic generation of the Son from the Father?

22. But if one considers God to be composite, as an essence in which there is accident, or to have any external covering and to be enveloped and concealed (*kaluptesthai*), or if one thinks that there is something around him (*peri auton*) which completes his essence, so that when we say "God" or name him "Father," we are not signifying the invisible and incomprehensible essence itself but something of what is around God, then let them censure the council for having written that "the Son is from the essence of God." But let them observe well that to think in this way is to blaspheme twice over, for they are insinuating the notion of a bodily god and they are falsely declaring that the Lord is not the Son of the Father himself

but of what is around the Father. But if God is simple, as indeed he is, then quite clearly when we say "God" and name the Father we are not naming something around him, but are signifying his very essence (*ousia*).[57] For even if it is impossible to comprehend what is the being and essence (*ousia*) of God, if only we understand that God is and consider that the Scriptures signify him in these terms, we intend to signify none other than him when we say "God" and "Father" and "Lord." Therefore when he says "I am who is" (Ex 3:14) and "I am the Lord God" (Ex 20:2) and whenever Scripture says "God" we recognize that this signifies nothing other than his incomprehensible essence (*ousia*) itself and we understand that the one of whom they speak is the one who is.

Therefore, let no one be shocked to hear that the Son of God is from the being of God. Rather, let him be receptive to the fathers who wrote "from the essence" (*ek tēs ousias*), according to a purified sense, as more explicit and yet equivalent to "from God." They considered that it was the same to say that the Word is "from God" as it is to say "from the essence of God," since, as I have said, "God" signifies nothing other than the essence (*tēn ousian*) of the One who is.[58] Therefore, if the Word is not from God as a genuine son who is from his father by nature, but is said to be from the Father in the same way that all creatures are said to be so, because of their having been created [by the Father], then indeed he is not from the being of the Father, nor is he a son according to essence (*kat ousian*), but because of virtue, as are we who are called sons by grace. But if he is alone from God as genuine Son, as indeed is the case, then it is well said that the Son is from the being of God.

23. The symbol (*paradeigma*) of the light and the radiance also has the same meaning.[59] For the sacred writers did not say that the Word was related to God like a fire which is ignited from the heat of the sun and which is usually extinguished again, for this is an external product and creation of its maker. But they all preached of him as Radiance,[60] in order to disclose his being properly and inseparably from the essence and his unity with the Father. Thus will his unchangeability and inalterability also be truly secured, for how can he be unchangeable and inalterable if he is not the proper (*idion*) offspring of the Father's essence? For it is necessary, in regard to this also, to safeguard his identity with his own Father.

Since this explanation is thus shown to be pious,[61] the enemies of Christ should not be shocked by the "*homoousios*" either, since this term also has a sound sense and rationale. For if we say that the Word is from the essence of God (let this at last be confessed by them!), what is that except to say that he is truly and eternally of the essence from which he is begotten? For he is not different in kind, as if he were something foreign and dissimilar (*anomoion*) that is mixed in with the essence of the Father. Nor is his likeness merely extrinsic, as if he were in some other respect or completely of a different essence (*heteroousios*), just as brass shines like gold and silver and tin.[62] These are foreign to one another and of different natures and are separate in their natures and their powers. Brass is not proper (*idion*) to gold, any more than a pigeon is from a dove. Even though they are considered to be like (*homoia*) each other, they are nevertheless different in essence. Therefore, if that is how the Son is, then he is a creature like us and not one in essence (*homoousios*). But if the Son is Word, Wisdom, Image of the Father, and Radiance, then it follows reasonably that he is "one in essence." Unless it is established that he is not from God but is an instrument, of a different nature and a different essence, then the council has decreed aptly and thought rightly.

24. Moreover, every bodily thought must be shunned in these matters. With a pure mind and transcending all conceptions that arise from sensation, let us contemplate with the mind alone[63] the authentic kinship of the Son and the Father and the Word's belonging to God (*logou tēn pros ton theon idiotēta*) and the unchanging likeness (*homoiotēta*) of the radiance to the light. Just as "offspring" and "Son" are terms that have not a human signification but one that is appropriate to God, and that is how they are used, so when we hear the term "*homoousios*," let us not fall back on our human senses and think of parts and divisions of divinity. Rather, let us bring to mind incorporeal realities and not tear asunder the unity of nature and the identity of light, for such is the proper (*idion*) relation of the Son to the Father, showing God to be truly Father of the Word.

Once again, the symbol (*paradeigma*) of the light and the radiance is indispensable. Who would dare to say that the radiance is unlike (*anomoion*) and foreign to the sun? Or rather, who, upon beholding the relation of the radiance to the sun and the identity of the light, would not confidently say that the light and the radiance are really one and that the one is shown in the other and the radiance is in the sun, so that the one who beholds this sees the other? How then can those who believe and see rightly refer to such a unity and natural identity (*idiotēta*) except as "offspring, one in essence"? And what should one fittingly and appropriately think about the offspring of God but that he is Word and Wisdom and

Power, of which neither is it legitimate to say that he is foreign to the Father, nor is it proper to fantasize that he is not eternally with the Father. For it is by this offspring that the Father has made all things and through whom he loves humanity, extending his providence to all things.

Therefore, he and the Father are one, as has been said.[64] But perhaps those perverse-minded people will dare to go further and say that the being of the Word is other than the light which is in him from the Father, so that the light which is in the Son is one with the Father, but he himself, as a creature, is foreign in essence.[65] But this is simply the belief of Caiaphas and the Samosatene, which the Church has banished and through which they fell from the truth and were declared to be heretics, and which these ones are now concealing. For if he participates wholly the light from the Father, why is he not himself what is participated, so that there be not found a medium between him and the Father?[66] For if he is not thus, then it no longer appears that all things have come into being through him, but rather that they have come to be through that which he himself also participates.[67] But if the Word is thus, being the Wisdom of the Father in whom the Father is revealed and known and creates and without whom the Father does nothing, then clearly he is "from the Father." For all things that came into being participate in him by participating the Holy Spirit. Being so, he is not "from non-being" nor a creature at all, but rather is the proper offspring from the Father, as the radiance is from the light.

25. It is in this same sense that those gathered in Nicaea decreed these terms. But let us now prove that they did not invent these things and manufacture them on their own, as these ones allege, but spoke what they received from those before them. So this pretence also will be snatched away from them. Learn, therefore, O Christ-fighting Arians, that Theognostus,[68] that learned man, did not shirk from saying "from the essence." Writing on the Son in the second book of the *Hypotyposes*, he speaks thus:

> The essence (*ousia*) of the Son is not something adjoined from outside, nor is it acquired from non-being, but it came forth from the essence of the Father, as the radiance of the light and the water's vapor. The radiance and the vapor are not the sun itself nor the water itself, yet neither is the relationship between them one of otherness. And neither is the essence (*ousia*) of the Son itself the Father, nor is it

other; but it is an outflow of the essence of the Father, which does not thereby undergo division. Just as the sun remains itself and is not lessened by the rays emanated by it, so neither does the essence of the Father undergo alteration in having the Son as an image of itself.

That is how Theognostus spoke, having previously investigated by way of enquiry and later putting this forward as his own opinion. As for Dionysius, bishop of Alexandria, he was writing against Sabellius and explaining in detail the economy of the Savior according to the flesh, thereby refuting the Sabellians and showing that it is not the Father who became flesh but his Word, as John said (Jn 1:14).[69] But since he was alleged to have said that the Son was something made, and came to be (*genēton*) and not of one essence (*homoousios*) with the Father, he wrote to his namesake, Dionysius the bishop of Rome, and defended himself, saying that this was a slander against him. He assured him that he did not say that the Son was made, but rather confessed him even to be "of one essence." His words are as follows:

I also wrote another letter, in which I refuted the false accusation which was brought against me to the effect that I did not say that the Son was of one essence (*homoousion*) with God. For although I say that I do not find this title anywhere in the holy Scriptures, yet the following proposals, of which they are silent, are not discordant with this meaning. I offered the example of human birth as being clearly a case of homogeneity and I said that surely the parents are other than the children only in that they are not themselves the children; otherwise there would necessarily be neither parents nor children. As I said before, I do not have this letter to hand, because of circumstances. Otherwise, I would have sent you the words used there, or rather a copy of the whole letter, which, if I find a way, I will still do. But I do know and recall that I offered many likenesses of kinship. I said that the plant which comes forth from the seed or the root is other than that from which it sprouts, and yet it is altogether of the same nature. And I said that the stream which flows from a fountain takes a different name, for neither is the fountain called a stream nor the stream a fountain; both are existent and the stream is the water from the fountain.[70]

26. You can also look to Dionysius, the bishop of Rome, to see that the Word of God is neither made nor a creature but is the inseparable and proper (*idion*) offspring of the Father's being, as the great council has written. He is writing against those who believe the doctrines of Sabellius and denounces those who dare to say these things. This is how he speaks:

> Next, it is proper that I should speak about those who divide and cut into pieces and destroy the most sacred preaching of the church of God, that of the divine monarchy, partitioning it into three powers and divided entities (*hypostases*) and divinities. It has become known to me that there are some among you, catechists and teachers of the divine word, who are leaders in this belief, which is, so to speak, diametrically opposed to the belief of Sabellius. For he blasphemed in saying that the Son is himself the Father and vice versa; while, on the other hand, these preach a kind of doctrine of three gods, separating the holy oneness (*monad*) into three entities that are foreign to each other and completely separated. But the divine Word must be united to the God of all, and the Holy Spirit must dwell and abide in God. For it is necessary to sum up and gather together the divine triad into one as into a kind of summit, I mean the God and Ruler of all. But the sundering and separation of the monarchy into three principles (*archas*) is the doctrine of the foolish-minded Marcion. It is a diabolical teaching, not belonging to the real disciples of Christ who are content with the Savior's teaching, and who know well that a triad is preached by the Holy Scriptures, but that neither the Old nor the New Covenant preaches three gods.
>
> One should not censure any less those who believe that the Son is made and who consider the Lord to have come into being as one of the things that have really come to be. The sacred utterances indeed witness to a birth that is befitting and appropriate to him, but not to some kind of fashioning or making. So it is no ordinary blasphemy, but a great one, to say that the Lord is some kind of handmade thing. For if he became Son, then there was when he was not (*en hote ouk en*). But he existed always, if indeed he is "in the Father," as he himself says, and if Christ is Word and Wisdom and Power. For the Sacred Scriptures say that

Christ is these things, as you know. But these are powers of God. Therefore, if the Son came into being, there was when these things were not; then there was a time when God was without these. But this is most absurd. Why, then, should I say anything more about these people to you, men who are bearers of the Spirit and who know clearly the absurdities that emerge from saying that the Son is made?

Those who expound this conception seem to me not to have taken account of all this, and so they have strayed completely from the truth, taking "He created me as a beginning of his ways," in a sense that is otherwise than what the holy and prophetic Scripture intends. As you know, there is not only one sense for "created." Here, "created" is to be taken as "He has set over the works which have come to be through him," which have come to be, that is, through the Son himself. For "created" does not here mean "made." "To make" differs from "to create." "Is he not your Father who has acquired you and made you and created you?" says Moses in the great song of Deuteronomy (Deut 32:6). And one could say to them: "O reckless people! Is he made, he who is the first born of all creation (Col 1:15), who is begotten from the womb before the morning star (Ps 110:3), who says as Wisdom, 'Before all the hills, he begets me' (Prov 8:25)?" And everywhere in the sacred utterances, one could find the Son spoken of as generated but not as having come into being (*gennesthai ... ou gegonenai*), from which those are clearly refuted who make false assumptions about the generation of the Lord and who dare to speak of his divine and ineffable generation as a making. Therefore, one must not partition the awesome and divine oneness (*monada*) into three divinities, nor dilute the honor and surpassing greatness of the Lord as something "made," but rather believe in God the Father and ruler of all and in Jesus Christ his Son and in the Holy Spirit, uniting the Word to the God of all. "For I," he says, "and the Father are one" (Jn 10:30) and "I am in the Father and the Father in me" (Jn 14:10). Thus both the divine triad and the holy preaching of the monarchy are secured.

27. As to the Word's being eternally coexistent with the Father and not of another essence or subsistence (*mē heteras* ousias *hypostaseos*) but belonging (*idion*) to the essence of the Father, as those in the

council said, you may hear this also from the diligent Origen. Those things which he has written by way of enquiry and speculation one should not take as his own beliefs but of those who are engaged in the contention of an enquiry that is undertaken with a view to debate. But it is the declarations that he makes when he is defining matters freely which represent the mind of that diligent one. Thus, after what he says to the heretics by way of tentative speculation, he immediately puts forward his own words in this way:

> If he is an image of the ineffable God, then he is an ineffable image. But I will be so bold as to add that, being the likeness of the Father, there is not [any time] when he was not. For when was it that God, who is called "Light" by John ("For God is light" (1 Jn 1:5)), did not have the radiance of his own glory, so that someone may dare to ascribe a beginning to the Son, as formerly not being? When was he not, who is the image of the ineffable and unnameable and unspeakable subsistence (*hypostasis*) of the Father, the reflection (Heb 1:3) and Word who "knows the Father" (Jn 10:15)? Let the one who dares to say, "there was when the Son was not," observe well that he is also saying that Wisdom once was not and the Word once was not and the Life once was not.[71]

And also in another place, he says, "But it is neither proper nor without danger if, through our weakness, we deprive God, as far as that lies within us, of his only begotten Word which coexists always with him, being the Wisdom in whom he rejoiced (Prov 8:30). In this way he will be conceived as not always rejoicing."[72]

See, then, how we prove that this conception has been transmitted from fathers to fathers. But you, O new Jews and disciples of Caiaphas, which fathers do you have to show for your sayings? You cannot speak of any among those who are understanding and wise, for all reject you, except only the devil. It is he alone who has become the father of such apostasy, he who from the beginning has sown this impiety in you and now has persuaded you to revile the ecumenical council because it did not decree your terms, but those which the eyewitnesses and servants of the Word from the beginning have handed down. For the faith which the council confessed in writing is that of the Catholic Church, and this is what was vindicated by the blessed fathers when they made their declaration the way they did and condemned the Arian heresy. But that is especially why these ones are trying to overturn the council. It is not the words that pain them, but the fact that by these words they are shown to be heretics and their heresy more audacious than the others.

28. Of course, when their own words were at that time shown to be thoughtless and easily refuted, once and for all, as impious, they resorted finally to the use of the term "unoriginated" (*agenētos*), which is from the Greeks, so that on the pretext of this term, they may again number the Word of God, through whom are all things that have come to be, among those very things which came to be and are created.[73] That is how shameless they are in their impiety and how contentious they are in their blasphemies against the Lord. If it is out of ignorance that they are so shameless in their use of this term, then they should have learned better from those who gave it to them. For these latter were not afraid to say that even Mind, which they say is from the Good, and Soul, which is from Mind, are unoriginated, even though it is known what they are from.[74] They realize that by saying this they are not detracting from the First, from whom these proceed. So let them either speak likewise or not speak at all about things they don't understand.

But if they think that they are knowledgeable, then they must be questioned, especially since the term is not from the Sacred Scriptures; for once again they are being contentious and speaking unscripturally. I have already explained the reason and the sense according to which the council with one voice decreed "from the being" (*ek tēs ousias*) and "one in essence" (*homoousios*). The synod, and the fathers who were before it, wrote and proclaimed this on the basis of what is signified about the Savior in the Scriptures. But now, let these ones answer also, if indeed they can, how they found this unscriptural term and in what sense they say that God is "unoriginated." Indeed, I have heard that the term has various senses. They say that what has not yet come into being but can become is "unoriginated"; and also what neither exists nor can come into being; and thirdly, the term signifies what exists but has neither come into being nor had a beginning of being, but is everlasting and imperishable.[75] Perhaps, then, they will wish to set aside the first two meanings, as issuing in absurdity. According to the first, both the things that have already come into being and those that are expected to come into being are unoriginated.[76] But the second is even more absurd. So they proceed to the third sense and use "unoriginated" in that sense. But in saying this, they are no less impious. For if they say that the unoriginated is what has no beginning of its being and has neither come into being nor is created but is everlasting, whereas the Word of God is the opposite of such, who does not see at once the villainy of these enemies of God? Who would not stone those who are so crazed?[77] Since they were ashamed to persist in uttering the original slogans of their myths, by which they were refuted, the wretched lot invented another way of again indicating the same meaning by using this term, "unoriginated." But if the Son is among those things which have come into being, then clearly he also came into being "from non-being"; and if he has a beginning of his being, then he was not before he was generated; and if he is not eternal, "there was once when he was not."

29. Therefore, since that is what they think, it was incumbent upon them to articulate their heterodoxy in their own words, and not to hide their perversity with the title of "unoriginated." But that is not what they do, these malicious ones! They do everything with deceit, in the style of their father the devil (cf. Mt 7:15). Just as he tries to deceive by using the appearance of others, so these have contrived the title of "unoriginated," so that, while pretending to speak well of God, they may harbor a hidden blasphemy against the Lord and, under this veil, communicate it to others.

But since this sophistry of theirs has been uncovered, let them say whatever else they have left over. "We have found," say the malicious, adding to their former words, "that what is unoriginated is that which does not have a cause (*aition*) for its being, but rather is itself the cause of the coming to be of what has come into being."[78] Thankless people and truly deaf to the Scriptures, who in all things act and speak not for the honor of God, but for the dishonor of the Son. They do not know that whoever dishonors the Son dishonors the Father. First of all, even if they call God by this title, it does not prove that the Word is among the things which come into being, since as offspring of the being of the Father, he is forever with him. Therefore, this title[79] does not take anything away from the nature of the Word, nor does the designation of "unoriginated" have its signification in relation to the Son, but in relation to the things which come to be through the Son. It is the same as when someone speaks to an architect and calls him a maker of a house or city; one does not include within that designation the son who is begotten of him, but calls him "maker" with a view to the skill and knowledge that go into his making, thus signifying that the architect is not the same as the things that come to be through him. But knowing the nature (*physin*) of the maker, one realizes that the one who is begotten from him is other than these things which are made by him. With reference to his son, one calls him father; but on account of the works which he makes, he is called creator and maker. Likewise, the one who thus calls God "unoriginated" (*agenēton*) names him from the works which he makes, signifying not only that he is not originated (*mē genēton*), but that he is also maker of the things that are originated (*genēton*).[80] Nevertheless, one recognizes that the Word is other than the things which originated in being and is alone the Father's own (*idion*) offspring, through whom all things came into being and are constituted.

30. The prophets also call God "ruler of all,"[81] but they do not call him so as if the Word were one of the "all"; for they knew that the Son is other than the things which came into being and is himself ruler of all, according to his likeness (*homoiotēta*) to the Father. They call God "ruler of all" because the Father rules over all the things which he has made through the Son, having granted authority over all these to the Son and in granting it, is still himself Lord of all things through the Word. Again, when they speak of God as the "Lord of powers" (cf. Ps 45:8), they do not say this as if the Word were one of these powers, but on account of the fact that whereas he is Father of the Son, he is also Lord of the powers which come into being through the Son. And, again, since the Word is "in the Father" (cf. Jn 14:10) he is Lord of all these powers and rules over all things; for everything that the Father has is the Son's (cf. Jn 16:15). Inasmuch as this is the sense contained in these titles, let the one who wishes to call God "unoriginated" do so, provided only that this implies not that the Word is one of the things that are originated, but rather, as I said before, that God is not originated and moreover that he is also Maker of originated things through his own Word.

Furthermore, even if the Father is called "unoriginated," the Word is still also the Image of the Father and of one essence (*homoousios*) with him. Being Image, he is other than originated things and other than all; for he has identity (*idiotēta*)[82] and likeness (*homoiōsin*) with the One whose Image he is. Therefore, the one who calls the Father unoriginated (*agenēton*) and almighty perceives in the Unoriginated and Almighty his Word and Wisdom, which is the Son. But these amazing people, so reckless in their impiety, did not discover the title of "unoriginated" in their efforts to honor God, but on account of their maliciousness concerning the Savior. If they were concerned about honor and praise, then they should have acknowledged God as "Father" and called him so; that would have been better than naming him "unoriginated." In calling God "unoriginated" they are speaking of him only as Maker, with reference to the things that have originated in being, as I said before, so that they can indicate the Son to be a work, according to their own fancy. But the one who calls God "Father" immediately signifies the Son also, who is in him, and is not ignorant that all things that came into being were created through the Son who is.

31.[83] Therefore, it would be more truthful to signify God by reference to the Son and call him Father than to call and name him "unoriginated," by reference only to his works. The latter title signifies the works which came into being from the will of God through his Word, whereas the title of "Father" acknowledges the integral (*idion*) offspring from his being. As much as the Word transcends the things which come into being, by so much and more does calling God "Father" surpass calling him "unoriginated." Indeed the latter is unscriptural and dubious, having multiple significations; whereas the former is simple and scriptural and more truthful and signifies only the Son. Moreover, the term "unoriginated" was fashioned by the Greeks, who do not know the Son, but the name of "Father" has been made known and granted to us by our Lord. Knowing whose son he was, he said, "I am in the Father and the Father in me" (Jn 14:10); and "the one who has seen me has seen the Father" (Jn 14:9); and "I and the Father are one" (Jn 10:30). We do not find it anywhere that he calls the Father "unoriginated." When teaching us to pray, he does not say, "When you pray, say 'God Unoriginated'" but rather, "When you pray, say 'Our Father who is in heaven'" (cf. Mt 6:9). It was his will also that the summit of our faith should have the same form, so he commanded us to be baptized not into the name of the unoriginated and the originated nor into the name of the uncreated and the created, but into the name of Father, Son and the Holy Spirit (Mt 28:19).[84] By this consecration, we too are truly made into sons, and saying the name of the Father, we also acknowledge through this name the Word who is in the Father. But if he wills that we call his own proper (*idion*) Father "our Father," we must not for that reason compare ourselves to the Son, who is so by nature. For the Father is called such by us on account of the Son. It is because the Word carried our body and came to be among us that God is called our Father, on account of the Word in us. The Spirit of the Word, in us and through us, names the Word's own Father as our Father, and this is the meaning of the apostle's saying, "God has sent forth the Spirit of his Son into our hearts, crying out, 'Abba, Father'" (Gal 4:6).

32. But since their ways are full of malice and they have been refuted as far as the name of "unoriginated," perhaps they will wish to say: "One should have spoken concerning our Lord and Savior Jesus Christ from what is written about him in the Scriptures, and not have introduced unscriptural terms." Well, sure, that is the way it should have been; and I would also say as much. For the manifestations of the truth that are derived from the Scriptures are more accurate than those from other places. But, as I said, it was the wrong-headedness and the untrustworthy deceitful impiety of Eusebius's party that forced the bishops to proclaim more explicitly terms that would over-turn their impiety. Moreover, it has been shown already that what was written by the council has a right sense, whereas it has become clear that the slogans of the Arians are rotten and that their ways are malicious. Even though the title of "unoriginated" has its own proper sense and can be applied piously, they interpret it according to their own will and fancy in a way that brings dishonor to the Savior, just to be contentious, like giants who war against God. But they did not remain uncondemned when they offered their earlier slogans and neither were they able now to escape detection when they interpreted the "unoriginated" so maliciously, although it can be understood rightly and piously. They were shamed in the midst of all and their heresy was everywhere stigmatized.

These things I have recalled, as much as I could, in order to clarify the things that took place at that time, at the council. Yet I know that the lovers of debate among those who war against Christ will still not wish to be converted even after hearing these things. They will persevere in seeking after other pretexts, and after these, they will invent yet others. According to the prophecy, "if the Ethiopian will change his skin and the leopard his spots" (Jer 13:23), then will those who have been taught impiety be willing to think piously. But you, beloved, read this by yourself when you receive it. If you judge it to have merit, let it be read to the brothers there present, so that they also, having learned these things, may embrace the council's zeal for the truth and the exactitude of its understanding, while condemning the impudence of the Christ-fighting Arians and the foolish allegations which they have labored to invent among themselves for the sake of their impious heresy. For glory, honor, and adoration is befitting to God the Father along with his Word and Son who with him is without beginning, together with the all-holy and life-giving Spirit, now and unto the endless ages of ages. Amen.

4

LETTERS TO SERAPION ON THE HOLY SPIRIT (1:15–33)

Introduction

The *Letters to Serapion on the Holy Spirit* were penned ca. 357, during Athanasius's third exile (356–362), which he spent in the refuge of monastic communities in the desert of Egypt. They were written in response to a request made to him by his friend and supporter the bishop Serapion of Thmuis, who a few years earlier, in 353, was head of a delegation that had traveled to Milan to plead the cause of Athanasius.[1] Serapion alerts Athanasius to the existence of a group of Christians who accepted the doctrine of the full divinity of the Son but shirked from extending that confession to the Holy Spirit. Using the language of Aetius and Eunomius, this group maintained that the Holy Spirit was "unlike" (*anomios*) to the Father and the Son in being. Aside from the general observation that the Scriptures do not directly refer to the Spirit as God, the scriptural warrants offered on behalf of this doctrine were Am 4:13 ("I am the one who establishes thunder and creates spirit and declares to people his Christ" (LXX)) and 1 Tim 5:21 (where the apostle exhorts, "I charge you in the sight of God and Christ Jesus and the elect angels that you observe these things without prejudice, doing nothing by partiality"). The first of these played an analogous role with regard to the doctrine of the Spirit, as did Prov 8:22 with regard to that of the Son; here, it was the Spirit that was claimed to be described as "created." The verse from Paul's *Letter to Timothy* was taken as an indication that the Spirit was an angel or "servant," as seems to be indicated also in Heb 1:14: "Are they not all ministering spirits sent to serve, for the sake of those who are to inherit salvation?"

Athanasius's response takes the form of a long letter, followed by two shorter ones which essentially summarize the contents of the first one.[2] The first half of the first letter (1–14) deals with the scriptural texts used by those who deny the divinity of the Spirit.

With regard to Am 4:13, Athanasius examines an array of scriptural texts in which reference is made to "spirit" in order to conclude that there are two distinct significations of the term in its scriptural usage: without the definite article, it refers to the human spirit or to wind or breath; with the definite article, it refers to the divine Spirit.[3] Since the text of Am 4:13 refers to "spirit," without the definite article, the reference is not to the Holy Spirit, and those who mistakenly understand it thus are forcing a figurative interpretation, or "trope," onto the passage.[4] Never at a loss for derogatory names for his opponents, Athanasius thus styles them "Tropici." Turning to 1 Tim 5:21, Athanasius points out that the text does not actually name the Spirit at all, and then launches into a demonstration that the scriptural depiction of the Spirit is in decisive contrast to that of angels.

The second half of the first letter (15–33), which is excerpted here, takes up the main theological argument of the "Tropici," that if the Spirit is not a creature, he must be a "brother" or "son" of the Son. Behind the seeming facetiousness of that argument, there is a concern that the uniqueness of the Son as "only-begotten" would be compromised by the assertion that the Spirit too fully shares in the divine being. Nevertheless, Athanasius exploits the seemingly indiscriminate application of the human analogy by his opponents in order to underscore his own conviction that theological reasoning by necessity includes an apophatic dimension: "God is not like a human being" (16). Yet, while guarding against the indiscriminate projection of human categories onto the divine, a "pious" use of reason has recourse to the scriptural symbolism (*paradeigmata*) by which the divine mystery is revealed to human beings. As he did with reference to the Son in earlier treatises, Athanasius now extends his analysis of scriptural symbolism to the Spirit in order to demonstrate that the Scriptures align the Spirit, in his person and work, with the Father and the Son. Moreover, the Spirit's work in creation and salvation can only be identified with divine agency, a fact that is sacramentally dramatized by the invocation of the Spirit, along with the Father and the Son, in the rite of baptism. With this defense of the Spirit's divinity, Athanasius's doctrine of God has become utterly conflated with the category of "Trinity" (*trias*), a term that is used here with notably greater frequency than in his earlier works which deal more narrowly with the question of the divinity of the Son. The significance of this treatise with regard to the development of the Christian doctrine of God lies primarily in the fact that it is the first thorough attempt to deal with the question of the divinity of the Spirit. Athanasius's arguments were to have a marked influence on later treatments of this issue, notably those of Basil of Caesarea and Gregory of Nazianzus, and they constitute a foundational phase in a trajectory of reflection that comes to resolution in the affirmation of the Spirit's divinity by the Council of Constantinople of 381.

The text of the *Letters to Serapion*, not available in a critical edition, can be found in Migne's *Patrolgia Graeca* 26:529–576.

Text

15. [565C] It seems to me that such is the sense of the divine sayings, which refutes the slander of these irrational people against the Holy Spirit. But they maintain their steadfast contention against the truth, as you have written, and no longer drawing upon the Scripture (for they find nothing there) but spewing out from the overflow of their own hearts (cf. Mt 12:34), they again assert: "If it is not a creature nor one of the angels, but proceeds from the Father, [568A] then it is itself also a son, and thus it and the Word are two brothers. And if it is a brother, how then is the Word 'only-begotten'?[5] And how is it that they are not the same, but one is named with reference to the Father, and the other is named with reference to the Son? And how, if it is from the Father, is it not said to be begotten also, or to be Son, but only 'Holy Spirit'? But if the Spirit is the Son's, then the Father is grandfather of the Spirit."

That is how they make sport, these dishonorable people, prying around[6] and intending to fathom the depths of God, which no one knows except the Spirit of God (1 Cor 2: 10–11), who is the one maligned by them. We should no longer answer them, according to the injunction of the apostle (cf. Titus 3:10), but, after the admonition of our preceding words, we should shun them as heretics. Or, we should ask them questions on a par with those which they ask, and [568B] demand an answer from them, as they demand from us. Let them say then whether the Father is from a father, and whether another has been begotten along with him, such that they are brothers from one father – what are their names and who, in turn, is their father and grandfather and who are the ancestors of these?[7] But they will say that there are none. Let them say, then, how is he Father if he is not himself begotten from a Father? Or how was he able to have a Son, without having himself been begotten as a son? I know that these questions are impious! But since they make sport of such matters, it is right to make sport of them, if only so that such an absurd and impious enquiry may cause them to become aware of their own mindlessness. For these conjectures have no basis in reality; far from it! It is not fitting to enquire in this way about divinity. God is not as a human being (Num 23:19), so that anyone should dare to ask human questions about him.[8]

16. [568C] As I said before, one should be silent about these things and not pay any attention to such people. But in order that our silence may not provide them with an occasion for their brazenness, let them hear this: Just as we cannot speak of a father of the Father, so we cannot speak of a brother of the Son. As is written above, there is no other God than the Father. Nor is there another Son, for he is only-begotten (Jn 1:14; Jn 1:18, 3:16, 3:18; 1 Jn 4:9). Therefore the Father is one and unique, and he is Father of one and only Son, and it is only in the Godhead that the Father and the Son have always been and forever are Father and Son.[9] Among human beings, [568D] if one is called father, he is nevertheless the son of another [569A] and if one is called son, he yet becomes the father of another. Thus, the names of father and son do not retain their proper significations among human beings. So Abraham, being the son of Nahor, became the father of Isaac and Isaac, being the son of Abraham, became the father of Jacob. This is the way of human nature, for human beings are parts of one another.[10] Each one who is begotten retains a portion of his father, so that he himself may also become father of another.

But it is not so in the case of the Godhead. God is not like a human being (Num 23:19), nor does he have a partitive nature.[11] Therefore, he does not beget the Son by way of partition, so that the Son may also become father of another, since the Father himself is not from a father. Neither is the Son a part of the Father. Therefore, he does not beget as he himself was begotten, but is whole image (*eikōn*) and radiance of the whole.[12] [569B] It is only in the Godhead that the Father is properly (*kyriōs*) Father and the Son properly Son; in their case, the Father is always Father and the Son always Son.[13] Just as the Father could never be Son, so also the Son could never be Father. And just as the Father will never cease to be uniquely Father, so also the Son will never cease to be uniquely Son. So it is madness to speak and even to think in any way of a brother of the Son, and to name the Father a grandfather. Neither is the Spirit called Son in the Scriptures, so as to be considered as a brother, nor is it called a son of the Son, lest the Father be conceived as a grandfather. But the Son is said to be Son of the Father, and the Spirit of the Son is said to be Spirit of the

Father.[14] Thus, there is one Godhead of the Holy Trinity, unto which there is also one faith.

17. [569C] That is also why it is madness to call the Spirit a creature. If it were a creature, it would not be ranked with the Triad, the whole of which is one God. It is sufficient to know that the Spirit is not a creature, nor is it counted among the things that are made. For no alien thing is intermixed with the Triad, but it is indivisible and homogenous with itself (*homoia heautē*). This much suffices for the faithful and this is the extent to which human knowledge attains, at which point the cherubim make a covering with their wings (cf. Isa 6:2). The one who seeks further and wishes to enquire beyond these things is disobeying him who says, "Do not be overwise, lest you be ruined" (Eccl 7:16). For the things that are handed down by faith should be understood not by human wisdom (cf. 1 Cor 2:13) but by the hearing of faith (cf. Gal 3:2). For what [572A] discourse can suitably interpret the things that are above originated nature? Or what hearing can understand what it is not possible for human beings to either hear or speak?

Paul spoke in this vein about what he heard (cf. 2 Cor 12:4); but about God himself, he said: "How unsearchable are his ways! Who has known the mind of the Lord? Or who has been his counselor?" (Rom 11:33–34). Thus Abraham did not pry and interrogate the one speaking to him, but "he believed and it was reckoned to him as righteousness" (Rom 4:3). Thus also Moses was called a faithful servant (Heb 3:5). But if those who think like Arius are unable either to understand or to believe in the indivisible and Holy Trinity, because wisdom will not enter into their crafty souls (Wis 1:4), let them not distort the truth on that account, nor let them say that what they cannot understand cannot be.

[572B] Indeed, their attitude has brought them to a most absurd end. Because they cannot understand how the holy Triad is indivisible, the Arians make the Son one with the creation, while the Tropici count the Spirit together with the creatures. But they should have either kept complete silence because of their lack of understanding – the former not counting the Son with creatures, nor the latter, the Spirit – or they should have acknowledged what is written and joined the Son to the Father and not divided the Spirit from the Son, so as to preserve truly the indivisibility and homogeneity of the nature (*homophyes*) of the Holy Trinity. Having learned these things, they should not have been presumptuous nor enquired in doubt as to how these things can be, so as to invent evil notions for themselves even if the one they ask is at a loss for words.

[572C] For it is impossible for any of those who have come into being (*tois genētois*), and especially for us human beings, to speak appropriately of the things that are ineffable. But then it is even more presumptuous to invent new terms other than those in the Scriptures for the things of which we cannot speak.[15] Such an attempt is madness, on the part of both the one asking and the one who even thinks of answering. The one who enquires in this way even about the things that are originated should not be considered to be in possession of his right mind.

18. Let those who are so facile in speaking about everything dare to answer and say how the heaven is constituted and from what material and what is its composition or how does the sun exist and each of the stars. But there is nothing remarkable [572D] about refuting their senselessness by referring to the things that are above, while we do not even know how is the nature of the trees here below, or the coming together of the waters or how is the formation of living beings and [573A] their constitution.[16] But they cannot say, since even Solomon, who attained a share of wisdom surpassing all, saw that it is impossible for men to find out these things, and said, "He put eternity into their hearts, yet without humanity's being able to discover the work which God has made from the beginning to the very end" (Eccl 3:11).

But then, since they cannot discover these things, do they profess that they do not exist? Indeed, they are bound to profess this, for their minds are corrupted. Therefore, it is fitting for someone to say to them: "You mindless and completely presumptuous people! Why don't you rather stop prying into the Holy Trinity, and simply believe that it exists? You have as a teacher in this regard the apostle, who says, 'It is necessary first to believe in God, that he exists, and that he rewards those who seek him' (Heb 11:6)." He did not [573B] say, "how he exists," but "that he exists." But if they are not subdued by this, let them say how the Father exists, that they may learn accordingly how his Word exists. But it is absurd, they will say, to enquire in this way about the Father. Therefore it is absurd, let it be said to them, to enquire in this way about his Word.

19. Therefore, since such an attempt is futile and a surplus of madness, let no one ask such questions any more, or else learn only what is in the Scriptures. For the symbols (*paradeigmata*)[17] in the Scriptures which pertain to these questions are sufficient and adequate. Thus, the Father is called "Fountain" and "Light": "They have forsaken me," it says, "the fountain of living water" (Jer 2:13).

And again in Baruch [573C]: "How is it, Israel, that you are in the land of enemies? You have forsaken the fountain of wisdom" (Bar 3:10,12). And according to John, "Our God is light" (1 Jn 1:5). But, in relation to the fountain, the Son is spoken of as the river: for "the river of God is filled with waters" (Ps 65:10). Relative to the light, he is called radiance, as Paul says: "who is the radiance of his glory, and the reflection of his being (*hypostaseōs*)" (Heb 1:3). Thus, the Father being light, while the Son is his radiance (for we cannot shrink from saying the same things about them many times), we can also see in the Son the Spirit, in whom we are enlightened: "that he may give you the Spirit of wisdom and revelation in the knowledge of him," it says, "enlightening the eyes of your heart" (Eph 1:17). But when we are enlightened by the Spirit, [573D] it is Christ who in the Spirit enlightens us. For "he was the true light," it says, "who enlightens every human being who comes into the world" (Jn 1:9). So, again, while the Father is fountain, and the Son is called river, we are said to drink of the Spirit. For it is written [576A] that "we have all been given to drink of one Spirit" (1 Cor 12:13). But when we are given to drink of the Spirit, we drink Christ; for "they drank from the spiritual rock that followed them, and that rock was Christ" (1 Cor 10:4). And again, while Christ is the true Son, we are made into sons when we receive the Spirit: "For you have not received," it says, "the Spirit of slavery that leads back to fear. But you have received the Spirit of sonship" (Rom 8:15). But when we are made sons by the Spirit, it is clearly in Christ that we receive the title of "children of God": "For to those who did accept him, he gave power to become children of God" (Jn 1:12). Then again, while the Father, as Paul says, is the "only wise one" (Rom 16:27), the Son is his wisdom: "Christ, the power of God and the wisdom of God" (1 Cor 1:24). But, the Son being wisdom, when we receive the Spirit of wisdom, we attain Christ [576B] and become wise in him. Thus it is written in the one-hundred-and-forty-fifth psalm: "The Lord sets prisoners free; the Lord grants wisdom to the blind" (Ps 146:7–8). And when the Spirit is given to us (for the Savior said, "Receive the Holy Spirit" (Jn 20:22)), it is God who is in us. Thus John has written: "If we love one another, God remains in us. In this we know that we remain in him and he in us, in that he has given us of his Spirit" (1 Jn 4: 12–13). But when God is in us, the Son also is in us, as the Son himself says: "The Father and I will come and make our dwelling with him" (Jn 14:23). Moreover, the Son is life (for "I am the life" (Jn 14:6) he says), and we are said to be made alive in the Spirit: for "the one

218

who raised [576C] Jesus Christ from the dead," it says, "will also bring to life your mortal bodies through his Spirit dwelling in you" (Rom 8:11). But when we are made alive in the Spirit, Christ himself is said to live in us: "I have been crucified with Christ," it says, "I live, yet it is no longer I who live, but Christ lives in me" (Gal 2:19–20). And again, as the Son said that whatever works he did were accomplished by the Father – "The Father," he says, "who dwells in me is doing his works. Believe me, that I am in the Father and the Father is in me. Or else, believe me because of the works themselves" (Jn 14:10–11) – so also, Paul said that the works that he accomplished in the power of the Spirit were the works of Christ: "I will not presume to speak of anything except what Christ has accomplished through me, for the sake of the obedience of the Gentiles, [576D] by word and work, in the power of signs and wonders, in the power of the Holy Spirit" (Rom 15:18–19).

20. Such being the correlation (*sustoichia*) and the unity of the Holy Trinity, who would dare to separate the Son [577A] from the Father, or the Spirit from the Son or from the Father himself? Or who would be so presumptuous as to say that the Trinity is unlike (*anomion*) and heterogenous (*heterophyē*) with respect to itself, or that the Son is of a different being (*allotrioousion*) than the Father, or that the Spirit is foreign to the Son?[18] But how can this be? If one were to enquire and ask again: How can it be that when the Spirit is in us, the Son is said to be in us, and when the Son is in us, the Father is said to be in us? Or, how is it really a Trinity if the three are depicted (*semainetai*) as one? Or how is it that when one is in us, the Trinity is said to be in us? Let such an enquirer begin by separating the radiance from the light, or wisdom from the one who is wise, or else let him say himself how these things can be. But if this cannot be done, then how much more is it the presumption of insane people to enquire into these things with respect to God?

Divinity is not handed down to us by demonstration of words, as it says (cf. 1 Cor 1:17), [577B] but in faith and through pious reasoning undertaken with reverence.[19] For if Paul preached about even those things which concern the saving cross "not in words of wisdom but in the demonstration of the spirit and power" (1 Cor 2:4), and in paradise "he heard ineffable things which no one may utter" (2 Cor 12:4), who can expound on the Holy Trinity itself? Yet one may remedy one's perplexity first of all through faith and then by recourse to the terms previously mentioned, which is to say: "image" and "radiance," "fountain" and "river," and "subsistence" and "expression."

For just as the Son is in the Spirit as in his own image,[20] so is the Father in the Son. Thus has the divine Scripture supplied a remedy [577C] for the impossibility of explaining and grasping these matters with words by granting us such symbols (*paradeigmata*), so that we may be able to speak more plainly in response to the faithlessness of those who are presumptuous and so that we may be able to speak without danger and to properly conceive and believe that there is one sanctification which is from the Father, through the Son, in the Holy Spirit.

Therefore, just as the Son is only-begotten, so also the Spirit, [580A] which is given and sent by the Son, is itself one and not many; neither is it one from among many but it is itself the only Spirit. Since the Son, the living Word, is one, so must his living energy and gift which sanctifies and illuminates be one, full, and perfect. It is said to proceed from the Father (Jn 15:26), since it shines forth and is sent and given by the Word who is confessed to be from the Father.[21] Certainly, the Son is sent from the Father, for "God so loved the world," it says, "that he sent his only-begotten Son" (Jn 3:16). On the other hand, the Son sends the Spirit, for "if I go," he says, "I will send the Paraclete" (Jn 16:7). The Son glorifies the Father, saying, "Father, I have glorified you" (Jn 17:4), whereas the Spirit glorifies the Son, who says, [580B] "He will glorify me" (Jn 16:14). The Son says, "Those things which I have heard from the Father are what I speak to the world" (Jn 8:26), while the Spirit, in turn, receives from the Son; "He will take from what is mine," he says, "and declare it to you" (Jn 16:14). The Son came in the name of the Father, whereas the Son also speaks of "the Holy Spirit whom the Father will send in my name" (Jn 5:43).

21. Therefore, since the Spirit has the same relation of nature and order with respect to the Son that the Son has with respect to the Father,[22] how can the one who calls the Spirit a creature escape the necessity of thinking the same about the Son? For if the Spirit is a creature of the Son, it follows that they should say also that the Son is a creature of the Father. [580C] These indeed were the fantasies of the Arians, who fell into the Judaism of Caiaphas. But if those who say such things about the Spirit pretend that they are not of a like mind with Arius, let them flee from his words and not become impious toward the Spirit. For just as the Son, who is in the Father and in whom the Father is (cf. Jn 14:10), is not a creature but belongs (*idios*) to the being (*ousia*) of the Father (and indeed you also claim to say this), so also the Spirit, who is in the Son and in whom the Son is, cannot legitimately be

ranked among creatures nor separated from the Word, so as to render the Trinity incomplete.

[580D] Enough has been said to refute the evil words that have issued from the ignorance of the Tropici about the sayings of the prophet and the apostle,[23] whose meaning they distort and so end up deceiving themselves. [581A] But let us finally look at the sayings about the Spirit in the divine Scriptures, taking them one by one, and like expert investigators let us determine well whether the Spirit has anything that belongs (*idion*) to creatures or whether it belongs (*idion*) to God.[24] In this way, we will be able to say whether it is a creature or whether it is other than creatures and belongs to and is one with the Godhead in the Trinity. Perhaps then they will become ashamed when they learn how much the words contrived by their blasphemy are discordant with the divine sayings.

22. Creatures come into being from non-being and have a beginning of their coming into being, for "in the beginning God made heaven and earth" and everything in them (Gen 1:1). But the Holy Spirit is said to be from God, for it is said "No one knows what pertains to a human being except the spirit that is in him. Likewise, no one knows what pertains to God except the Spirit of God. We have not received the spirit of the world but the Spirit that is from God" (1 Cor 2:11–12). So, on the basis of these words, what kind of kinship is there between the Spirit and creatures? Creatures used not to be, but God is the one who is (Ex 3:14), from whom also the Spirit is. But what is from God can neither be from non-being, nor a creature. Otherwise, according to their thinking, the one from whom the Spirit is will also be considered a creature. Who can stand such senseless people, who thus say in their hearts that there is no God (Ps 13:1)? For if it is true that just as no one knows what pertains to a human being except the spirit that is in him, so no one knows what pertains to God except for the Spirit that is in him, how is it not foul speech to say that the Spirit that is in God and that searches even the deep things of God (1 Cor 2:10) is a creature? On the basis of these assertions one will learn to say, [581C] on the one hand, that the spirit of a human being is extrinsic to the human being and, on the other hand, that the Word which is in the Father is a creature.

Moreover, the Spirit is and is called the Spirit of holiness and of renewal. For Paul writes: "He was established as Son of God in power according to the Spirit of holiness, through resurrection from the dead, Jesus Christ, our Lord" (Rom 1:4). And again he says:

"But you were sanctified, you were justified in the name of our Lord Jesus Christ and in the Spirit of our God" (1 Cor 6:11). And when writing to Titus, [584A] he said: "But when the kindness and love of God our Savior appeared, not because of righteous deeds that we had done but because of his mercy, he saved us through the bath of rebirth and the renewal of the holy Spirit, whom he richly poured out on us through Jesus Christ our Savior, so that we may be justified by his grace and become heirs in hope of eternal life" (Titus 3:4–7). As for creatures, however, they are sanctified and renewed, for "You will send forth your spirit and they will be created and you will renew the face of the earth" (Ps 104:30). Paul also says, "For it is impossible for those who have once been enlightened and have tasted the heavenly gift and have attained participation in the Holy Spirit" (Heb 6:4).

[584B] 23. But how can that which is not sanctified by another and which does not participate in holiness but is itself participated – the one in which all of creation is sanctified – itself be one of the all? How can it belong among those who participate in it? It would be necessary, then, for those who say this to say also that the Son, through whom all things come into being, is himself one of the "all."

The Spirit is called "life-giving." For it says, "The one who raised Jesus Christ from the dead will also give life to your mortal bodies, through his Spirit that dwells in you" (Rom 8:11). While the Lord is life itself[25] and, as Peter said, "the author of life" (Acts 3:15), the Lord himself said, "The water which I will give to him will become in him a fount of water welling up to eternal life ... He said this concerning the Spirit that those who believed in him were to receive" (Jn 4:14, 7:39). [584C] But, as we have said, creatures are granted life through the Spirit. So then how can that which does not participate in life but is itself participated and in fact grants life to creatures have any kinship with things that come into being? Or how can the Spirit be in any way one of the creatures which are granted life in the Spirit by the Word?

The Spirit is spoken of as "anointing" and is "seal."[26] So John writes: "As for you, the anointing that you received from him remains in you, and you have no need of someone to teach you. But his anointing," his Spirit, "teaches you about everything" (1 Jn 2:27). In the prophet Isaiah, it is written: "The Spirit of the Lord is upon me, because he has anointed me" (Isa 61:1). Paul says, "Having believed in him you have been sealed for the day of redemption" (cf. Eph 1:13).[27] But, as for creatures, they are sealed

LETTERS TO SERAPION ON THE HOLY SPIRIT

and anointed by the Spirit and [585A] taught everything by the Spirit. Now, if the Spirit is "anointing" and "seal," as the one in whom the Word anoints and seals all things, what kind of likeness or commonality of identity (*idiotēs*) can there be between the unction and seal and those who are anointed and sealed? So, on this account also, the Spirit is not among all things, for the seal cannot be from among the things that are sealed; neither can the unction be from among the things that are anointed, but rather belongs (*idion*) to the anointing and sealing Word. The unction has the fragrance and breath of the one who anoints and those who are anointed, when they partake of this unction, say: "We are the fragrance of Christ" (2 Cor 2:15). The seal possesses the form of Christ who seals, while those who are sealed participate in it, and become conformed to it, as the apostle says: "My children, for whom I am again in labor, until Christ is formed in you" (Gal 4:19). [585B] When we are sealed in this way, we properly become sharers in the divine nature, as Peter says (2 Pet 1:4), and so the whole creation participates of the Word, in the Spirit.

24. Moreover, all things are said to be participants of God through the Spirit. For it says, "Do you not know that you are the temple of God and that the Spirit of God dwells in you? If anyone destroys the temple of God, God will destroy that one. For the temple of God, which you are, is holy" (1 Cor 3:16,17). But if the Holy Spirit were a creature, there would not be for us any participation of God in the Spirit. Indeed, if we were merely united to a creature, we would still be foreigners to the divine nature, having no participation in it.[28] [585C] But now that we are called participants of Christ and participants of God, it is thereby shown that the unction and seal which is in us is not of a created nature but of the nature of the Son, who unites us to the Father through the Spirit that is in him. This is what John teaches, when he writes, as has been cited above, "This is how we know that we remain in God and he in us, in that he has given us his Spirit" (1 Jn 4:13). But if we become sharers in the divine nature through participation in the Spirit, one would have to be crazy to say that the Spirit is of a created nature and not of the nature of God, [588A] for that is how those in whom the Spirit is become divinized. But if the Spirit divinizes, it is not to be doubted that it is of the nature of God himself.[29]

And for a still clearer negation of this heresy, the psalmist sings in the one-hundred-and-third psalm, as we have previously quoted: "You will take away their spirit and they will perish and return to their dust. You will send forth your spirit and they will be created, and you will renew the face of the earth" (Ps 104:29–30). And Paul writes to Titus: "Through the bath of regeneration and the renewal of the Holy Spirit, which he poured out richly upon us through Jesus Christ" (Titus 3:5–6). But if the Father creates and renews all things through the Son and in the Holy Spirit, what likeness or kinship can there be between creatures and the Creator? Or how can it at all be the case that the one in whom everything [588B] is created is a creature?

Such foul talk would consistently lead to blasphemy against the Son, so that those who say that the Spirit is a creature should say also that the Son, through whom all things were created, is a creature as well. For the Spirit is said to be and is the image of the Son; for "those whom he foreknew he also predestined to be conformed to the image of his Son" (Rom 8:29). Therefore, if it is confessed even by them that the Son is not a creature, then neither could his image be a creature. For as the image is, so must be that of which it is an image. Therefore, the Son is quite fittingly and properly confessed not to be a creature, since he is the Image (*eikōn*) of the Father. Yet, the one who counts the Spirit among creatures will surely end up counting the Son also among creatures and uttering impropriety against the Father through this [588C] improper speech about his Image.

25. Thus, the Spirit is other than the creatures, and is shown rather to belong (*idion*) to the Son and to be not foreign to God. But then there is that foolish question they ask: "If the Spirit is from God, why is it not also called Son?" This question has already been shown to be rash and reckless in what we have said above, and we will equally show it to be so now. Even though it is not called "Son" in the Scriptures but "Spirit of God," nevertheless it is said to be in God himself and from God himself, as the apostle has written (cf. 1 Cor 2:11–12). If the Son belongs (*idios*) to the being of the Father because he is from the Father, then necessarily [589A] the Spirit also, who is said to be from God, belongs (*idion*) to the being of the Son. Of course, the Lord is Son; but then the Spirit is called the Spirit of sonship (Rom 8:15).[30] And, again, while the Son is Wisdom (1 Cor 1:24) and Truth (cf. Jn 14:6), it is written that the Spirit is Spirit of Wisdom (cf. Isa 11:2) and Truth (cf. Jn 14:17, 15:26). Yet again, while the Son is Power of God (1 Cor 1:24) and Lord of glory (1 Cor 2:8), the Spirit is said to be Spirit of Power and Spirit of glory. And that is how Scripture speaks of each of them, respectively. So Paul writes to the Corinthians: "If they had known,

they would not have crucified the Lord of glory" (1 Cor 2:8); and in another place, "For you did not receive a spirit of slavery to fall back into fear, but you received a spirit of sonship" (Rom 8:15),[31] and furthermore, "God sent the Spirit of his Son into our hearts, crying 'Abba, Father'" (Gal 4:6). Peter [589B] wrote: "If you are insulted for the name of Christ, blessed are you, for the Spirit of glory and of God rests upon you" (1 Pet 4:14). As for the Lord, he said that the Spirit is Spirit of Truth and Comforter (Jn 14:16), which shows that the Trinity is complete in the Spirit. Therefore, it is in the Spirit that the Word glorifies creation and presents it to the Father by divinizing it and granting it adoption. But the one who binds creation to the Word could not be among the creatures and the one who bestows sonship upon creation could not be foreign to the Son. Otherwise, it would be necessary to look for another spirit to unite this one to the Word.[32] But that is senseless. Therefore, the Spirit is not among the things that have come into being but belongs (*idion*) to the divinity of the Father, and is the one in whom the Word divinizes the things that have come into being. But the one in whom creation is divinized cannot be extrinsic to the divinity of the Father.

[589C] 26. That the Spirit is above creation and other than the nature of originated beings, but rather belongs to divinity, is something that can also be gleaned from the fact that the Holy Spirit is unchangeable and inalterable.[33] For it says, "The Holy Spirit of discipline will flee deceit and withdraw from senseless thoughts" (Wis 1:5). Moreover, Peter says, "in the incorruptibility of the gentle and calm Spirit" (1 Pet 3:4). And again, in *Wisdom*, "For your incorruptible Spirit is in all things" (Wis 12:1). [592A] If "no one knows the things of God except the Spirit of God who is in him" (1 Cor 2:11), and, as James said, "there is no alteration or shadow caused by change" (Jas 1:17) in God, then insofar as the Holy Spirit is in God, it is necessarily unchanging and invariable and incorruptible.

Conversely, the nature of originated and created beings is changeable insofar as it is external to the being of God and comes into subsistence from non-being. For it says, "every human being is a liar" (Ps 116:11); and "all have sinned and fallen short of the glory of God" (Rom 3:23), while "the angels who did not cling to their own origin[34] but deserted their proper dwelling, he has kept in eternal chains, in gloom, for the judgment of the great day" (Jude 6). And in Job: "If he puts no trust in his holy angels (Job 15:15) ... and finds fault with his angels (Job 4:18) ... and the stars are not [592B] pure in his sight (Job 25:5)." So Paul writes: "Do you not know that we will judge angels? Then why not everyday matters?" (1 Cor 6:3). We have also heard that the devil, though he was "in the midst of the cherubim" (cf. Ezek 28:14) and was "the seal of the likeness" (cf. Ezek 28:12), fell from heaven like lightening (cf. Lk 10:18). If such then is the nature of created beings and such things are written even of the angels, while the Spirit is the same and unchanging and possesses the inalterability of the Son, with whom he remains inalterable forever, what kind of likeness is there between the inalterable and the alterable?[35] It should be clear enough that insofar as the Spirit is not a creature, then neither is his being in any way that of the angels, since they are changeable while he is Image of the Word and proper (*idios*) to the Father.

Moreover, "the Spirit of the Lord fills the world" (Wis 1:7). So David sings, [592C] "Where shall I go from your Spirit?" (Ps 139:7). And it is also written in Wisdom, "Your incorruptible Spirit is in all things" (Wis 12:1). But all the creatures that have come into being exist in their allotted places: the sun, moon and stars are in the firmament (cf. Gen 1:17); the clouds, in the air. He has set the boundaries of the nations for people (cf. Deut 32:8). The angels are "sent for service" (cf. Heb 1:14); "and the angels came to stand before the Lord" (Job 1:6), as it is written in Job. And "Jacob the Patriarch had a dream and, behold, a stairway rested on the ground, with its top reaching to heaven and the angels of God ascended and descended upon it" (Gen 28:12). But if the Spirit fills all things and, in the Word, is present in all things, while the angels are inferior to the Spirit [593A] and present only where they are sent, it cannot be doubted that the Spirit is not among the things that have come into being, nor is the Spirit at all an angel, as you say, but is above the nature of angels.[36]

27. It can also be seen from the following that the Holy Spirit is participated and does not participate.[37] (For we must not hesitate to repeat ourselves.) Scripture says: "For it is impossible that those who have once been enlightened and tasted the heavenly gift and participated in the holy Spirit and tasted the good word of God" (Heb 6:4–5), etc. But as for the angels and other creatures, they are participants of the Spirit itself. Therefore, they are capable of falling away from that which they participate.[38] The Spirit, however, is always the same and is not among those who participate, whereas all things participate in it. But if the Spirit is always the same [593B] and is the one who is participated, while creatures participate in it, then the Holy Spirit cannot be an angel or any creature at all, but is

proper (*idion*) to the Word, from whom the Spirit is given, and is thus participated by creatures. Otherwise, they will end up saying that the Son too, of whom we have all become participants in the Spirit, is a creature.

Moreover, the Holy Spirit is one, while creatures are many. For there are "thousands of thousands" and "myriads of myriads" (Dan 7:10) of angels and the stars are many, and so are the thrones and dominions and heavens, as well as the cherubim and seraphim, and the many archangels. In short, creatures are not one, but they are all many and diverse. But if the Holy Spirit is one, while creatures are many and angels are many, what likeness is there between the Spirit and originated beings? It is a matter without any ambiguity [593C] that the Spirit is not among the many and is not an angel, but rather is one and belongs (*idion*) to the one Word, and accordingly belongs (*idion*) to the one God and is of the same being (*homoousion*).[39]

Taken even by themselves, these [scriptural] sayings about the Holy Spirit demonstrate that it has nothing in common with or proper (*idion*) to the nature or essence of creatures, but that it is other than originated beings and belongs to (*idion*) and is not foreign to the being and divinity of the Son, through which it belongs to the Holy Trinity. This puts their senselessness to shame.

28. Moreover, aside from these scriptural utterances, let us also consider the tradition and teaching and faith of the Catholic Church from the beginning, that which the Lord has given, the apostles preached, and the fathers [596A] guarded. This is the foundation on which the Church is established, and the one who strays from it is not a Christian and should no longer be called so: The Trinity is holy and perfect, confessed as God in Father, Son, and Holy Spirit, having nothing foreign or extrinsic mingled with it, nor compounded of creator and created, but is wholly Creator and Maker. It is identical with itself and indivisible in nature, and its activity (*energeia*) is one.[40] For the Father does all things through the Word and in the Holy Spirit. Thus the oneness of the Holy Trinity is preserved and thus is the one God "who is over all and through all and in all" (Eph 4:6) preached in the Church – "over all," as Father, who is beginning (*archē*) and fountain; "through all," through the Son; and "in all" in the Holy Spirit.[41] It is Trinity [596B] not only in name and linguistic expression, but Trinity in reality and truth. Just as the Father is the "One who is" (Ex 3:14), so likewise is his Word the "One who is, God over all" (Rom 9:5). Nor is the Holy Spirit non-existent, but truly exists and subsists.[42]

The Catholic Church does not think of less than these three, lest it fall in with Sabellius and with the present-day Jews who follow Caiaphas, nor does it invent any more than these three, lest it be dragged into the polytheism of the Greeks. Let them learn that this is indeed the faith of the Church by considering how the Lord, when he sent the apostles, exhorted them to establish this as a foundation for the Church, saying: "Go and make disciples of all nations, baptizing them in the name of the Father and the Son and the Holy Spirit" (Mt 28:19). [596C] So the apostles went and taught likewise, and this is the preaching that has made its way into all the Church under heaven.

29. Since this is the foundation of the Church's faith, let them once again speak up and give an answer: Is it Trinity or Dyad?[43] If it is a dyad, then let them number the Spirit among the creatures. But then your conception is no longer of the one God who is "over all" and "through all" and "in all" (Eph 4:6), for you do not have the "in all," having sundered and excluded the Spirit from the divinity. Indeed, according to your own thinking, the baptismal consecration which you think that you are performing is not entirely an entrance into divinity, for you have appended [597A] a creature to the divinity.[44] Like the Arians and the Greeks, you too call the creation "God," along with the God who created it, through his own Word.[45]

If this is how things stand with you, where is your hope? For who will join you to God if you do not have the Spirit of God himself but one that belongs to creation? What is this presumption and recklessness of yours, demoting the Father and his Word to the level of creatures and raising the creature to the same level as God? This is what you do in fact when you imagine that the Spirit is a creature but then count him along into the Trinity. What again is this madness of yours, "speaking iniquity against God" (Ps 75:6), to the extent that you number with God and his Word not even as much as the totality of angels or the totality of creatures, but merely one among the creatures? For if, according to you, the Spirit is an angel and a creature [597B] and is yet counted into the Trinity, then not only one but all the created angels must be counted in also. No longer then would there be a Trinity, but some innumerable throng of divinity. In that case, the consecration to which you pretend would again be fragmented every which way, and would be unstable (*abebaios*) because of this multiplicity.[46] Your sacramental rites and those of the Arians are indeed of such a kind – you who pursue disputations against the divinity and worship the creature instead of God, the Creator of all (cf. Rom 1:25).

30. These are the sorts of absurdities that you run up against when you speak of God as a dyad. But if God is Trinity, which he actually is, and a Trinity which has been shown to be indivisible and not dissimilar to itself (*ouk anomios*),[47] then its holiness must be one, and its eternity one, and its immutable nature. [597C] The faith in the Trinity, which has been handed down to us, is one, and it is this faith which unites us to God, whereas anyone who takes anything away from the Trinity and is baptized in the name of the Father only, or in the name of the Son only, or in the name of the Father and the Son apart from the Spirit, receives nothing but remains empty and unsanctified – both he and the one who appears to be administering the consecration. After all, it is a consecration in the Trinity! Likewise, the one who divides the Son from the Father or demotes the Spirit to the level of creatures has neither the Son nor the Father but is godless and worse than an unbeliever (1 Tim 5:8) and anything but a Christian. And this is just and right, for as the baptism given in the Father and the Son and the Holy Spirit is one and the faith in the Trinity is one, as the apostle says (Eph 4:5), [600A] so the Holy Trinity, which is identical with itself and united with itself, has nothing of what is originated within it. This is the indivisible unity of the Trinity and faith in this Trinity is one.

But if, according to the invention of you Tropici, it is not actually so, and you have been induced by your dreams to say that the Holy Spirit is a creature, then your faith is no longer one and neither is your baptism one but two – one of them being in the Father and the Son, and another in an angel who is a creature. But at this point nothing is left secure[48] for you and nothing true. For what kind of communion can there be between an originated being and the Creator?[49] Or what kind of oneness can there be between the creatures below and the Word who has made them? The blessed Paul, who knew this, did not divide the Trinity, as you do, but taught its unity when he wrote to the Corinthians about the spiritual gifts [600B] and summed them all up by referring them to the one God and Father, saying: "There are different gifts but the same Spirit; there are different forms of service but the same Lord; there are different workings but the same God who works all of them in everyone" (1 Cor 12:4–6). For that which the Spirit imparts to each is provided from the Father through the Son. Everything that belongs to the Father belongs to the Son (Jn 16:15, 17:10); thus, what is given by the Son in the Spirit are the Father's gifts. And when the Spirit is in us, the Word who gives the Spirit is also in us, and the Father is in the Word. So it is that "I and my Father will come and make our dwelling in him" (Jn 14:23), as it is said. For where the light is, there is the radiance; and where the radiance is, there is its [600C] active energy (*energeia*) and luminous grace. Paul taught this again when he wrote back to the Corinthians and said, in his second epistle: "The grace of our Lord Jesus Christ and the love of God and the communion of the Holy Spirit be with you all" (2 Cor 13:13). For the gift and the grace that is given are given in the Trinity: from the Father, through the Son, in the Holy Spirit. Just as the grace that is given is from the Father and through the Son, so there would be among us no communion in the gift except in the Holy Spirit. For it is by our participation in the Spirit that we have the love of the Father and the grace of the Son and the communion of the Spirit itself.

31. Thus, it has been shown that the activity (*energeia*) of the Trinity is one. [600D] For the apostle does not mean that what is given by each [of the Trinity] is different and separate but rather [601A] that what is given is given in the Trinity, and it is all from the one God. How then is it not outright impiety against the Son himself to call a creature one who, far from being a creature, is united to the Son just as the Son is united to the Father, and who is glorified with the Father and the Son[50] and confessed as God (*theologoumenon*) along with the Word, and who activates (*energoun*) everything that is worked by the Father through the Son? For there is nothing which is not brought into being and actuated through the Word, in the Spirit.

This is what is sung in the psalms: "By the word of the Lord, the heavens were established and by the breath (*pneumati*) of his mouth all their power" (Ps 33:6).[51] And in the one-hundred-and-forty-seventh psalm: "He will send his word and melt them; he will pour forth his spirit and the waters will flow" (Ps 147:18). And we are justified, as the apostle says, "in the name of our Lord [601B] Jesus Christ and in the Spirit of our God" (1 Cor 6:11). The Spirit indeed is inseparable from the Word. So when the Lord says, "I and the Father will come" (Jn 14:23) the Spirit also comes with them and dwells in us no differently than the Son, as Paul writes to the Ephesians: "that he may grant you in accord with the riches of his glory to be strengthened with power through his Spirit in the inner self, and that Christ may dwell [in your hearts through faith]" (Eph 3:16–17). But if the Son is in us, so is the Father, as the Son says: "I am in the Father and the Father in me" (Jn 14:10). So when the Word comes to the prophets, they prophesy in the Holy Spirit itself. Therefore, when Scripture says, "the Word of the Lord came" to a certain prophet, it indicates that he is prophesying in the Holy Spirit. [601C] In Zechariah it is written, "Only receive my words and my ordinances, which I decree in my spirit to my servants, the prophets" (Zech 1:6). And when rebuking the people, a little later on, he said: "They have made their hearts disobedient so as not to hear my laws and the words which the Lord of hosts has sent by his spirit through the former prophets" (Zech 7:12). In Acts, Peter said, "Brothers, the Scriptures which the Holy Spirit had spoken beforehand had to be fulfilled" (Acts 1:16). And the apostles cried out together: "Master, who has made heaven and earth and sea and all that is in them, who spoke by the holy spirit through the mouth of your child, [604 A] our father David" (Acts 4:24–25). And when Paul was in Rome, he spoke boldly to the Jews who approached him, saying, "Well did the holy Spirit speak to your fathers through Isaiah the prophet" (Acts 28:25). To Timothy, he wrote, "the Spirit says explicitly that in the last times some will turn away from the sound faith by paying attention to deceitful spirits" (1 Tim 4:1). Therefore, when the Spirit is said to be in someone, it is understood that the Word is in that person, giving the Spirit. So when the prophecy was being fulfilled, "I will pour out my spirit upon all flesh" (Joel 2:28), Paul said, "according to the support of the Spirit of Jesus Christ which is in me" (Phil 1:19). And to the Corinthians he wrote, "Are you looking for proof of Christ speaking in me?" (2 Cor 13:3). But if it was Christ who was speaking [604B] in him, then clearly the Spirit that was speaking in him was Christ's Spirit. So when Christ was speaking in him, he again said, in Acts, "But, now compelled by the Spirit, I am going to Jerusalem. What will happen to me there I do not know, except that in one city after another the holy Spirit has been testifying to me that imprisonment and hardships await me" (Acts 20:22–23).

Therefore, when the saints[52] say, "Thus says the Lord," they are not speaking otherwise than in the Holy Spirit; and, speaking in the Holy Spirit, they speak these things in Christ. When Agabus says, in Acts, "Thus says the Holy Spirit" (Acts 21:11), this does not happen otherwise than by the Word's coming to him and it is thereby that the Spirit enables him to speak in the Spirit and to testify to what is about to happen to Paul in Jerusalem. [604C] Certainly, when the Spirit gave testimony to Paul (cf. Acts 20:23), Christ himself was speaking in Paul, (605A) insofar as the testimony issued from the Spirit of the Word. Thus it was that when the Word came to the holy Virgin Mary, the Spirit also entered with him (cf. Lk 1:35), and the Word, in the Spirit, fashioned and joined a body to himself, wishing to unite creation to the Father and to offer it to the Father through himself and to reconcile all things in his body, "making peace among the things of heaven and the things of earth" (cf. Col 1:20).

32. The divine Scriptures thus unanimously demonstrate that the Holy Spirit is not a creature but belongs to (*idion*) the Word and to the divinity of the Father. This is the consensus of the teaching of the saints on the holy and indivisible Trinity and this is the one faith of the Catholic Church. But the extremely irrational myth-making of the Tropici is discordant with the Scriptures and consistent rather with the irrationality of the Ariomaniacs. [605B] It is just like them to dissemble in order to deceive the simple.[53] But thanks be to the Lord that, as you write, they have not been able to veil themselves with their feigned controversy with the Arians. Although they are hated by the Arians because they say that only the Spirit is a creature and not also the Word, they are also condemned by everyone as people who make war against the Spirit.[54] They are indeed close to death, desolate and bereft of the Spirit. In the words of the blessed apostle, they are natural people (*physikoi anthropoi*) who were incapable of receiving what pertains to the Spirit of God because these things are judged spiritually (cf. 1 Cor 2:14–15). But those who attend to the things that belong to the truth "judge all things and are not themselves subject to judgment by anyone" (1 Cor 2:15), having within them the Lord [605C] who, in the Spirit, reveals himself to them and, through himself, reveals the Father.

33. As for me, although I am residing in the desert, I have written briefly to your reverence because the shamelessness of those who have deviated from the truth has stirred me to disregard those who would wish to ridicule the weakness and lowliness of my exposition. I strongly urge that when you read this, you may correct what requires correction and excuse what is inadequately expressed. What I hand down to you is in accordance with the apostolic faith handed down to us by the fathers and I have invented nothing extraneous to it. I have expressed what I have learned, which is in conformity with the holy Scriptures and is consistent with the passages from the holy Scriptures that have been cited previously as confirmation.

[605D] It is not an invention brought in from the outside, but the Lord Jesus Christ himself personally taught the Samaritan woman – and through her, he teaches us – the perfection of the Holy

Trinity as one inseparable Godhead. The Truth herself gives witness when she says to the Samaritan woman: "Believe me, woman, the hour is coming, [608A] and is now here, when true worshippers will worship the Father in Spirit and Truth. And indeed the Father seeks such people to worship him. God is Spirit, and those who worship him must worship in Spirit and Truth" (Jn 4:21,23–24). It is clear from this passage that Truth is the Son himself, for he says, "I am the Truth" (Jn 14:6). It is he who was invoked by the prophet David when he said, "Send out your light and your truth" (Ps 43:3). Therefore, the true worshippers indeed worship the Father, but in Spirit and Truth, confessing the Son and in him, the Spirit. For the Spirit is inseparable from the Son, as the Son is inseparable from the Father. Truth herself gives witness when she says, "I will send you the Paraclete, [608B] the Spirit of Truth, who proceeds from the Father (Jn 15:26), whom the world cannot receive (Jn 14:17)" – that is to say, those who deny that the Spirit is from the Father and in the Son.

It is necessary therefore to confess and cling to the Truth, according to the model of true worshippers. As for those who after all this are still unwilling to learn and incapable of understanding, let them at least cease from foul speech and not separate the Trinity, lest they be separated from life. Let them also not number the Holy Spirit among creatures, so that they may not be like the Pharisees of another time who attributed the works of the Spirit to Beelzebub (cf. Mt 12:24), matching their presumption and suffering with them the punishment which is unpardonable both here and hereafter.[55]

5

LETTER 40: TO ADELPHIUS, BISHOP AND CONFESSOR, AGAINST THE ARIANS

Introduction

Athanasius's *Letter to Adelphius* was written ca. 370. Adelphius was the bishop of Onuphis, a town located on the Nile Delta, and he is listed as one of the signees of the *Tome to the Antiochenes*, which was the product of an Alexandrian synod convened by Athanasius in 362 to deal with the division among pro-Nicene camps in Antioch over Trinitarian terminology.[1] Adelphius is also mentioned among the names of pro-Nicene bishops who had been exiled during the tenure of George of Cappadocia,[2] and presumably it is for this reason that he has been granted the title of "Confessor." It is difficult to ascertain the precise contents of the doctrine being refuted in this letter, not least because of Athanasius's style of dramatizing his opponent's views by contriving self-damning monologues for them.[3] Moreover, given Athanasius's penchant for depicting anti-Nicene theology as being in organic continuity with all previous doctrinal error, his characterization of the teaching reported by Adelphius as "Arian" cannot spontaneously be taken at face value. Athanasius asserts that these "Arians" have now devised a new variation on their heresy, advancing from disbelief in the genuine divinity of the Word to a denial of the Word's becoming human. He accuses them furthermore of separating the Word from the flesh and of refusing to worship the Incarnate Word.

At first blush, it is difficult to see how such teachings are consistent with what we know of the doctrines of Arius and his supporters, which, even as elsewhere reported by Athanasius himself, do not include a denial of the Incarnation nor an outright refusal to worship Christ. Yet, once we take into account Athanasius's tendency to conflate his opponents' statements with what he considers to be their logical consequences, both of Athanasius's accusations can be made intelligible. With regard to the denial of the doctrine that the Word has become

234

human, the issue in question is not simply whether an incarnation took place but who it was who became incarnate. Arius and Asterius taught that the Word who became incarnate in Christ is other than the Word and Wisdom who is an uncreated eternal attribute of God.[4] When Athanasius accuses the "Arians" of this letter of "separating the body from the Word" (3, 8), it is likely that he has in mind the cleavage in such doctrine between the human body of Christ and the eternal Word, which is strictly consequent upon the separation of the "created" Word who became incarnate from the eternal Word.[5] Moreover, the letter's preoccupation with worship also seems to evoke a divergence between Nicene and anti-Nicene parties. In *Orations against the Arians*, Athanasius made much of the point that insofar as the "Arians" worship Jesus Christ and yet assert that the Word is a creature, they are involved in the idolatry of rendering worship to a creature.[6] But there are indications that those who did not believe that the Son was fully divine found ways to interpret Christian worship in a way that circumvented that difficulty. One of the early supporters of Arius, Theognis of Nicaea, explained that worship is rendered to "the Father alone," even though "we reverence (*veneramur*) the Son, because we are certain that his glory ascends to the Father."[7] The later development of "Neo-Arianism," beginning in the 350s, led to an even stronger emphasis that "the Son 'properly speaking' cannot be worshipped,"[8] even if Christian worship is always directed to the unoriginated God through the mediation of the Son.

Between the lines of the following letter, one can plausibly reconstruct an anti-Nicene counter-accusation, namely that it is the Nicene supporters who worship a creature since they do not at all qualify their worship of Christ even while acknowledging that the humanity of Christ is created. Such an accusation would explain why Athanasius, despite his aggressive rhetoric, substantially assumes a defensive posture in this letter: "We do not worship a creature. Never!" Athanasius's response – and herein lies the enduring value of the letter – presents his own Christology in a direction that anticipates the later Christological controversies and shows the direct link between his Christological thinking and that of his successor, Cyril. Central to the Christological vision propounded here is the inseparability of the divinity and humanity of the Incarnate Word as a single subject of salvific agency and a single object of worship. In a typical vein, the position attacked is styled "impious," and the "right faith" bears the mark of "piety" (*eusebeia*), which consists in gratitude for the coming of the Word in the flesh.

The text, not available in a critical edition, can be found in Migne's *Patrologia Graeca* 1072A–1084B.

Text

[1072A] 1. We have read what your Reverence has written, and we truly welcome your piety toward Christ. First of all, we glorify God for having given you the grace to be both right-minded and yet cognizant, as far as possible, of the stratagems of the devil (cf. 2 Cor 2:11).[9] On the other hand, we were amazed at the perversity of the heretics, seeing that they have fallen into such a pit of impiety that they are no longer in possession of their senses and their minds have become completely corrupt. This venture of theirs is at the instigation of the devil and is an imitation of the lawless Jews who, when they were thoroughly refuted, invented new pretexts for themselves in order only to deny the Lord. But they did this only to their own detriment and in order to draw upon themselves what was prophesied against them.[10] In the same way, these also, [1072B] seeing themselves to be shunned on all sides and recognizing that their heresy has become loathsome to everyone, have become inventors of new evils (cf. Rom 1:30) so that they may not stop their wars against the truth but may [1073A] truly persevere in being enemies of Christ.

Where has this evil of theirs erupted from? Just how did they dare to utter this new slander against the Savior? But it seems that indeed the impious man is useless and "degenerate in matters which pertain to faith" (2 Tim 3:8). At first, they denied the divinity of the only begotten Son of God, while at least making a pretence of confessing his incarnate coming. But now, culminating a gradual decline, they have fallen from this supposition of theirs and become altogether godless, to the extent that they neither acknowledge him to be God nor believe that he has become human. If they had believed this, they would not have said the kinds of things which your Reverence has written against them.

2. But you, truly and dearly beloved, have done what is consistent with ecclesiastical tradition and [1073B] piety toward the Lord by refuting and exhorting and censuring the likes of those. Urged on by their father the devil, "they did not know nor understand," as it is written, "but wander in darkness" (Ps 82:5). Therefore, let them learn from your Reverence that such a perversity as theirs

belongs to Valentinus, Marcion, and Manichaeus. Of these, some substituted appearance for reality and the others separated what is inseparable, denying that "the Word became flesh and dwelt among us" (Jn 1:14). So then why do they not claim their ownership of the heritage of these names, since they are of the same mind as them? It makes sense that they should have the names of those whose perversity they retain, so that from now on they should be called Valentinians and Marcionites and Manichees.[11] Perhaps then [1073C] they will become ashamed because of the bad odor of these names and so they will be enabled to perceive into what depth of impiety they have fallen. Indeed, it would have been just not to answer them at all, in accordance with the apostolic exhortation, "After a first and second warning, break off contact with a heretic, realizing that such a person is perverted and sinful and self-condemned" (Titus 3:10–11) – especially since the prophet too says of such people, "the fool will speak foolishly and his heart will contrive vain things" (Isa 32:6). But since they too, in the style of their leader, go around like lions seeking whom they can devour among the simple (cf. 1 Pet 5:8), it has become necessary for us to write back to your Reverence so that the brothers may be taught again by your admonition and so may further refute the vacuous discourse of these people.

3. We do not worship a creature. Never! [1073D] Such an error belongs to the pagans and the Arians. But we do worship the Lord of creation, the Word of God who has become incarnate. While that flesh, on its own, [1076A] is a part of creation, it nevertheless became the body of God. And neither do we separate that body from the Word and worship it on its own, nor do we cast the Word far from the flesh when we want to worship him. But knowing, as we said before, that "the Word became flesh" (Jn 1:14) we acknowledge him as God even when he comes in the flesh. Who then would be so senseless as to say to the Lord, "Stand aside from your body so that I may worship you"? Or who would be so impious as to join the Jews who did not understand and say to him, because of the body, "Why do you, a human being, make yourself to be God?" (Jn 10:33).

The leper, however, was not such as these. He worshipped the God who was in the body and recognized that he was God, saying, "Lord, if you wish, you can make me clean" (Mt 8:2). He did not [1076B] consider the Word of God to be a creature on account of the flesh, nor did he disparage the flesh because the Word who wore it was the Maker of all creation. But he worshipped the Creator of all as being in a created temple, and so he was cleansed. Likewise, the hemorrhaging woman, who believed and merely touched the hem of his garment, was healed (Mt 9:18–22, Mk 5:25–34); and the sea with foaming waves heard the Incarnate Word and stopped its storm (Mt 8:23–27 and par.); and the man who was blind from birth was healed by the Word through the spit of the flesh (Jn 9:6). And what is even greater and more wonderful (though maybe this also scandalized these most impious of people), is that when the Lord was hanging on the cross itself (for the body was his, and the Word was in it), the sun became darkened and the earth shook, the rocks were split and the veil [1076C] of the temple was torn, and many of the bodies of the dead saints were raised (cf. Lk 23:45, Mt 27:51).

4. These things took place, and yet no one made it a point of debate, like the Arians dare to do now, as to whether one must believe in the Word's becoming flesh. Though they saw a human being, they recognized him to be their Maker. When they heard a human voice, they did not say that the Word was a creature because the voice was human. Instead, they trembled and recognized that the human voice was nonetheless being spoken from a holy temple. How then are these impious people not afraid that "since they did not see fit to acknowledge God, they may be handed over to their undiscerning mind to do what is improper" (Rom 1:28)? For creation does not worship a creature, [1076D] but neither did it decline to worship its Lord because of his flesh. It discerned its own Maker in the body and "in the name of Jesus every knee" bowed – and will bow – "of those in heaven [1077A] and on earth and under the earth and every tongue shall confess" – even if it displeases the Arians – "that Jesus Christ is Lord to the glory of God the Father" (Phil 2:10–11). For the flesh did not detract from the glory of the Word. Far from it! Rather, it is the flesh which was glorified by the Word. Nor was the Son's divinity diminished because he who is in the form of God received the form of a servant (cf. Phil 2:6–7). Rather, he became the Liberator of all flesh and of all creation (cf. Rom 8:21).[12] And if God sent his Son born of a woman (cf. Gal 4:4), this is not a deed that brings us shame but glory and great grace. He became a human being that we might be divinized in him; he came to be in a woman and was begotten of a virgin in order to transport our errant race into himself and in order that from then on we may become a holy race and [1077B] "partakers of the divine nature" (2 Pet 1:4), as the blessed Peter has written. And "what the law, weakened by the

flesh, was powerless to do, this God has done; by sending his own Son in the likeness of sinful flesh and for the sake of sin, he condemned sin in the flesh" (Rom 8:3).

5. Since the flesh was assumed by the Word in order to liberate all human beings and to raise all from the dead and to make ransom for sin, how can those who devalue it and those who, because of it, slander the Son of God as a creature and as something that was made not appear ungrateful and worthy of all contempt? They might as well cry out to God and say: "Do not send your only begotten Son in the flesh. Do not make him take flesh from the Virgin, [1077C] or he will free us from death and sin. We do not want him to come in a body or he will undergo death on our behalf. We do not want the Word to become flesh, so that by its means he may become the Mediator of our way to You and so that we may dwell in the heavenly mansions (cf. Jn 14:2). Let the gates of heaven be closed shut, so that your Word may not consecrate the way into the heavens for us by the veil of his flesh (cf. Heb 10:20)." These are their words, uttered with the same diabolical presumption which led them to invent such perversities for themselves.

But those who do not want to worship the Word who has become flesh show no gratitude for his humanization. And those who separate the Word from the flesh negate the belief that there is one redemption from sin and [1077D] one destruction of death.[13] Just how will these impious ones ever find the flesh assumed by the Savior all by itself, so that they may dare to say: "We do not worship the Lord with his flesh but we separate the body and worship him alone." Yet the blessed Stephen saw the Lord standing at the right hand in the heavens (Acts 7:55); and the angels said to the disciples, "He will come in the same way as you have [1080A] seen him going into heaven" (Acts 1:11), and the Lord himself addressed the Father and said, "I wish that where I am, they may also be with me" (Jn 17:24). If the flesh then is inseparable from the Lord, must they not altogether cease this error and henceforth worship the Father in the name of our Lord Jesus Christ? But if they do not worship so and if they do not render service (*latreuontas*)[14] to the Lord who has come in the flesh, then let them be completely cast out and let them not be counted as Christians but as pagans or Jews.

6. This is their madness and presumption, as we have described it above. But ours is the right faith, which issues from the apostolic teaching and the tradition of the fathers and has its confirmation in both the Old and [1080B] New Testaments. For the prophets say,

"Send out your Word and your Truth" (Ps 43:3) and "Behold, the Virgin will conceive and bear a son and they shall call his name Emmanuel, which means 'God is with us'" (Isa 7:14, Mt 1:23). What is this about except God's coming in flesh? Then there is the teaching of the apostolic tradition, where the blessed Peter says, "Christ suffered for us in the flesh" (1 Pet 4:1) and Paul writes, "We await the blessed hope and the appearance of the glory of our great God and Savior Jesus Christ, who gave himself for us to redeem us from all sin and to cleanse for himself a people as his own, [1080C] eager to do good works" (Titus 2:13–14). But how did he give himself for us unless he had put on the flesh? For he gave himself for us by making an offering of his flesh, so that in it he may undergo death and "destroy the devil who has the power of death" (Heb 2:14).

Consequently, we always give thanks in the name of Jesus Christ and we do not reject the grace that has come to us through him. For the coming of the Savior in the flesh has become the ransom and salvation of all creation. My dearly beloved ones, let those who love the Lord be mindful of these things. But as for those who have imitated Judas and abandoned the Lord to join Caiaphas, let them find in these words a better teaching than what they have held – if indeed they are willing and have reached the point of being ashamed. Let them know, at least, that when we worship the Lord in the flesh, we are not worshipping a creature but, as we said before, we are worshipping the Creator clothed with a created body.

[1080D] 7. Moreover, we would like your Reverence to pose to them the following question: When Israel was commanded to go up to Jerusalem to worship in the temple of the Lord, where there was the ark and above it the cherubim of glory overshadowing the mercy-seat (cf. Heb 9:4–5), was this a good deed or a bad one? If they were doing a bad deed, why is it that those who did not heed this law were consigned to punishment? For it is written that the one who disregards it and does not go up is to be cut off from among the people (cf. Lev 17:9, Num 9:13). But if they were doing a good deed, [1081A] through which in fact they were pleasing to God, must not these defiled Arians, whose heresy is the most shameful of all, be utterly deserving of destruction? For in that case, they commend the ancient people for the honor rendered by them to the temple but do not wish to worship the Lord who is in his flesh, as in a temple.[15] And yet the old temple was fashioned from rocks and gold and was merely a shadow, but when the reality arrived the image[16] was henceforth annulled, according to the

240

words of the Lord, and there did not remain a stone upon another stone, that was not thrown down (cf. Mt. 24:2).

Although they saw that the temple was made of stones, the [ancient people] did not think that the Lord speaking in the temple was a creature, nor did they scorn the temple and go far off from it to worship. But, in accordance with the law, they went into the temple and served the Lord who spoke from the temple. This being so, [1081B] how can one not worship the all-holy and all-sacred body of the Lord, which was announced by the angel Gabriel and fashioned by the Holy Spirit and became a garment for the Word? For the Word raised the woman with a fever by extending his bodily hand (cf. Mk 1:30–31) and raised Lazarus by giving utterance to his human voice (Jn 11:43). When he extended his hands upon the cross, he overthrew "the ruler of the power of the air, who is at work in the sons of disobedience" (Eph 2:2) and cleared the way to heaven for us.[17]

8. Therefore, the one who dishonors the temple dishonors the Lord who is in the temple and the one who separates the Word from the body rejects the grace that was granted to us in the Word. As for these most impious Arian fanatics, [1081C] let them not think that the Word is a creature because his body is created. Nor should they impugn his body because the Word is not a creature. Their perversity is overwhelming; they confuse and mix everything up and contrive pretexts just so that they can count the Creator among the creatures.

But let them listen to this: If the Word were a creature, he would not have assumed a created body in order to enliven it. For what help can there be from one creature, itself in need of salvation, to another? But it is because the Word is Creator and is himself the Maker of creatures that "at the end of the ages" (Heb 9:26) he put on the creature in order that he, the Creator, may restore the creature and consecrate it anew. [1081D] A creature cannot ever be saved by another creature, any more than creatures are created by a creature.[18] This would not have happened unless [1084A] the Word were the Creator.

Therefore, let them not falsify the divine Scriptures nor scandalize the simple ones in the community. If they are willing, let them change their minds and no longer serve the creature instead of God, the creator of all. But if they want to persist in their impieties, let them take their fill of them by themselves and let them grind their teeth like their father the devil, because the faith of the Catholic Church knows that the Word of God is the creator and maker of everything. We know that "in the beginning was the Word and the Word was with God" (Jn 1:1) and we worship the Word who has become human for our salvation, not as if he has become equal to the body, but as the Master taking on the form of a servant, [1084B] and as the Creator and Maker coming to be in a creature so that, by granting freedom to all in himself, he may present the world to the Father and give peace to all, in heaven and on earth. Thus do we acknowledge his divinity, which is that of the Father, and we worship his incarnate presence, even if the Arian fanatics burst.

Greet all who love our Lord Jesus Christ. Most truly and dearly beloved, we pray that you may be in good health and that you may commend us to the Lord. If necessary, let Hieracas the presbyter read this.[19]

NOTES

1 INTRODUCTION

1 *History* 22.16.17; English translation (hereafter ET): Bowman (1986) 224.
2 Philo, *Flaccus* 55, 65–71.
3 *Expositio totius mundi et gentium* 37 (*SC* 124).
4 Canon 6: "The ancient customs of Egypt, Libya, and Pentapolis shall be maintained, according to which the bishop of Alexandria has authority over all these places, since a similar custom exists with reference to the bishop of Rome." Tanner, *Decrees of the Ecumenical Councils*, Vol. I (1990) 8–9.
5 Roberts (1979, 54) conjectures that Valentinus and Basilides were teachers at the catechetical school.
6 See Stroumsa (1986).
7 Roberts (1979) contends that Irenaeus's writings were available in Egypt "not long after the ink was dry on the author's manuscript" (53).
8 We cannot be sure of the exact date of his birth. The date of 295 follows the Coptic *Encomium of Athanasius* in *Testi Copti* 21 (1968) 6–8, which states that Athanasius was 33 years old at the time of his consecration as bishop in 328. See M. Tetz, *Theologische Realenzyklopädie*, Bd. 4 (1979) (hereafter *TRE*) 333. A later date makes more plausible the accusations later brought against him that he was below the canonical age of 30 at the time of his consecration as bishop (cf. *Festal Index* 3).
9 *Patrologia Orientalis* I, 4 (407).
10 *Patrologia Orientalis* I, 4 (408). Tetz summarizes this "little known story" and judges it to be "not unlikely": *TRE* 334.
11 *Ibid.*
12 *History of the Arians* 64.
13 Cf. *Encomium of Athanasius* in *Testi Copti* 17.
14 Stead (1988) makes a plausible case that the letter *"Henos Somatos"* (Urk. 4b) was written by the young Athanasius.
15 Gregory Nazianzus, *Oration* 21:6.
16 On Athanasius's affinities with Middle Platonic doctrine, see, especially, Meijering (1968).
17 Stead (1976) concludes that it is not unlikely that Athanasius had "at least a nodding acquaintance" with rhetorical textbooks; at any rate, he

243

employs classical rhetorical methods which he might have simply "absorbed ... by imitation" of other theologians (121).

18 *Oration* 21:6

19 Greek: *philoponos*; lit., "labor-loving." *On the Council of Nicaea* 27.

20 *Ibid.*; on the question of the authenticity of Athanasius's quotations of Dionysius of Alexandria, see below, n. 37.

21 On the influence of Irenaeus on Athanasius, see Anatolios (2001).

22 Defense against the Arians (Apologia Contra Arianos/Apologia Secunda) 6.

23 Harnack (1968), Vol. 3, 139.

24 Epiphanius, *Panarion* 68.

25 Martin (1996) 286–298.

26 Martin (1996) 298.

27 Socrates, *Ecclesiastical History* I:9, ET: L'Huillier (1996) 28.

28 Epiphanius, *Panarion* 68.

29 The doctrinal debates of the fourth century have traditionally been referred to as the Arian controversy. Such nomenclature is misleading on two counts: first, it seems to imply that the doctrinal issues at stake were all settled in place until the Arians introduced a foreign way of thinking into the clear calm of "orthodoxy"; and secondly, it adopts the misleading strategy, practiced by Athanasius himself, of conflating all opposition to Nicene doctrine and formulation as Arian, although there was some significant variety in anti-Nicene positions. It is impossible to name a historical event or process without implying a perspectival interpretation. In referring to the controversy as the "Nicene crisis," the perspective adopted here is one that acknowledges that the issues at stake were decisively broached at the Council of Nicaea and that their resolution, as far as the mainstream Christian tradition is concerned, came to be associated with that event in particular. This association itself owed no small part of its construction to the work of Athanasius; see, especially, his *On the Council of Nicaea*, below. On the construction and use of the category of "Arianism," see, especially, Wiles (1996).

30 The student of this controversy nevertheless now has the advantage of several magisterial monographs produced in the last two decades, to which the present exposition is indebted. Among the most helpful are Simonetti (1975), Hanson (1988), Arnold (1991), Barnes (1993), and Martin (1996); on Arius himself, most helpful is Williams (1987, 2001).

31 *Ecclesiastical History* I.5.

32 *Ecclesiastical History* I.15.1–6.

33 *On First Principles* I, 2, 2; *Commentary on John* 1:204, 2:8–9.

34 *On First Principles* I, 2, 10.

35 *Commentary on John* 2:32.

36 *Commentary on John* 2:72.

37 The authenticity of the quotations from Dionysius of Alexandria and his Roman namesake has been denied by Abramowski (1982), who has proposed that both sets of quotations were penned in the mid-fourth century by someone attempting to mediate between Marcellus of

Ancyra and Eusebius of Caesarea, shortly before the Council of Sardica of 343. Abramowski's hypothesis has been supported by Heil (1999), but rejected by Lorenz (1986) 81, n. 59; Hanson (1988) 75, n. 76; Fiege, *Die Lehre Markells von Ankyra in der Darstellung seiner Gegner*, EThSt 58 (Leipzig, 1991) 113–118; Simonetti, *Studi sulla cristologia del II e III secolo* (Rome, 1993) 274; and Williams (2001) 151, 325, n. 292. Heil does bring to light some differences in style between the supposed fragments of Dionysius quoted by Athanasius in *On the Thought of Dionysius* (*De Sententia Dionysii*), but these are not completely convincing; see the cautionary remarks by J. Leemans (review in *Vigiliae Christianae* 56: 329–333) and M. Vinzent (*Theologische Literaturzeitung* 126 (2001) 10: 1053–1055).

38 *On the Opinion of Dionysius* 4.
39 *Ibid.*
40 *On the Opinion of Dionysius* 15.
41 *On the Council of Nicaea* (*De Decretis*) 2.
42 Photius, *Bibliotheca*, Cod. 106.
43 *Letter to Alexander of Thessalonika*, Opitz, Urk. 14.
44 Thalia, in Athanasius, Orations against the Arians 1:5, and On the Councils of Ariminum and Seleuceia (De Synodis) 15.
45 Opitz, Urk. 17.
46 Biblical references are to the New American Bible translation of Scripture texts, with some modification.
47 *On the Council of Nicaea* 19–20.
48 Opitz, Urk. 24.
49 The reconciliation between Arius and Constantine likely followed upon a local council at Nicaea or Nicomedia, which would explain the seeming reference to a "second session" of the Council of Nicaea by Eusebius of Caesarea in his *Life of Constantine* 3:23 (see Hanson (1988) 174–178).
50 Cf. *Festal Index* 2.
51 Scholarly opinion differs considerably on the issue of the dating of this treatise, ranging from a date prior to the Nicene Council to one late in the 350s. For a good summary of the issues, see Leemans (2000) 132–135.
52 This is the opinion of Kannengiesser (1970).
53 See *Festal Letter* IV:5; cf. *Festal Index* 8.
54 *Defense against the Arians* 87.
55 Sozomen, *Ecclesiastical History* II.31.
56 *Defense against the Arians* 87.
57 *Defense against the Arians* 3–20.
58 *Festal Index* 10.
59 On the rivalry between Athanasius and his opponents in enlisting monastic support, see Gregg and Groh (1981).
60 Bartelink (1994) 314–318.
61 Socrates, *Ecclesiastical History* II, 9; Sozomen, *Ecclesiastical History* III, 6.
62 *Encyclical Letter* 2
63 While a native of Cappadocia, it seems that Gregory had studied in Egypt. See Gregory Nazianzus, *Oration* 21:15.

64 *History of the Arians* 9.

65 *Encyclical Letter* 3; Gregory Nazianzus compares the sufferings of Athanasius's supporters under Gregory with the trials of Job: *Oration* 21:17. A modern historian (Barnes (1993) 45) counters that "Athanasius suppresses the fact that there was violence on both sides … it is highly improbable that his partisans failed to resist the imposition of a new bishop with all the force that they could muster." Theoretically, that is a reasonable surmise, though the question in this particular case is just how much force Athanasius's supporters could muster in the face of the overwhelming show of force by imperial troops.

66 This central theme in Athanasius is given its due prominence by Tetz (1979) 304–338.

67 NPNF IV, 535, adapted. The *Festal Letters* were Athanasius's epistles to the Church of Egypt anticipating the celebration of Easter, in keeping with the traditional practice of the bishop of Alexandria. On the manuscript tradition and dating of the *Festal Letters*, see, especially, Camplani (1989), Lorenz (1986), and Barnes (1993) 183–191; for a good overview of the secondary literature on this subject, see Leemans (2000) 163–167.

68 NPNF IV, 537, adapted. This letter was probably written while Athanasius was still in Egypt. See Martin (1996) 407.

69 *Festal Letter* XI:13; NPNF IV, 537, adapted.

70 *Syntagmation*, Fr. 14, Vinzent (1993).

71 *Syntagmation*, Fr. 10, Vinzent (1993) 86.

72 Arius, *Thalia*, in Athanasius, *On the Councils of Ariminum and Seleucia* (*De Synodis*) 15. See also *Encyclical Letter of Alexander of Alexandria* (Urk. 4b), where Arius is reported as saying that the Son is "not like the Father in substance" (Opitz, *AW* III/I, 7:21–22).

73 For comparisons of the theological perspectives of Arius and Asterius, see Kopecek (1979) 29–34; Hanson (1988) 32–41; Vinzent (1993) 63–67.

74 The authenticity of the third oration was at one time challenged by Kannengiesser (1983b, 310–416; 1993; 1995). However, the third oration is far too similar to both the other two orations and Athanasius's corpus in general to warrant such a conclusion. For the similarity in theological thought and vocabulary, see, especially, Meijering (1996a, 11–23; 1996c); for the similarity in polemical style, see Schmidtz (1988). At an oral communication presented at the 14th International Conference on Patristics Studies in Oxford, "Die Datierung des apologetischen Früwerks und der Arianerreden," on 19 August 2003, Kannengiesser retracted his earlier position.

75 There are only two direct internal indications of the date of composition: a reference to the death of Arius (I:3) and the reign of Constantius II (I:10; III:25); these place the work between 337 and 361. Athanasius's manifest reluctance to use the term "*homoousios*" in this treatise indicates a date prior to the mid-350s, at which point he began actively promoting the use of the term as the only sure safeguard against the "Arian heresy." That the treatise was written during his

exile in Rome is suggested by the fact that Athanasius refutes Asterius by direct quotation, to which he would have access in Rome through Marcellus, who himself had published a refutation of Asterius (ca. 336). Athanasius's use of language similar to that of the "Dedication Creed" of Antioch (341), such as references to the Son as "exact image" of the Father (I:26) and "like" (*homoion*; I:26) the Father, has been taken as an indication that it was written before that date. The basis for this position is that a date posterior to that creed would signal Athanasius's approval of that creed (cf. Moutsoulas (1985)). However, it was typical of Athanasius to use his opponent's words against themselves and to press the point that the very use of such terms can only coherently lead to an acknowledgement of the full divinity of the Son (cf. *Oration* III:11, *On the Councils of Ariminum and Seleucia* 38). A date after the Council of Antioch of 341 therefore cannot be ruled out. There are intratextual indications that the second oration was written some time after the first (cf. *Oration* II:1) and a passage in the third oration directs the reader to a passage in the second, as having been articulated "a short while" ago (III:11, apparently referring to II:42; see Meijering (1996a) 18, 23, 123). These indications point to a gradual process of composition, as has been suggested by Kannengiesser (1983b). Abramowski (1991) makes a good case for placing the third oration just prior to the Council of Sardica in 343. For a succinct overview of the debates regarding the dating of the *Orations*, see Leemans (2000) 138–144.

76 Kannengiesser (1993) 378.
77 *AW* II/III, 107.
78 *AW* II/III, 108–109.
79 This creed is reproduced by Athanasius in his *On the Councils of Ariminum and Seleucia* 23.
80 Hanson (1988) 301 (translation slightly modified).
81 Lienhard categorizes the debate in terms of "miahypostatic" and "dihypostatic" traditions (1987; 1999, 28–46). It should be noted that the categories of "East" and "West" are only valid in a general, not an absolute and exceptionless sense. Athanasius and Marcellus of Ancyra were allied with the "Western" bishops, and the "Western" contingent of the Council of Sardica included representatives from Palestine, Arabia, and Greece.
82 Perhaps contributing to the emperor's change of tone was the debacle involving Stephen, the bishop of Antioch, who arranged for a prostitute to be stripped naked and clandestinely brought by night into the room of the sleeping Bishop Euphrates, one of the delegates sent by the Council of Sardica. Upon seeing the old man, the prostitute experienced compunction and betrayed her commissioner. Stephen was deposed and replaced by a bishop of anti-Nicene tendencies but irenic character, Leontius. The incident seems to have shaken Constantius's confidence in the integrity of the anti-Nicene camp as well as the veracity of their allegations against Athanasius and others. See *History of the Arians* 20.

83 In Socrates, *Ecclesiastical History* II:19; Athanasius, *On the Councils of Ariminum and Seleucia* 26

84 Barnes (1993) 92; cf. *Festal Index* 18

85 *AW* II/V, 196–197. On Athanasius's success in aligning the monastic movement with his own person and doctrinal convictions, see Brakke (1995).

86 On the dating, see Barnes (1993) 198–199; on the problems involved in dating this work, see below.

87 We have no extant record of such a formula. Nevertheless, the strength of the Western bishops' resistance to Constantius at these councils suggests as much; Hanson (1988, 334) conjectures that the bishops were presented with a "formula which was not openly Arian but was patient of an Arian interpretation."

88 *AW* II/III, 84–85. Cf. *Historia Acephala* 1.9–11 (Martin); *Festal Index* 28.

89 *Defense before Constantius* 30.

90 *History of the Arians* 51; cf. Gregory of Nazianzus, *Oration* 21:16.

91 There was at this point no clear differentiation between the terminology of origination (*agen(n)etos*) and generation (*gen(n)etos*); see Prestige (1923).

92 See Epiphanius, *Panarion* 73.

93 ET: Hanson (1988) 364.

94 *Dialogue against the Luciferians* 19.

95 The Athanasian authorship of the *Life of Antony* is attested to by all the manuscript evidence. It has only lately been questioned, most notably by Barnes (1986) and Barnard (1994). Responses to Barnes's position and arguments in support of Athanasian authorship are ably set forth by Braake (1994) and Louth (1988). A good overview of the debate is found in Leemans (2000) 153–161.

96 *Letter I to Serapion* 27.

97 *Oration* 21:33; ET: NPNF 7, 278.

98 The incident is mentioned with gruesome terseness in *Historia Acephala* 2:10.

99 *Letter* 51.

100 *Historia Acephala* 5:2 (Martin).

101 *Festal Index* 35; *Historia Acephala* 3:4.

102 *Letter to Jovian* 4; PG 26:817C–819A.

103 *Historia Acephala* 5:2 (Martin).

104 *Historia Acephala* 5:6–7 (Martin).

105 *Letter* 109; PL 54:1016B.

106 *Oration* 21:37.

107 Journal entry for 14 April 1838, in *The Journals of Søren Kierkegaard*, tr. Alexander Dru (London: Oxford, 1938) 58.

108 This portrait is represented most forcibly in Schwartz (1959) and Barnes (1981), who has famously labeled Athanasius as "a gangster" (230). For a good overview of the history of the interpretation of Athanasius's character, see Arnold (1991) 11–23.

109 Louth (1988) 505.

110 See, for example, Von Campenhausen (1959) 73.

111 For a thorough treatment of this issue, see Arnold (1991) 62–89.

112 *AW* II/VI, 201.

113 Hanson (1988) 319.

114 Brakke (2000, 1107) offers a quotation, in partially elided form, from a Coptic fragment of one of Athanasius's festal letters that purports to reveal him as advocating the whipping of those who exploited the martyrs' relics for financial gain. However, the elision is misleading and the text, as translated by Brakke himself elsewhere, seems to suggest that the transgressors will be punished by Christ, just as were the money-changers in the temple, rather than to recommend their being whipped by others. This interpretation is consistent with Athanasius's common practice of assimilating his opponents to scriptural images of villainy. The text, in Brakke's unelided translation, runs as follows: "This resembles the crookedness of Jeroboam, who sold <the priesthood and those who sold> and bought doves in the temple of God, as it is written (1 Kings 12:31; Mt 21:12–13; par.). Rather it is clear without a doubt that it is those who are lawless now and are being driven out by whippings to whom the Lord said, 'Do not make my Father's house a house of trade' (Jn 2:16). They too will hear him say, 'Do not sell the body of my martyrs and do not make their good confession a business for the sake of greed.' For it is necessary for those who commit such a sin to receive the same punishment" (Brakke (1998) 478).

115 See *Orations against the Arians* (hereafter *Or. Ar.*) 1:1.

116 *AW* I/I.II (= Bd. I, Teil I, Lief. 2), 117.14–19.

117 *Letter to Marcellinus* 15–26.

118 On this theme, see, especially, Tetz (1979).

119 PG 26:1447C–1448A.

120 Translations of *Against the Greeks – On the Incarnation* are based on the critical edition of Thomson (1971); this passage is found in Thomson (1971) 6.

121 Thomson (1971) 94.

122 On Athanasius's anthropology, one may still usefully consult Bernard (1952) and Roldanus (1968); see also Anatolios (1998) 53–67.

123 Thomson (1971) 140.

124 *On the Council of Nicaea* 11.

125 *Ibid.*; *AW* II/I, 10.

126 *Or. Ar.* 1:20.

127 *Thalia*, in *Or. Ar.* 1:5; *To the Bishops of Egypt* (*Ad Episcopos Aegypti*) 12.

128 *Or. Ar.* 1:15–16.

129 The verb *sunkatabainō* (to descend with) is applied to the act of creation in *Against the Greeks* 47; God's creation is characterized as "mercy" in *On the Incarnation* (hereafter *Inc.*) 3, 8, 11.

130 Thomson (1971) 6.

131 For some nuances of this general view, see Armstrong (1972) 35ff.

132 Thomson (1971) 8.

133 *Republic* IV: 440–441C.

134 *Against the Greeks* 32.

135 See Plato, *Phaedrus* 246.

136 Thomson (1971) 12, 14; the image of the charioteer is found in Plato's *Phaedrus* 246/247. On Athanasius's understanding of the human body, see Pettersen (1990) and Anatolios (1998) 62–64.

137 *Against the Greeks* 8.

138 *SC* 400; 188–192.

139 *Inc.* 1.

140 Thomson (1971) 164. The contrast drawn here between humanity as rational (*logikon*) and as irrational (*alogon*) bears implicit reference to the status of its participation in the *Logos*.

141 On human fall and descent, see *Against the Greeks* 8, 9, 19, 22, 23, and *Inc.* 16; on the Word's condescension in the Incarnation, see *Inc.* 3, 8, 15.

142 Thomson (1971) 22, 24.

143 Meijering (1991).

144 Thomson (1971) 168, 170.

145 *Or. Ar.* 1:37–1:45; cf. *Or. Ar.* 3:11–14.

146 *Against the Heresies* III, 24, 2; IV, 20, 1.

147 See Grillmeier (1975) 308–328.

148 Thomson (1971) 166.

149 Hanson (1988) 450.

150 *Inc.* 44.

151 Thomson (1971) 152–154.

152 On the theme of the Eucharist as "sacrifice" in the early Church, see Moll (1975) and Young (1979).

153 *Inc.* 41; see Grillmeier (1975) 311 and Kelly (1978) 285.

154 *Inc.* 7.

155 Thomson (1971) 154–158. Among the many passages in which Athanasius speaks of Christ's relation to his body in terms of "offering" and "sacrifice," see *Inc.* 8, 9, 10, 16, 20, 21, 25; *Or. Ar.* 1:41, 2:7, 2:14, 2:69; *On the Council of Nicaea* 14; *To Epictetus* 4, 5, 6; *To Adelphius* 6.

156 *AW* I/I.II, 183.10–184.30.

157 See also *Or. Ar.* 2:55, 2:65, 2:69.

158 Cf. Kelly (1978) 378–379.

159 *Inc.* 20, 14; *Or. Ar.* 2:63.

160 Thomson (1971) 154.

161 *Inc.* 10

162 *Or. Ar.* 2:61, 2:74. The same terminology is explicitly applied by Cyril of Jerusalem, Athanasius's contemporary, to refer to the act of Eucharistic communion. See Cyril of Jerusalem, *Mystagogy* IV, 1; see also *Alexandrian Liturgy of St. Basil*, PG 31:1648A; John of Damascus, *Exposition of the Orthodox Faith* 4:13.

163 *Inc.* 13.

164 See, for example, Origen, *On First Principles* I, 5, 5; I, 8, 3.

165 The psalms especially are pervaded by this motif: for example, Ps 15:5, 16:8, 21:8, 46:6, 93:1, 125:1. On the Jewish and Hellenistic background to the theme of stability, see Williams (1985).

166 Heb 12:28.

167 *Against the Greeks* 41, 42; *Inc.* 3.

168 See, for example, *Or. Ar.* 1:45, 1:50, 2:70, 3:38, 3:40.
169 See Bromiley, *Theological Dictionary of the New Testament*, Vol. 4, 574–576.
170 Thomson (1971) 140, 142.
171 *AW* I/I.II, 246.3–11.
172 See, for example, *Against the Greeks* 36; *Or. Ar.* 1:17, 1:20, 2:2, 2:57, 3:62, 3:64.
173 Literally, "the realm of dissimilitude"; cf. Plato, *Politicus* 273d.
174 Thomson (1971) 242, 244, 246; cf. *CA* 2:56, 2:68.
175 Greek: *logotheisēs*; PG 26:396A.
176 PG 26:393B–396A.
177 Williams (1983) 58–59. Williams suggests that Arius's rejection of this term was based on his interpretation of it according to Porphyry's definition in which it indicated a property predicated of a substance, rather than a substance itself.
178 *On the Council of Nicaea* 25.
179 PG 26:393A–393B; for the connections between this passage and other writings of Athanasius, see Meijering (1996b) 81–89.
180 See *Or. Ar.* 2:70.
181 Lapidge (1979).
182 On the Incarnation as an "extension" of the lordship of the Word, see also *Inc.* 45.
183 *AW* I/I.II, 190.9–191.24; cf. *To Epictetus* 9, *To Adelphius* 4, *To the Egyptian Bishops* 17, *Or. Ar.* 1:42.
184 NPNF IV, 531, adapted; see also *To Adelphius* 4.
185 *To Epictetus* 6.
186 *Or. Ar.* 2:55.
187 Greek: *theologoi*.
188 Thomson (1971) 176.
189 See *Or. Ar.* 2:46.
190 *AW* I/I.II, 221.
191 PG 26:396C.
192 PG 26:388C–389C.
193 On the "*idios*" motif in Alexandrian Christology, see Louth (1989); for an exposition of Cyril's Christology that takes due note of Athanasius's influence on Cyril, see McGuckin (1994) 175–226.
194 Cyril of Alexandria's Second Letter to Nestorius, 5; Wickham (1983) 6.
195 This pertains to the biblical writer.
196 *AW*, II/I, 52.
197 *Against the Greeks* 9; cf. 19, 27, 29.
198 See, for example, *Inc.* 7, 8.
199 See, for example, *Inc.* 19, 40, 54.
200 Thomson (1971) 122.
201 Thomson (1971) 128.
202 *Against the Greeks* 40.
203 *Or. Ar.* 1:50.
204 See *Or. Ar.* 1:46ff.; cf. 3:24, 3:25, 3:38.
205 See *Or. Ar.* 1:11, 2:62, 3:4, 3:59. See also Pelikan (1962).
206 *Or. Ar.* 2:42–43; see also Williams (1993).

207 "Either they must teach us not to baptize in the manner we have been taught, or else not to believe as we were baptized, or not to glorify as we believe. Can anyone deny that the sequence of relationship in these acts must necessarily remain unbroken" (*On the Holy Spirit* 68).

208 *On First Principles* I, 2, 1–10; *Commentary on John* I:125ff. On Origen's theology of Christological titles, see Crouzel (1989) 189–192; cf. Lorenz (1979) 67–94.

209 Stead (1976).

210 See *Or. Ar.* 2:32 and *Letters to Serapion* 1:20; see also Pelikan (1962), Sieben (1974), and Torrance (1995) 254–259.

211 The "exactness" (*akribeia*) of scriptural language is a common motif in Athanasius; see *Or. Ar.* 2:33, 2:71, 3:52.

212 *Or. Ar.* 1:22. For strong statements on the distinct subsistences of Father, Son, and Spirit, from Athanasius's later period, see, for example, *On the Councils of Ariminum and Seleucia* 41 and *Letters to Serapion* 1:28.

213 On the "*skopos*" of Scripture in Athanasius, see Pollard (1959) 422–25; Ernest (1993); Torrance (1995) 235–244.

214 *Or. Ar.* 1:54; cf. *Or. Ar.* 2:8 and *On the Council of Nicaea* 14. See also Ernest (1993) and Sieben (1974).

215 PG 26:385A–388A; for resonances between this passage and other writings of Athanasius, see Meijering (1996b) 49–59.

216 *Letters to Serapion* 1:19; Athanasius is referring to 1 Cor 12:13, "we were all given to drink of one Spirit," and Eph 1:17, "that the God of our Lord Jesus Christ, the Father of glory, may give you the spirit of wisdom and revelation in the knowledge of him, having the eyes of your hearts enlightened."

217 *Letters to Serapion* 1:20.

218 *Letters to Serapion* 1:24.

219 *Letters to Serapion* 3:2.

220 With reference to the real subsistence of the Spirit, see *Letters to Serapion* 1:28.

221 Thomson (1971) 274–276. On the importance of the theme of imitation of the scriptural saints in Athanasius, see Tetz (1979).

222 See Louth (1970).

223 *Festal Letter* 13:1.

224 *Second Letter to Virgins* 6.

225 *Letter to Amoun*; *First Letter to Virgins* 12–30.

226 *First Letter to Virgins* 43.

227 NPNF IV, 531, adapted.

2 SELECTIONS FROM *ORATIONS AGAINST THE ARIANS*

1 *Or. Ar.* 1:22, 1:37, 2:24.

2 See Kannengiesser (1983b) 24.

3 Opitz III/I, Urk. 4b, 8.2–3; see also Arius, *Thalia*, in *Or. Ar.* 1:5.

4 It would seem that in Arius's understanding, this proleptic bestowal was conferred upon the Son even in his pre-existent state. He explic-

itly rejects the notion that the Son "previously existed and was later begotten or reestablished as a Son" (*Statement of Faith of Arius*, *AW* III/I, Urk. 6, 13.1–2). Athanasius seems to acknowledge that a simple adoptionism was rejected by the early supporters of Arius in *On the Council of Nicaea* 6; cf. Williams (1987, 2nd edn.) 104–105. Williams entertains the possibility that the assertion of the Son's mutability could be a mere deduction of Athanasius's imposed on Arius's doctrine of the creatureliness of the Son, but then dismisses it because of "the attention Athanasius expends on the exegetical issues connected with this" (1987, 105). We may also note the testimony of Alexander of Alexandria along with the explicit anathematization of this teaching by both the Council of Antioch of 325 and the Council of Nicaea. For a positive evaluation of the doctrine of the Son's change-ability in early Arianism, see Gregg and Groh (1981) esp. 13–42.

5 *AW* III/I, Urk. 14, 27.13.

6 *AW* III/II, Urk. 24.

7 See all of Gregg and Groh (1981).

8 See, for example, Asterius, *Syntagmation*, Fr. 45, Vinzent (1993) 110, from Alexander of Alexandria's letter to Alexander of Thessalonica.

9 This interpretation is closely aligned with the thesis of Lorenz, who considers Arian "Logos-theology" to be dependent on Origen's theology of the Incarnation; see Lorenz (1979) 211–224.

10 *On First Principles* I, 2, 10 (Butterworth (1973) 25–26).

11 Cf. *Against Celsus* VI: 79, 150–151.

12 Cf. *On First Principles* I, 2, 10; I, 6, 2; I, 8, 3.

13 Asterius, *Syntagmation*, Fr. 44, Vinzent (1993) 108.

14 This is a telling rhetorical question; Athanasius seems more concerned that "those who belong to the Church" be viscerally horrified at the impiety of Arian doctrine than that they should be capable of refuting them in argument. See Chapter 1, pp. 36–37.

15 Cf. Symbol of Nicaea (*AW* III/II, Urk. 24).

16 That God does not "progress" is an important part of Athanasius's Trinitarian theology; see, for example, *Or. Ar.* 1:17. There is a similar stress in Origen's doctrine of God; cf. *On First Principles* I, 2, 10.

17 Here, Athanasius is directing his attack against the teaching of Asterius, who could speak of the Son as "exact image" of the Father (*Syntagmation*, Fr. 10, Vinzent (1993)). It is aimed generally against those anti-Nicene "*homoians*" who were willing to confess that the Son is like the Father while ascribing to him changeability. The point would not hold against Arius, who reportedly asserted that Father, Son, and Spirit are wholly "unlike" (*Thalia*, in Athanasius, *Or. Ar.* 1:5). Athanasius's point is that to say that the Father is unchangeable while the Son is changeable makes it self-contradictory to maintain that the Son is like the Father.

18 This is a typical instance of Athanasius's technique of inserting Arian theology into Scriptural statements that speak of the correlation of Father and Son, in order to highlight, by jarring effect, the discordance of Arian theology with Scripture.

NOTES

19 Asterius referred to the Son as "image," which gives Athanasius another opportunity to make the point that it is self-contradictory to say that the changeable Son is the image of the unchangeable Father. Cf. "Creed of the Council of Antioch of 341," in Athanasius, *De Synodis* 23).

20 On the significance of this term for Athanasius's theology, see Chapter 1, pp. 66–74; Louth (1989).

21 For the notion that those who do not properly honor the divinity of the *Logos* become themselves irrational (*alogoi*) and prone to irrational thoughts, see *Against the Greeks* 9, 19, 34; *Inc.* 12; *On the Council of Nicaea* 2.

22 The Son is referred to as the "fruit" (*karpos*) of the Father in *Against the Greeks* 46.

23 It is not clear whether Athanasius has a particular event of Jesus's life in mind here, such as the Transfiguration. He could simply be making the point, which is typical with him, that the "works" of Christ are ample demonstration of his divinity and provide a counter-witness to those who would take him for a mere human being. Cf. *Inc.* 15, 30, 31, 54; Origen, *On First Principles* I, 2, 8.

24 Greek: *hoi hagioi*; in Athanasius, this term usually refers to the writers of the Scriptures.

25 According to Aristotelian teaching, an accident is that which does not exist in itself but in an underlying subject (*ousia*); see *Categories* 4, 1b25–27, and *Topics* I 9, 103b22–23. Aristotle lists as accidents quantity, quality, relation, location, time, position, state, action, and passion. Athanasius's reasoning is that if the Son's being "Word" and "Wisdom" were accidental to him and thus susceptible to variation, there is nothing to ensure that he will persist in being Word and Wisdom. This logic owes something to Origen, who argued that goodness is not stable in creatures because it is accidental to their natures (see, for example, *On First Principles* I, 2, 4; I, 2, 10; I, 5, 5). Of course, the Arians would counter that this capacity to persist is granted to him by God, as a grace.

26 Greek: *echrise*; lit., "christened."

27 Asterius, *Syntagmation*, Fr. 45, Vinzent (1993) 110.

28 This is a reference to Eusebius of Nicomedia; see Chapter 1, p. 10.

29 Here, Athanasius is constructing his own deductions in order to push Arian doctrine into a kind of adoptionism, quite ignoring the doctrine of a reward proleptically awarded to the Son in anticipation of his future merits. His larger point, however, still stands – namely that this conception makes the Son "gain" divine prerogatives as a consequence of his human career, a conception which he apparently considers to entail "logical" if not temporal adoptionism.

30 Paul of Samosata was bishop of Antioch (ca. 260–268), and was condemned by Antiochian synods in 264 and 268. While it is difficult to reconstruct with any assurance his genuine thought, it appears that he denied the pre-existence of Christ and was thus routinely represented as teaching that Christ was a mere man (*psilos anthropos*).

31 Athanasius often likens the "Arians" to the Jews. While this motif rightly bears an ill savor in the post-holocaust world, it should be noted that the taunts of Athanasius are part of a strategy of excluding the "Arians" from the boundaries of Christian identity. Typically, this strategy is worked out by projecting the "Arians" onto the scriptural landscape and aligning them with those who refuse to acknowledge the lordship of Christ in the evangelical accounts. Thus, they are identified not only with the Jews, but also with Pilate, Herod, etc. Likewise, they are aligned with previous groups of heretics who have been excluded from the communion of the Church, such as the Valentinians, the Manichees, and the Marcionites. For a critique of Athanasius's strategy of identifying his opponents with the Jews, see Brakke (2001).

32 Athanasius's opponents would agree that even if the Son himself is divine by grace, he is still the mediator of grace to others. But in that case, he asks, how was the grace of being "sons" of God granted through the mediation of the Son even before the Son himself attained to the grace of divinity? While it may still be contended that the grace of being Son was granted even prior to creation, through God's foreknowledge of his merits (see n. 4, above), Athanasius is concerned at this point with establishing at least that the Son's divinity was not consequent upon his human career, and thus not consequent upon the abasement to which the text of Philippians 2 refers.

33 Lit., "there is no sonship apart from the true Son."

34 Once again, Athanasius is trying to show that the exegesis of his opponents suffers from self-contradiction. On Asterius's doctrine of the likeness between Father and Son, see nn. 17 and 19 above. In his exposition of the proceeding of the Nicene Council (*On the Council of Nicaea* 20), Athanasius portrays Eusebius and his supporters as accepting the formula that the Son is "like the Father in all things."

35 Greek: *kata patrikēn idiotēta*.

36 Reading *ton genomenon anthrōpon* (with OSBc3Ac), rather than merely *ton genomenon*. Cf. *AW* I/I, 152.

37 Cf. *Inc.* 6, 13. Athanasius's use of this theme seems to have a distinctly Irenaean flavor; see Irenaeus, *Against the Heresies* III, 23, 1; IV, 20, 7.

38 Greek: *tous sussōmous autou*; see Chapter 1, p. 61, and accompanying note.

39 That the victory wrought by the Word's Incarnation and death on the cross is manifest in the conversion of the nations to Christ, the decline of idolatry, and the spreading of the knowledge of God is an important theme in Athanasius's earlier treatise, *Against the Greeks – On the Incarnation*. See *Against the Greeks* 1; *Inc.* 1, 30, 31, 45, 46, 47, 52, 55. A similar conception is found in Origen, *On First Principles* IV, 1, 1; IV, 1, 5.

40 It is striking that for Athanasius, the very fact that Jesus is worshipped is a sign of his divinity. A parallel argument is found in *Inc.*, where the Church's faith in him is considered to be a manifestation of Christ's active divinity. See *Inc.* 53.

41 In these *Orations*, Athanasius typically refers to the "kinship" (*sungeneia*) that human beings have with Christ's body. See *Or. Ar.* 2:63, 2:69, 3:53.

42 Greek: *tēn dianoian ... ekklēsiastikēn*; cf. *Against the Greeks* 6, 7, 33; *On the Council of Nicaea* 3.

43 Greek: *bebaia*; see Chapter 1, pp. 61–63.

44 See *Or. Ar.* 3:11–13.

45 Lit., "according to his own paternal (*patrikēn*) divinity and perfection."

46 This text from the psalm is applied to Christ in Heb 1:8–9. For Origen's treatment of this text with reference to the soul of Christ, see *On First Principles* II, 6, 4. Cf. Asterius, *Syntagmation*, Fr. 45, Vinzent (1993); on the authenticity of this fragment, see Vinzent (1993) 253–255.

47 Greek: *metochous*; in the original context of the psalm, the term refers to the "fellow kings" over whom the Israelite king stands pre-eminent. The term *metochos* means "partner," and it also means "partaker," one who "participates in" (*metechein*). It therefore lends itself readily to being interpreted in light of the framework of "participation." For Athanasius, all creatures participate in God, while the Son, as God, is participated by creatures. On one occasion, Athanasius concedes that one might be able to speak of the Son as participating the Father, but this is an altogether unique case of "whole participation"; see *Or. Ar.* 1:15–16. On Athanasius's doctrine of participation, see Bernard (1952) 32–38; Meijering (1974) 62–64; Kolp (1979); Anatolios (1998) 50–52, 104–109, 137–138.

48 Athanasius's treatment of the Son's Incarnate reception of the Spirit on our behalf is close to that of Irenaeus: cf. *Against the Heresies* III, 9, 3; III, 17, 1–2; III, 18, 3; *Demonstration of the Apostolic Faith* 6. See also Roldanus (1968) 236–252; Anatolios (2001) 474–475.

49 Cf. Eusebius of Caesarea, commenting on the same text: "the Anointer, who is the Supreme God, is far superior to the Anointed, who is God in a different sense" (*Demonstration of the Gospel* IV, 15; PG 22:305A).

50 For Athanasius, "Image" (*eikōn*) is one of the names of the Son. Consequently, he speaks of humanity not in terms of being God's image, but of being "*kat' eikona* – according to the image." See Bernard (1952) 21–24; Roldanus (1968) 38–65. The same usage is found in Origen; cf. *Commentary on John* 1:105.

51 Greek: *metochos*; see above, n. 47.

52 Greek: *tēn patrikēn basileian* – i.e. the Son's kingdom is that of the Father.

53 See Chapter 1, pp. 61–63; cf. *Or. Ar.* 3:12–13.

54 Asterius, *Syntagmation*, Fr. 45, Vinzent (1993) 110, 253–255.

55 Athanasius's stress on the instability of created beings in goodness as something rectified by the humanization of the Word is derived from Origen; see, for example, *On First Principles* I, 2, 4: "Or again, since it was to happen that some of those who were created would prove unable, in consequence of the good being within them as an accident and not by nature, that is, not essentially, to remain firm and steadfast and to abide for ever in the just and temperate use of their original

NOTES

blessings, but would turn and change and fall away from their first
state, the Word and Wisdom of God became the Way" (Butterworth
(1973) 17).

56 Hanson (1988) 434.

57 Hanson (1988) 825.

58 *Commentary on John* 1:111, 118.

59 It is also true, however, that there was a much thinner stream of tradition that identified "Wisdom" with the Spirit, rather than with Christ;
thus Irenaeus, *Against the Heresies* IV, 20, 3, and even in the fourth
century, Gregory of Elvira, *On the Orthodox Faith* 27–29.

60 See Chapter 1, pp. 80–82.

61 Arius held that God was not eternally Father (*Thalia*, in Athanasius,
Or. Ar. 1:5), but Asterius maintained that while the Son is not eternal,
God is always Father by virtue of his generative capacity (Asterius,
Syntagmation, Fr. 14, Vinzent (1993), in Athanasius, *On the Councils of
Ariminum and Seleucia* (*De Synodis*) 19).

62 In the background here is Origen's doctrine that if God is eternally
almighty, there must always be a creation over which God is sovereign
(*On First Principles* I, 2, 10). Athanasius transposes this line of
reasoning to argue that if God *is* Creator, he must be eternally in
possession of his creative agency, which is biblically identified as the
Son/Word/Wisdom. The same argument is made in *Or. Ar.* 1:26, 29.
On the Origenian background to this argument, see Anatolios (1999).

63 Cf. *Or. Ar.* 3:63. Origen also speaks of the generation of the Son from
the Father as "an act of his will proceeding from the mind" (*On First
Principles* I, 2, 6; I, 2, 9; IV, 4, 1). Even more directly, Clement of
Alexandria speaks of the Word as "the Father's will" (*thelēma*) in his
Exhortation 12; see also Justin Martyr, *Dialogue with Trypho*, 128.

64 Greek: *poiēsanti*; in this context, usually translated as "appointed." The
text to which Athanasius refers speaks of Jesus as "the apostle and high
priest of our confession, who was faithful to the one who appointed
(*poiēsanti*) him."

65 Given the fact that what is at issue is precisely whether the words of
Scripture designate the essence of the Word to be that of a creature,
Athanasius seems to be quite begging the question here by asserting
that the words of Scripture themselves have to be interpreted consistently with the essence to which they apply. But his point, ultimately,
is that the essence of the Word cannot be determined by the single use
of a particular term but in light of the overall patterns of terminology
and plot throughout the Scriptures. Thus, he will go on to argue that
the overall scriptural designation of the Word differentiates him from
creatures and posits a strict correlativity of the Father and the
Word/Wisdom/Son.

66 Greek: *tōn akerainōn*; see Kannengiesser (1983b) 24.

67 Cf. *Or. Ar.* 1:22.

68 Greek: *autexousios*; cf. Arius, *Thalia*, in Athanasius, *Or. Ar.* 1:5 (=
Asterius, *Syntagmation*, Fr. 43, Vinzent (1993)).

69 Cf. *Letter of Arius and his Party to Alexander of Alexandria*, AW III, Urk. 6.

70 Cf. *Confession of Faith of Arius and his Supporters to Alexander of Alexandria*, AW III, Urk. 6; the Nicene confession repudiates this teaching by insisting that the Son is "begotten not made" (AW III, Urk. 24).

71 The diversity among creatures is an important concern for Origen; cf. *On First Principles* II, 1, 1–4 and II, 9, 5–8, although Origen's universe is decidedly more hierarchical than that of Athanasius. The latter typically makes the point that all creation is equal with respect to God and equally in need of divine help; cf. *Against the Greeks* 35–44.

72 On creation's order, harmony, and manifest lack of self-sufficiency as indications of the Creator, see *Against the Greeks* 27, 28, 35–44.

73 The sense of this passage is admittedly obscure. A large part of the difficulty is that Athanasius's very point is to display the non-sense and absurdity of the notion of a self-creating creature. This notion is the result of the *reductio ad absurdum* that he has conceived by combining (1) the "Arian" acknowledgment of the Son as Creator; (2) the "Arian" doctrine that the Son is himself created; and (3) the Scriptural notion that whatever the Father makes, the Son also makes (cf. Jn 10:37–38, 14:10). The result is a self-creating Son and, by general inference, the conception of creatures that create themselves and thus, instead of being brought into being from nothing by God's word, are already in existence such as to be able to hear the very word that is supposed to create them! That God's creating word would thus be redundant for the creation of these already existent beings is precisely Athanasius's point!

74 Valentinus, Basilides, and Marcion were all attacked by Irenaeus for holding the doctrine that this world was not created by the true God (cf. Irenaeus, *Against the Heresies* II, 2, 1–4; II, 3, 1). Athanasius reproduces some of Irenaeus's arguments against this conception; see Anatolios (2001) 470–471. For Athanasius, the Arians imitate the teachings of Valentinus, Marcion, and Basilides in their asserting that the Creator-Word is not fully divine by nature. Hence, in their view too, the creator of this world is not "*the* true God." Athanasius likens his opponents to Valentinus also in *Or. Ar.* 2:70. On the other hand, it seems that the opponents of Alexander and Nicene theology similarly accused Nicene theologians of affinity with Valentinus and Marcion. From that perspective, the reasoning was that the Nicene theologians' defense of the full divinity of the Son posited two Unbegottens and thus two Gods. See *Letter of Arius to Alexander of Alexandria*, Urk. 6, and the defensive remarks of Athanasius in *On the Councils of Ariminum and Seleucia* 52.

75 Cf. *Inc.* 2–3.

76 The designation of the work of the Word as "assistance" (*hypourgein*) and his identification as subordinate assistant (*hypourgos*) is attributed by Athanasius to the teaching of Asterius; see below, *Or. Ar.* 2:28 (Asterius, *Syntagmation*, Fr. 26, Vinzent (1993)) and *On the Council of Nicaea* 7 (Asterius, *Syntagmation*, Fr. 28, Vinzent (1993)). It is a designation that is also employed by Eusebius of Caesarea: see *Hist. Eccl.* I,

2, 2–3; *Dem. Ev.* IV, 10, 16; V, 5, 3. See, further, Vinzent (1993) 206–207.

77 Greek: *dia to idion tēs ousias kai tēn kata panta homoiotēta tou hiou pros ton patera*; the depiction of the Son's relationship to the Father as "complete likeness" was proposed at the Council of Nicaea, according to Athanasius's account in *On the Council of Nicaea* 20.

78 Arius taught that the Son does not fully know the Father or even his own essence; see Athanasius's version of the *Thalia*, in *On the Councils of Ariminum and Seleucia* 15. Asterius considerably modified the apophatic tone of Arius's theology, as well as Arius's emphasis on the "unlikeness" between Father and Son; see Vinzent (1993) 68–69.

79 *Letter of Arius to Alexander of Alexandria*, Urk. 6; Asterius, *Syntagmation*, Fr. 35, Vinzent (1993).

80 See Heb 1:4–14.

81 Athanasius is countering the doctrine of Asterius, *Syntagmation*, Frs. 26, 28, Vinzent (1993), in which the Word "alone" is directly created by God and then becomes a mediatorial "assistant" of God's creative activity. That God is not so weak as to need "assistance" for the work of creating is a motif which Athanasius borrows from Irenaeus: cf. *Against the Heresies* IV, 7, 4; V, 4, 2. Athanasius will make the same point in *On the Council of Nicaea* 7 and *On the Councils of Ariminum and Seleucia* 52. See Anatolios (2001) 471.

82 See *Encyclical Letter of Alexander of Alexandria and his Clergy*, AW III/I, Urk. 4b; Athanasius's ascription of such teaching to Asterius (*Syntagmation*, Fr. 26, 28, Vinzent (1993)) appears to be authentic (see Vinzent (1993) 202–210). Cf. Eusebius of Caesarea; see also *Hist. Eccl.* I, 2, 2–3; *Dem. Ev.* IV, 10; V, 5.

83 The same point is made by Irenaeus, *Against the Heresies* II, 2, 1, and repeated by Athanasius in *On the Council of Nicaea* 7.

84 That is, the creative agency itself (*demiourgia*) originates in the Father, while the Son applies this creative agency to the task of making creatures. This conception is consistent with the notion of the Son as instrument of God's creative activity and a subordinate "assistant" to the Father. Cf. Eunomius, *Apology* 20: "He who creates by his own power is entirely different from him who does so at the Father's command and acknowledges that he can do nothing of his own accord" (ET: Vaggione (1987) 61).

85 A similar line of reasoning is employed by Irenaeus against the Valentinians (cf. *Against the Heresies* II, 1, 3–4) as well as by Methodius of Olympus, in defense of the belief that God alone is Creator: *On Free Will* 5.

86 Of course, the Arians came to no such conclusion. Athanasius is not actually arguing that they did, but rather that their logic (the doctrine in question is that of Asterius) leads to an infinite regress which makes the given fact of creation a logical impossibility.

87 Vinzent (1993, 260) considers this passage to originate from the writings of Asterius, *Syntagmation*, Fr. 47.

88 Insisting on the "oneness" of the Word undercuts Arius's emphasis on "oneness" as the primary designation of divinity; cf. *Thalia*, in *On the*

Councils of Ariminum and Seleucia 15. In distinction to Arius's teaching, Asterius placed less emphasis on the "oneness" of divine being; for him, the primary designation of divinity was "Unbegotten/Unoriginated": see Vinzent (1993) 64–67.

89 Vinzent (1993, 200) considers this quotation to originate in Asterius, *Syntagmation*, Fr. 24.

90 Cf. *Against the Greeks* 27–28.

91 Asterius, *Syntagmation*, Fr. 34, Vinzent (1993) 222–224.

92 A pejorative reference to Asterius's sacrificing to the pagan gods in order to escape punishment during the Diocletian persecution.

93 Origen also contrasts what pertains to the Word by nature and is therefore stable, and what pertains to creatures not by nature but accidentally and is therefore unstable and liable to loss: see *On First Principles* I, 2, 4; I, 2, 10; I, 5, 5; I, 6, 2; I, 8, 3.

94 The quotation is quite out of context. The verse in the Septuagint runs: "I am full [i.e. 'have had enough'] of whole-burnt rams and the fat of sheep; I do not desire the blood of bulls and goats." That God has "no need of anyone" is emphasized also in *Against the Greeks* 28; there is a similar stress in Irenaeus (cf. *Against the Heresies* I, 22, 1; II, 1, 5; IV, 14, 1; IV, 20, 1).

95 A certain subordinationism, whereby women are equally in the image of God and yet hierarchically ordered to the authority of men, is typical of the Fathers of the early Church. Often, such a view draws on 1 Cor 11:7–9: see, for example, Ambrose, *On Paradise* IV, 24; Augustine, *Literal Commentary on Genesis* XI:42; John Chrysostom, *Discourse 2 on Genesis* 2. See, further, Clark (1983) 27–76.

96 In attempting to deconstruct the logic of his opponents from within, Athanasius seems to lapse momentarily into a position that he explicitly rejects, i.e. that the Son is the effect of the Father's will. However, Athanasius is not here directly articulating his own position but working from the Arian position toward his own by showing that its self-contradictions lead one toward what he considers to be the correct view. His own position is more directly articulated in the following chapter, where he says that the Word is himself the will of the Father.

97 Athanasius is employing the imagery of Irenaeus, who refers to the Son and Spirit as God's "two hands": *Against the Heresies* IV, Pref., 1; IV, 20, 1. The image is based on scriptural texts (e.g. Job 10:8, Ps 119:73). See also, below, *Or. Ar.* 71; *On the Council of Nicaea* 7.

98 See above, 2:2 and n. 96.

99 Greek: *hagioi*, writers of Scripture.

100 The tactic of recasting Arius's "there was once when the Son was not" into biblical linguistic patterns was one to which Athanasius constantly returned. The substance of his reasoning is already present in Origen, *On First Principles* IV, 4, 1; cf. *Letter of Alexander of Alexandria*, AW III/I, Urk. 14, 23–24.

101 Asterius, *Syntagmation*, Fr. 76, Vinzent (1993).

102 On the *akribeia* of Scripture and the significance of scriptural images (*paradeigmata*), see Chapter 1, pp. 78–80; Pelikan (1962).

103 Arius's concern that *"homoousios"* implies division and partition of the Godhead is evident in his *Letter of Arius to Alexander of Alexandria* (Opitz, *AW* III/I, Urk. 6).

104 Asterius, *Syntagmation*, Fr. 75, Vinzent (1993) 140, 321–323.

105 Athanasius's statement that the *Logos* is not *prophorikos* amounts to a repudiation of an important aspect of the theology of some of the Greek apologists of the second century, particularly Theophilus (*To Autolycus* 22). See also Tatian (*Address to the Greeks* 5) and Athenagoras (*A Plea for the Christians* 10). Cf. *Against the Greeks* 40, where Athanasius repudiates the identification of the Word as *Logos spermatikos*.

106 A similar apophaticism as to the generation of the Son is expressed in the *Letter of Alexander of Alexandria*, Urk. 14.

107 See n. 102, above.

108 Origen typically approached the doctrine of Christ by investigating the names or conceptions, *epinoiai*, applied to Christ in the Scriptures (cf. *On First Principles* I, 2, 1ff. and *Commentary on John* 1, 31, 221ff.). Origen divides these *epinoiai* into two sets, those that apply to the Son in himself and those that apply to the Son in relation to creation (*Commentary on John* 2, 18, 128). Arius collapsed this distinction and tended to understand all the *epinoiai* of the Son as ways of conceiving the Son's relation to creation. In particular, the Son is Word and Wisdom not in himself and not as such but only improperly speaking and due to his graced participation in the essential Word and Wisdom which is integral to the divine essence and because of his agency in manifesting the divine Word and Wisdom to creation. See Arius, *Thalia* (= *De Synodis* 15), where he speaks of the Son as "conceived (*epinoieitai*) according to countless conceptions (*epinoiais*) – spirit, power, wisdom, God's glory, truth and image" – and *Encyclical Letter of Alexander of Alexandria*, where Arius is quoted as saying that the Son is "neither like (*homoios*) the Father in being, nor is he the Father's true Word by nature, nor his true Wisdom ... but is improperly (*katachrēstikōs*) called Word and Wisdom since he came into being by the proper Word of God and the Wisdom which is in God" (*AW* III/I, Urk. 4b, 7.21–8.2); see also *Or. Ar.* 1:9 and *Letter to the Bishops of Egypt and Libya* 12. On Origen's doctrine of *epinoiai*, see Crouzel (1989) 188–192. For a comparison of Arius and Origen on the *epionoiai* of Christ, see Lorenz (1979) 81–85. The teaching that the Son was not strictly speaking the true Word and Wisdom of God was also adopted by Asterius, who seems to be Athanasius's immediate source here; cf. *Syntagmation*, Fr. 64, 69, Vinzent (1993) (= *Or. Ar.* 2:37), and *Syntagmation*, Fr. 66, Vinzent (1993) (= *De Synodis* 18); see also Vinzent (1993) 310–312. On the history of the concept of *epioniai*, see Orbe (1955).

109 Cf. Arius, *Thalia*, in Athanasius, *Or. Ar.* 1:5.

110 *Ibid.*

111 Asterius, *Syntagmation*, Fr. 64, Vinzent (1993).

112 Asterius, *Syntagmation*, Fr. 66, Vinzent (1993).

113 The critical text of *AW* I/I.II, 214.30, here reads *aidion* (eternal), but it seems more likely that this is another instance where Athanasius is presenting opposing conceptions with reference to his recurrent motif that the Son is *idion tēs ousias* ("proper to the being") of the Father. The reading of *idion* is attested in the manuscript tradition: OSBclAc.

114 = Asterius, *Syntagmation*, Fr. 72, Vinzent (1993); cf. Arius, *Thalia*, in Athanasius, *De Synodis* 15. The Creed of the synod of Antioch of 325 insisted that "the Scriptures call him a begotten son in a proper and true sense (*kyriōs kai alethōs*)" (Opitz, Urk. 18, 39).

115 Here, Athanasius asserts his own doctrine of the distinction between the Father and the Son. As is customary with him, he succeeds in turning the table on the Arian accusation that the doctrine of the co-eternal and co-equal subsistence of the Son leads to a positing of "two Unbegottens." He retorts that their own admission of "an unbegotten Wisdom" is vulnerable to the same accusation, which they admittedly deflect by asserting that this Wisdom is simply an attribute of "the Father himself." But at this point, Athanasius uses the occasion to state that Wisdom coexists with the Father and is thus distinct. Such a statement is at variance with the modalistic conception of his supporter, Marcellus of Ancyra.

116 For similar reasoning employed by Athanasius in likening his Arian opponents to the Manichees, see his *Letter to the Bishops of Egypt* 16. While this strategy is clearly part of a rhetorical and polemical campaign to associate his opponents with recognized heretics, Athanasius does make an attempt to provide some intelligible substance for the accusation. His rationale amounts to the argument that what the Arians and the Manichees have in common is the implied notion of a *Deus absconditus*, or "hidden God." The Manichees hold that the true God is not the God present and active in creation, while the Arians hold that the true Word and Wisdom is other than the Word and Wisdom which is active in creation, and which is identified by the Scriptures with Jesus Christ. On Athanasius's alignment of the Arians with other recognized heresies, see Lyman (1993b). Athanasius's criticism of a God "without witnesses" echoes that of Irenaeus, *Against the Heresies* II, 9, 1–2; II, 10, 1.

117 Asterius, *Syntagmation*, Fr. 32, Vinzent (1993).

118 Asterius, *Syntagmation*, Fr. 33, Vinzent (1993).

119 Asterius, *Syntagmation*, Fr. 67, Vinzent (1993) (in Athanasius, *Or. Ar.* 1:5). Athanasius's contention that the doctrine of his opponents is self-contradictory can be easily deflected by noting that they used such terms as "Wisdom," "Power," and "Word" equivocally, sometimes referring to an uncreated attribute of the divine essence while at other times referring to the created participation in these attributes, which is exemplified by the Son. The foundation of Athanasius's logic is precisely that such equivocation is scripturally unwarranted and results in the "Manichean" notion of a true God behind the God manifested by Scripture and creation.

120 On Athanasius's appeal to baptismal practice, see Williams (1993). As Williams points out, non-Nicene theologians also appealed to

baptismal practice and the formula of Mt 28:19, using it to substantiate a pluralist theology in which each of the *hypostases* is truly (*alethōs*) distinct. Cf. *Second Creed of Antiochene Synod of 341*, in Athanasius, *On the Councils of Ariminum and Seleucia* 23.

121 See n. 31, above

122 Athanasius's assertion of the necessary consistency between teaching, faith, and baptismal initiation is taken up by Basil of Caesarea, in his treatise *On the Holy Spirit* 68.

123 On the Manichees and Paul of Samosata, see, respectively, nn. 116 and 30, above. The Phrygians were an ancient cult, with Eastern roots but later transported to Rome, dedicated to the worship of Cybele, "Mother of the Gods," and her young consort, Attis. See Vermaseren (1977).

124 The reference to "human patronage" might be an allusion to Eusebius of Nicomedia and his considerable influence at the imperial court.

125 The invalidity of Arian baptism is again asserted in *Letters to Serapion* 1:29–30.

126 Thus, the question of identifying the subject of the verse (the Word as God and not a creature) is determined by reference to the whole range of scriptural language *before* Athanasius takes up the disputed verse. Once "the person" (*to prosopon*) is identified, the sense will be interpreted accordingly.

127 *Paroimiai* means both "proverbs" and "parables." That the fact that this is a "proverb" necessitates that it be treated as a parable, *paroimiōdiōs* – i.e. with a view to a hidden meaning – is also asserted by Marcellus of Ancyra, Fr. 29, Vinzent (1997) 30.

128 Of course, this stratagem of accommodating the sense of the passage to the "person" (*prosopon*) completely begs the question by supplanting the apparent description of the "person" rendered by the passage (as created) with that which is *presumed* to belong to the person, quite apart from the passage in question. The implied logic of Athanasius's overall strategy is that "the person" of Wisdom cannot be delineated merely from this one passage, but from the whole plot and "scope" (*skopos*) of the scriptural designation of the Son. The identification of the person of the Son is thus to be construed both from the overall plot with its Christological center of "a double account of the Savior" and from the larger *patterns* of linguistic correlations by which the various designations of the Son are brought together.

129 The same interpretation is given by Marcellus of Ancyra (e.g. Frs. 26, 28, Vinzent (1997) 30) and later taken up by Hilary of Poitiers (*On the Trinity* XII: 44–50) and Gregory of Nazianzus (*Theological Oration* 30:2). It was rejected by Eusebius of Caesarea (*Ecclesiastical Theology* I, 10; III, 2).

130 The substance of Athanasius's argument is that the predication of "created" does not in itself define the being of the subject of the statement, which would be the case if the *persona* of Wisdom had simply said, "I *am* a creature." Rather, such a predication can merely state an event pertaining to the subject of the statement, thus leaving open the possibility that the subject of that statement transcends that

event. Concretely, of course, Athanasius is reading the text in the framework of his belief that the human "creation" of the Incarnate Word is an event that pertains to the subject of the Word but does not define the Word's being and nature. He is arguing that the text as it stands does not preclude such a reading. As negative support for his point, he goes on to cite passages in which creatures are simply so called, which is not the case in this text. The argument that the word "created" does not always designate a creature seems to be adopted by Athanasius from Eusebius of Caesarea, *Ecclesiastical Theology* III, 2, 22ff. See Meijering (1974) 100.

131 The same series of texts is quoted by Eusebius of Caesarea to make the same point: cf. *Ecclesiastical Theology* III, 2, 11–12; see also Meijering (1974).

132 Athanasius is following the customary interpretation whereby the "two peoples" are Jews and Gentiles.

133 A modern reader may well respond with the popular wisdom that in fact each thing is unique (i.e. "no two snowflakes are the same"), but Athanasius's point is not that single instances of created beings do not each have unique features – with respect to this point, he concedes readily that every created being is different and so all are *equally* different. His point remains that nevertheless there is no created being who is *completely* unique, most principally because every creature has in common with every other creature the original feature of being created.

134 Athanasius's argument is that if one rejects the interpretation that Wisdom's saying "He created me" refers to the Incarnation, the adjoining phrase "for the works" must be interpreted to mean that the creation of Wisdom is posterior (whether chronologically or logically) to creation ("the works"). The latter alternative makes the Word to be inferior to creation.

135 On "this rhetoric of reversal" by which the Incarnation changes the Father's relationship to the Son from "Father" to "Lord" and humanity's relationship to the Father from "Lord" to the "Father," see Anatolios (1998) 133–138. It is adopted by Gregory of Nazianzus, *Theological Oration* 30:8.

136 Cf. *Inc.* 1, 7.

137 The same line of reasoning is followed later by Gregory of Nazianzus in his explication of this passage; cf. *Theological Oration* 30:2.

138 On the salvific efficacy of Christ's death, see *Inc.*, *inter alia*, 8, 9, 13, 16, 19, 20, 25, 31. See also Chapter 1, pp. 56–61.

139 A similar reasoning is found in *Inc.* 44; see also below, 2:68.

140 Greek: *diastēmatikēn archēn tou einai echei*. The contrast between the lack of distance or interval (*diastēma*) between Father and Son and creation's beginning as associated with such an "interval" is found in *Letter of Alexander of Alexandria to Alexander of Thessalonica*, AW III/I, Urk. 14, 22.16. It is also taken up and elaborately developed by Gregory of Nyssa; see, for example, *Against Eunomius* I: 25–26.

141 Greek: *en tō ginesthai metreitai*. This is to say that creatures do not possess being entirely and simultaneously but their being is, as it

were, "meted out"; becoming (*ginesthai*) is this "rationing out" of being.

142 Both Arius (*Thalia*, in Athanasius, *On the Councils of Ariminum and Seleucia* 15 and *Epistle to Alexander*, Urk. 6; *Letter to Eusebius of Nicomedia*, Urk. 1) and Asterius (*Syntagmation*, Fr. 66, Vinzent (1993)) reserved the title of *anarchos* ("without beginning") to the Unbegotten God. On the other hand, Alexander of Alexandria had spoken of the generation of the Son as *anarchon*; Urk. 14, 28. That the Son is *anarchos* is denied by Eusebius of Caesarea, for whom such a designation would conjure up the conception of "two Unbegottens"; see *Ecclesiastical Theology* II, 6.

143 In the original context, these passages are from the "Song of Moses" in the book of Deuteronomy and refer to the people of Israel as "God's children," albeit, because of their disobedience, as "God's degenerate children." See Deut 32: 5ff.

144 This is a preferable reading to the critical text of *AW*, which leaves out *mē*, thus reading: "If the Word was a creature by nature and being and there was a difference ..." The latter reading makes little sense on its own and less so considering that Athanasius is countering precisely the position that the categories of creature and offspring are indifferent; the alternative manuscript tradition represented here is found in Euthymius Zigabenus, *Panoplia dogmatica* (see *AW* III/I, 237).

145 cf. *Or. Ar.* 2:48.

146 Accepting the addition of "of God" (in 76cZig) omitted in the critical edition of *AW* III/I, 238.

147 In applying the title of "firstborn" to the Incarnation, Athanasius is countering the doctrine of Asterius who, according to Marcellus of Ancyra, took "firstborn" as equivalent to "only-begotten," both taken as signifying the origin of the Son. See *AW* III/I, 238, n. 61:13; cf. Marcellus of Ancyra, Fr. 10, Vinzent (1997) 12–13.

148 This is to contradict the doctrine of Arius and Asterius on the two Words and Wisdoms of God: see *Thalia*, in Athanasius, *Or. Ar.* 1:5; Asterius, *Syntagmation*, Frs. 33, 62, 64, 65, 70, Vinzent (1993).

149 Asterius, *Syntagmation*, Fr. 25, Vinzent (1993) 94, 201–202.

150 Athanasius is now dealing with a different text, Rom 8:29, which he takes to be a clear reference to the Incarnation. He uses this text as a demonstration of his logical-linguistic point that to be first "of all" is to be excluded from the category of this "all." Thus, Rom 8:29 speaks of Christ as "the firstborn *among* many brothers" in order to include Jesus Christ within the category of brothers.

151 Asterius spoke of the Son as mediating the unmitigated transcendence of the Father (*Syntagmation*, Fr. 26, Vinzent (1993), in Athanasius, *Or. Ar.* 2:24). Athanasius here relocates this mediation away from the nature of the Son and ascribes it to the *condescension* of the Son. On the significance of the category of "condescension" for Athanasius's presentation of Christ, see Chapter 1, pp. 49–56ff.

152 Cf. 1 Cor 15:47.

153 cf. *Inc.* 6; Irenaeus, *Against the Heresies* III, 23, 1.

154 On the inappropriateness of an unredeemed humanity, see *Inc.* 6; on Christ's redemption as repayment of "debt" (*opheilē, opheilēma*) on our behalf, see *Inc.* 9, 20.

155 Vinzent conjectures this to be a reference to Asterius; cf. *Syntagmation*, Fr. 37, Vinzent (1993) 225–227.

156 This objection is treated in a similar manner in *Inc.* 44.

157 On the close parallels between this section and Irenaeus, *Against the Heresies* III, 18, 7, see Anatolios (2001) 472–473

158 On the Incarnation as rendering salvation secure (*bebaia*), see Chapter 1, pp. 61–66.

159 On the Word as instrument of God's creative activity, see Arius, *Thalia*, in Athanasius, *Or. Ar.* 1:5, and Asterius, Frs. 26–30, Vinzent (1993).

160 Greek: *meta paratērēseōs akribous*; cf. *Or. Ar.* 2:33, 2:51; see also Chapter 1, p. 79

161 The preposition *eis* can denote purpose as in the English "for", or spatial movement as in the English "into"; Athanasius will play on this equivocality.

162 On the Word as "hand" of God, see n. 97, above.

163 Cf. Dan 3:58–90.

164 At this point, Athanasius is seeking to interpret what the Scriptures say about Christ as Wisdom in relation to the designation of Christ as "Son." His point will be that the designation of Christ as "Son" and "Word" is predicated of him absolutely, while the "creation" of Wisdom in Prov 8:22 is qualified by its being said to be "as a beginning of the ways" and "established as a foundation" (Prov 8:23). Because some of the primary scriptural names for the Word/Son/Wisdom are applied to him absolutely and not merely with a view to creation, his person as such cannot be conceived merely as associated with the work of creation.

165 In Athanasius, the designation of God as "good and lover of humanity" (*agathos kai philanthropos*) typically introduces an account of how God overcomes human weakness in order to ensure humanity's communion with him: see *Against the Greeks* 35, 41; cf. *Inc.* 15.

166 Note the contrast here between remaining mortal and remaining immortal, in close parallel to *Inc.* 3. See also Chapter 1, pp. 61–66.

167 The motif of God's goodness as compensating for our weakness recalls a prominent motif in *Against the Greeks – On the Incarnation*: see *Against the Greeks* 2, 35, 41; *Inc.* 2, 7, 11. See also Anatolios (1998) 32–35; Pettersen (1998).

168 This analogy is reminiscent of Plotinus, *Enneads*, I, 6, 3, where the intelligible realm is compared to the bodily realm through recourse to the analogy of an architect's plan in relation to the material building. More proximately, it echoes Origen, *Commentary on John* 1:114: "For I think that just as a house and a ship are built or devised according to the plans of the architect, the house and the ship having as their beginning the plans and thoughts in the craftsman, so all things have come to be according to the thoughts of what will be,

which were prefigured by God in wisdom, 'For he made all things in wisdom'" (Heine, 57).

169 Presuming the principle of intertextuality, Athanasius assumes that the referent of the passage must be considered in terms of the other ways in which it is referred to in the rest of the Scriptures. Wisdom is elsewhere described as creator; therefore its being said to be "created" raises the question: how can the creator be created? He has already provided the Christological answer in terms of the *skopos* of Scripture.

170 Athanasius here conceives the incarnation as the act whereby uncreated Wisdom assumes the created wisdom which is its copy (*typos*) and which is constituted by participation in uncreated Wisdom.

171 See n. 50, above.

172 On the universe as a harmonious body ordered to unity through the active presence of the Word, see *Against the Greeks* 35–40, 43, 44. The conception of the harmony of the universe as indicative of divine agency is commonplace in Hellenistic philosophy (cf. Plato, *Laws* X 886A and *Timaeus* 30A), and especially the Stoics (e.g. Pseudo-Aristotle, *On the World* 399a 1–14), as well as in earlier Christian literature (e.g. *Letter of Clement to the Church of Corinth* 20).

173 In Athanasius's Greek, the personal pronoun switches from feminine when the subject is Wisdom (*sophia*) to masculine when the subject is the Word (*Logos*) or the human being (*anthropos*) which the Word became.

174 Cf. Mt 11:27, Lk 10:22, Jn 10:15, Jn 14:7.

3 ON THE COUNCIL OF NICAEA (DE DECRETIS)

1 Cf. Schwartz (1959) 85; Opitz, *AW* II/I, *De Decretis* 2.15; Quasten (1960) 61; Altaner and Stuiber (1966) 271; Tetz, *TRE* 339; Young (1983) 76; Barnes (1993) 198–199. The latter dates the work at 352–353, still accepting the evidentiary value of this accusation by Athanasius: "Schwarz was certainly correct in holding that the fact that Athanasius writes as if violence were threatening but had not yet been employed excludes a date after he was dispossessed of his see in February, 356" (199).

2 For this view, see, especially, Brennecke (1984) 11, n. 41; Abramowski (1982) 259, n. 71; Heil (1999) 22–35.

3 There is of course also the "argument from silence" that Athanasius does not actually mention the so-called "Blasphemy of Sirmium" in this treatise and, moreover, that he fails to treat the scriptural proof-texts alluded to in that creed (i.e. Jn 14:28, "The Father is greater than I," and 1 Cor 15:28, "When all things are subjected to him, then the Son himself will also be subjected to him who put all things under him"). Rather, he seems for the most part to be focused on refuting the teachings of Asterius. Furthermore, the assertion that the dissatisfaction with Nicene non-scriptural *ousia*-language only comes into view at 357 is radically undercut by noting that the issue is already very much evident in Athanasius's *Or. Ar.* 1:30ff.

4 Cf. the inflamed rhetoric of his encyclical *To the Bishops of Egypt and Libya* 22, 23.

5 This is a reference to Eusebius of Nicomedia, an early supporter of Arius and a leader of the anti-Nicene party in the East; see Chapter 1. The identity of Athanasius's addressee is not known, though Athanasius's language suggests that it is a bishop. By way of mere conjecture, it has been suggested that it is Pope Liberius (Barnes (1993) 199).

6 This is a fairly typical instance of Athanasius's attempt to drive home the point that the Arians' refusal to acknowledge the full divinity of Christ renders them not Christians but "contemporary Jews." See *Or. Ar.* n. 31.

7 Cf. Mt 11:5, Jn 2, Mt 14:13–21.

8 Prov 18:1: "A man seeks a pretext, when he wishes to separate himself from friends."

9 The accusation that "in a little while they will turn to outrage (*eis hubreis*)" has often been taken as an indication that this treatise was composed at a time of relative calm threatened by the anticipation of imminent persecution of the pro-Nicenes. See n. 1, above.

10 That the absence of right belief in the *Logos* leads to irrationality is an important motif in Athanasius: cf. *Against the Greeks* 9, 19, 34; *Inc.* 12; *Or. Ar.* 1:35.

11 As he goes on to say, Athanasius appended this letter penned by Eusebius of Caesarea to his treatise; see *AW* II/I, 28–31. The reference to Eusebius's having "denied the day before" could be an allusion to the Council of Antioch of 325, which took place shortly before that of Nicaea, and whose anti-Arian statement of faith was rejected by Eusebius; see Hanson (1988) 146–151.

12 "We considered that the anathema proclaimed by them at the end of the [confession of] faith was harmless, since it forbade the use of unscriptural words, which are the cause of almost all the confusion and disorder of the church. Therefore, since no divinely inspired Scripture had used the words, 'out of non-being' and 'once he was not' and the rest that follow, it did not seem fitting to use or teach them" (*AW* II/I (= Bd. II, Lief. 1), 30.41–31.4).

13 Acacius of Caesarea, one of the main targets of Athanasius's polemic in this letter, was a leader of the anti-Nicene "*homoian*" party. He was the successor to Eusebius as bishop of Caesarea and a proponent of his predecessor's subordinationist theology. See Hanson (1988) 579–583. As he seems to imply here, Athanasius typically depicts Acacius as an opportunist who is motivated by the desire to curry favor with the emperor Constantius. Cf. *On the Councils of Ariminum and Seleucia* 39.

14 The reference again is to Eusebius of Caesarea; see n. 12, above.

15 Cf. *Shephard of Hermes* 9:9.

16 The designation of "saints" (*hoi hagioi*) refers to the scriptural writers. On the harmony and mutual "agreement" of Scriptures, see also Athanasius's *Letter to Marcellinus* 9.

17 Cf. *Or. Ar.* 1:1.

18 By subsuming all anti-Nicenes under the category of "Arian," Athanasius can accuse them of inconsistency and "reversal." In this case, he is exploiting the discrepancy between the present "Eusebian party" which is rejecting Nicene *ousia*-language and the position of Eusebius of Caesarea who (albeit reluctantly) accepted Nicene terminology.

19 There is no record of this letter, unless Athanasius is here referring to the earlier *Or. Ar.*

20 The Arian doctrine represented here seems to be that of Arius himself; cf. *Thalia*, in Athanasius, *Or. Ar.* 1:5, and *On the Councils of Ariminum and Seleucia* 15. Cf. Athanasius's statement of Arius's views in his *Letter to the Bishops of Egypt and Libya* 12.

21 See *Or. Ar.* 1:35–51.

22 Asterius, *Syntagmation*, Fr. 29, Vinzent (1993) 96.

23 Asterius, *Syntagmation*, Fr. 28, Vinzent (1993). This also seems to have been the view of Eusebius of Caesarea: cf. *Hist. Eccl.* I, 2, 2–3; *Dem. Ev.* IV, 10, 16; V, 5, 3. Athanasius's response to this doctrine is a close paraphrase of his previous treatment of it in *Or. Ar.* 2:25ff.

24 On the Word as the "hand" of God, see *Or. Ar.* 2:31, 2:71. The terminology is distinctly Irenaean: see *Against the Heresies* IV, Pref.; IV, 20, 1.

25 Asterius, *Syntagmation*, Fr. 27, Vinzent (1993).

26 On Asterius, see Chapter 1, pp. 18–19.

27 The following is a close paraphrase of *Or. Ar.* 2:26. That the Son is "mediator" was a doctrine taught by Alexander of Alexandria (cf. Urk. 14, 44), Athanasius's predecessor, though without any hint of Asterius's conception of the Son as "shielding" creation from divine immediacy.

28 Reading *autourgethēnai* (following the manuscript tradition of B (Basiliensis gr. A III 4)) rather than *hypourgethēnai*, as given in *AW* II/I, 8.4.

29 Athanasius's argument runs as follows: The "Arians" associate the coming into being of the Son with the function of mediating God's creative activity to creatures. But in positing the Son as a creature who does not require such mediation activity, they thereby contradict their own premise of the necessity for such mediation; and since such mediation is associated with the very being of the Son, his being would be "superfluous"!

30 Asterius, *Syntagmation*, Fr. 31, Vinzent (1993) 98.

31 The logical-linguistic argument that "greater" and "lesser" are qualifications that are not applicable to different natures is also made by Irenaeus, *Against the Heresies* IV, 9, 2.

32 On Paul of Samosata, see *Ch 2,* note 30.

33 The fear that the conception of the Son as generated from the divine essence implies the attribution of passibility to God and the partitioning of the divine essence is a constant concern of anti-Nicene theology, beginning with Arius himself: cf. his *Letter to Alexander of Alexandria* (Urk. 6); *Or. Ar.* 2:34.

34 The hermeneutical principle that words must be interpreted in light of the nature of the subject of which they are predicated is enunciated by Athanasius earlier in his *Or. Ar.*; cf. 2:44.

35 The formulations of God's relation to the world in terms of a divine "containing" of the world and of God's being in all things by his power and outside everything according to his nature are typical of Athanasius: see *Against the Greeks* 42; *Inc.* 17, 42. These conceptions are pervasive in early Christian theology: cf. *Shepherd of Hermas* 1.1; Origen *Against Celsus* IV, 92; VII, 34. On formulations of transcendence and immanence in early Christian theology, see Prestige (1964) 25–54.

36 On the impassible generation of the Father, see Origen, *On First Principles* I, 2, 4; I, 2, 6; *Letter of Alexander of Alexandria* (Urk. 14).

37 On the revelatory significance of scriptural *paradeigmata*, see *Or. Ar.* 2:33; *Letters to Serapion* 1:19. See also Chapter 1, pp. 79; Pelikan (1962).

38 For Athanasius's treatment of this verse, see *Or. Ar.* 2:18–82.

39 For examples of Athanasius's own application of this rule, see *Or. Ar.* 2:8, 2:44, 3:43. On this hermeneutical rule in Athanasius, see Sieben (1974).

40 Thus, the "time" signified by the scriptural passage is not the time of its composition but the "time" within the Christological narrative plot (*skopos*) of Scripture. Principally, for Athanasius, the scriptural plot divides into two "times": before and after the Incarnation (cf. *Or. Ar.* 3:29).

41 It is a typical Christological formulation for Athanasius to distinguish what belongs properly to the flesh and then immediately assert that the flesh itself belongs to the Word. See Chapter 1, pp. 66–71; Anatolios (1998) 138–155.

42 On the Word's not being "lessened" by the body, see *Inc.* 17; *Or. Ar.* 1:42, 3:34; *To Adelphius* 8. Cf. *Letter of Alexander of Alexandria*, Urk. 14, 28.17–18. This passage essentially reproduces *Or. Ar.* 1:42.

43 Arius, *Thalia*, in Athanasius, *Or. Ar.* 1:5; cf. the anathemas of the Nicene Council.

44 This seems to be a standard ancient rule of exegesis; it is given expression by Jerome: "when the lesser is likened to the greater, the greater is harmed by the comparison, while the lower benefits" (*Against Jovinian* 1:3). Thus, in his exegesis of Psalm 1, he rejects the allegorical interpretation by which the "happy man" is Christ, explaining that the "happy man" of the psalm is likened to a tree (v. 3): "for if Christ is compared to a tree, he is less than the tree since in a comparison the thing compared is less than that to which it is compared; hence, the tree would be greater than the Lord who is compared to it" (Homily 1 on Psalm 1; ET: FOC, Vol. 48, 3–4).

45 It is likely that Athanasius is here rephrasing and dramatizing Arius's conception (shared by Asterius) that there are two Words, the one immanent in God and the other being the created "Word" which participates in God's immanent Word (see Arius, *Thalia*, in *Or. Ar.* 1:5, and *On the Council of Ariminum and Seleucia* 15). The authenticity of the

quotation is not implausible insofar as it seems to be an instance of a typical strategy employed by anti-Nicene theologians of devaluing the distinction of the scriptural titles of Christ by showing that they are also applicable to other creatures. See Hanson (1988) 838–839, with other examples.

46 Athanasius's argumentation here bears considerable resemblance to that of Eusebius of Caesarea, *Demonstration of the Gospel* IV:3.
47 At the Council of Nicaea; cf. the accounts in *Letter to the Bishops of Africa (Ad Afros)* 5, and *On the Councils of Ariminum and Seleucia* 36.
48 Cf. *On the Councils of Ariminum and Seleucia* 36.
49 *Shepherd of Hermes* 1:1.
50 A similar list of mistaken conceptions of creation is found in *Inc.* 2. Those who speak of an origination of the world by chance are the Epicureans; those who speak of another creator are the followers of Marcion, the Manichees, and the "Gnostics." In his polemic against the Valentinians, Irenaeus counters those who believe that the world was created by angels (*Against the Heresies* II, 2, 1).
51 Thus, Athanasius is asserting his own definition of what constitutes the Son's being "alone" or "unique" (*monos*). Arius tended to restrict the title to "*the* God" in distinction from the created Word (*Thalia*, in *On the Councils of Ariminum and Seleucia* 15); Asterius was more ready to apply it to the Word who is the pre-existent Christ in the sense that this Word is "alone" directly created by God (*Syntagmation*, Frs. 28, 29, Vinzent (1993); see above, *On the Council of Nicaea* 7, 8). Having argued against this latter interpretation, Athanasius now asserts his own definition of the Son's being alone in a way that is basically equivalent to "*homoousios*."
52 The verse is taken quite out of context. It runs: "for we who live are always being given up to death for the sake of Jesus." But Asterius, not unlike Athanasius, is here simply concerned with establishing scriptural linguistic rules; his point is that the word "always" is used of ordinary people and not only Christ. See n. 45, above.
53 As he immediately goes on to say, Athanasius has been quoting Asterius (*Syntagmation*, Fr. 46, Vinzent (1993)). The section from the beginning of 19 up to this point is essentially reproduced in *Letter to the Bishops of Africa* 5. Athanasius's account of the Council of Nicaea in *On the Councils of Ariminum and Seleucia* 35–36 is closely dependent on the account presented here.
54 *Symbol of Nicaea*, Urk. 25, 52.
55 Presumably, referring to phrases like "there was once when he was not," perhaps in allusion to Eusebius of Caesarea's admission that such phrases are unscriptural. See the *Letter of Eusebius of Caesarea to his Church*, AW II/I, 30. See also n. 12, above.
56 Eusebius of Caesarea takes this text as applying to the Incarnation: *Dem. Ev.* IV, 15, 47ff.
57 Cf. *On the Councils of Ariminum and Seleucia* 34, 35.
58 On Athanasius's identification of God with Being, see Meijering (1974) 7, 126, and Ricken (1978).

59 On the significance of this scriptural image in Athanasius's theology, see Pelikan (1962).

60 Greek: *apaugasma*; see Heb 1:3, Wis 7:26.

61 That is, the explanation of the Nicene phrase "from the essence" (*ek tēs ousias*).

62 The doctrine that the Son is unlike the Father in essence (*anomios, heteroousios*) began to be popularized in the 350s by the "neo-Arians" Aetius and Eunomius, but Arius had already spoken of the unlikeness of essence between Father, Son, and Spirit; cf. *Thalia*, in *Or. Ar.* 1:5. On "neo-Arianism," see all of Kopecek (1979).

63 True contemplation of God involves transcending material conceptions; cf. *Against the Greeks* 2.

64 Jn 10:30; see above.

65 This appears to be the teaching of Asterius: *Syntagmation*, Fr. 77, Vinzent (1993) 140.

66 *AW* II/I, 20. Newman translates: "For if he partakes in fullness the light from the Father, why is he not rather that which others partake, that there be no medium introduced between him and the Father?" (NPNF IV, 166). In the original text, there is no mention of "others" partaking the Son; that addition is supplied by Newman to elucidate the sense in which he construes the text. (Athanasius asks: *"diati mē mallon autos esti to metechomenon?"*) Newman's translation has obscured rather than clarified Athanasius's argument. First of all, the "Arians" (especially Asterius, who seems to be in view here) did not disagree with the notion that others partake of the Son, so it would not make any sense for Athanasius to ask, "why is he not ... that which others partake?" Secondly, that others partake of the Son does not in itself rule out the introduction of a medium between the Son and the Father. Rather, Athanasius's argument is that if one speaks of the Son as wholly participating the Father, then (precisely because the participation is *whole*) the Son *is* what he participates (i.e. shares fully in the being of the Father). Thus, the argument here essentially reduplicates the line of thought and articulation that is found in *Or. Ar.* 1:15–16; there, Athanasius asserts that "what is partaken" (*to metechomenon*) is directly the essence of the Father, which is thus also the essence of the Son (1:15; *AW* I/I.II, 125.25–26), and "what is partaken of the Father is the Son" (*to de ek tou patros metechomenon, touto estin ho huios*)" (1:16; *AW* I/I.II, 125.6). This construction fits in consistently with the immediate context. First, the "Arians" as well as Paul of Samosata (as represented by Athanasius) would not agree that the Son is what he participates. Secondly, saying that the Son is what he participates ensures that there is no "medium" in this case between the Son who wholly participates and the Father who is wholly participated. For an analysis of the closely parallel argument in *Or. Ar.* 1:15–16, see Anatolios (1998) 105–109. The awkwardness of saying that the Son participates the Father and is himself what he participates highlights the terminological deficiency under which Athanasius is laboring, in that he does not have distinct terms for the distinction and sameness between Son and Father. Nevertheless, the distinction remains even in

this model of participation, in that the Son is what he participates precisely as the one who participates and not the one who is participated. Ironically, the exposition of the argument in *Or. Ar.* 1:15–16 is clearer because of the use of *ousia*-language: what the Son participates is the *ousia* of the Father, which is also the *ousia* of the Son. Given that Athanasius is on the defensive here with respect precisely to the use of *ousia* language, he seems to be trying to make his argument without such terminology.

67 That is to say, if the Son is not himself the same in being as the light which he participates (i.e. the Father's divinity), then creation has not come to be through the agency of the Son himself but through the agency of the light in which he participates and in relation to which he is other.

68 See Chapter 1, p. 5, 8–9.

69 Dionysius was head of the catechetical school of Alexandria (ca. 233–248) and then bishop of Alexandria (248–265). Sabellius (third century) was understood to have advocated a modalism by which Son and Spirit are "modes" of divine being.

70 This supposed excerpt from Dionysius reappears in *On the Thought of Dionysius* 18 and *On the Councils of Ariminum and Seleucia* 44. On the question of the authenticity of these excerpts, see Chapter 1, n. 37.

71 Origen, *On First Principles* IV, 4, 1; cf. Koetschau, Fr. 32 (from Justinian, *Ep. ad Mennam* (Mansi IX 525) (H. Görgemanns and H. Karpp (eds) *Origenes. Vier Bücher von den Prinzipien*, Texte zur Forschung 24 (Darmstadt, 1976) 784)).

72 *Ibid.*

73 For parallel treatments of the different meanings of "unoriginated," see *Or. Ar.* 1:30ff.; *On the Councils of Ariminum and Seleucia* 46.

74 Perhaps what Athanasius has in mind is the statement by Plotinus that intelligible realities are unoriginated (*agenēta*) in the sense that they do not have a beginning (*archē*) in time but originated in the sense that they do have a beginning (*archē*) (*Enneads* II, 4, 5, 25ff.). In *Or. Ar.* 1:31, Athanasius had made a similar distinction in saying that the Son could be said to be "unoriginated" insofar as he does not begin to be but exists eternally, notwithstanding that his eternal existence is derived from the Father. In this treatise, he falls short of repeating the assertion that the Son could be called "unoriginated" in a certain sense. Between the writing of *Or. Ar.* and this treatise, the anti-Nicene Council of Antioch of 344, in its *"Macrostich"* or "Long-lined" creed, had explicitly anathematized anyone who referred to the Son as "without beginning" (*anarchos*, or *agennētos*) (see *On the Council of Ariminum* 26). Much of the difficulty involved in this discussion can be traced to the fact that there was no clearly held distinction at this point between *agenēton* ("uncreated") and *agennēton* ("ungenerated," or "unbegotten"). See Prestige (1923).

75 There is no ascertainable direct source for Athanasius's reporting of the three definitions of *agenētos*. However, categorization of the various senses of "unoriginated" goes back to Aristotle's *On the Heavens* I, 11, in which three definitions are also given: (1) "whenever something now

is, which formerly was not, no process of becoming or change being involved. Such is the case, according to some, with contact and motion, since there is no process of coming to be in contact or motion"; (2) "when something which is capable of coming or of having come to be does not exist"; and (3) "where there is a general impossibility of any generation" (tr. J.L. Stocks, in J. Barnes (ed.) *The Complete Works of Aristotle*, Bollingen Series LXXX.2 (Princeton, 1984) 465). The third definition reported by Athanasius was the one articulated by Asterius as applicable to God. It has resonances with Plato's definition of the unoriginated principle (*archē agenēton*) as that which is the origin of all which comes into being but which is itself without an origin (*ouk ex archēs*) (*Phaedrus* 245d). Vinzent also suggests that Asterius was influenced by the Aristotelian conception of the first principle as Reason and Unmoved Mover (*Metaphysics* ? 8. 1073 a). Cf. *Or. Ar.* 1:30 (= Asterius, *Syntagmation*, Fr. 2, Vinzent (1993) 153–154. See also Opitz, *AW* II/I, 25.

76 The assertion that things that have already come into being would be unoriginated according to the definition of the term as "what has not yet come into being but can become" seems inconsistent. Presumably, Athanasius means that according to this definition, all things that have come into being *were* unbegotten before they came into being.

77 The inflammatory language underscores Athanasius's point that the Arian position, as a "blasphemy," should induce outrage; he expresses this outrage in biblical terms. Cf. Ex 19:13, 21:17.

78 Asterius, *Syntagmation*, Fr. 4, Vinzent (1993) 153–154.

79 That is to say, the title of "*agenēton*." Newman translates: "For the name *of offspring* does not detract from the nature of the Word" (NPNF IV, 170), but that is clearly inconsistent with the context.

80 Athanasius's discussion of this point reproduces his argumentation in *Or. Ar.* 1:33.

81 *Pantokrator*: the title is pervasive throughout the Scriptures; among the prophets, it occurs most frequently in Zephaniah.

82 "*Identity*" (*idiotēta*) here does not mean "identical," but refers to the correlation between Father and Son that is designated by the term *idios*; see Chapter 1, pp. 66–74.

83 The following section is a virtually identical reproduction of *Or. Ar.* 1:34.

84 Cf. *Or. Ar.* 2:41–43; *Letters to Serapion* 1:29–30.

4 LETTERS TO SERAPION ON THE HOLY SPIRIT
(1:15–33)

1 *Historia Acephala* 1.7 (Martin).

2 While the *Letters* have been traditionally divided into four, the second and third letters constitute a single whole. What is known as the second letter contextualizes Athanasius's defense of the divinity of the Holy Spirit by reasserting the divinity of the Son, while "the third letter" is essentially an abridgement of the first. The latter part of the fourth letter (4:8–23), a short commentary on Mt 12:32, appears to be

a distinct composition. On the manuscript tradition of the *Letters to Serapion*, see Opitz (1935) 163–164; Shapland (1951) 11–16; Lebon (1947) 17–22; Cattaneo (1986) 12–15.

3 The same rule is articulated in Rufinus's version of Origen's *On First Principles* I, 3, 4.

4 See 1:7.

5 The scriptural reference to the Son as "only-begotten" (*monogenēs*) (Jn 3:16, 1 Jn 4:9) was of crucial significance for both Nicene and anti-Nicene theology. For Athanasius, it signified the uniqueness of the Son's being, as altogether of a different order than that of creation. For Arius and Asterius, and anti-Nicene theology in general, it is a term that differentiates the Son from the "unoriginated/uncreated" (*agen(n)ētos*) God, although for Asterius it also indicated the unique status of the Son as the only one who is directly created by God. Here, the argument is being made by the "Tropici" that if the Spirit proceeds from the Father, then the title signifying the Son's uniqueness is being subverted.

6 Greek: *periergazomenoi*; cf. 2 Thess 3:11. Athanasius goes on to give the counter-example of Abraham, who did not pry (*oute perieirgasato*) but accepted God's word in faith; see below, 1:17.

7 Athanasius is here transposing to his argumentation on behalf of the Spirit's divinity his typical strategy of referring questions posed about the Son back to the Father, with the intention of showing that such questions are simply inapplicable and unanswerable because they project creaturely categories and conundrums into the realm of the divine. Cf. *Or. Ar.* 1:22, 1:25, 3:63; Gregory of Nazianzus, *Oration* 31:7.

8 For Athanasius, valid theological reasoning always makes allowance for the difference between God and creation; any analogy between human experience and divine being involves an abstraction from creaturely limitations and a consideration of divine perfection. Cf. *Or. Ar.* 1:28; *On the Council of Nicaea* 11.

9 This is a repeated theme in Athanasius: cf. *Or. Ar.* 1:21, 1:28, 3:4; *On the Council of Nicaea* 11, of which this section is a fairly close paraphrase.

10 Greek: *merē ... eisin allēlon*; cf. Rom 12:5, Eph 4:25.

11 That the relation of the Son and the Father does not involve "partition" was a common concern for both Nicene and anti-Nicene theologians, from the outbreak of the controversy onwards; cf. *Letter of Arius to Alexander* (Urk. 6), *Letter of Alexander of Alexandria* (Urk. 14).

12 On the relation of the Son to the Father as "whole" of the "whole," see *Or. Ar.* 1:16, 2:35.

13 For the expression "always Father, always Son," see *Letter of Alexander of Alexandria* to Alexander of Thessalonica (Urk. 14, 26).

14 Accepting the emendation of Shapland, following the reading of BA, rather than Montfaucon's adoption of RS; see Shapland (1951) 103, n. 10.

15 Cf. *On the Council of Nicaea* 20.

16 Gregory of Nazianzus adopts a similar maneuver by beginning his exposition of Trinitarian theology with the incapacity of the human mind to comprehend even creaturely realities; cf. *Oration* 30:31.

17 On scriptural *paradeigmata*, see Chapter 1, pp. 79ff; Pelikan (1962). Cf., *inter alia*, *Or. Ar.* 2:33, 2:71, 3:52; *On the Council of Nicaea* 12.

18 The language of unlikeness being refuted here is indicative of the influence of Aetius and Eunomius on those whom Athanasius is opposing. Athanasius seems to be begging the question, insofar as he is already presuming that the Trinity is a single entity, so that the positing of unlikeness is considered as attributing a lack of *self*-consistency to the Trinity. But he has just shown, to his satisfaction at least, that the singleness of the Trinity is manifest from the scriptural witness to the common activity of Father, Son, and Spirit.

19 On "pious reasoning," see *On the Thought of Dionysius* 2; *Or. Ar.* 1:9. For Athanasius, this means reasoning that is anchored in the patterns of scriptural narrative and symbols.

20 The Spirit is called "image" of the Father in Irenaeus, *Against the Heresies* IV, 7, 4. As here, Athanasius tends to speak of the Spirit as image of the Son (cf. below, 1:24; *Letters to Serapion* 4:3; see Bernard (1952) 127–130). This identification is also used by Cyril of Alexandria (*Thesauras* 33) and John Damascene, *On the Orthodox Faith* 1:13.

21 The notion of the Spirit's procession as involving a "shining forth" from the Son becomes significant in later Byzantine theology, with Gregory of Cyprus and Gregory Palamas; see Staniloae (1980) 11–44.

22 Cf. Basil, *On the Holy Spirit* 43.

23 The reference is to the proof-texts of Am 4:13 and 1 Tim 5:21.

24 Athanasius will now proceed to recount the scriptural "names" of the Spirit, as he has done elsewhere with regard to the Son. (e.g., *inter alia*, *Against the Greeks* 46; *Or. Ar.* 1:16, 1:19, 1:20). The same method will be employed by Basil, *On the Holy Spirit* 22ff., and Gregory Nazianzus, *Orations* 33:29. Throughout, Athanasius is concerned to show that, within the divine–human relation, the Spirit is an active agent and not a passive recipient. Such arguments are resonant of the Stoic polarity of *to poioun* ("the active") and *to paschon* ("the passive"); see Chapter 1, pp. 68ff.

25 Greek: *autozōē*. Cf. *Against the Greeks* 47; *Inc.* 20; Origen, *Against Celsus* 3:41.

26 On the Spirit as an "anointing" mediated by the Incarnate Word, see *Or. Ar.* 1:46ff.

27 It would have suited Athanasius's argument here to have quoted the whole text: "In him [Christ] you also, who have heard the word of truth, the gospel of your salvation, and have believed in him, were sealed *with the promised holy Spirit*, which is the first installment of our inheritance toward redemption as God's possession, to the praise of his glory." Presumably, he was counting on his audience to know that the sealing referred to the Spirit.

28 A creature cannot join other creatures to God and grant other creatures participation in divine life. This argument had been used by

Athanasius in defense of the divinity of the Son; cf., for example, *Or. Ar.* 2:41, 2:69, 2:70. This reasoning is taken up by Gregory of Nazianzus, *Oration* 31:4.

29 Cf. Basil, *On the Holy Spirit* 36.

30 Having elaborated on the names and designations of the Spirit's work in the Scriptures, Athanasius now focuses on the scriptural patterns of correlating the Spirit and the Son.

31 In the Pauline text cited by Athanasius, the adoption granted by the Spirit is identified with "glorification," which is presumably what Athanasius has in mind when referring to this passage for evidence that the Spirit is "Spirit of glory." Cf. Rom 8:16: "The Spirit itself bears witness with our spirit that we are children of God, and if children, then heirs, heirs of God and joint heirs with Christ, if only we suffer with him so that we may also be glorified with him."

32 The same argument is used by Athanasius in reference to the Son's joining the world to the Father; cf. *Or. Ar.* 2:26, *On the Council of Nicaea* 8.

33 Cf. *Or. Ar.* 1:35ff., on the inalterability of the Son.

34 As far as concerns the biblical phrase, considered in itself, it would be better translated as "the angels who did not keep to their own domain (*archēn*)," as does the *New American Bible*. However, given Athanasius's theological perspective, he would be inclined to understand the *archē* referred to in the biblical text as the origination of the angels from God.

35 cf. *Or. Ar.* 1:35.

36 On "filling all things" as a divine attribute, see Chapter 3, n. 35; cf. Basil, *On the Holy Spirit* 54. In subsequent Byzantine liturgical tradition, the Spirit is typically described as "Heavenly Consoler ... present in all places and filling all things."

37 For a parallel Christological argument, that the Son does not participate but is participated, see *Against the Greeks* 46; *Inc.* 17.

38 Cf. Origen, *On First Principles* I, 2, 4; I, 5, 5; I, 6, 2; I, 8, 3; cf. Didymus, *On the Spirit* 5.

39 This is the only instance of Athanasius's direct application of the term "*homoousios*" to the Holy Spirit. It is sometimes claimed that the designation is repeated in 2:6 (Hanson (1988) 752, n. 70) or 3:1 (Shapland (1951) 133, n. 7), but in both these cases the term is applied to the Son's relation to the Father.

40 The identity of activity among the three "Persons" indicates identity of being; this becomes a fundamental principle of the Trinitarian theology of Cyril of Alexandria as well as of the Cappadocians. See Prestige (1936) 257–260.

41 cf. Irenaeus, *Against the Heresies* V, 18, 2; *Demonstration* 5; Hippolytus, *Against Noetus* 14; Athanasius, *Or. Ar.* 3:15; *Letters to Serapion* 3:6.

42 The emphatic assertion that the Spirit "truly exists and subsists" (*hyparchei kai hyphestēken alēthos*), as well as the preceding stress that the Trinity is such not only in name but "in reality and truth" (*alētheia kai hyparxei trias*), inserts an anti-Sabellian insistence on the reality of the distinct existence of each of the three within the unity of Godhead.

The willingness to articulate such an emphasis, perhaps in response to concern that anti-Nicene theology is equivalent to modalism, separates Athanasius from the modalist theology of Marcellus of Ancyra. This stress on the distinct and real existence of each of the Trinity is fundamental to Origen's Trinitarian theology: see *On First Principles* I, 2, 2; I, 2, 9; I, 3, 1.

43 Arius refers to the "Monad" which always was and the "Dyad" that came to be when the Son was created; see *Thalia*, in Athanasius, *On the Councils of Ariminum and Seleucia* 15.

44 For the argument from baptism as applied to the Son, see *Or. Ar.* 2:41; see also Williams (1993) 149–180.

45 On the performative "idolatry" involved in referring divine honor and worship to one who is yet confessed to be a creature, see *Or. Ar.* 2:14, 3:16; *Letter to the Bishops of Egypt* 13.

46 Athanasius also casts doubts on "Arian" baptism in *Or. Ar.* 2:41; cf. Basil, *On the Holy Spirit* 28. On the importance of the category of "stability" in Athanasius's theology of redemption, see Chapter 1, pp. 61–66.

47 That Father, Son, and Spirit are "unlike" (*anomios*) each other in being was the teaching of Aetius and Eunomius, whose followers were thus styled "anomeans."

48 Greek: *asphalēs*; see n. 46, above.

49 cf. *Or. Ar.* 2:41.

50 The Nicene–Constantinopolitan creed of 381 professes faith in the Holy Spirit as the one who is "honored and glorified (*sundoxazomenon*) with the Father and the Son" (Denzinger-Schönmetzer, 150). It is pointed out that Athanasius never directly calls the Spirit "God" (Hanson (1988) 752), but the assertion that the Spirit is confessed to be God along with the Word certainly amounts to that, as does his reference to the Spirit as "*homoousios*"; see above, 1:27.

51 A similar application of this text to the Son and Spirit is found in Irenaeus, *Against the Heresies* I, 22, 1; *Demonstration* 5.

52 The bibilical writers.

53 Athanasius typically presents his defense of what he considers to be correct doctrine in terms of a pastoral concern for the simple (*hoi akeraioi*) who are being "deceived" by the teachers of incorrect doctrine; cf. *Or. Ar.* 1:1, 1:13, 1:32, 2:18, 3:16.

54 Greek: *pneumatomachountes*. The appellation of *Pneumatomachoi*, or "Spirit-fighters," coined by Athanasius (cf. the reference in Acts 5:39 to *theomachoi*), came to be a common taunt addressed by pro-Nicene theologians to those who denied the divinity of the Spirit.

55 A reference to the sin against the Holy Spirit: "But whoever speaks against the holy Spirit will not be forgiven, either in this age or the age to come" (Mt 12:32).

5 LETTER 40: TO ADELPHIUS, BISHOP AND CONFESSOR, AGAINST THE ARIANS

1 See *Tome to the Antiochenes* 10

2 *History of the Arians* 72; *Defense of his Flight* 7.

3 See below, 5.

4 Cf. *Thalia*, in Athanasius, *Or. Ar.* 1:5; Asterius, Fr. 64, Vinzent (1993); Athanasius, *Or. Ar.* 2:37; *On the Councils of Ariminum and Seleucia* 18.

5 This interpretation is in accord with Moutsoulas (1974) and Lebon (1935) 748, n. 3. Roldanus (1968, 228–229, n. 1) considers that the doctrine represented here is not Arian but belongs to a group with "Antiochene" tendencies. His reasoning does not take sufficient account of the Arian two-Words doctrine and of Athanasius's method of conflating his opponents' stated doctrine with its logical consequences (cf. Stülcken (1899) 68). For a refutation of this argument, see Moutsoulas (1974) 327–328.

6 See *Or. Ar.* 2:14, 3:16; cf. *Letter to the Bishops of Egypt* 13: "If they say that the Lord is a creature and yet worship him as a creature, how are they any different from the gentiles?" See also *Letter to the Bishops of Egypt* 4.

7 *Sermones Arianorum*, Fr. 16, in Bardy (1936) 212.

8 Kopecek (1985) 171.

9 The victory of Christ over the devil bestows on the disciples of Christ knowledge of the devil's stratagems; see *Or. Ar.* 1:51.

10 Here again, Athanasius's strategy of denying Christian identity to the "Arians" begins with depicting them as akin to the Jews; see *Or. Ar.*, n. 31. He goes on to align them with the Marcionites, Manichees, and Valentinians; see 2, below.

11 Cf. *Or. Ar.* 2:70.

12 That it is not the Word who is lessened but humanity which is elevated by Christ's redemption is a fundamental motif of Athanasius's Christology: cf. *Inc.* 17; *Or. Ar.* 1:42, 2:14, 3:34.

13 This is a classic statement of Athanasius's correlation of the unity of subject in Christ and the integrity of Christian salvation. It is also a good example of how Athanasius conflates his opponents' statements with what he considers to be their logical consequences. Obviously, the position being refuted here does not include the explicit negation that "there is one redemption from sin and one destruction of death." However, for Athanasius, the integrity of the transformation effected by Christ's salvation necessarily involves the unity in Christ of the humanity which is in solidarity with our condition and the divinity which possesses the resources for healing and transforming our condition to the point of deification. To sever these dimensions of Christ's single salvific agency is to fragment the saving action which emanates from that agency. See *Or. Ar.* 2:70.

14 The term *latreuō* refers to the service of worship, as is clear from below, 7, where Athanasius speaks of the Jews serving the Lord in the temple. Cf. Augustine, *On the Trinity* 1:13; John Damascene, *On the Divine Images* 1:8.

15 The conception of Christ's body as a temple is prominent in Athanasius's *Inc.*; see, for example, 8, 9, 20, 26, 31.

16 Greek: *typos*; cf. Heb 8:5. This whole passage, with its contrast of the old cult of the temple and the new cult centered on the person of

Christ, and the characterization of that contrast in terms of "shadow" and "reality," is replete with echoes of Heb 8–9. Cf. *Festal Letter* **XIX**.

17 Cf. *Inc.* 25.

18 Cf. *Inc.* 7, 14; *Or. Ar.* 2:41; Irenaeus, *Against the Heresies* **IV**, 33, 4.

19 Hieracas is mentioned in the same list as Adelphius as being one of those banished by the Arians during the tenure of George of Cappadocia (*Defense of his Flight* 7; *History of the Arians* 72).

BIBLIOGRAPHY

The following bibliography is weighted in favor of major works in English and works on Athanasius explicitly cited in Chapter 1 and in the notes accompanying the translations. Fuller bibliographical data can be found in C. Butterweck (1995) *Athanasius von Alexandrien: Bibliographie*, Abhandlungen der Nordrhein-Westfälischen Akademie der Wissenschaften 90 (Opladen: Westdeutscher Verlag). Important and informative annotated bibliographies and overviews of recent Athanasius scholarship can be found in C. Kannengiesser (1985) "The Athanasian decade 1974–84: a bibliographical report," *Theological Studies* 46: 524–541, and in J. Leemans (2000) "Thirteen years of Athanasius research (1985–1998): a survey and Bibliography," *sacris erudiri* 39: 105–217. One can find bibliographies that comprise the extensive recent scholarship on the Nicene crisis in R.P.C. Hanson (1988) *The Search for the Christian Doctrine of God: The Arian Controversy* (Edinburgh: T&T Clark) 878–900, and in A. Martin (1996) *Athanase D'Alexandrie et L'église D'Egypte Au IVe Siècle (328–373)*, Collection de l'Ecole française de Rome 216 (Rome: Ecole Française de Rome) 835–891.

Texts and translations

Barnard, Leslie W. (tr.) (1994) *The Monastic Letters of Saint Athanasius the Great*, Fairacres Publication 120 (Oxford: SLG).

Bartelink, G.J.M. (ed. and tr.) (1994) *Vie d'Antoine. Athanase d'Alexandrie. Introduction, texte critique, traduction, notes et index*, Sources Chrétiennes 400 (Paris: Éditions du Cerf).

Butterworth, G.W. (1973) *On First Principles* (Gloucester, MA: Peter Smith).

Camelot, P.T. (ed. and tr.) (1977) *Athanase d'Alexandrie. Contre les Païens. Texte grec, introduction et notes*, Sources Chrétiennes 18 (Paris: Éditions du Cerf).

Gregg, Robert C. (tr.) (1980) *The Life of Antony and the Letter to Marcellinus* (New York: Paulist Press).

Heil, Uta (ed. and tr.) (1999) *Athanasius von Alexandrien: De Sententia Dionysii: Einleitung, Übersetzung, und Kommentar* (Berlin: Walter de Gruyter).

Kannengiesser, Charles (ed. and tr.) (1973) *Athanase d'Alexandrie. Sur l'incarnation du Verbe. Introduction, texte critique, traduction, notes et index*, Sources Chrétiennes 199 (Paris: Éditions du Cerf).

Kirchenväter-Kommission der Preussichen Akademien der Wissenschaften (ed.) (1934–2000) *Athanasius Werke*: I/I (ed. M. Tetz): *Epistula ad Episcopos Aegypti et Libyae, Orationes I et II Contra Arianos, Oration III Contra Arianos*; II/I (ed. H.-G. Opitz): *De Decretis, De Sententia Dionysii, Apologia de fuga sua, Apologia contra Arianos, Epistula encyclica, De Morte Arii, Historia Arianorum, De Synodis, Apologia ad Constantium*; III/I: *Urkunden zur Geschichte des Arianischen Streites 318–328* (Berlin).

Lebon, J. (tr.) (1947) *Lettres à Serapion sur la divinité du Saint Esprit*, Sources Chrétiennes 15 (Paris: Éditions du Cerf).

Lefort, T. (1955) *Lettres festales et pastorales en copte* (edn. and tr.), CSCO, Vols. 150–151 (= *Scriptores Coptici* 19–20) (Löwen).

Martin, Annik (ed.) (1985) *Historie "Acéphale" et index syriaque des lettres festales d'Athanase d'Alexandrie: introduction, texte critique, traduction et notes*, Sources Chrétiennes 317 (Paris: Éditions du Cerf).

Meijering, E.P. (1984) *Athanasius: Contra Gentes* (introduction, translation, and commentary), Philosophia Patrum, Interpretations of Patristic Texts, Vol. 7 (Leiden: E.J. Brill).

Meijering, E.P. and van Winden, J.C.M. (1989) *Athanasius, De incarnatione verbi. Einleitung, Übersetzung, Kommentar* (Amsterdam: Gieben).

Montfaucon, B. (1857) *S.P.N. Athanasii archiepiscopi Alexandrini opera omnia quae exstant* (J.P. Migne, PG 25–26) (Paris).

Orlandi, Tito (ed.) (1968) *Testi Copti 1) Encomio di Atanasio 2) Vita di Atanasio*, Testi e documenti per lo studio dell' antichità 21 (Milan: Istituto Editoriale Cisalpino).

Robertson, Archibald (1994) *Athanasius: Select Works and Letters*, Vol. 4 in Nicene and Post-Nicene Fathers, 2nd series (Peabody, MA: Hendrickson).

Shapland, C.R.B. (1951) *The Letters of Saint Athanasius Concerning the Holy Spirit* (London: Epworth Press).

Stockhausen, A. (2002) *Athanasius von Alexandrien. Epistula ad Afros. Einleitung, Kommentar und Übersetzung*, Patristische Texte und Studien 56 (Berlin and New York: Walter de Gruyter).

Thomson, R.W. (1971) *Athanasius: Contra Gentes and De Incarnatione*, Oxford Early Christian Texts (Oxford: Clarendon Press).

Vinzent, Markus (1993) *Asterius von Kappadokien. Die Theologischen Fragmente. Einleitung, Kritischer Text, Übersetzung & Kommentar* (Leiden: E.J. Brill).

——(1997) *Markell von Ankyra. Die Fragmente der Brief an Julius von Rom* (Leiden: E.J. Brill)

Secondary sources

Abramowski, Luise (1982) "Dionys von Rom (268) und Dionys von Alexandrien (264/5) in der arianischen Streitigkeiten des 4 Jahrhunderts," *ZKG* 93: 240–272.

——(1991) "Die dritte Arianerrede des Athanasius. Eusebianer und Arianer und das westliche Serdicense," *ZKG* 102: 389–413.

Altaner, B. and Stuiber, A. (1966) *Patrologie* (Freiburg).

Anatolios, Khaled (1998) *Athanasius, the Coherence of His Thought*, Routledge Early Church Monographs (London and New York: Routledge).

——(1999) "Theology and economy in Origen and Athanasius," in W.A. Bienert and U. Kühneweg (eds.) *Origeniana Septima* (Leuven: Peeters).

——(2001) "The influence of Irenaeus on Athanasius," in M.F. Wiles and E.J. Yarnold (eds.) *Studia Patristica*, Vol. 38 (Leuven: Peeters).

Armstrong, A.H. (1972) "Neoplatonic valuations of nature, body and intellect: an attempt to understand some ambiguities," *Augustinian Studies* 3: 35–59.

Arnold, Duane W.H. (1991) *The Early Episcopal Career of Athanasius of Alexandria*, Christianity and Judaism in Antiquity Vol. 6 (Notre Dame: University of Notre Dame Press).

Bardy, G. (1936) *Recherches sur Lucien d'Antioche et son École* (Paris).

Barnard, L.W. (1994) "Did Athanasius know Antony?" *Ancient Society* 24: 139–149.

Barnes, M. and Williams, D.H. (eds.) (1993) *Arianism after Arius: Essays on the Development of the Fourth Century Trinitarian Conflicts* (Edinburgh: T&T Clark) 65–81.

Barnes, Timothy (1981) *Constantine and Eusebius* (Cambridge, MA: Harvard University Press).

——(1986) "Angel of light or mystic initiate? The problem of the *Life of Antony*," *Journal of Theological Studies* (n.s.) 37: 353–368.

——(1993) *Athanasius and Constantius: Theology and Politics in the Constantinian Empire* (Cambridge, MA: Harvard Universtiy Press).

Bernard, Regis (1952) *L'Image de Dieu d' après saint Athanase*, Théologie 25 (Paris: Aubeir).

Bouyer, L. (1943) *L'Incarnation et l'Église-corps du Christ dans la théologie de saint Athanase* (Paris).

Bowman, Alan K. (1986) *Egypt After the Pharaohs* (London: British Museum Publications).

Brakke, David (1994) "The Greek and Syriac versions of the *Life of Antony*," *Le Museon* 107: 29–53.

——(1995) *Athanasius and the Politics of Asceticism* (Oxford: Clarendon), reprinted as (1998) *Athanasius and Asceticism* (Baltimore: Johns Hopkins University Press).

——(1998) "Outside the places, within the truth," in David Frankfurter (ed.) *Athanasius of Alexandria and the Localization of the Holy: Pilgrimage and Holy Space in Late Antique Egypt* (Leiden) 445–481.

——(2000) "Athanasius," in Phillip Esler (ed.) *The Early Christian World* (London and New York: Routledge) 1100–1119.

——(2001) "Jewish flesh and Christian spirit in Athanasius of Alexandria," *Journal of Early Christian Studies* 9(4): 453–481.

Brennecke, H.C. (1984) *Hilarius von Poitiers und die Bischofsopposition gegen Konstantius II. Untersuchungen zur dritten Phase des arianischen Streites (337–361)*, Patristische Texte und Studien 26 (Berlin and New York: Walter de Gruyter).

Camplani, Alberto (1989) *Le lettere festali di Atanasio di Alessandria: Studio storico-critico*, Corpus dei manoscritti copti letterari (Rome: C.I.M.).

Cattaneo, E. (1986) *Atanasio. Lettere a Serapione. Lo Spirito Santo*, Collana di testi patristici 55 (Rome) 12–15.

Clark, Elizabeth (1983) *Women in the Early Church*, Message of the Fathers of the Church 13 (Michael Glazier Books).

Cross, F.L. (1945) *The Study of St. Athanasius* (Oxford: Clarendon Press).

Crouzel, H. (1989) *Origen*, tr. A.S. Worall (Edinburgh: T&T Clark).

Ernest, J.D. (1993) "Athanasius of Alexandria: the scope of Scripture in polemical and pastoral context," *Vigiliae Christianae* 47: 341–362.

Florovsky, G. (1962) "The concept of creation in St. Athanasius," *Studia Patristica* 6: 36–52.

Frend, W.H.C. (1976) "Athanasius as an Egyptian Christian leader in the fourth century," in *Religion, Popular and Unpopular in the Early Christian Centuries* (London) 20–37.

Gregg, Robert C. (ed.) (1985) *Arianism: Historical and Theological Reassessments*, Papers from the 9th International Conference on Patristic Studies, 5–10 September 1983, Oxford, England, Patristic Monograph Series 11 (Cambridge, MA: Philadelphia Patristic Foundation).

Gregg, Robert C. and Groh, Dennis (1981) *Early Arianism – a View of Salvation* (Philadelphia: Fortress Press).

Grillmeier, Aloys (1975) *Christ in Christian Tradition*, 2nd edn. (New York: Sheed and Ward).

Hanson, R.P.C. (1988) *The Search for the Christian Doctrine of God: The Arian Controversy* (Edinburgh: T&T Clark).

Harnack, Adolph (1968) *History of Dogma*, tr. Neil Buchanan from the 3rd German edn. (New York: Dover).

Kannengiesser, Charles (1970) "La date de l'apologie d'Athanase 'Contre les paiens' et 'sur l'incarnation,'" *Recherches de Science Religieuse* 58.

——(1973) "Athanasius of Alexandria and the foundation of traditional Christology," *Theological Studies* 34: 103–113.

——(1979) "Athanasius of Alexandria: three orations against the Arians: a reappraisal," in Elizabeth A. Livingstone (ed.) *Studia Patristica*, Vol. 17, Part 3 (Oxford: Pergamon Press) 981–995.

——(1983a) "Arius and the Arians," *Theological Studies* 44: 456–475.

——(1983b) *Athanase d' Alexandrie. Évêque et Écrivain: Une lecture des traités contre les Ariens*, Théologie historique 70 (Paris: Beauschesne).

——(1993) "Athanasuis' so-called third oration against the Arians," *Studia Patristica* 26: 378.

——(1995) "Die Sonderstellung der dritten Arianerrede des Athanasius," *ZKG* 106: 18–55.

——(ed.) (1974) *Politique et Théologie chez Athanase d'Alexandrie*, Actes du Colloque de Chantilly, Théologie historique 27 (Paris: Beauschesne)

Kelly, J.N.D. (1978) *Early Christian Doctrines* (San Francisco: Harper-Collins).

Kolp, A.L. (1979) "Partakers of the divine nature: the use of 2 Peter 1:4 by Athanasius," in Elizabeth A. Livingstone (ed.) *Studia Patristica*, Vol. 17, Part 3 (Oxford: Pergamon Press) 1018–1023.

Kopecek, T.A. (1979) *A History of Neo-Arianism*, 2 vols. (Cambridge, MA: Philadelphia Patristic Foundation).

——(1985) "Neo-Arian religion: the evidence of the *Apostolic Constitutions*," in Gregg (1985).

Lapidge, M. (1979) "Stoic cosmology," in J. Rist (ed.) *The Stoics* (Berkeley: University of California Press) 161–186.

Lebon, J. (1935) "Altération doctrinale de la 'Lettre à Epictète' de saint Athanase," *RHE*.

L'Huillier, Peter (1996) *The Church of the Ancient Councils: The Disciplinary Work of the First Four Ecumenical Councils* (Crestwood, NY: St. Vladimir's Seminary Press).

Lienhard, J.T. (1987) "The 'Arian' controversy: some categories reconsidered," *Theological Studies* 48: 415–437.

——(1999) *Contra Marcellum. Marcellus of Ancyra and Fourth-century Theology* (Washington: CUA Press).

Lorenz, R. (1979) *Arius judaizans? Untersuchungen zur dogmengeschichtlichen Einordnung des Arius*, Forschungen zur Kirchen- und Dogmengeschichte 31 (Göttingen: Vandenhoeck & Ruprecht).

——(1986) *Der Zehnte Osterfestbrief des Athanasius von Alexandrien. Text, Übersetzung, Erläuterungen*, BZNW 49 (Berlin and New York).

Louth, A. (1970) "Reason and revelation in St. Athanasius," *Scottish Journal of Theology* 23: 385–396.

——(1981) *The Origins of the Christian Mystical Tradition from Plato to Denys* (Oxford: Clarendon Press; New York: Oxford University Press).

——(1988) "St. Athanasius and the Greek *Life of Antony*," *Journal of Theological Studies* 39: 504–509.

——(1989) "The use of the term 'idios' in Alexandrian theology from Alexander to Cyril," *Studia Patristica* 19: 198–202.

Lyman, Rebecca J. (1993a) *Christology and Cosmology: Models of Divine Activity in Origen, Eusebius and Athanasius* (Oxford and New York: Clarendon Press).

——(1993b) "A topography of heresy: mapping the rhetorical creation of Arianism," in Barnes and Williams (1993) 45–62.

McGuckin, J. (1994) *St. Cyril of Alexandria. The Christological Controversy. Its History, Theology, and Texts*, supplements to *Vigiliae Christianae* 33 (Leiden: E.J. Brill).

Martin, Annik (1996) *Athanase D'Alexandrie et L'église D'Egypte Au IVe Siècle (328–373)*, Collection de l'École française de Rome 216 (Rome: Ecole Française de Rome).

Meijering, E.P. (1968) *Orthodoxy and Platonism in Athanasius: Synthesis or Antithesis?*, 2nd edn. (Leiden: E.J. Brill).

——(1975) "Athanasius on the Father as the origin of the Son", in *God Being History* (Amsterdam: North Holland Publishing Co.; New York: American Elsevier Publishing Company) 89–102.

——(1989) *De Incarnatione Verbi. Einleitung, Übersetzung, Kommentar*, in co-operation with J.C.M. van Winden (Amsterdam).

——(1991) "Struktur und Zusammenhang des apologetischen Werkes von Athanasius," *Vigiliae Christianae* 45: 313–326.

——(1994) "Zur Echtheit der dritten Rede des Athanasius gegen die Arianer (*Contra Arianos* 3, 59–67)," *Vigiliae Christianae* 48: 135–156.

——(1996a) *Athanasius: Die dritte Rede gegen die Arianer. Teil I (Kapitel 1–25): Einleitung, Übersetzung und Kommentar* (Amsterdam).

——(1996b) *Athanasius: Die dritte Rede gegen die Arianer. Teil II (Kapitel 26–58): Übersetzung und Kommentar* (Amsterdam).

——(1996c) "Zur Echtheit der Dritten Rede des Athanasius gegen die Arianer (*Contra Arianos* III: I)," *Vigiliae Christianae* 50: 364–387.

——(1998) *Athanasius: Die dritte Rede gegen die Arianer. Teil III (Kapitel 59–67): Übersetzung, Kommentar, theologiegeschichtlicher Ausblick* (Amsterdam).

Moll, Helmut (1975) *Die Lehre von der Eucharistie als Opfer. Eine Dogmengeschichtliche Untersuchung vom Neuen Testament bis Irenäus von Lyon* (Köln-Bonn: Peter Hanstein Verlag).

Moutsoulas, E.D. (1974) "La lettre d'Athanase d'Alexandrie a Épictète," in Kannengiesser (1974).

——(1985) "Le problème de la date des 'Trois Discours' contre les Ariens d'Athanase d'Alexandrie," *Studia Patristica* 16: 324–341.

Nordberg H. (1961) "A reconsideration of the date of St. Athanasius' *Contra Genties – De Incarnatione*," *Studia Patristica* 3: 262–266.

Opitz, Hans Georg (ed.) (1935) *Untersuchungen Zur Überlieferung der Schriften des Athanasius*, Arbeiten zur Kirchengeschichte 23 (Berlin: Walter de Gruyter).

Orbe, A. (1955) *La Epinoia. Algunos preliminares historicos de la distinction kat' epinoian* (Rome).

Pelikan, Jaroslav (1962) *The Light of the World: A Basic Image in Early Christian Thought* (New York: Harper).

Pettersen, Alvyn (1982) "A reconsideration of the date of the *Contra Gentes – De Incarnatione* of Athanasius of Alexandria," *Studia Patristica* 18.

——(1990) *Athanasius and the Human Body* (Bristol: Bristol Classical Press).

——(1995) *Athanasius* (Harrisbug, PA: Morehouse).

——(1998) "A good being would envy none life: Athanasius on the goodness of God," *Theology Today* 55: 59–69.

Pollard, T.E. (1957) "Logos and Son in Origen, Arius and Athanasius," in Kurt Aland and F.L. Cross (eds.) *Studia Patristica* 2 (*Texte und Untersuchungen* 64) (Berlin: Akademie-Verlag) 282–287.

——(1959) "The exegesis of Scripture and the Arian controversy," *BJRL* 41: 414–429.

Prestige, G.L. (1923) "*agen(n)etos* and *gen(n)etos* and kindred words in Eusebius and the early Arians," *Journal of Theological Studies* 24: 486–496.

——(1964) *God in Patristic Thought* (London: S.P.C.K.).

Quasten, J. (1960) *Patrology* 3 (Utrecht, Antwerp, and Westminster, MD).

Ricken, Friedo (1978) "Zur Rezeption der platonischen Ontologie bei Eusebios von Kaisareia, Areios und Athanasios," *THPH* 53: 321–352.

Roberts, Colin H. (1979) *Manuscripts, Society and Belief in Early Christian Egypt* (Oxford: Oxford University Press).

Roldanus, J. (1968) *Le Christ et l'homme dans la théologie d'Athanase d'Alexandrie. Étude de la conjunction de sa conception de l'homme avec sa christologie* (Leiden: E.J. Brill).

Schmidtz, D. (1988) "Schimpfwörter in Athanasius' Rede gegen die Arianer," in M. Wisseman (ed.) *Roma Renascens. Beiträge zur Spätantike und Rezeptionsgeschichte (Fs. Ilona Opelt)* (Frankfurt).

Schneemelcher, Wilhelm (1951) "Anthanasius von alexandrine als Theologe und als Kirchenpolitiker," *ZNW* 43: 242–56.

Schwartz, Eduard (1959) *Gesammelte Schriften*, Vol. 3, *Zur Geschichte des Athanasius* (Berlin: Walter de Gruyter).

Sieben, Hermann-Josef (1974) "Herméneutique de l'exègése dogmatique d'Athanase," in Kannengiesser (1974) 195–214.

Simonetti, Manilo (1975) *La crisi ariana nel IV secolo* (Rome: Institum Patristicum Augustinianum).

Slusser, Michael (1986) "Athanasius, '*Contra Gentes*' and '*De Incarnatione*': place and date of composition," *Journal of Theological Studies* 37: 114–117.

Staniloae, D. (1980) "Trinitarian relations and the life of the Church," in *Theology and the Church* (Crestwood, NY: St. Vladimir's Seminary Press) 11–44.

Stead, Christopher (1964) "The Platonism of Arius," *Journal of Theological Studies* 15: 16–31.

——(1976) "Rhetorical method in Athanasius," *Vigilae Christaianae* 30: 121–137.

——(1977) *Divine Substance* (Oxford: Clarendon Press).

——(1978) "The *Thalia* of Arius and the testimony of Athanasius," *Journal of Theological Studies* 29: 20–52.

——(1982) "The Scriptures and the Soul of Christ in Athanasius," *Vigilae Christianae* 36: 233–250.

——(1988) "Athanasius' earliest written work," *Journal of Theological Studies* (n.s.) 39: 76–91.

——(1994) "Arius in modern research," *Journal of Theological Studies* 45.

Stroumsa, G. (1986) "The Manichaean challenge to Egyptian Christianity," in B. Pearson and J. Goehring (eds.) *The Roots of Egyptian Christianity*, Studies in Antiquity and Christianity (Philadelphia: Fortress Press) 307–319.

Stülcken, A. (1899) *Athanasiana*, Literar- und dogmengeschichtliche Untersuchungen, TU 19, 4 (Leipzig).

Tetz, M. (1979) "Zur Biographie des Athanasius von Alexandrien," *ZKG* 90(2–3): 304–338.

——(1995) *Athanasiana: Zu Leben und Lehre des Athanasius*, BZNW 78 (Berlin and New York).

Torrance, T.F. (1975) "Athanasius: a study in the foundations of Classical theology," in *Theology in Reconciliation: Essays toward Evangelical and Catholic Unity in East and West* (London: G. Chapman) 215–266.

——(1989) "The doctrine of the Holy Trinity according to St. Athanasius," *Anglican Theological Review* 71: 395–405.

——(1995) "The hermeneutics of Athanasius," in *Divine Meaning* (Edinburgh: T&T Clark) 229–288.

Vaggione, R.P. (1987) *Eunomius: The Extant Works*, Oxford Early Christian Texts (Oxford: Clarendon Press).

van Winden, J.C.M. (1975) "On the date of Athanasius's Apologetical Treatises," *Vigilae Christianae* 29: 291–295.

Vermaseren, M.J. (1977) *Cybele and Attis: The Myth and the Cult* (London).

von Campenhausen, Hans (1995) *The Fathers of the Greek Church*, ET tr. Stanley Godman (NY: Pantheon).

Wickham, L. (ed.) (1983) *Cyril of Alexandria: Select Letters* (Oxford: Clarendon Press).

Widdicombe, Peter (1994) *The Fatherhood of God from Origen to Athanasius* (Oxford: Clarendon Press).

Wiles, Maurice (1962) "In defence of Arius," *Journal of Theological Studies* 13: 339–347.

——(1989) "The philosophy in Christianity: Arius and Athanasius," in G. Vesey (ed.) *The Philosophy in Christianity*, Royal Institute of Philosophy Lecture Series 25, 41–52.

——(1996) *Archetypal Heresy: Arianism through the Centuries* (Oxford: Clarendon Press).

Williams, M. (1985) *The Immovable Race: A Gnostic Designation and the Theme of Stability in Late Antiquity* (Leiden: E.J. Brill).

Williams, Rowan (1983) "The logic of Arius," *Journal of Theological Studies* 34: 56–81.

——(1987) *Arius: Heresy and Tradition* (London: Darton, Longman & Todd) (2nd edn. 2001).

——(1993) "Baptism and the Arian controversy," in Barnes and Williams (1993).

Young, F.M. (1971) "A reconsideration of Alexandrian Christology", *Journal of Ecclesiastical History* 22: 103–114.

——(1979) *The Use of Sacrificial Ideas in Greek Christian Writers from the New Testament to John Chrysostom*, Patristic Monograph Series 5 (Cambridge, MA: Philadelphia Patristic Foundation).

——(1983) *From Nicaea to Chalcedon: A Guide to the Literature and its Background* (Philadelphia: Fortress Press).

INDEX